THE BUSINESS BOOK

OTHER BIG IDEAS

SIMPLY EXPLAINED

THE BUSINESS BOOK

SENIOR EDITOR
Sam Atkinson

PROJECT ART EDITOR
Amy Child

EDITORS
Scarlett O'Hara, Alison Sturgeon

US EDITORS
Margaret Parrish, Jane Perlmutter

PICTURE RESEARCHER
Sumedha Chopra

MANAGING EDITOR
Esther Ripley

MANAGING ART EDITOR
Karen Self

PUBLISHER
Sarah Larter

ART DIRECTOR
Phil Ormerod

ASSOCIATE
PUBLISHING DIRECTOR
Liz Wheeler

PUBLISHING DIRECTOR
Jonathan Metcalf

JACKET DESIGNER
Laura Brim

JACKET EDITOR
Manisha Majithia

JACKET DESIGN
DEVELOPMENT MANAGER
Sophia Tampakopoulos

ILLUSTRATIONS
James Graham

PRODUCER, PRE-PRODUCTION
Rebecca Fallowfield

PRODUCER
Gemma Sharpe

4.2019

original styling by
STUDIO8 DESIGN

produced for DK by
COBALT ID

ART EDITORS
Darren Bland, Paul Reid

EDITORS
Richard Gilbert, Diana Loxley,
Sarah Tomley, Marek Walisiewicz

This American Edition, 2018
First American Edition, 2014
Published in the United States
by DK Publishing
345 Hudson Street
New York, New York 10014

Copyright © 2014, 2018
Dorling Kindersley Limited
DK, a Division of Penguin Random House LLC
18 19 20 21 22 10 9 8 7 6 5 4 3 2 1
001–196652–Nov/2018

Published in Great Britain by
Dorling Kindersley Limited.

A catalog record for this book is
available from the Library of Congress.
ISBN: 978-1-4654-7588-6

DK books are available at special discounts
when purchased in bulk for sales promotions,
premiums, fund-raising, or educational use.
For details, contact: DK Publishing Special
Markets, 345 Hudson Street,
New York, New York 10014
SpecialSales@dk.com

Printed and bound in China

A WORLD OF IDEAS:
SEE ALL THERE IS TO KNOW

www.dk.com

CONTRIBUTORS

IAN MARCOUSE, CONSULTANT EDITOR

Ian Marcousé lectures in business and economics education at the Institute of Education in London. He has written a host of business text books for A-level and BTEC students, including the popular *A–Z Business Studies* handbooks, and is the founder and director of A–Z Business Training Ltd.

PHILIPPA ANDERSON

Philippa Anderson is a communications consultant and business writer who has authored articles, magazine features, and books on numerous aspects of business, from market research to leadership. She also provides communications consultancy for multinational firms, including 3M, Anglo American, and Coca-Cola.

ALEXANDRA BLACK

Alexandra Black studied business communications before embarking on a writing career that led her to Japan and stints with financial newspaper group Nikkei Inc. and investment bank J. P. Morgan. She later worked for a direct marketing publisher in Sydney, Australia, before moving to Cambridge, UK. She writes on a range of subjects, from business to history and fashion.

DENRY MACHIN

Denry Machin is an associate tutor at Keele University, UK, and is working at doctoral research on the application of business thinking within education. He also works for Harrow International Management Services as projects manager, assisting in the development of Harrow School's presence in Asia. He is the author of several business books, journals, and magazine articles.

NIGEL WATSON

Nigel Watson has taught business and economics for A-Level and International Baccalaureate students for 25 years. He has authored and co-authored books and magazine articles in both subjects.

CONTENTS

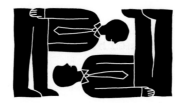

MAKING MONEY WORK
MANAGING FINANCES

WORKING WITH A VISION
STRATEGY AND OPERATIONS

SUCCESSFUL SELLING
MARKETING MANAGEMENT

CTION

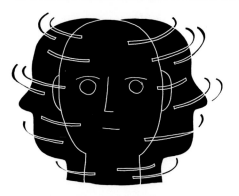

From the time that goods and services began to be traded in early civilizations, people have been thinking about business. The emergence of specialized producers and the use of money as a means of exchange were methods by which individuals and societies could, in modern terms, gain a "business edge." The ancient Egyptians, the Mayans, the Greeks, and the Romans all knew that wealth creation through the mechanism of commerce was fundamental to the acquisition of power, and formed the base on which civilization could prosper.

The lessons of the early traders resonate even today. Specialism revealed the benefits of economies

> The art of administration is as old as the human race.
> **Edward D. Jones**
> **US investment banker**
> **(1893–1982)**

of scale—that production costs fall as more items are produced. Money gave rise to the concept of "value added"—selling an item for more than it cost to produce. Even when barter was the norm, producers still knew it was advantageous to lower costs and raise the value of goods. Today's companies may use different technologies and trade on a global scale, but the essence of business has changed little in millennia.

An era of change
However, the study of business as an activity in its own right emerged relatively recently. The terms "manager" and "management" did not appear in the English language until the late 16th century. In his 1977 text *The Visible Hand*, Dr. Alfred Chandler divided business history into two periods: pre-1850 and post-1850. Before 1850 local, family-owned firms dominated the business environment. With commerce operating on a relatively small scale, little thought was given to the wider disciplines of business.

The growth of the railroads in the mid-1800s, followed by the Industrial Revolution, enabled businesses to grow beyond the immediate gaze of friends or family, and outside the immediate locale. To prosper in this new—and

increasingly international— environment businesses needed different, and more rigorous, processes and structures. The geographic scope and ever-growing size of these evolving businesses required new levels of coordination and communication—in short, businesses needed management.

Managing production
The initial focus of the new breed of manager was on production. As manufacturing moved from individual craftsmen to machinery, and as ever-greater scale was required, theorists such as Henri Fayol examined ever-more-efficient ways of operating. The theories of Scientific Management, chiefly formulated by Frederick Taylor, suggested that there was "one best way" to perform a task. Businesses were organized by precise routines, and the role of the worker was simply to supervise and "feed" machinery, as though they were part of it. With the advent of production lines in the early 1900s, business was characterized by standardization and mass production.

While Henry Ford's Model T car is seen as a major accomplishment of industrialization, Ford also remarked "why is it every time I ask for a pair of hands, they come with

 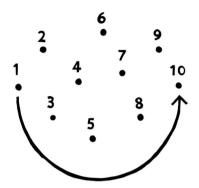 

a brain attached?" Output may have increased, but so too did conflict between management and staff. Working conditions were poor and businesses ignored the sociological context of work—productivity mattered more than people.

Studying people

In the 1920s a new influence on business thinking emerged—the Human Relations Movement of behavioral studies. Through the work of psychologists Elton Mayo and Abraham Maslow, businesses began to recognize the value of human relations. Workers were no longer seen as simply "cogs in the machine," but as individuals with unique needs. Managers still focused on efficiency, but realized that workers were more productive when their social and emotional needs were taken care of. For the first time, job design, workplace environments, teamwork, remuneration, and nonfinancial benefits were all considered important to staff motivation.

In the period following World War II, business practice shifted again. Wartime innovation had yielded significant technological advances that could be applied to commerce. Managers began to utilize quantitative analysis, and

were able to make use of computers to help solve operational problems. Human relations were not forgotten, but in management thinking, measurability returned to the fore.

Global brands

The postwar period saw the growth of multinationals and conglomerates—businesses with multiple and diverse interests across the globe. The war had made the world seem smaller, and had paved the way for the global brand. These newly emerging global brands grew as a result of a media revolution—television, magazines, and newspapers gave businesses

Entrepreneurship is about survival, which nurtures creative thinking. Business is not financial science, it's about trading—buying and selling.
Anita Roddick
UK entrepreneur (1942–2007)

the means to reach a mass audience. Businesses had always used advertising to inform customers about products and to persuade them to buy, but mass media provided the platform for a new, and much broader, field— marketing. In the 1940s US advertising executive Rosser Reeves promoted the value of a Unique Selling Proposition. By the 1960s, marketing methods had shifted from simply telling customers about products to listening to what customers wanted, and adapting products and services to suit that.

Initially, marketing had its critics. In the early 1960s hype about the product became more important than quality, and customers grew dissatisfied with empty claims. This, and competition from Japanese manufacturers, had Western companies embracing a new form of business thinking: Total Quality Management (TQM) and Zero Defects management. Guided by management theorists, such as W. Edwards Demming and Philip B. Crosby, quality was seen as the responsibility of the entire company, not just those on the production line. Combining Human Relations thinking and the customer-focused approach of marketing, many companies »

adopted the Japanese philosophy of *kaizen*: "continuous improvement of everything, by everyone." Staff at all levels was tasked with improving processes and products through "quality circles." While TQM is no longer the buzzword it once was, quality remains important. The modern iteration of TQM is Six Sigma, an approach to process improvement that was developed by Motorola in 1986 and adapted by Jack Welch during his time as CEO of General Electric.

Gurus and thinkers
Business history itself emerged as a topic of study in the 1970s. Dr. Alfred Chandler progressed the study of business history from the purely descriptive to the analytical—his course at Harvard Business School stressed the importance of organizational capabilities, technological innovation, and continuous learning. Taking their cue from Chandler, in the 1980s and 1990s management experts—such as Michael Porter, Igor Ansoff, Rosabeth Moss Kanter, Henry Mintzberg, and Peter Drucker—encouraged businesses to consider their environments, to consider the needs of people, and to remain adaptable to change. Maintaining

the conditions for business growth, and the correct positioning of products within their market, were considered key to business strategy. Moreover, what distinguished these gurus from their predecessors—who had tended to focus on operational issues—was a focus on leadership itself. For example, Charles Handy's *The Empty Raincoat* revealed the paradoxes of leadership, and acknowledged the vulnerabilities and fragilities of the managers themselves. Leadership in the context of business, these writers recognized, is no easy undertaking.

Digital pioneering
Just as television and mass media had done before, the growth of the Internet in the 1990s and early

Business can be a source of progressive change.
Jerry Greenfield
US businessman, co-founder of Ben and Jerry's ice cream (1951–)

2000s heralded a new era for business. While early hype led to the failure of many online start-ups in the dot-com bubble of 1997 to 2000, the successful e-commerce pioneers laid the foundations for a business landscape that would be dominated by innovation. From high-tech garage start-ups—such as Hewlett-Packard and Apple—to the websites, mobile apps, and social-media forums of the modern business environment, technology is increasingly vital for business.

The explosion of new businesses thanks to technology also helped to expand the availability of finance. During the 1980s and 1990s finance had grown into a distinct discipline. Corporate mergers and high-profile takeovers became a way for businesses to grow beyond their operational limits; leverage joined marketing and strategy as part of the management lexicon. In the late 1990s this expanded to venture capital: the funding of small companies by profit-seeking investors. The risk of starting and running a business remains, but the opportunities afforded by technology and easier access to finance have made taking the first step a little easier. With micro-finance, and the support of online

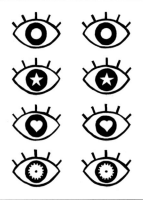

networks and communities of like-minded people dispensing business advice, enterprise has never been more entrepreneurial.

Recent business thinking has brought diversity and social responsibility to the fore. Businesses are encouraged, and increasingly required by law, to employ people from diverse backgrounds and to act in an ethical manner, wherever they operate in the world. Businesses such Nike and Adidas require suppliers to prove that labor conditions in their factories meet required standards. Sustainability, recycling, diversity, and environmentalism have entered business thinking alongside strategic management and risk.

New horizons
If business thinking has shifted, so too has the nature of business itself. Where once a company was constrained by its locality, today the opportunities are truly global. Globalization does, however, mean that business is more competitive than ever. Emerging markets are creating new opportunities and new threats. They may be able to outsource production to low-cost countries, but as their economies grow, these emerging nations are breeding new competition. China,

for example, may be "the world's factory," but its home-grown companies are also starting to represent a threat to Western businesses. As the global recession of 2007–08 and ongoing economic uncertainty have proven, business in the 21st century is increasingly more interdependent and more challenging than ever before. Starting a business might be easier, but to survive entrepreneurs need the tenacity to take an idea to market, the business acumen to turn a good plan into a profitable enterprise, and the financial skill to maintain success.

Continual change
For centuries social, political, and technological factors have forced companies and individuals to create new ways of generating profits. Whether bartering goods with a neighboring village or seeking ways to make profits from social networking, business thinking has changed, shifted, and evolved to mirror the wants and needs of the societies whose wealth it creates. Sometimes, as in the 2008 financial crisis, business failed in its efforts. In other examples—the legacy of Apple's game-changing products, for example—companies have been spectacularly successful.

Business is a fascinating subject. It surrounds us and affects us daily. A walk down the street, a wander around a supermarket, an Internet search on almost any topic will reveal commerce in its many and varied forms. At its core business is, and always has been, about survival and surplus—about the advancement of self and of society. As the world continues to open up, and as opportunities for enterprise multiply, an interest in business has never been more relevant, or more exciting. Moreover, for those with entrepreneurial spirit, business has never been more rewarding. ■

Business, more than any other occupation, is a continual dealing with the future; it is a continual calculation, an instinctive exercise in foresight.
Henry R. Luce
US magazine publisher (1898–1967)

START S

THINK B

STARTING AND GROWING THE BUSINESS

MALL,
G

All businesses start from the same point: an idea. It is what happens to that idea that determines business success.

According to *Entrepreneur* magazine, nearly half of all new start-ups fail within the first three years. Beating the odds at start-up is tough. First and foremost an idea, no matter how good, must be combined with entrepreneurial spirit, defined as the willingness to take risk. Without entrepreneurial spirit a great idea might never be pursued. Not all ideas are good ones though; it would be a foolish entrepreneur who rushed a product to market without careful thought, research, and detailed planning. Risk might be inherent in business enterprise, but successful entrepreneurs are those who are not only willing to take risks, but are also able to manage risk.

Realistic propositions

Having an idea is the first step—the next hurdle is finance. Some start-ups require very little capital, and a few require none at all. However, many require significant backing, and most will need to seek funding at some stage in the growth process. An entrepreneur must be able to convince financial backers that the concept is valid

and that they have the skills and knowledge to turn the original concept into a successful business.

It follows that the idea must be profitable. Sometimes, an idea may look great on paper, but turn out to be uncommercial when put into practice. Determining whether an idea has potential requires a study of the competition and the relevant market. Who is competing for customers' time and money? Are these competitors selling directly competitive products or possible substitutes? How are competitors perceived in the market? How big is the market?

Most markets are increasingly global, crowded, and competitive. Few companies are lucky enough to

The only thing worse than starting something and failing … is not starting something.
Seth Godin
US entrepreneur (1960–)

find a profitable niche—to succeed, companies need to do something different in order to stand out in the market. The strategy for most companies is to differentiate; this means demonstrating to customers that they offer something that is not available from competitors—a Unique or Emotional Selling Proposition (USP or ESP).

Such attempts to stand out are everywhere. Every business, and at every stage of production, from raw-material extraction to after-sales service, tries to distinguish its products or services from all others. Walk into any bookstore, for example, and you will see countless examples of books, often on the same topic, using design, style, and even size (large or small) to stand out from the competition.

Gaining an edge often depends on one of two things: being first into a new market niche, or being different from the competition. For example, in 1995 eBay was first into the online auction market, and has dominated it ever since. Similarly, Volvo was first to identify the opportunity for luxury bus sales in India, and has enjoyed healthy sales. In contrast, Facebook was by no means the first social network, but it is the most successful; its edge was having a better product.

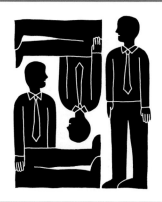

Once a company is established, the challenge shifts: the objective now is to maintain sales and grow in the short- and long-term.

Adapting to survive

Long-term business survival depends upon the company constantly reinventing and adapting itself in order to remain ahead of the competition. In dynamic markets, which are growing and evolving all the time, the idea on which the company was founded may become irrelevant over time, and rivals will almost certainly copy it. The ecosystem in which a business operates is rarely, if ever, static. Corporations exist in these ecosystems as living organisms that must adapt to survive. In their 2013 book, *Reinventing Giants*, Bill Fischer, Umberto Lago, and Fang Liu noted that the Chinese home appliances company Haier had reinvented itself at least three times in the past 30 years. In contrast, Kodak, a US giant of the 20th century, was slow to react to the rise of digital photography, and went bankrupt.

Moreover, just as the enterprise must adapt, so too must the owner. Most businesses start small, and remain small. Few entrepreneurs are willing or know how to take the second step of employing people who are neither family nor previously known friends. This is the start of a move from entrepreneur to leader, and it requires a new set of skills, as new demands are placed on the business founders. Where once energy, ideas, and passion were enough, evolving businesses require the development of formal systems, procedures, and processes. In short, they require management. Founders must develop delegation, communication, and coordination skills, or they must employ people who have them.

As Larry Greiner described in his 1972 paper, "Evolution and Revolution as Organizations Grow", as a business grows, the demands on it change. The Greiner Curve is a graphic that shows how the initial stages of growth rely on individual initiative, and that evolving ad-hoc business practice into sustainable and successful growth can only be achieved by experienced people and rigorous systems. Professional management, as opposed to entrepreneurial spirit, becomes essential to business evolution.

Some leaders, such as Bill Gates and Steve Jobs, for example, are able to make the transition from entrepreneurial founder to corporate leader. Many others, however, struggle to make the necessary changes; some try and fail, while others decide to remain small.

Finding a balance

Determining how fast to grow is, therefore, a balance of the founder's skills and desires. But in order to survive, the idea must be unique enough to define its own niche, and the individual or group behind it must demonstrate entrepreneurial spirit. They need the flexibility to adapt the idea—and themselves—as business and market pressures demand. Luck will play a part, but it is the balance of these factors that determines whether a small start-up becomes a giant. ∎

When you have to prove the value of your ideas by persuading other people to pay for them, it clears out an awful lot of woolly thinking.
Tim O'Reilly
Irish entrepreneur (1954–)

IF YOU CAN DREAM IT, YOU CAN DO IT

BEATING THE ODDS AT START-UP

IN CONTEXT

FOCUS
Business start-ups

KEY DATES
18th century The term "entrepreneur" is used to describe someone who is willing to risk buying at certain prices and selling at uncertain prices.

1946 Professor Arthur Cole writes *An Approach to Entrepreneurship*, sparking interest in the phenomenon.

2005 The micro-finance, nonprofit site Kiva.com launches to make small loans to very small businesses.

2009 Crowdfunding websites, such as Kickstarter.com, allow individuals to provide funding for businesses.

2013 A study by Ross Levine and Yona Rubinstein finds that as teenagers, many successful entrepreneurs exhibited aggressive behavior, broke the rules, and got into trouble.

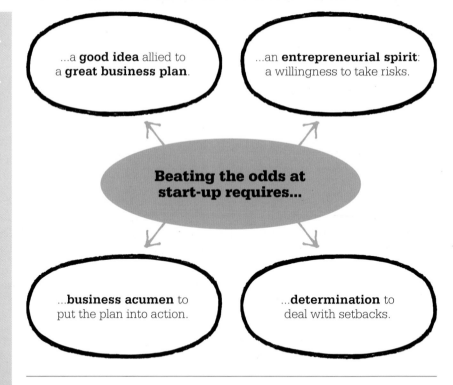

...a **good idea** allied to a **great business plan**.

...an **entrepreneurial spirit**: a willingness to take risks.

Beating the odds at start-up requires...

...**business acumen** to put the plan into action.

...**determination** to deal with setbacks.

The reasons for starting a business are many. Some people dream of being their own boss—of turning their hobby into a profitable enterprise, of expressing their creativity, or of being richly rewarded for their hard work. Although Walt Disney's maxim "if you can dream it, you can do it" holds true for some, pursuing the dream is risky. Those who attempt it must have the entrepreneurial spirit to fearlessly quit a well-paid job, go it alone, and face a future filled with uncertainty. Others might need a push; often being laid off (and its associated lump-sum payment) can be a springboard.

Younger entrepreneurs are increasingly a part of the start-up scenario. They may have gained the necessary skills for business by their early twenties, and enjoy the excitement and freedom of running their own venture.

Keeping the faith

While the reasons for start-up may vary, what all entrepreneurs have in common is the willingness to take risks. Few entrepreneurs get it right first time—it takes resilience and tenacity to keep going in the face of failure, and it takes perseverance to remain positive when customers, banks, and financial backers repeatedly say "no." Faith in the idea is essential. While some start-ups require very little capital, most require funding during their early growth phases. A business owner must be able to convince banks, or other financial backers, that their concept is valid and that they have the skills to turn the idea into a profitable venture, even though this may take some time. It took Amazon six years to make a profit.

In recent years, securing finance for start-ups has become a little easier. Many governments offer loan plans or grants. Entrepreneurs with big ideas can access large funds of money and managerial support from venture capitalists, whose sole purpose is to incubate start-ups. For smaller start-ups, and for people with very little of their own capital, micro-loans and crowdfunding finance—such as that offered by Kickstarter.com—are increasingly popular.

The business plan

The key to securing financing is a business plan. A good plan will outline the idea itself, detail any supporting market research, describe operational and marketing activities, and give financial predictions. The plan should also outline a strategy for long-term growth and identify contingencies (alternative ideas or markets) if things do not go as planned.

Most importantly, a good business plan will acknowledge that the biggest reason for business failure is a lack of cash. While loan capital can help for a while, eventually a business must fund its operations from revenue. A good business plan will analyze future cash flows and identify any potential shortfalls.

Beating the odds at start-up is defined by the tenacity to take an idea to market, the ability to secure sufficient finance, and the business acumen to turn a good plan into a long-term, profitable enterprise. ▪

Sustaining a business is a hell of a lot of hard work, and staying hungry is half the battle.
Wendy Tan White
UK business executive (1970–)

"Tony" Fernandes

Tan Sri Anthony "Tony" Fernandes was born in Kuala Lumpur in 1964 to an Indian father and Malaysian mother. He went to school in England and graduated from the London School of Economics (LSE) in 1987. He worked briefly for Richard Branson at Virgin Records as a financial controller before becoming Southeast Asia Vice President for Warner Music Group in 1992. In 2001, Fernandes left Warner to go it alone. He mortgaged his home to raise the finance needed to buy the struggling young airline, AirAsia. His low-cost strategy was clear in the company's tagline: "Now everyone can fly." One year after his takeover, the airline had cleared its debts of $11 million and had broken even. Fernandes estimates that around 50 percent of its travelers are first-time flyers. The company is now widely regarded as the world's best low-cost airline.

In 2007 Fernandes founded Tune Hotels, a low-cost hotel chain that promises "Five-star beds at one-star prices." He advises potential entrepreneurs to "dream the impossible. Never take no for an answer."

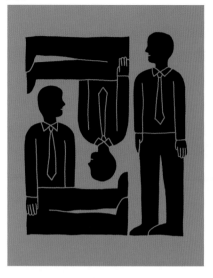

THERE'S A GAP IN THE MARKET, BUT IS THERE A MARKET IN THE GAP?

FINDING A PROFITABLE NICHE

IN CONTEXT

FOCUS
Positioning strategy

KEY DATES

1950s and 60s Markets are dominated by large companies offering mass-produced items, such as Coca-Cola. Choice is limited, but the scope for products targeted at new sectors of the market is high.

1970s and 80s Markets become more segmented as companys generate new products and market them toward narrower groups.

1990s and 2000s Companies and brands position themselves ever-more aggressively and distinctively in the overcrowded marketplace.

2010s Finding and sustaining market niches is assisted by the promotional capabilities of the Internet, which allow "one-to-one" marketing and customization of products.

Many markets are crowded, with multiple sellers chasing the same customers.

⬇

For these sellers, **competition lowers profitability**.

⬇

Market gaps—a new product or sector of the market—offer the enticing prospect of **healthy profitability**.

⬇

But does the gap contain enough business to **generate a profit**?

⬇

There's a gap in the market, but is there a market in the gap?

Finding a space in the market that is unchallenged by competition is the Holy Grail of positioning strategy. Unfortunately these spaces—known as market gaps—are often illusive, and the benefits of finding one are often equally illusory.

Although competition is a fact of life, it makes business difficult, contributing to an ever-downward pressure on prices, ever-rising costs (such as the funding of new product development and marketing), and an incessant need to outmaneuver and outsmart rivals. In contrast, the benefits of finding a market gap—a small niche segment of a market that is unfettered by competition—are obvious: greater control over prices, lower costs, and improved profits.

The identification of a market gap, combined with a dose of entrepreneurial spirit, is often all that is needed to launch a new business. In 2006, Twitter founder Jack Dorsey combined short-form communication with social media, providing a service that no one else had spotted. Free to most users, revenue comes from companies who pay for promotional tweets and profiles: Twitter earned advertising revenues of $582 million in 2013.

See also: Stand out in the market 28–31 ▪ Gaining an edge 32–39 ▪ Reinventing and adapting 52–57 ▪ Porter's generic strategies 178–83 ▪ Good and bad strategy 184–85 ▪ The value chain 216–17 ▪ Marketing mix 280–83

Not all gaps are lucrative, however. The Amphicar, for instance, was an amphibious car produced in the 1960s for US consumers who wanted to drive on roads and rivers. It was a quirky novelty, but the market was too small to be profitable. This was also true for bottled water for pets—launched in the US in 1994, Thirsty Cat! and Thirsty Dog! failed to entice pet owners.

A sustainable niche

Snapple, the manufacturer of healthy tea and juice drinks, is a company that has successfully found a sustainable and profitable niche. A glance at the beverage counter of any supermarket reveals that dozens of brands compete for sales. Many companies have failed in this ultra-competitive market: for example, Pepsi tried to capture a nonexistent market for morning cola with its short-lived, high-caffeine drink, AM.

Success for Snapple came from positioning the product as a unique brand—Snapple was one of the first companies to manufacture juices and drinks made completely from

Snapple's positioning in the crowded US beverage marketplace was the key to its success. By focusing on a niche healthy product and marketing itself as a quirky company, Snapple was able to wrestle a large market share (indicated here by circle size) from its rivals.

natural ingredients. Its founders ran a health store in Manhattan, and the company used the slogan: "100% Natural." Snapple targeted students, commuters, and lunch-time office workers with a new healthy "snack" drink, combining its Unique Selling Proposition (USP) with irreverent marketing and small bottles that were designed to be consumed in

one sitting. Distribution was through small, inner-city stores where customers could "grab-and-go." These tactics helped to secure a profitable and sustainable niche, distinguishing Snapple from its rivals in the 1980s and 1990s. In 1994 sales peaked at $674 million.

Unoccupied market territory can present major opportunities for companies, but the challenge lies in identifying which gaps are profitable and which are traps. During the 1990s, many companies became excited about the potential of the "green" market, across a whole range of goods. But this market has failed to materialize in any profitable way. This marks one of the potential pitfalls in identifying market gaps based on market research: sometimes consumers have strong attitudes or opinions on trends or issues—such as ecology—that they are disinclined to consider when purchasing products, especially if they affect cost. Many market gaps, it seems, are tempting, but illusory. ▪

Snapple

A contraction of the words "snappy" and "apple," Snapple was launched in 1978 by Unadulterated Food Products Inc. The company was founded in 1972 by Arnold Greenberg, Leonard Marsh, and Hyman Golden in New York, US.

Such was the popularity of Snapple that the company has been subject to numerous buyouts. Unadulterated was purchased by Quaker Oats for $1.7 billion in 1994 but, following differences in strategic

vision that led to falling sales, was sold to Triarc in 1997 for $300 million. Triarc then sold the Snapple brand to Cadbury Schweppes for $1.45 billion in September 2000, with a further deal in May 2008 seeing Snapple become part of what is now the Dr Pepper Snapple Group.

Marketed as "Made From the Best Stuff on Earth," Snapple's unusual blends of ready-to-drink teas, juice drinks, and waters are sold in more than 80 countries around the world.

YOU CAN LEARN ALL YOU NEED TO KNOW ABOUT THE COMPETITION'S OPERATION BY LOOKING IN HIS GARBAGE CANS
STUDY THE COMPETITION

IN CONTEXT

FOCUS
Analytical tools

KEY DATES
1950s Harvard academics George Smith and C. Roland Christensen develop tools to analyze companies and competition.

1960s US management consultant Albert Humphrey leads a research project that yields SOFT analysis, the forerunner to his later SWOT analysis.

1982 US professor Heinz Weihrich develops the TOWS matrix which uses the threats to a company as the starting point for formulating strategy.

2006 Japanese academics Shinno, Yoshioka, Marpaung, and Hachiga develop computer software that combines SWOT analysis with AHP (Analytic Hierarchy Process).

Whether a company is long established or in its start-up phase, a key strategic issue is its competitive advantage—the factor that gives it an edge over its competitors. The only way to establish, understand, and protect competitive advantage is to study the competition. Who is competing with the company for its customers' time and money? Do they sell competitive products or potential substitutes? What are their strengths and weaknesses? How are they perceived in the market?

For Ray Kroc, the US entrepreneur behind the success of fast-food chain McDonalds, this reportedly involved inspecting competitors'

See also: Stand out in the market 28–31 ▪ Gaining an edge 32–39 ▪ Thinking outside the box 88–89 ▪ Leading the market 166–69 ▪ Porter's generic strategies 178–83 ▪ The MABA matrix 192–93 ▪ Porter's five forces 212–15

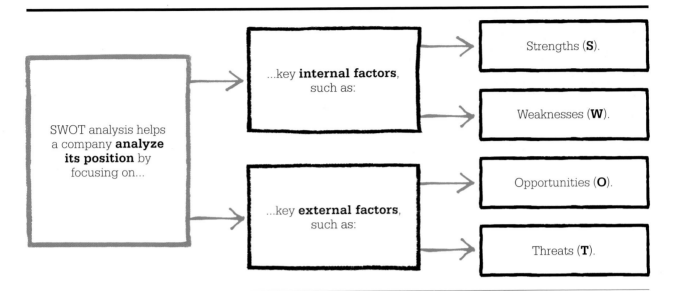

SWOT analysis helps a company **analyze its position** by focusing on...

...key **internal factors**, such as:

Strengths (**S**).

Weaknesses (**W**).

...key **external factors**, such as:

Opportunities (**O**).

Threats (**T**).

trash. But there is a range of more conventional tools to help companies to understand themselves, their markets, and their competition.

SWOT analysis
The most popular such tool is SWOT analysis. Created by US management consultant Albert Humphrey in 1966, it is used to identify internal strengths (S) and weaknesses (W), and to analyze external opportunities (O) and threats (T). Internal factors that can be considered as either strengths or weaknesses include: the experience and expertise of management; the skill of a work force; product quality; the company's financial health; and the strength of its brand. External factors that might be opportunities or threats include market growth; new technologies; barriers to entering markets; overseas sales potential; and changing customer demographics and preferences.

SWOT analysis is widely used by businesses of all types, and it is a staple of business management

courses. It is a creative tool that allows managers to assess a company's current position, and to imagine possible future positions.

A practical tool
When well-executed, a SWOT analysis should inform strategic planning and decision-making. It allows a company to identify what it does better than rivals (or vice versa), what changes it may need to make to minimize threats, and what opportunities may give the company competitive advantage. The key to strategic fit is to make sure that the company's internal and external environments match: its internal strengths must be aligned with the external opportunities. Any internal weaknesses should be addressed so as to minimize the extent of external threat.

When undertaking a SWOT analysis, the views of staff and even customers can be included—it should provide an opportunity to solicit views from all stakeholders. The greater the number of views

included, the deeper the analysis and the more useful the findings. However, there are limitations. While a company may be able to judge its internal weaknesses and strengths accurately, projections about future events and trends (which will affect opportunities and threats) are always subject to error. Different stakeholders will also be privy to different levels of information about a company's activities, and therefore its current position. Balance is key; »

If you go exactly where your competitors are, you're dead.
Thorsten Heins
German-Canadian former CEO of Blackberry (1957–)

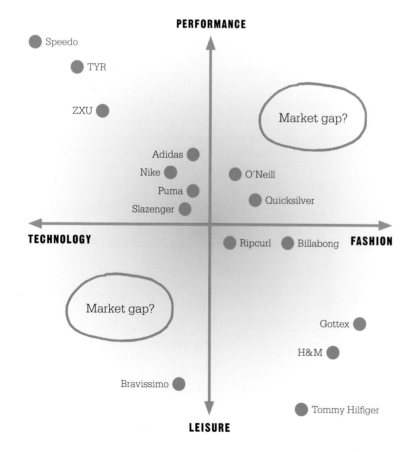

senior managers may have a full view of the company, but their perspective needs to be informed by alternative views from all levels of the organization.

As with all business tools, the factor that governs the success of SWOT analysis is whether or not it leads to action. Even the most comprehensive analysis is useless unless its findings are translated into well-conceived plans, new processes, and better performance.

Market mapping

A slightly narrower but more sophisticated tool for analyzing a company's position and competition is "market mapping" (also known as "perceptual mapping"). Market maps are diagrams that represent a market and the placement of products within that market, providing a visual means of studying the competition. The process is useful both internally (to help an organization understand its own products) and externally (to chart how consumers perceive the brand in relation to the competition).

To draw up a market map, a company identifies several consumer purchase-decision factors that stand in opposition to one another. In the fashion market, an example might include "technology" *vs.* "fashion," and "performance" *vs.*

"leisure." Additional factors could include the item's price (high *vs.* low), quality of production (high *vs.* low), stylish *vs.* conservative, or durable *vs.* disposable. Two of these dimensions, or opposing pairs, are then plotted onto a horizontal or vertical axis.

Based on market research or the knowledge of managers, all of the products within a particular market can be plotted onto the map. The market share of each product can be represented by the size of its corresponding image on the map, but more often, analysts choose to simply make a rough sketch of the market, ignoring market size.

A company may choose to compile several market maps, each of which depicts a different set of variables, and then analyze them—individually and in combination—to gain an overall view of the company's position in the market.

Finding the gap

The goal of market mapping is to identify opportunities where a company can differentiate itself from its competitors. These are areas where the company offers unique value, and they can be used to inform marketing messages. The map will also reveal overcrowded segments, which signify heightened competitive threat.

For a new start-up, a market map can be used to identify a viable gap in the market—a good place to position a company when it is struggling to establish itself. Established businesses can use market mapping combined with SWOT analysis to discover opportunities and decide whether the company has the strengths to exploit one of those opportunities. The market map helps to inform the strategy (the need to reposition a product away from competitors'

Market mapping plots opposing qualities of products along two axes. By identifying the two main oppositional factors for any product, it is easy to see gaps in the market.

The apparel market is a competitive sector with a host of finely delineated fashion brands. Speedo's market positioning is built around producing high-performance, technical products.

offerings, for example) and the tactics (moving from conservative to sporty, for example) that will help the company to achieve that strategic goal.

Market analysis such as this may, for example, have helped luxury Singaporean tea shop TWG Tea to identify an opportunity in the market. Launched in 2008, TWG targets a slightly older, wealthier customer base than coffee shops and other "lifestyle" cafés. TWG has opened new locations across the world, based on studying the competition, identifying a market gap, and designing its products and services to fill that gap.

Internal focus

As a company grows it might choose to draw up a map including just its own products. Analysis of the results can help identify any overlap between different products (informing decisions about which products to drop, and which to concentrate research and development and marketing spend, for example). It can also be used to ensure that the company's marketing message stays on track, helping to avoid strategic drift.

Perceived as a technical performance product, Speedo, for example, needs to ensure that its marketing reflects that view; a campaign that promotes Speedo as a fashionable label would risk confusing customers and could damage the brand.

The key to successful market mapping is market research. While it can be useful to compare internal and external perceptions of a product, and the products of the competition, it is the customers' views that matter most. When

based on such data, even though managers may disagree, the market map cannot be "wrong"—it simply represents, for better or worse, how the brand is perceived. The challenge for management is to use the map, and knowledge of internal strengths and weaknesses, to plan the appropriate strategic response.

Both SWOT analysis and market mapping allow a company to better understand itself, its market, and, most importantly, the competition. Equally, being aware of weaknesses can help avoid costly strategic mistakes, such as producing overly ambitious products or making an entry into a crowded market position. An appreciation of the opportunities and threats of the market, and the relative and shifting positions of competing products, is essential to long-term successful strategic planning. To plan where you are going, it helps to know where you are—and where your competitors are too. ∎

Albert Humphrey

Born in 1926, Albert Humphrey was educated at the University of Illinois, US, and at the Massachusetts Institute of Technology (MIT), where he gained a master's degree in Chemical Engineering. He later went on to earn an MBA from Harvard University. While working with the Stanford Research Institute (now SRI International) between 1960 and 1970, Humphrey came up with the Stakeholder Concept, which has since been used by business leaders and politicians. He also undertook research to identify why corporate planning failed, by holding interviews with more than 5,000 executives at over 1,100 companies. As a result of the findings, he invented SOFT analysis: "what is good in the present is Satisfactory, good in the future is an Opportunity; bad in the present is a Fault, and bad in the future is a Threat." Fault was later softened to the more acceptable Weaknesses, and Satisfactory became Strengths. The now-ubiquitous acronym SWOT was born.

THE SECRET OF BUSINESS IS TO KNOW SOMETHING THAT NOBODY ELSE KNOWS

STAND OUT IN THE MARKET

IN CONTEXT

FOCUS
Differentiation

KEY DATES
1933 US economist Edward Chamberlin's *Theory of Monopolistic Competition* describes differentiation as a means for a company to charge more for its products or services by distinguishing them from the competition.

1940s The concept of the Unique Selling Proposition (USP) is put forward by Rosser Reeves, advertising executive at New York advertising agency Ted Bates, Inc.

2003 US marketing professor Philip Kotler outlines the need for USPs to be superseded by Emotional Selling Propositions (ESPs) in his book *Marketing Insights from A to Z*.

Few businesses enjoy the privileges of monopoly power in their chosen fields of operation. Most markets are increasingly global, increasingly crowded and, therefore, increasingly competitive. In order to achieve commercial success companies need to do something different—as Greek shipping magnate Aristotle Onassis recommended, they need to "know something that nobody else knows" in order to stand out from the competition.

Unique Selling Propositions

Faced with competition, the strategy for most companies is to differentiate. This involves offering

See also: Finding a profitable niche 22–23 ▪ Gaining an edge 32–39 ▪ Reinventing and adapting 52–57 ▪ Porter's generic strategies 178–83 ▪ Good and bad strategy 184–85 ▪ The value chain 216–17

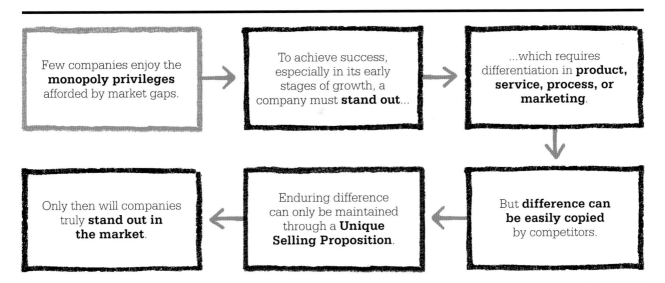

Few companies enjoy the **monopoly privileges** afforded by market gaps.

To achieve success, especially in its early stages of growth, a company must **stand out**...

...which requires differentiation in **product, service, process, or marketing**.

But **difference can be easily copied** by competitors.

Enduring difference can only be maintained through a **Unique Selling Proposition**.

Only then will companies truly **stand out in the market**.

customers something that the competition cannot or does not offer—a Unique Selling Proposition (USP). The concept was developed by US advertising executive Rosser Reeves in the 1940s to represent the key point of dramatic difference that makes a product salable at a price higher than rival products. Tangible USPs are hard to acquire and hard to copy, which is what makes them unique.

Companies must distinguish their product or service from the competition at every stage of production—from raw material extraction to after-sales service. Products such as Nespresso coffee-makers and Crocs footwear, and service providers such as majority Asian-owned hotel group Tune Hotels, are all heavily differentiated, each having a strong USP.

The primary benefit of uniqueness, however it is achieved, is greater customer loyalty and increased flexibility in pricing. Differentiation guards products and services from low-priced competition; it justifies higher prices and protects profitability; and it can give businesses the competitive advantage needed to stand out in the market.

The challenge of difference

By definition, not all products can be unique. Differentiation is costly, time consuming, and difficult to achieve, and functional differences are quickly copied—"me-too" strategies are commonplace. Touchscreen technology was introduced to the cell-phone market as a point of differentiation for Apple's iPhone, but is now a feature of most smartphones. Differentiation often does not remain a point of difference for long.

With functional uniqueness being so elusive, marketing guru Philip Kotler suggested that companies focus instead on an Emotional Selling Proposition (ESP). In other words, that the task of marketing is to generate an emotional connection to the brand that is so strong that customers perceive difference from the competition. For example, while the design and functionality of Nike and Adidas sneakers are distinct, the differences are so small that they amount to only a marginal difference in performance. The products' differences are, however, magnified in the perception of the consumer through marketing and the power of branding—uniqueness is achieved through brand imagery, promotion, and sponsorship.

Apple achieved differentiation in the fledgling digital-music market by combining easy-to-use software »

There is no such thing as a commodity. All goods and services are differentiable.
Theodore Levitt
US economist (1925–2006)

with well-designed hardware and a user interface that integrated the two. The product itself—the iPod portable music device—was functionally little different than existing MP3 players, but combined with the iTunes software to create a unique customer experience. This experience is Apple's ESP, which the company promoted with its "Think Different" advertising campaign.

Standing out

One company that has achieved uniqueness is the British fashion label Superdry, which has grown to include more than 300 stores in Europe, Asia, North and South America, and South Africa. Drawing a novel, international influence from Japanese graphics and vintage Americana, combined with the values of British tailoring, Superdry quickly established a strong position in the hypercompetitive clothing market from its launch in 2004. The business started life in university towns across the UK, a positioning that gave the brand a youthful appeal. Despite limited advertising and abstaining from celebrity endorsements, Superdry's popularity rapidly grew. The company's distinctive look quickly caught the

eye of celebrities (a jacket worn by soccer player David Beckham became one of its best-selling products, and Beckham himself became an unoffical talisman of the brand), providing free publicity.

Superdry focused on offering clothing with a fashionably tailored fit and attention to detail (even down to garment stitching). Worn by off-duty office workers, students, sports stars, and celebrities alike, the brand was able to appeal to a broad customer base. Most differentiation strategies involve targeting one segment of the market; Superdry chose to target them all. The brand's unique blend of fashion with ease of wear, comfort with style, and the presence of mysterious but meaningless Japanese writing, has proved a difficult mix for competitors to replicate.

Maintaining uniqueness

As many companies discover, popularity can be the enemy of difference. While Superdry clothing has become increasingly ubiquitous around the world, its uniqueness and difference have declined. The challenge for Superdry, like all companies, is to protect its uniqueness while also

expanding its reach—to stand out from the crowd, while welcoming those crowds into its stores.

Differentiation can occur at any point in the value chain. Standing out is not limited to products or services—it can occur in any number of internal processes that translate into an improved customer experience. Swedish furniture retailer IKEA, for example, differentiates itself not only through contemporary design and low prices, but through the entire customer retail experience. The company's low prices are achieved, in part, through its self-picking and self-assembly retail model—the customer experience involves picking products from the company's vast showrooms and warehouses and then, once they have transported the goods home, assembling the furniture.

Even the way IKEA "guides" shoppers on a one-way, defined route through its showrooms is unique. While this tactic encourages spontaneous purchases, it also helps to reinforce IKEA's points of difference—customers are exposed to predesigned rooms and furniture layouts that emphasize the brand's contemporary style. Price is kept low since fewer store assistants are required to direct customers around the store.

Different but the same

Paradoxically, familiarity can also be a source of differentiation. The entire McDonald's organization revolves around providing almost identical fast-food products, with the same service, in identical

Fashion label Superdry is a young company that has successfully carved out market share. Rapid growth since its founding in 2004 is thanks in part to a highly differentiated, faux-vintage look.

Differentiation is not so important when a company's products match the desires of the customer and do not overlap with the competition. Although the risks might be high, differentiation is most effective when your products are popular, but overlap with those of the competition.

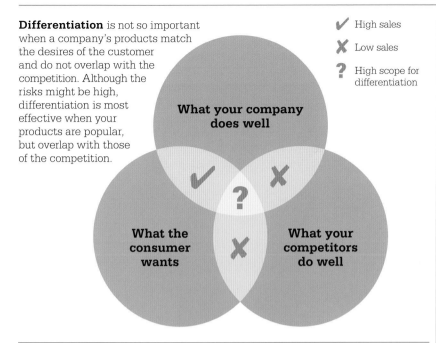

✔ High sales

✘ Low sales

? High scope for differentiation

What your company does well

What the consumer wants

What your competitors do well

restaurants the world over. This familiarity differentiates McDonald's from unknown local offerings, and from other global competitors who cannot maintain the same degree of consistency across their operating territories.

In a market in which rival companies promote the uniqueness of their products in ever-louder and more complex ways, consumers have become increasingly savvy when it comes to distinguishing reality from rhetoric. While differences do not have to be tangible—the evidence shows that an Emotional Selling Proposition (ESP) is often enough—the challenge for businesses is that points of differentiation do have to be genuine and believable. Developing an emotional connection with the customer requires that the differentiation is understood and consistently delivered throughout the organization. Well-defined core principles that celebrate a company's uniqueness should inform the customer experience at

every point of contact—difference has to be believable, and it is only believable if it is dependable.

Sustaining differentiation
Once established, uniqueness—whether functional or emotional—requires nurturing and protecting. Standing out from the crowd is a constant battle that is fought in the hearts and minds of the company's staff, as well as customers. As legal clashes between rivals—such as Apple and Samsung—demonstrate, uniqueness might also have to be contested in the courtroom.

Every industry has leaders and followers—what separates them is that the leaders are usually those with the most defensible points of differentiation. Whether in features and functionality, brand image, service, process, speed, or convenience, uniqueness must be established and communicated for a company and its offerings to stand out in the market. The key to long-lasting success is making that differentiation sustainable. ■

Rosser Reeves

US advertising executive Rosser Reeves (1910–84) held the maxim that an advertisement should show off the value of a product, not the cleverness of the copywriter. After a brief spell at the University of Virginia, from where he was expelled for drunken misconduct, Reeves worked as a journalist and then copywriter before joining advertising agency Ted Bates, Inc. in New York in 1940. His exceptional talent saw him rise to become Chairman of the company in 1955. He is credited with redefining television advertising and, among many others, for formulating slogans such as "It melts in your mouth, not in your hand" for chocolate confectionary brand M&Ms. Reeves's Unique Selling Proposition, first outlined in the 1940s, was described in his 1961 book *Reality of Advertising*. Such was his impact on the advertising industry that his legacy lives on long after his death—his pioneering style of leadership was the inspiration for the lead character in US television series *Mad Men*.

In order to be irreplaceable one must always be different.
Coco Chanel
French fashion designer (1881–1971)

BE FIRST OR BE BETTER

GAINING AN EDGE

IN CONTEXT

FOCUS
Competitive advantage

KEY DATES
1988 US scholars David Montgomery and Marvin Lieberman write "First-Mover Advantage," outlining the competitive advantages of being first to market.

1995 Amazon.com launches, the first of a new breed of online retailers.

1997–2000 Adopting the "be first" mantra, dot-com companies race to market; many fail when the promised advantages do not materialize.

1998 Montgomery and Lieberman question their original findings in their paper, "First-Mover (Dis)Advantages."

2001 Amazon.com returns its first profit. The company's first-mover advantages were significant, but a good business model mattered more.

First-movers have no competition and have the potential to **become market leaders**…

…but **unless the market is static**, and technological innovation is limited, **the risk of failure is high**.

Later entrants enter a recognized market and **know what mistakes to avoid**.

They stand to benefit most in a **rapidly changing market**, in which **technological innovation** is advanced.

In order to gain an edge, either be first, or be better.

If you need to buy a book online, which website do you visit first? If you want to research the author of the book, which search engine do you use? The answers, most probably, are Amazon and Google, respectively. Such is the dominance of these two Internet giants that their names define their respective markets.

Both organizations have a significant edge in the markets they lead, but they achieved that dominance by different means. Amazon, launched in 1995, gained its advantage by being the first business to enter the online retail market, establishing its brand name, and building a loyal customer base. Google, by contrast, was by no means first. When Google launched in 1998, the market was already dominated by several large players; Google's edge came from offering a superior product—not only was it faster, but it produced more accurate search results than any of its competitors.

Getting into a market first has significant advantages, but there are also benefits to being second. The key is that in order to gain a competitive edge in the market, a business needs either to be first, or it needs to be better.

Market pioneers
The benefits of being first into a market are known as "first-mover advantage," a term popularized in 1988 by Stanford Business School professor David Montgomery and his co-author, Marvin Lieberman. Although introduced a decade previously, Montgomery and Lieberman's idea took particular hold during the dot-com bubble between 1997 and 2000. Spurred

See also: Beating the odds at start-up 20–21 ▪ Stand out in the market 28–31 ▪ How fast to grow 44–45 ▪ The Greiner curve 58–61 ▪ Creativity and invention 72–73 ▪ Changing the game 92–99 ▪ Balancing long- versus short-termism 190–91

Amazon.com was a first-mover in the online retail market. It has dominated the industry since its launch in 1995, creating strong brand recognition and a loyal customer base.

on by the example of Amazon, businesses spent millions pitching themselves headlong into new online markets. Conventional wisdom was that being first ensured that the company's brand name became synonymous with that segment, and that early market dominance would create barriers to entry for subsequent competition.

In the end, however, overspending, overhype, and overreaching into markets where little demand existed was the downfall of many fledgling dot-coms. With notable exceptions, businesses found that promised returns were not being realized and funds quickly ran short—and for many of these first-movers, failure followed.

First-mover advantage
Being first out of the block undoubtedly has its advantages, and in the case of the dot-coms, those advantages were exaggerated to the extreme. First-movers often enjoy premium prices, capture significant market share, and have

a brand name strongly linked to the market itself. First-movers also have more time than later entrants to perfect processes and systems, and to accumulate market knowledge. They can also secure advantageous physical locations (a prime location on a main street of a city, for example), secure the employment of talented staff, or

First-mover advantages accrue when a company gains a first-mover opportunity (through proficiency or luck) and is able to maintain an edge despite subsequent entry.
David Montgomery and Marvin Lieberman

access beneficial terms with key suppliers (who may also be eager to enter the new market). Additionally, first-movers may be able to build switching costs into their product, making it expensive or inconvenient for customers to switch to a rival offering once an initial purchase has been made. Gillette, for example, having invented the safety razor in 1901, has consistently leveraged its first-mover advantage to create new products, such as a "shaving system" that combines cheap handles with expensive razor blades.

Market strategies
In the case of Amazon.com, first-mover advantage consisted of a combination of factors. In the newly emerging e-commerce market, customers were eager to try online purchasing, and Amazon was well placed to exploit this growing curiosity. Books represented a small and safe initial purchase, and Amazon's simple web design made buying easy and enjoyable. Early sales enabled the organization to adapt and perfect its systems, and to adjust its website to match customer needs—adding, for example, its OneClick ordering system to enable purchases without entering payment details.

Amazon was also able to build distribution systems that ensured quick and reliable delivery of its products. Although competitors could replicate these systems, customers already trusted Amazon, and the brand loyalty »

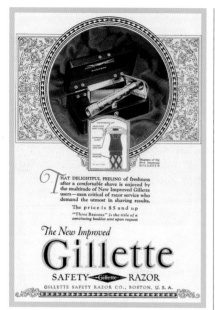

Gillette invented the safety razor in 1901 and later consolidated its first-mover advantage by developing a "shaving system" that made it difficult for customers to switch brands.

the organization enjoyed created significant emotional switching costs; even today, Amazon enjoys the benefits of this trust and loyalty, and almost a third of all US book sales are made via Amazon.com.

A recent example of how important first-mover advantage remains are the "patent wars" contested between most of the leading smartphone makers (including Apple, Samsung, and HTC). Patents help a company to defend technological advantage. In the hypercompetitive smartphone industry, being first to market with a new technological feature offers critical, albeit short-term, advantage. In an industry in which consumers' switching costs are high, even short-term advantages can have a significant impact on revenue.

Since the publication of Montgomery and Lieberman's original paper in 1988, academic research has indicated that significant advantages accrue to market pioneers, which can be directly attributable to the timing of entry. The irony is that in a retrospective paper that appeared in 1998, "First-Mover (Dis) Advantages," Montgomery and Lieberman themselves backed off their original claims concerning the benefits of being the first to enter a market.

Building on the work of, among others, US academics Peter Golder and Gerard Tellis in 1993, Montgomery and Lieberman's 1998 paper questioned the entire notion of first-mover advantage. In their research, Golder and Tellis had found that almost half the first-movers in their sample of 500 brands, in 50 product categories, failed. Moreover, they found that there were few cases where later entrants had not become profitable or even dominant players—in fact, their research identified that the failure rate for first-movers was 47 percent, compared to only 8 percent for fast followers.

Learning from mistakes

The challenge for first-movers is that the market is often unproven; industry pioneers leap into the dark without fully understanding customer needs or market dynamics. First-movers often launch untried products onto unsuspecting customers; and it is rare that they get it right first time. Large companies may be able to take the losses of such early-market entry mistakes; small companies, on the other hand, may soon find that their cash is running out and their tenuous business models are collapsing.

Later entrants have the advantage of learning from the mistakes of the first-movers, and from entering a proven market. They are also able to avoid costly investment in risky and potentially flawed processes or technologies; first-movers, by contrast, may have accrued significant "sunk costs" (past investment) in old, less-efficient technologies, and may be less able to adapt as the industry matures. Followers can enter at the point at which technology and processes are relatively well established, with both cost and risks being lower.

Followers may have to fight to overcome the first-movers' brand loyalty, but simply offering a superior product that better addresses customer needs is often sufficient to secure a market. Brand recognition is one thing, but technical and product superiority can give that all-important competitive edge. Moreover, with investment costs being much lower, followers often have surplus cash to use on marketing, thereby offsetting the branding advantages of the first-mover.

When Google, for example, entered the Internet search business in 1998, the market was dominated by the likes of Yahoo, Lycos, and AltaVista, all of whom had established customer bases and brand recognition. However, Google was able to learn from the

Good artists copy; great artists steal.
Steve Jobs
US former CEO of Apple (1955–2011)

> If later entrants can leapfrog pioneers, companies could be better off entering late.
> **Peter Golder and Gerard Tellis**

mistakes of these earlier entrants and, quite simply, build a better product. The organization realized that with so much information on the Internet people wanted search results that were comprehensive and relevant; the various market incumbents offered a variety of systems for filtering search results, but Google was able to take the best of these systems and build its own unique algorithm that led to market dominance.

First-mover failures

There are numerous examples in corporate history of first-movers that were unable to achieve or maintain a competitive advantage. Famous failures in the online sphere include Friends Reunited and MySpace. Although both companies still exist, their first-mover advantage was not sufficient to offset the might (and product superiority) of Facebook. Similarly, eToys.com, launched in 1999, was one of a new breed of online retailers, but first-mover advantage was not enough to sustain the business and the company declared bankruptcy in 2001—by coincidence, the same year that Amazon started to sell toys. (Resurrected some years later, etoys.com is now owned by Toys R

Us.) The online clothing retailer boo.com is an example of a first-mover that had technological superiority, but was ahead of its time—the site was too resource-heavy for most consumers' slow Internet connections. Launched in 1999, boo.com went into receivership the following year—being first is not a guarantee of success if the basic business model is flawed.

Despite the evidence presented by Golder and Tellis, and examples such as Google, it remains the case that first-mover advantage has captured corporate imagination. Mirroring the earlier dot-com gold rush, the recent boom in the market for web-based smartphone- and tablet-accessed applications (the "app" market) is fueled by a desire to be first. Thousands of apps have launched in the hope of staking their claims on lucrative segments

of this new market. But success is not guaranteed—a 2012 study revealed that on average, 65 percent of users delete apps within 90 days of installing them.

Timing is everything

The reason a first-mover does not always yield its promised advantages is that much depends on timing, and therefore luck. In their 2005 paper, "The Half-Truth of First-Mover Advantage," US business scholars Fernando Suarez and Gianvito Lanzolla identified technological innovation and the speed at which the market is developing as crucial in determining whether or not being a first-mover is advantageous.

Their findings suggest that when a market is slow-moving and technological evolution is limited, first-mover advantage can be »

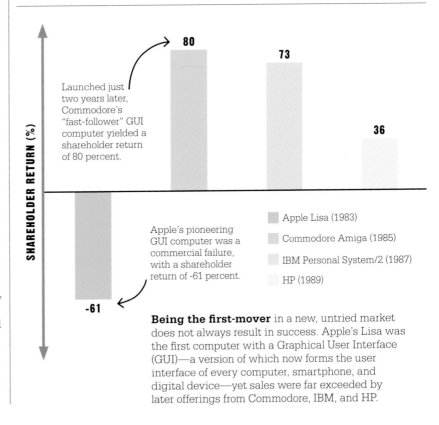

Launched just two years later, Commodore's "fast-follower" GUI computer yielded a shareholder return of 80 percent.

Apple's pioneering GUI computer was a commercial failure, with a shareholder return of -61 percent.

SHAREHOLDER RETURN (%)

80
73
36
-61

■ Apple Lisa (1983)
■ Commodore Amiga (1985)
■ IBM Personal System/2 (1987)
□ HP (1989)

Being the first-mover in a new, untried market does not always result in success. Apple's Lisa was the first computer with a Graphical User Interface (GUI)—a version of which now forms the user interface of every computer, smartphone, and digital device—yet sales were far exceeded by later offerings from Commodore, IBM, and HP.

significant. They give the example of the market for vacuum cleaners, and, in particular, of the long-term market leader, Hoover. Until the relatively recent introduction of Dyson cleaners, the market was benign and technological advancement slow. Having been first to market in 1908, Hoover enjoyed several decades of advantage—an advantage that was (and, in some places, still is) reflected in the widespread use of the company's brand name as the verb "to hoover."

In other industries, however, where technological change or market evolution is rapid, first-movers are often at a disadvantage. The first search engines are examples of businesses that had too much invested in early iterations of a technology to keep up with the rapid pace of change.

Early advantage quickly becomes obsolete in changeable markets. As the market evolves, later entrants are those that seem to be cutting edge, offering innovative features that build on the market-knowledge as well as learning from the mistakes of the first-mover. The first-mover may have enjoyed short-lived advantage but in dynamic markets such an advantage is rarely durable. Even Apple, who enjoyed significant early-entrant advantage in the smartphone market with the iPhone, is not immune from first-mover disadvantage. Competitors, Samsung in particular, were able to listen to customer complaints about iPhones, analyze customer needs, and produce products with features and functionality welcomed by the market. Apple, locked into previous technology iterations, took time to react and iPhone sales suffered as a result.

Customer needs

To gain an edge, therefore, you do not always need to be first. Indeed, US multinational Procter & Gamble, for example, prefers only to enter those markets in which it can establish a strong number one or number two position over the long-term—rarely is this achieved in a blind rush to be first.

Procter & Gamble seeks markets that are demographically and structurally attractive, with lower capital requirements, and higher margins. But most

> 66
> If you do things well,
> do them better.
> **Anita Roddick**
> **UK entrepreneur (1942–2007)**
> 99

importantly, the organization insists on a deep understanding of customer needs in any market they enter. In other words, they would rather enter mature markets than be first into new ones.

The company values long-term relationships with its customers and suppliers; its view of innovation is different from small companies who, in attempting to capture market share, strive to gain an edge through the introduction of disruptive technology—innovative technology that seeks to destabilize the existing market. Procter & Gamble, perhaps heeding the research, considers such strategies to be short-lived. They realize that overly rapid innovation runs the risk of cannibalizing their own sales and reducing the returns on new product investment. In the market for disposable baby diapers, for example, Procter & Gamble was more than ten years behind the first mover. The company's now famous Pampers brand was launched in 1961, following some way behind Johnson & Johnson's Chux brand,

The PalmPilot, launched in 1997, was a successful fast-follower product. It followed Apple's unsuccessful Newton, which was the first personal digital assistant (PDA) to enter the market.

which was launched in 1949. At the time, disposable diapers were a new innovation, and customers were wary of their use. Procter & Gamble waited until customers had come to accept the product before entering the market. Moreover, they spent nearly five years researching and addressing each of the major problems with Chux and developed a product that was more absorbent, had lower leakage, was more comfortable for the baby, offered two sizes, and could be produced at a significantly lower cost. Today, *Forbes* magazine lists Pampers as one of the world's most powerful brands, valued at over $8.5 billion, with the diapers being purchased by 25 million consumers in over 100 countries. By contrast, Chux was phased out by Johnson & Johnson in the 1970s due to shrinking sales.

Securing a foothold

In reality, then, while it is readily assumed that speed is good when entering a market, gaining an edge might depend less on timing than it does on appropriateness. Whether a company is first, second, or last to market is important; but it is less important than the suitability of a company's products or services to that market, and its ability to deliver on brand promises. Both these factors can have a profound impact on long-term viability and business success.

Amazon may have enjoyed lasting first-mover advantage, but that alone is insufficient to account for its phenomenal success. Amazon leverages its first-mover advantage into a sustainable competitive edge; its website is continually made easier to use, it offers a range of complimentary products, and it continues to drive down costs, enabling it to offer market-beating prices. Most notably, Amazon did not return a profit until 2001—the company spent its earlier years building a better product. The foundations of success may have been laid by first-mover advantage, but Amazon's edge has been built on long-term good business practice.

First-movers undoubtedly have a natural competitive edge. Whether it is a lasting impression on customers, strong brand recognition, high switching costs, control of scarce resources, or the advantages of experience, that edge can help to secure a strong, and long-term, foothold in the market. But as research shows, second-movers, and their followers, may sometimes be in an advantageous position. Learning from the mistakes of early entrants, they frequently offer superior products at lower prices. With the aid of skillful marketing, these benefits can be leveraged to offset the advantages enjoyed by first-movers. To become a market leader, a business needs either to be first, and impressive, or it needs to be better. The companies we remember, the Amazons and the Googles, are those that were either first or better—the ones we forget are those that had no edge at all. ■

To suffer the penalty of too much haste, which is too little speed.
Plato
Greek philosopher (429–347 BCE)

Jeff Bezos

Born on January 12, 1964 in Albuquerque, New Mexico, US, Jeff Bezos had an early love of science and computers. He studied computer science and electrical engineering at Princeton University, and graduated *summa cum laude* in 1986.

Bezos started his career on Wall Street, and by 1990 had become the youngest senior vice-president at the investment company D. E. Shaw. Four years later, in 1994, he quit his lucrative job to open Amazon.com, the online book retailer—he was barely 30 years old at the time.

As with many Internet start-ups, Bezos, with just a handful of employees, created the new business in his garage; but as operations grew, they moved into a small house. The Amazon.com site was launched officially on July 16, 1995. Amazon became a public limited company in 1997; the company's first year of profit was 2001. Today, Bezos is listed by *Forbes* magazine as one of the wealthiest people in the US; and Amazon stands as one of the biggest global success stories in the history of the Internet.

PUT ALL YOUR EGGS IN ONE BASKET, AND THEN WATCH THAT BASKET
MANAGING RISK

IN CONTEXT

FOCUS
Risk management

KEY DATES
1932 The American Risk and Insurance Association is established.

1963 Robert Mehr and Bob Hedges publish *Risk Management in the Business Enterprise*, claiming that the objective of risk management is to maximize a company's productive efficiency.

1970s Inflation and changes to the international monetary system (the ending of the Bretton Woods agreement) increase commercial risks.

1987 Merrill Lynch becomes the first bank to open a risk-management department.

2011 The US Financial Crisis Inquiry Commission says that the 2008 financial crisis was caused partly by financial companies "taking on too much risk."

Entrepreneurs are defined by their willingness to bear risk—particularly the risk of business failure. This is especially true for those starting new companies, because more than half of start-ups fail within the first five years. Lesser risks in established businesses include the possible failure of new products, or damage to the brand or a manager's reputation. Whatever the level or type, however, risk is something that all businesses need to be aware of and manage carefully. US businessman Andrew Carnegie was pondering these issues when he suggested that in terms of

Risk is an **inevitable part** of business.

But it **can be quantified** and action taken...

...through **oversight and good management**.

Part of this process involves deciding **what level of risk is "acceptable"**...

...and **where to place the risk**—on all the "eggs in the basket," or just one?

Managing risk is a **strategic process**, balancing cost against reward.

managing risk, it might be best to put all your eggs in one basket, then watch that basket.

From the collapse of Lehman Brothers (2008), to BP's Deepwater Horizon disaster (2010), events of the early 21st century fundamentally changed how organizations perceive risk. Companies now think in terms of two factors: oversight and management. "Risk oversight" is how a company's owners govern the processes for identifying, prioritizing, and managing critical risks, and for ensuring that these processes are continually reviewed. "Risk management" refers to the detailed procedures and policies for avoiding or reducing risks.

Inherent risks

Risk is inherent in all business activity. Start-ups, for example, face the risk of too few customers, and therefore insufficient revenue to cover costs. There is also the risk that a competitor will copy the company's idea, and perhaps offer a better alternative. When a company has borrowed money from a bank

there is a risk that interest rates will rise, and repayments will become too burdensome to afford. Start-ups that rely on overseas trade are also exposed to exchange-rate risk.

Moreover, new businesses in particular may be exposed to the risk of operating in only one market. Whereas large companies often diversify their operations to spread risk, the success of small companies is often linked to the success of one idea (the original genesis for the start-up) or one geographic region, such as the local area. A decline in that market or area can lead to failure. It is essential that new businesses are mindful of market changes, and position themselves to adapt to those changes.

The Instagram image-sharing social-media application, for example, started life as a location-based service called Burbn. Faced with competition, the business changed track into image-sharing. Had Instagram not reacted to the risks, and been savvy enough to diversify its offering (regularly adding new features), it may not have survived.

> It's impossible that the improbable will never happen.
> **Emil Gumbel**
> **German statistician (1891–1966)**

At its heart, risk is a strategic issue. Business owners must carefully weigh the operational risk of start-up, or the risks of a new product or new project, against potential profits or losses—in other words, the strategic consequences of action *vs.* inaction. Risk must be quantified and managed; and it poses a constant strategic challenge. Fortune favors the brave, but with people's lives and the success of the business at stake, caution cannot simply be thrown to the wind. ▪

BP's Deepwater Horizon incident led to huge fines and US government monitoring of its safety practices and ethics for four years.

In deep water

Even large and diverse organizations can find it hard to successfully balance risk against potential financial reward. On April 20, 2010, Deepwater Horizon, an offshore oil rig chartered by British Petroleum (BP), exploded, killing 11 workers and spilling tens of thousands of barrels of crude oil into the Gulf of Mexico.

The incident was blamed on management failure to adequately quantify and manage risk; the official hearing cited a culture of "every dollar counts." Analysts who examined the disaster claimed that BP had prioritized financial return over operational risk. Chief executive Tony Hayward, who took the post in 2007, had suggested that the organization's poor performance at the time was due to excessive caution. Coupled with increasing pressure from shareholders for better returns, the bullish approach that followed led to significant cost cutting and, eventually, risk-management failures.

LUCK IS A DIVIDEND OF SWEAT. THE MORE YOU SWEAT, THE LUCKIER YOU GET

LUCK (AND HOW TO GET LUCKY)

IN CONTEXT

FOCUS
Maximizing opportunity

KEY DATES
1974 3M employee Art Fry uses the adhesive developed— and rejected as defective—by a colleague six years earlier to attach a bookmark in his hymnbook. This chance usage leads to the Post-it Note.

2009 A *Harvard Business Review* article "Are 'Great' Companies Just Lucky?" reports that in only half of the 287 high-performing companies surveyed could success be attributed to distinguishable practices or features of the organizations themselves.

2013 Five years' hard work yields music group Daft Punk's aptly titled song "Get Lucky". A result of industry collaboration, market research, and strong marketing and publicity, the song's commercial success demonstrates the value of business planning.

Luck is usually regarded as something over which businesses have no control. Yet, as McDonald's CEO Ray Kroc said, "the more you sweat, the luckier you get," suggesting that luck can be created. The reality is that both are true. As global markets become more volatile and less predictable, luck plays an inevitable part in business success. Launch a start-up at the same time as a rival and it may be luck that determines who succeeds, and who fails.

Making your own luck
A well-considered business plan is designed to dispense with reliance on luck. A good idea, underpinned by detailed market research and solid financial planning, may help a start-up to ride the whims of the market. A good plan charts a course of action in turbulent markets, protects against the unknown, and prepares the company for contingencies.

In addition, a well-conceived plan can ensure that a company is in a position to benefit from favorable

The first rule of luck in business is that you should persevere in doing the right thing. Opportunities will come your way if you do.
Ronald Cohen
UK venture capitalist (1945–)

market conditions. In other words, what might seem like luck is often the result of planning. Take the famous example of 3M Post-it Notes. The invention of a reusable glue was accidental, but it was business insight that turned the lucky discovery into a commercial success.

With so many variables, luck is likely to play a part in the survival of a start-up. But a good plan reduces how much luck a company needs. ∎

See also: Beating the odds at start-up 20–21 ∎ Gaining an edge 32–39 ∎ Understanding the market 234–41 ∎ Forecasting 278–79

BROADEN YOUR VISION, AND MAINTAIN STABILITY WHILE ADVANCING FORWARD
TAKE THE SECOND STEP

The business landscape may appear to be dominated by corporate goliaths, but the reality is that small businesses outnumber large companies by a significant margin. In fact, most businesses never grow beyond the scope of the owner—they start small and stay small. In the US, more than 99 percent of companies employ fewer than 500 people. In 2012, there were almost 5 million small businesses (with fewer than 49 employees), but only 6,000 companies employing more than 250 people.

Aspiration, or its lack, is a key factor for small-scale companies. Many small-business owners are content with the lifestyle the business allows them, and have no desire for growth. But he biggest reason for a lack of growth is finance. Growth requires access to capital, which is difficult and expensive to access for small companies. Moreover, unlimited liability means that an owner's personal assets (such as the family home) are at risk if the business fails—a risk that many are unwilling to take.

Entrepreneurial spirit is defined as the willingness to take risks. Business owners who do aspire to growth must be willing to take the risky but important second step. For most small-business owners, this means employing the first nonfamily member and beginning to acquire the necessary leadership and management skills to scale the business and manage the people, systems, and processes. ∎

Large businesses might appear to be towering oaks, but most have acornlike beginnings. A common difference between them and companies that stay small is the willingness to take risks.

See also: Beating the odds at start-up 20–21 ▪ Managing risk 40–41 ▪ The Greiner curve 58–61 ▪ Who bears the risk? 138–45 ▪ Small is beautiful 172–77

NOTHING GREAT IS CREATED SUDDENLY

HOW FAST TO GROW

IN CONTEXT

FOCUS
Business growth

KEY DATES
1970s McKinsey & Company consultants develop the MABA matrix to help conglomerates decide which divisions to grow, and how quickly.

2001 Neil Churchill—professor at INSEAD business school, France and John Mullins—professor at London Business School, UK—write *How Fast Can Your Company Afford to Grow*, introducing the self-financeable growth rate (SFG).

2002 Toyota announces plans to be the world's largest car producer. Eight years later, after recalling more than 8 million cars due to quality issues, it admits to growing too fast.

2012 Edward Hess writes *Grow to Greatness: Smart Growth for Entrepreneurial Businesses*, describing growth as recurring change.

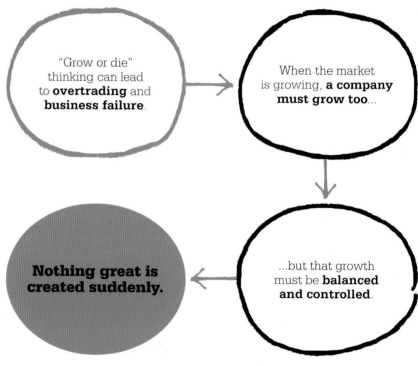

"Grow or die" thinking can lead to **overtrading** and **business failure**.

When the market is growing, **a company must grow too**...

...but that growth must be **balanced and controlled**.

Nothing great is created suddenly.

One reason many new businesses fail is, perhaps surprisingly, because they grow too fast. Excessively rapid growth can cause companies to overreach their ability to fund growth: they simply run out of cash to pay for day-to-day operations. A major challenge for any manager is to balance income with expenditure, ensuring that there is sufficient cash to meet the rising costs of the business.

In 2001, business professors Neil Churchill and John Mullins created a formula for calculating the pace at which a company can expand from internal financing alone. Known

See also: Managing risk 40–41 ▪ Luck (and how to get lucky) 42 ▪ The Greiner curve 58–61 ▪ Hubris and nemesis 100–03 ▪ Profit versus cash flow 152–53 ▪ Small is beautiful 172–77 ▪ The MABA matrix 192–93

as the self-financeable growth rate (SFG), it helps managers to strike the right balance between consuming and generating cash. It does this by measuring three things: the amount of time a company's money is tied up in inventory before the company has paid for its goods or services; the amount of money needed to finance each dollar of sales; and the amount of cash that is generated by each dollar of sales.

Sustainable growth

When accurately applied, the SFG formula determines the rate at which a company can sustain growth through only the revenues it generates—without needing to approach external funding agencies for more cash. Essentially, it predicts a sustainable growth rate and helps to avoid overtrading. When a market is growing faster than a company's SFG, Churchill and Mullins identified three ways for managers to exploit the growth opportunity: speed up cash flow; reduce costs; or raise prices.

Each of these "levers" helps to generate the cash needed to fuel faster growth.

As a young start-up business, the fashion brand Superdry enjoyed phenomenal growth. From its inception in the UK in 2004, the company rapidly added new stores throughout the world. In 2012, however, after several profit warnings, it became clear that Superdry had become a victim of its own success. Critics suggested that the brand was so focused on growth that it had forgotten its fashion roots, failing to update products on a seasonal basis. Other reasons for the decline included supply issues, accounting mistakes, and an inability to react quickly enough to fierce competition. In a tacit acknowledgement that excessive growth was to blame, the company announced plans to review its new store openings.

Business-growth expert Edward Hess suggests that growth can add value to a company, but if it is not properly managed, it can "stress a business's culture, controls,

The fate of the exploding Helix Nebula resembles the decline of a company that has expanded too rapidly: after using up all its energy resources, the star collapses on itself and dies.

processes and people, eventually destroying its value and even leading the company to grow and die." Growth is not a strategy, he claims, but a complex change process, which requires the right mindset, the right procedures, experimentation, and an enabling environment. ▪

A profitable company that tries to grow too fast can run out of cash— even if its products are great successes.
Neil Churchill and John Mullins

Edward Hess

A graduate of the universities of Florida, Virginia, and New York, Edward Hess has been teaching and working in the world of business for more than 30 years. He began his career at the oil company Atlantic Richfield Company, and later became a senior executive at several other leading US organizations, including Arthur Andersen.

Hess specializes in business growth, and especially in debunking the "myths" that growth is always good and always linear. Contrary to the dictum that companies must "grow or die," he suggests that they are likely to "grow and die."

Hess is the author of ten books and more than 100 practitioner articles and case studies. He is currently professor of business administration at the University of Virginia, US.

Key works

2006 *The Search for Organic Growth*
2010 *Smart Growth*
2012 *Grow to Greatness*

THE ROLE OF THE CEO IS TO ENABLE PEOPLE TO EXCEL
FROM ENTREPRENEUR TO LEADER

IN CONTEXT

FOCUS
Business growth

KEY DATES
1972 Professor Larry Greiner suggests the various stages of business growth are preceded by crisis, the first being a crisis of leadership.

2001 Leadership and change expert John Kotter writes the paper "What Leaders Really Do." Published in *Harvard Business Review*, it draws a distinction between the roles of manager and leader.

2008 Indian business scholar Bala Chakravarthy and Norwegian economist Peter Lorange's paper "Driving Renewal: The Entrepreneur-Manager" is published in *Journal of Business Strategy*. In it, the authors calls for a new breed of entrepreneurship in management, in order to manage business renewal.

As a business grows, its **demands change**.

→ **Entrepreneurship** is needed to spark a business into life, but...

↓

...**management discipline** is required to support that growth...

← ...and **leadership skills** are required to maintain **long-term growth**.

↓

Founders must adjust from being the sole decision-maker to **delegating**...

→ ...and **make the transition** from entrepreneur to **leader**.

In the early days of a new business the most valuable skill a founder can have is entrepreneurship—the vision to identify opportunities, and the willingness to take risks. But as the business grows, demands change. Disciplined management skills and corporate expertise are required to co-ordinate a growing enterprise. Some entrepreneurs are able to make the transition to leadership successfully, while others struggle.

An Ernst & Young report in 2011 identified entrepreneurs as people who are nonconformist, driven and tenacious, passionate and focused, with an opportunist mind-set.

See also: Take the second step 43 ▪ The Greiner curve 58–61 ▪ Leading well 68–69 ▪ Effective leadership 78–79 ▪ Develop emotional intelligence 110–11 ▪ Mintzberg's management roles 112–13 ▪ The value chain 216–17

Other studies report entrepreneurs as mavericks, unafraid of failure and driven by a passion for success. While there is some overlap, absent from these findings are the traits that define good leaders and managers: organization, an eye for detail, communication, emotional intelligence, and the ability to delegate. And as Indian executive Vineet Nayar advised, effective leadership involves encouraging others within the company to realize their potential, and excel.

Making the transition

Canadian business guru Professor Henry Mintzberg proposed that management can be broken down into three categories: managing by information, through people, and through action. Many entrepreneurs have difficulty managing through information—they often lack the skills to build the systems and communication networks on which large businesses are built.

Cyprus-born Stelios Haji-Ioannou, entrepreneur and founder of easyGroup, is known for rarely staying still. His company launched in 1998 with a low-cost airline, easyJet, and now includes more than 20 "easy" businesses that operate on a similar low-cost model. Haji-Ioannou has shown an aptitude for strategy, and an eye for detail; but he has also been criticized for lacking leadership skills, for micromanaging, and, common to entrepreneurs, for an inability to delegate and let managers manage.

US professor Larry Greiner identified leadership—the ability of a start-up founder to transition from entrepreneur to leader—as one of the major crises that businesses face as they grow. Greiner suggests that successful growth often requires the employment of professional managers who bring to the business an understanding of the requirements of financial markets, banks, and—most importantly—have the leadership skills needed to manage complex organizations. Entrepreneurs may possess bountiful ideas, but it takes management discipline to turn those ideas into successful ventures, and leadership skills to move the start-up beyond its entrepreneurial roots.

Start-ups require the spark of entrepreneurship; but growth requires a different set of skills: a founder must transition from being sole decision maker to being a disciplined manager and a successful leader. Those who are unable to make this transition often need to step aside and let the professionals take over. But this is often easier said than done. ▪

The function of leadership is to produce more leaders, not more followers.
Ralph Nader
US political activist (1934–)

Zhang Yin

Chinese entrepreneur and paper-recycling tycoon Zhang Yin was born in Guangdong in 1957. Recognizing that the Chinese export sector faced a shortage of paper-packaging materials, Zhang (her Cantonese name is Cheung Yan) opened a paper-trading business in Hong Kong in 1985.

Quickly moving from entrepreneur to established business leader, Zhang moved to Los Angeles, US, where she co-founded the paper-exporting company America Chung Nam in 1990. The business quickly became the leading paper exporter in the USA, and the largest overall exporter to China. In 1995, after returning to Hong Kong, Zhang cofounded Nine Dragons Paper with her husband and her brother. The company went on to become the world's largest maker of packaging paper.

In 2006, at the age of 49, Zhang became the first woman to top the list of richest people in China, according to the magazine *Hurun Report*. The following year, Ernst & Young awarded her "Entrepreneur of the Year in China 2007."

CHAINS OF HABIT ARE TOO LIGHT TO BE FELT UNTIL THEY ARE TOO HEAVY TO BE BROKEN

KEEP EVOLVING BUSINESS PRACTICE

IN CONTEXT

FOCUS
Middle management

KEY DATES
Pre-1850 The business landscape is dominated by small, family-run firms.

1850s and 60s A rapid expansion of the railroad systems and new industrial technology in Europe and America create greater possibilities for entrepreneurial businesses.

From 1880s As family businesses grow ever larger, administration becomes important and they begin to employ professional managers.

1982 UK economist Norman Macrae predicts a future trend of "intrapreneurs": managers with entrepreneurial thinking.

People are important in organizational life. Whether it is the initiative of a single entrepreneur or the combined energy of thousands of employees, it is people who get things done. However, that energy and initiative would count for little without managers to foster it. The creation, implementation, and management of organizational processes is what molds individual energies into a coherent whole—and as a company evolves, it is the experience of management that is essential in redefining those processes.

While management experience can liberate a business, it can also enslave it. Experience quickly gives

See also: Beating the odds at start-up 20–21 ▪ Take the second step 43 ▪ Reinventing and adapting 52–57 ▪ The Greiner curve 58–61 ▪ The weightless start-up 62–63 ▪ Beware the yes-men 74–75 ▪ The capability maturity model 218–19

It is the structure of the organization, rather than the employees alone, which holds the key to improving the quality of output.
W. Edwards Deming
US business professor (1900–93)

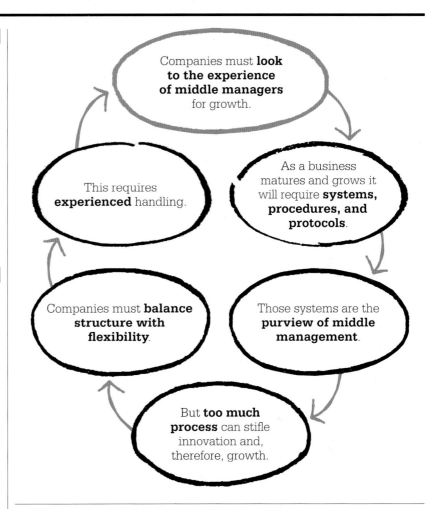

Companies must **look to the experience of middle managers** for growth.

As a business matures and grows it will require **systems, procedures, and protocols**.

This requires **experienced** handling.

Those systems are the **purview of middle management**.

Companies must **balance structure with flexibility**.

But **too much process** can stifle innovation and, therefore, growth.

way to the comfort of habit, and in ever-dynamic markets habit can too easily lead to stasis and stagnation. The danger for management is that, as US investor Warren Buffet warned, "chains of habit are too light to be felt until they are too heavy to be broken."

Middle management

The importance of middle management was described by business historian Alfred Chandler in his 1977 text, *The Visible Hand*, a play on economist Adam Smith's "invisible hand" metaphor, which explains the self-regulating forces of the market. Chandler noted that before 1850, family firms dominated business in the USA. These firms had poor communication networks and limited access to educated staff, so rarely grew beyond groups of family and friends who could be educated, trained, and trusted to manage the business.

However, with the growth of national railroad networks in the 1850s, the management landscape began to change. Improvements in transportation and communication allowed firms to grow beyond the immediate gaze of friends or family, and beyond the immediate locale. But to prosper in this new environment, companies needed more rigorous processes and structures. The increasing geographic scope and size of businesses required new levels of coordination and communication. Businesses had grown too unwieldy for one person to manage; they required the oversight of a team of people. This marked the emergence and rise of the professional manager.

As standardization and mass production emerged in the early 20th century, the role of management grew. Business was taking place on an increasingly global scale. Even before mechanization, coordination from managers enabled mass production. Standardization turned management into a science, and managers into a vital cog in the organizational machine.

Enablers and enterprise

In a 2007 *Harvard Business Review* article "The Process Audit," US businessman Michael Hammer » summarized the science of management (which is essentially the management of business process) into two factors: enablers and enterprise capabilities. Enterprise capabilities stem from senior management, and include culture, tight governance mechanisms, and strategic vision. Enablers, however, are the task of middle management. They include design, infrastructure, process, protocol, responsibilities, and performance management. The enablers turn vision into reality.

Realizing the vision

Hammer claimed that while the aspiration for business growth might come out of the boardroom, it is a company's infrastructure—designed and implemented by middle management—that makes growth possible. Vision without infrastructure is just a dream—it cannot become a reality. Leaders of growing companies know that, regardless of their own aspirations, the building blocks of growth are laid by middle management.

At the Japanese brewer Asahi, for example, it was a team of middle managers who developed Super Dry Beer, starting a craze in Japan for dry beer and allowing the company to capture more market share. Similarly, a group of Motorola middle managers was lauded for successfully developing a new wireless digital system for a client in under one year (the process usually takes two to three years).

Sitting between senior leaders and operational staff, middle managers are the communications conduit through which executives remain attuned to day-to-day business and personnel issues. Middle managers, as the Asahi and Motorola examples show, are often at the heart of corporate inspiration and perspiration—they generate ideas and they work to realize ideas in practice. Middle management is also the driver of functional efficiency: improvements in cost, quality, speed, and reliability are delivered by middle management and the processes it introduces.

Growing the business

As a business evolves, so must the management processes that enable it. Whereas initial stages of growth rely on individual initiative and entrepreneurial spirit, evolving ad-hoc practices into sustainable growth needs to be based on

Middle management as a technology enables the organization as we know it.
Alfred Chandler
US business historian (1918–2007)

lessons learned through business experience. The true science of management is the conversion of experience into repeatable and reliable process—today's problems become tomorrow's processes and next year's capabilities.

Process is the "stuff" of management. Business processes are essential to maintaining order; like a country's rail system and the rules that accompany it, processes are the infrastructure around which a company organizes. Business practice must evolve as the business grows from a single outlet to a chain, from one staff member to many, and from national to multinational.

Cath Kidston

English fashion designer, author, and entrepreneur Catherine Kidston was born in 1958. Raised with her three siblings near Andover in Hampshire, she was educated at a number of English boarding schools, before moving to London at 18.

After working as a store assistant, she ran a vintage curtain business with a friend on London's King's Road for five years. In 1992 she sold the business and a year later opened a store selling vintage home goods, wallpaper, and fabric. With about $23,000 in her pocket, she had to buy her stock carefully, mixing her own fabrics and wallpaper with items from tag sales and fabric from eastern Europe. Gingham ordered from Europe arrived already made into duvet covers and pillowcases, rather than as a fabric bolt. Kidston realized she would have to improvise, so decided to "cut it up and make it into other things." She kept some of the bedding, but altered most items into products such as toiletry bags. The Cath Kidston brand was born.

The development of infrastructure and the strength of a new layer of middle management were key factors in the evolution of UK retailer Cath Kidston from a single store in 1993 to more than 120 global branches and concessions by 2013, with stores throughout Europe and Asia, and plans to expand into North America. Widely renowned for its vintage fabrics, wallpapers, and brightly painted junk furniture, Kidston's initial growth, as is common with many single-founder start-ups, was slow. In the early days, monthly accounts took six weeks to prepare and clashes between IT systems caused issues with cash-flow projections and supply-chain management. It took nine years to open a second branch, and another two before the third.

Following a buy out in 2010, Cath Kidston became partly owned by a US private-equity group, with Kidston herself retaining about 20 percent of stock. As expansion took hold, the company started to move from ad-hoc processes to a more planned approach. Specialized managers and consultants were brought in to help build capacity for growth. New departments were added, including design, buying, and merchandising, and systems were introduced. Most importantly, middle management gained experience of what it takes to open and run a new store. The lessons from earlier mistakes were integrated into procedures and policies; by building on experience, every new store opening became easier than the last.

Excess and habit

The dangers of processes and of hierarchy (if it becomes excessive) are that they may begin to grip the organization too tightly. Protocol and bureaucracy can wear people

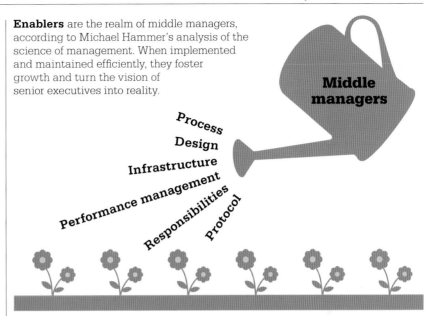

Enablers are the realm of middle managers, according to Michael Hammer's analysis of the science of management. When implemented and maintained efficiently, they foster growth and turn the vision of senior executives into reality.

Process
Design
Infrastructure
Performance management
Responsibilities
Protocol

Middle managers

down, stifling innovation and hindering growth. As markets and technology move ever faster, process must not blind managers to opportunity, and systems must not restrict strategic agility. For example, Motorola continued to invest in satellite technology throughout the 1990s even after competitors had switched to cheaper, more effective ground-based cell towers.

Habit can also twist logic. So habitual, for example, were the claims of ethical behavior from Dennis Kozlowski, CEO of Swiss security company Tyco International, that he seemed able to divorce the reality of his own behavior from his rhetoric—in 2005 he was convicted of corporate fraud. Habit can also lead to hubris. Buoyed by his business's accomplishment in electronics, in 1994 Samsung CEO Lee Kun-Hee believed that the same approach would lead to success in the car market, but the venture struggled and was rescued in 2000 by Renault. The experience (and habits) of Renault's managers

have since helped Renault Samsung Motors gain a footing within the South Korean automotive market.

Business leaders dismiss the value of middle management, and the value of process, at their peril. Without middle managers who are able to evolve a leader's vision into reality, many businesses would be stuck like those of the pre-railroad era, destined to remain small, local, and family run. It is the science of management that enables business evolution and growth. ∎

If you can't describe what you are doing as a process, you don't know what you're doing.
W. Edwards Deming

A CORPORATION IS A LIVING ORGANISM

IT HAS TO CONTINUE TO SHED ITS SKIN

REINVENTING AND ADAPTING

IN CONTEXT

FOCUS
Process and product

KEY DATES
1962 US professor Everett Rogers writes *Diffusion of Innovations*, showing how innovation moves through social systems.

1983 US business consultant Julien Phillips publishes the first change-management model in the journal *Human Resource Management*.

1985 In *Innovation and Entrepreneurship*, Peter Drucker describes the best approach to managing change as one that "always searches for change, responds to it, and exploits it."

1993 US change expert Daryl Conner uses the metaphor of "the burning platform" to describe the high cost of a business that stays the same.

Just as human beings are organisms that grow, change, and adapt, so do successful businesses. In 1970, the US futurist Alvin Toffler published *Future Shock*, a book that predicted the coming phenomenon of "a perception of too much change in too short a period of time." The pace of change, he said, would also spread to the world of business, as companies were forced to adapt their products and processes to maintain advantage in an increasingly competitive market.

Toffler's ideas of the effects of rapid technological change were viewed at the time as far-fetched, but with the invention of computers and the Internet, change has accelerated even more rapidly than he predicted. Toffler presciently claimed that we would live in a state of "high transience," in which we would give ideas, organizations, and even relationships an ever-shorter amount of our time. Social media websites are witness to this idea in action, providing a platform for the new ways we have begun relating to one another; they also demonstrate new ways of starting, growing, and building businesses.

The reinvention of daily life means marching off the edge of our maps.
Bob Black
US activist (1951–)

In 1989, US computer scientist Alan Kay claimed that it took 10 years for an innovation to go from the laboratory to everyday life, but by 2006 Twitter had managed to cut this down to just four years. Products can now be bought online from anywhere in the world, and customer feedback is instant and global. The challenge for companies to adapt and reinvent is huge.

Products and processes
The personal and business landscape has changed so radically since the 1960s that no industry or corporation has proved immune to

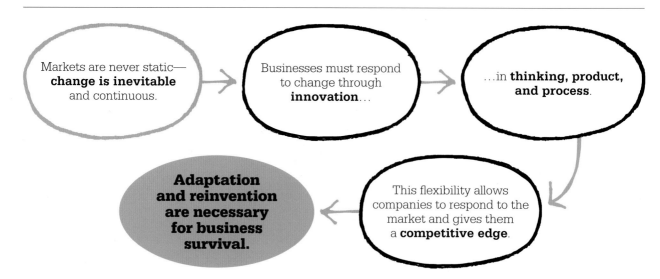

Markets are never static—**change is inevitable** and continuous.

Businesses must respond to change through **innovation**...

...in **thinking, product, and process**.

This flexibility allows companies to respond to the market and gives them a **competitive edge**.

Adaptation and reinvention are necessary for business survival.

its effects. Consider, for example, the music and movie industries. New technology has completely, and very rapidly, changed the way that movies and music are purchased and consumed. For the big movie and music businesses (and all their associated suppliers and producers), survival has required a high level of reinvention and adaptation.

This reinvention has come in the form of both new products and new processes. Product adaptation involves updates and redesign—essentially, innovation and invention. The movie industry has undergone many transformations since the early days of black-and-white moving pictures, or "movies." It has reinvented itself through technology (from adding sound to creating "impossible" computer-generated images); marketing devices, such as monthly access cards; events, such as outdoor screenings; and the growth of the multiplex to multiply visitor numbers and reduce turnaround times. The newest product aimed at luring viewers away from illegal downloads and back into movie houses is Stereoscopic-3D—itself a reinvention of an older idea.

Around the turn of the 21st century, the music industry was also struggling because of the drop in sales of CDs, and began to refocus on live music and merchandise. However, both the music and movie industries found new life through digitization, such as Apple's iPod and iTunes. This revolutionary combination of product and process—Apple's hardware and software—made legal downloads of music and movies more attractive than illegal versions. In 2013 the Apple iTunes store offered 60,000 movies across 119 countries, and 35 million songs.

Innovative methods

Process adaptation involves finding new ways to do things; it involves introducing or removing processes. Competition from online sales and pirate streaming continue to affect movie distribution companies such as Netflix. The response of this highly popular video streaming service was to make all the episodes of one television series (*House of Cards*) available for download simultaneously; the rationale being that the risk of piracy would be lower if consumers were able to legally buy all episodes at once.

For Netflix this bold strategy was not just a radical new process; it was also an adaptation of the company's entire business model. Still in the adolescent stages of growth, in 2012 Netflix was primarily an online streaming service, but for *House of Cards* it entered the world of production. By producing and distributing, Netflix was able to capture more profit and gain more control over content. Netflix did not »

Excellent companies don't believe in excellence—only in constant improvement and constant change.
Tom Peters
US business expert (1942–)

Product adaptation in the music industry demonstrates the steady use of new technology—from gramophone to vinyl, cassette, CD, minidisc, and MP3 digital music file—as companies have sought to broaden the market for music.

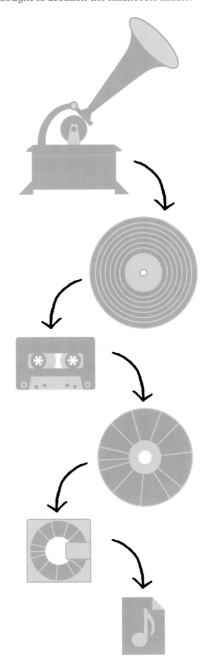

know if the *House of Cards* experiment would work. It did know, however, that in order to maintain the momentum of early growth, it needed to adapt and reinvent—in this case reinvention as television producers as well as distributors.

Internal changes

Reinvention and adaptation can also be internally focused on systems, recurrent tasks, or operational activities. Whether improvement of this type is based on data from formal process improvement frameworks (such as Total Quality Management) or simply on the experience and intuition of managers, internal process adaptation allows companies to maximize revenue while also reducing costs.

The McDonalds McSnack Wrap, for example, takes staff only 21 seconds to make—the shorter the preparation time, the greater the number of customers that can be served by the fewest staff. At R Griggs Group Ltd, manufacturer of Dr. Martens shoes, a reinvention of

Dr. Martens footwear grew from a niche fashion item to an international mainstream hit within a matter of years. R Griggs, the brand's producer, had to reinvent processes to match demand.

internal systems allowed the company to exploit global sales opportunities. In 1994, due to the brand's growing popularity, demand far exceeded manufacturing capability. Poor planning and coordination led to delayed production and lost sales. The solution was a reinvention of internal systems based around an integrated IT system. The product itself—the classic "1460" eight-laced leather boot—changed very little, although more designs were later added to the product range. The key change was the adaptation of internal processes, which ensured supply could match demand.

Adapting in a recession

Internal process adaptation is even more important in markets where demand is static or falling. Operational efficiencies, rather than revenue growth, are the key to profit. For insurance companies, for example, scope for new product adaptation is limited, so competition is price-based—especially in a recession, when customers are particularly price sensitive. The key to maintaining profitability while remaining price competitive is continual process improvement— the reinvention of internal systems that deliver the same product to customers, but at a lower cost and, therefore, increased profitability. The days of the door-to-door insurance salesperson have long since been replaced by telesales and an e-commerce approach.

Reinventing the company

A notable company that has successfully reinvented itself is Samsung Electronics. Established in 1969, Samsung Electronics is a subsidiary of the Samsung Group, which aimed to exploit opportunities in the emerging technology

> Those who initiate change will have a better opportunity to manage the change that is inevitable.
>
> **William ("Bill") Pollard**
> US businessman (1938–)

industry. The company began with black-and-white televisions and moved into home appliances during the 1970s. In the 1980s, production grew to PCs and semiconductors.

In 1986, Samsung released its first car phone, the SC-100. The product was a disaster—the quality was so poor that many customers complained. This reputation for poor quality blighted Samsung for much of its early life, since consumers regarded its goods as inferior to premium Japanese products.

On June 7, 1993, chairman Lee Kun-Hee gathered senior Samsung executives and declared that the company needed to reinvent itself. His famous instruction "Change everything except your wife and children" shows how seriously he took the situation. Lee also recognized shifting market dynamics, telling colleagues that the company needed to "produce cell phones comparable to Motorola's by 1994 ... or Samsung will disengage itself from the cell-phone business." The "new management" initiative that followed, supported by product and process innovation, put the emphasis on the quality and innovation that Samsung is now renowned for, and galvanized

When processes evolve they may create new jobs or cause existing ones to disappear. The manual switchboards of the old ztelephone system were soon replaced by faster, automatic ones.

its foundation for future growth. Samsung's transformation was not yet complete, however—the Asian financial crisis of the late 1990s forced the company to reinvent itself yet again. Adapting its process turned Samsung into a more market-focused and consumer-friendly brand. Since then the company's efforts, particularly in the cell-phone industry, have been based on constant attrition, reinvention, and adaptation.

Long-term survival

Few businesses survive without adaptation or reinvention. Products such as Kellogg's Cornflakes and Heinz Beans—products that have not changed in decades—are rare. Even when a product has not changed, many of the processes used in its manufacture, distribution, and marketing have altered dramatically. The factories of 100 or 50 years ago were very different than today's, where many

tasks are automated and fulfilled by computers and robots. Promotions have also adapted to fit changed consumer demographics, globalized markets, and customer preferences. Even established brands cannot avoid reinvention.

Truly successful business transformation is rarely due solely to discovering and commercializing bold new ideas, technologies, and products. The most successful businesses know that reinvention is

a continual process. Social media, for example, has created a market shift that has required businesses of all types to adapt; even record labels now embrace the promotional value of websites such as YouTube.

The ecosystem in which a business operates is rarely, if ever, static. Corporations exist in these ecosystems as living organisms that must adapt to survive; great leaders know that failure to adapt leads to extinction. ∎

Lee Kun-Hee

Born on January 9, 1942, Lee Kun-Hee is Chairman of the South Korean conglomerate Samsung. Holding an economics degree from Waseda University in Tokyo, Japan, and an MBA from George Washington University in the US, Lee Kun-Hee joined the Samsung Group in 1968 and succeeded his father as Chairman on December 1, 1987.

Samsung is the quintessential example of a *chaebol*, a uniquely Korean conglomerate that mixes Confucian values with family ties and government influence. Under Lee's stewardship, the company

has been transformed from a Korean budget brand into a major international force and, alongside Sony, is one of the world's most prominent Asian businesses. Samsung Electronics, the conglomerate's most famous subsidiary, is a leading developer of semiconductors, TV screens, and cell phones—with its smartphones even outselling the iPhone in many markets.

The *Forbes* 2013 Rich List recorded Lee as the world's 69th richest billionaire, and the richest Korean.

WITHOUT CONTINUAL GROWTH AND PROGRESS, SUCCESS HAS NO MEANING

THE GREINER CURVE

IN CONTEXT

FOCUS
Business growth

KEY DATES
1972 Larry Greiner outlines
five stages of business growth,
and their related crises, in
"Evolution and Revolution
as Organizations Grow."

1988 Macedonian business
expert Ichak Adizes writes
Corporate Lifecycles, in which
he describes the growth of
corporations as a series
of five "S" curves.

1994 Professor David Storey
claims that all forms of "stage"
models have limitations. He
suggests looking at growth
through categories of
companies instead: failures,
trundlers, and flyers.

1998 In a reprint of his 1972
article, Greiner updates his
theory and adds a sixth stage
to the Curve.

A side from the financial
rewards that they offer to
entrepreneurs, start-ups
can be exciting places to work.
Amid the chaos, continual change,
ever-evolving policies and
procedures, and the abundance of
work required, these environments
buzz with energy, initiative, and
ideas. But as business growth
places increasing pressure on
people and systems, excitement
can turn into frustration.

Periods of chaos often occur in
a start-up's early life. As it matures,
the new business will pass through
various conceptual thresholds. In
1972 Larry Greiner identified these
as "crises of growth," which he

See also: Beating the odds at start-up 20–21 ▪ Take the second step 43 ▪ How fast to grow 44–45 ▪ From entrepreneur to leader 46–47 ▪ Keep evolving business practice 48–51 ▪ The weightless start-up 62–63

Start-ups are **exciting places** to work...

...but growth brings inevitable **crises**.

These crises **are predictable and can be managed** by using the Greiner Curve.

illustrated on a graph that came to be known as the Greiner Curve. He noticed that companies of all types go through periods of growth followed by inevitable crises, when major organizational change is needed to maintain momentum.

Stages of growth

Greiner initially identified five stages of growth, but later added a sixth. The first of these stages is "growth through creativity." During this stage, the start-up is small and growth is fueled by the enthusiasm of its founders. Management procedures, communications—and even interactions with customers— are usually informal and ad hoc. However, as more staff joins and production expands, more capital

will be required (perhaps from banks or venture capitalists), and the need for formal systems and procedures increases. The founders—who are likely to be technically or entrepreneurially oriented—find themselves faced with their first crisis, as they become burdened by management responsibilities that they are ill-equipped to deal with. This first crisis is therefore one of leadership: who will lead the company out of confusion and solve the new management problems?

Change of leadership required for phase two may only be a question of internal reorganization and a change in style, abandoning the casualness of the company's early days in favor of greater formality and more rigid systems and procedures. But in

many cases the original founders have neither the skills nor the desire to take on more formal leadership. In 2002, chef Jamie Oliver founded Fifteen, a chain of restaurants that also provide training opportunities for disadvantaged young people. As the chain grew, he handed over the management to a CEO, so that he could return to doing what he does best: being a commercially successful celebrity chef.

Under professional managers, business growth continues in an environment of more formal structures and budgets, and with the establishment of separate functions, such as production and marketing. This is the second stage of growth, known as "growth through direction." As the new »

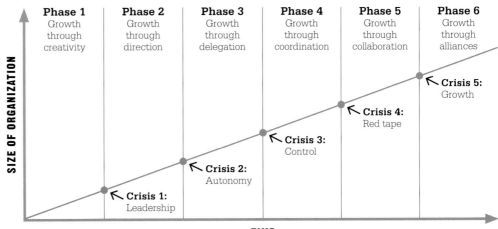

The Greiner Curve illustrates the six stages of growth that any company might undergo during its development. Each growth phase generates a crisis, the resolution of which leads to the next growth stage.

Phase 1 Growth through creativity

Phase 2 Growth through direction

Phase 3 Growth through delegation

Phase 4 Growth through coordination

Phase 5 Growth through collaboration

Phase 6 Growth through alliances

SIZE OF ORGANIZATION

Crisis 1: Leadership

Crisis 2: Autonomy

Crisis 3: Control

Crisis 4: Red tape

Crisis 5: Growth

TIME

manager takes responsibility for direction, mid-level supervisors or managers act more as functional specialists, but after a while they begin to demand more freedom to make decisions, leading to the second crisis: "autonomy." This crisis can be solved by freeing the mid-level managers from bureaucracy and allowing the company to achieve "growth through delegation"—Greiner's third stage of growth. Unburdened by the need to manage day-to-day issues, senior management can shift its attention to strategy and long-term growth.

Stay small or grow?

At this point a start-up faces perhaps the biggest crisis of all: a crisis of control. The founders or senior management may find it hard to give up responsibility for decision making, even to trusted boards. When this happens, the founder may decide to remain small—in essence, to limit growth to the extent of their own control.

Such decisions are laudable. Not all companies can be global and all-conquering, and in fact, small- and medium-sized enterprises dominate the business landscape. Some

One can choose to go back towards safety or forward towards growth.
Abraham Maslow
US psychologist (1908–70)

entrepreneurs start a small company to escape the stresses, politics, and office-bound purgatory of corporate life and so, for them, it may make sense to limit growth at this stage.

Other entrepreneurs—such as Virgin chief, Richard Branson—are enthused by the early phases in the life of a new business, but become bored as the bureaucratic demands increase. Branson likes to guide a business through its start-up phase then hand it over to professional managers, so he can move on to new, more exciting, projects. Choosing to remain small does not mean that a business will be crisis-

free. All businesses, of all sizes, and regardless of growth aspirations, will face uncertainties and challenges. It does mean, however, that the business will avoid the requirements of the next stage: "growth through coordination."

During this fourth stage, increasing centralization is common. By this time the company may be relatively large, with operations controlled through a head office. The company may appoint executives with experience of managing large, diverse businesses and introduce standard operating procedures.

However, the introduction of standard policies eventually leads to the next crisis: a "red-tape crisis," in which increasing bureaucracy stifles operations, and growth falters as a result.

A return to informality

Paradoxically, the fifth stage, "growth through collaboration," requires, in part, a return to the earlier days of flexibility. Systems allow greater spontaneity, teamwork is introduced, and matrix (network) structures are used to recapture the collaborative nature of a start-up—in other words, the organization tries to operate like a lean, creative company once again.

Once this has been attained, the next crisis relates to the limits of internal growth. Under pressure from shareholders to continually improve returns, further growth can only be achieved by developing partnerships with complementary organizations. By this sixth stage a company is already big, possibly very big. "Growth through alliances" therefore suggests that expansion will continue through mergers, outsourcing, or joint ventures—the company needs to look beyond its own internal

Larry Greiner

Larry Greiner is a professor of management and organization at the University of Southern California, US. He received a BA degree from the University of Kansas, and an MBA and doctorate from Harvard Business School.

Greiner is the author of numerous publications on the growth and development of organizations, management consulting, and strategic change. His 1972 article, "Evolution and Revolution as

Organizations Grow", is regarded as an all-time classic. Greiner has acted as a consultant to companies and government agencies in the US and abroad, such as Coca-Cola, Merck, Andersen Consulting, Times Mirror Company, and KinderCare.

Key works

1972 "Evolution and Revolution as Organizations Grow"
1998 *Power and Organization Development*
1999 *New CEOs and Strategic Change, Across Industries*

Spotify CEO Daniel Ek worked with co-founder Martin Lorentzon to build a large but agile company. It avoids Greiner's growth problems by working in small squads overseen by "tribes."

capabilities, and the capacity of its core markets, and seek external growth.

The actual rate of growth—in terms of customer numbers, revenue, or profits—within each phase of the Greiner Curve will vary, depending on the individual company. Organizations such as Facebook were already large by the time they started to face crises of delegation and control. Others may remain small for many years, perhaps never even reaching the leadership-crisis stage.

Using the Greiner Curve
Knowledge of the Greiner Curve can help start-up founders to predict and manage the inevitable crises of growth. Even when enjoying the heady days of early growth, entrepreneurs need to be mindful of the steps required to build the business further. They must put structures in place as soon as possible; the earlier that formal systems and professional management are introduced, the less they will be resented and resisted, and the stronger the foundations for continued growth.

In this regard, the various crises identified by the Greiner Curve can be seen as natural transitions. An organization must manage its way through such transitions and growing pains as it continually defines and redefines the scope of its operations, its values, and its overall purpose. As Benjamin Franklin observed, "without continual growth and progress, such words as improvement, achievement, and success have no meaning."

Large but agile
One company that seems to have heeded the lessons of the Greiner Curve is the Internet music-streaming service, Spotify. The organization's Swedish founders, Daniel Ek and Martin Lorentzon, knew at the company's inception in 2008 that their aim was growth. They also knew that they were not willing to compromise the benefits that accompany the excitement of a start-up business.

Spotify organizes itself around project-based teams, called "squads." The organization is divided into small clusters of squads, with each squad running

as a start-up business. Mirroring the benefits enjoyed by companies in Greiner's first stage, every squad is fully autonomous, has direct contact with its stakeholders, and operates with minimal dependency on other squads.

To deal with the various crises of growth (such as autonomy and red-tape), related squads are grouped into "tribes." The function of the tribe is to support and enable the activities of each squad, in essence mirroring the role of venture capitalists in incubating new start-ups. The operation is kept small and agile by limiting the head count for each tribe to 100.

Spotify appears to have managed to maintain a balance between the benefits of growth and the feel-good elements of a start-up. The founders nevertheless admit that the system is not flawless, and as the demand for an organization-wide strategy grows, it may be that even Spotify will not escape the crises of growth predicted by the Greiner Curve. ∎

All growth depends upon activity. There is no development physically or intellectually without effort, and effort means work.
Calvin Coolidge
US former President (1872–1933)

IF YOU BELIEVE IN SOMETHING, WORK NIGHTS AND WEEKENDS— IT WON'T FEEL LIKE WORK
THE WEIGHTLESS START-UP

IN CONTEXT

FOCUS
Start-ups

KEY DATES
1923 Walt Disney starts making professional cartoons in his uncle Robert's garage.

1976 The first 50 Apple computers are built in the spare room of Steve Jobs's parents' house. A few months later Apple moved "upscale" to his parents' garage.

1978 Indian master brewer Kiran Mazumdar-Shaw founds biotechnology company, Biocon, in the garage of her rented house in Bangalore, India.

2004 Kevin Rose quits his television job to found Digg, a news aggregator website that attracts 38 million users a month during its peak. The "office" is his bedroom.

Many start-ups require **skill, not capital outlay**.

⬇

In a weightless start-up, the risk is **time, not money**.

⬇

The work can be done initially on **weekends and evenings, but**...

⬇

...**if you believe in what you're doing, it won't feel like work.**

Starting a business requires almost boundless energy, unwavering commitment, and the resilience to deal with risk. But increasingly, the commercial potential of the Internet is allowing a growing number of "weightless" start-ups to take flight. These ventures are low on financial resources, but high on individual skill and the investment of time to bring an idea to fruition.

Personal passion is an essential ingredient in a successful start-up. As Kevin Rose, founder of Internet start-ups Digg, Revision3, and Milk, put it: "If you believe in something, work nights and weekends—it won't feel like work." Even global greats such as Nestlé foods and Siemens electronics grew from the dreams and aspirations of a small group of people. These entrepreneurs faced the risk of a new business because they deeply believed in something, and were driven to realize their dream, despite long hours, stress, and, often, a string of failures large or small. These are quickly forgotten when people are doing something they love.

Traditionally, the main barriers to enterprise were time and capital. Entrepreneurs from nonwealthy

See also: Beating the odds at start-up 20–21 ▪ Luck (and how to get lucky) 42 ▪ The Greiner curve 58–61 ▪ Changing the game 92–99 ▪ Small is beautiful 172–77

Hewlett-Packard (HP) began life in Dave Packard's garage. The company has restored the garage, which in 1987 was named a California landmark as "the birthplace of Silicon Valley."

backgrounds usually needed a full-time job to meet the living costs of themselves and their families. Without sufficient savings, few people could risk a new business venture in the 20th century, but today, starting a business is easier.

Micropreneurism

In the mid-2000s, the notion of a micropreneur began to emerge. This was an individual who ran a very small business, often in addition to full-time employment. The concept gained popularity alongside the rise of e-commerce, which made it possible to launch a commercial website and manage it nights and weekends. Sales platforms, such as those provided by eBay and the Chinese online marketplace Taobao, made it even easier, since they dispensed with the need for a website or payment systems.

These micropreneurs, who sell everything from homemade fashion items to antiques and secondhand electronics, are risking very little other than their own time—the capital outlay can be as much or as little as they are willing to risk. The micropreneur's skill lies in spotting the right opportunity. In this way the business can be as small or large as time, and desire, allows.

For those who aspire to more than running a business as a part-time hobby, the lean start-up path is well trodden. Large companies such as Hewlett-Packard and Indian biotech Biocon both started in their founders' garages. Passion was key—with very limited capital, essential equipment was begged and borrowed; friends and family were used as (free) staff; and sleep was sacrificed. The main resources were time, skill, and tenacity.

The path is not straightforward, however, and requires a deep commitment, often in the face of failure. As Jeff Bezos warned, "invention requires a long-term willingness to be misunderstood." ▪

Hewlett-Packard

Bill Hewlett, born 1913, and Dave Packard, born 1912, were close friends who graduated as electrical engineers from Stanford University. After his marriage, Packard moved into an apartment in Palo Alto, California, with his wife, while Hewlett camped out in a shed on the grounds. A garage belonging to the property became a decidedly low-tech workshop. From 1938 to 1939 the garage served as home, think tank, lab, office, and production department. Bill and David developed the 200A and 200B audio oscillators, which became Hewlett-Packard's first products.

Believed to be the first US technology company to launch in a garage, Hewlett-Packard was founded by the two friends on an investment of just $538. Today the organization is one of the world's largest technology companies, with sales in excess of $27 billion in 2012. The garage is designated a historic landmark and is listed on the United States National Register of Historic Places.

You have to really believe in yourself and know that, in the worst-case scenario, if it doesn't work out, you still built something really cool.
Kevin Rose

LIGHTIN
THE FIR
LEADERSHIP AND HUMAN RESOURCES

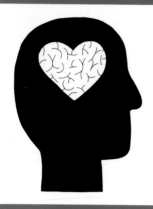

Growth from a small start-up to a large multinational company cannot be achieved without leaders who are passionate about their business and who are inspirational to their staff. Leading a business is, at its core, about harnessing the power of people.

One popular business aphorism claims that "there are no business problems, only people problems." Managing people is not easy; every organization is a collection of individuals, each with their own philosophies, vulnerabilities, drives, strengths, and weaknesses. Effective leadership embraces these differences and creates a culture in which people can make

Good leadership consists of showing average people how to do the work of superior people.
J. D. Rockefeller
US industrialist (1839–1937)

the most of their talent. In other words, leadership is about creating capacity in others. It is about imagining the future, determining strategic direction, and aligning the organization and its people to a particular vision.

Leaders and managers
The very best leaders, as Steve Jobs said, "put a dent in the universe." These leaders are not bound by convention; they are able to think outside the box, embracing one-of-a-kind ideas that disrupt the status quo in their favor. In today's hypercompetitive markets, the leaders we celebrate do not only outthink, outsmart, and outcompete their rivals, they disrupt entire industries. They change the game.

Rarely, though, do leaders achieve greatness alone. Leaders rely on managers. While leadership is about vision, management is about process, planning, budgeting, structuring, and staffing—tasks that help an organization to keep doing what it does. In *The Manager's Job* (1975), Henry Mintzberg identified three broad management roles: informational (managing by information); interpersonal (managing through people); and decisional (managing through action). Importantly,

Mintzberg noted that none of these roles is exclusive or privileged. Leading well often involves shifting seamlessly between leadership and management, and knowing when, contextually, each role is most appropriate to adopt.

Creating the organizational capacity for continued success also means putting together teams and managing talent. An effective team is a powerful thing. Individuals perform better in teams; they are more productive and more innovative. Teams can also be self-managing; individuals support each other and strive not to let the team down. Effective teams require less supervision and less direction than individuals, and performance is guided by group norms, not by one individual's expectations.

It is not surprising, then, that great organizations recognize the value of teams. Google, for example, designs workstations so that staff can easily collaborate. "Hangout spaces" are adorned with funky furniture and supplied with food to allow teams to work and socialize. Leaders at Google want employees to interact; they recognize that by encouraging teamwork, employees enjoy greater job satisfaction and creativity, and as a result, innovation rises. To the benefit of

its staff and its bottom line, Google knows that the best workplaces feel like playgrounds—places where people can imagine and invent.

Satisfaction and challenge

Creating an organizational culture that embraces teamwork and encourages creativity helps companies address the perennial question: "is money the motivator?" Most find the answer is "no." Higher pay might encourage an individual to take a new job, it might encourage people to move a little faster or to work a little harder, but people soon forget about the money and start to focus on other things—such as job satisfaction, challenge, and respect from managers. Virgin Atlantic airline, for example, is not known as one of the highest payers, but is regarded as a great place to work.

A strong organizational culture is, therefore, essential to success. Through tradition, history, and structure, companies build a sense of identity—a unique personality defined by the characteristic rituals, beliefs, stories, meanings, values, norms, and language that determine the way in which "things are done around here."

Importantly for leaders, managing people also means managing oneself. Business history is littered with examples of leaders who, blinded by success, leapt into ill-conceived initiatives or made "bet-the-farm" decisions that proved disastrous. "Deal fever" can mean that warning signs are ignored by leaders who feel they can do no wrong. Successful leaders, however, know that they must fight against the illusion of invulnerability. They also realize the dangers of wanting to be liked or to conform. Great leaders know that they must guard against groupthink and "yes-man" mentalities in themselves and others, because such approaches leave decisions unchallenged, and allow ill-judged projects to proceed without sufficient due diligence.

Everyone experiences tough times; it is a measure of your determination and dedication how you deal with them.
Lakshmi Mittal
Indian entrepreneur (1950–)

The best leaders accept that they are not gods of management, and that, in fact, occasionally being told "no" can be more important than always hearing "yes."

Emotionally intelligent

Creating a culture where this kind of challenge is the norm depends upon diversity. In companies with employees from diverse backgrounds, where gender, race, and age are balanced, the different perspectives mean decisions are more likely to be questioned.

Perhaps most importantly then, and as recent research indicates, the single most important trait for successful leaders is emotional intelligence. In his bestselling book, *Emotional Intelligence* (1995), Daniel Goleman describes five domains of Emotional Intelligence (EQ): knowing your emotions; managing them; motivating yourself; recognizing and understanding other people's emotions; and managing relationships. Without EQ, a leader can be technically brilliant and full of great ideas, but still ineffective. This is because a sole trader may be able to survive on intuition alone, but as soon as someone else is employed, EQ becomes key. Lighting the fire means keeping the sparks flying for everyone. ∎

MANAGERS DO THINGS RIGHT, LEADERS DO THE RIGHT THINGS
LEADING WELL

IN CONTEXT

FOCUS
Organizational roles

KEY DATES
1977 US professor Abraham Zaleznik writes an article asking "Managers and Leaders: Are They Different?"

1985 In *Leaders: Strategies for Taking Charge*, Warren Bennis and Burt Nanus suggest four leadership strategies to help leaders do the right things.

1990 US leadership expert John Kotter publishes *What Leaders Really Do*.

1997 Robert House and Ram Aditya claim that management consists of implementing the vision and direction provided by leaders.

2005 Warren Bennis publishes *Reinventing Leadership: Strategies to Empower the Organization*.

Leaders **develop a vision** for the organization.

They **conquer** in any context—even in the most turbulent of times.

Leaders advocate **change and new approaches**...

...that **managers then implement** to make a new, stable environment.

Managers do things right, leaders do the right things.

Good managers do not necessarily make good leaders, and good leaders can be poor managers. This is because the two jobs are not the same, despite sharing similar characteristics—principally the need to drive human (and therefore organizational) capacity. As Warren Bennis and Burt Nanus noted in 1985, "managers do things right; leaders do the right thing." Leaders "conquer" their surroundings—the competitive environment—through vision and strategy, and it is the role of managers to then implement these strategies effectively.

Effective management is crucial to organizational success. It takes care of processes, planning,

See also: The value of teams 70–71 ▪ Gods of management 76–77 ▪ Effective leadership 78–79 ▪ Organizing teams and talent 80–85 ▪ Develop emotional intelligence 110–11 ▪ Mintzberg's management roles 112–13

budgeting, structure, and staffing; tasks that help an organization to keep doing what it does. Without management, no matter how well led, an organization would disintegrate into disorganized chaos. However, management is not leadership—it will not lead the company in new directions.

Decisive leadership

In 1990, John Kotter argued that leadership is about dealing with change and developing a vision for the organization, often within turbulent times. Leaders then communicate their vision to the rest of the company, and motivate staff—especially managers—to act in ways that will bring about the required change. Leadership is about setting the agenda and empowering people to produce useful change.

"Leading well" does not always mean making people happy; likability and success rarely go together. The direct, tough, and sometimes even rude leadership styles of some of the most highly regarded leaders—such as Jack Welch of General Electric, Steve Jobs of Apple, and Jill Abramson of *The New York Times*—have been well documented.

Leaders have to be brave in the face of uncertainty, standing firmly behind their vision for the company. They need to hold staff accountable when things do not go as planned, and make difficult decisions about who to hire or fire in order to develop an organizational culture capable of achieving their strategic vision.

The next generation

Truly great leaders know that they will not be around forever, and one of their most important tasks is to hire, train, and nurture their successor. They lead well by making sure somebody is ready and waiting to take over from them. Nine years before his retirement, General Electric CEO Jack Welch said, "from now on, choosing my successor is the most important decision I'll make. It occupies a considerable amount of thought almost every day."

Jill Abramson was the first woman to become executive editor of *The New York Times*. She found that unpopularity came "with the territory," as *Times*' chairman Arthur Sulzberger had warned.

It is common practice in many companies to privilege leadership over management, but it is unwise. Great organizations value both: leaders who can spot opportunities, and managers who can make those opportunities a reality. ▪

Leadership is lifting a person's vision to high sights, raising their performance to a higher standard, building a personality beyond its normal limitations.
Peter Drucker
US management consultant
(1909–2005)

Blending leadership and management

Inspirational leadership skills are the hallmark of Portuguese soccer coach José Mourinho. His teams won two European Cups and 14 trophies in eight years, elevating him to sit alongside some of the greats of soccer management.

Successful sports teams, like great organizations, are a blend of good management and good leadership, and Mourinho achieves the rare feat of excelling in both. As a leader, he makes his mark immediately. When he first took over Chelsea Football Club in London, England, he called a team meeting and urged any naysayers to speak up, or stay silent from then on. He learned his management skills from Bobby Robson and Louis van Gaal, for whom he worked as an assistant coach and translator at the Spanish soccer team FC Barcelona. Under their guidance he also learned how to study opponents, form strategies, and build strong, winning teams.

NONE OF US IS AS SMART AS ALL OF US

THE VALUE OF TEAMS

IN CONTEXT

FOCUS
Teamwork

KEY DATES
1924–1932 The Hawthorne Studies, conducted by Elton Mayo, highlight the importance of groups in affecting the behavior of individuals at work.

1930s The Human Relations Movement is sparked by Mayo's work. It proposes that worker satisfaction and productivity depend on careful management and consideration of groups.

1940s As a result of Abraham Maslow's findings, and the earlier work of Mayo, businesses begin to recognize the value of teamwork.

21st century Workplace design moves from the solo workspaces and closed offices of the 20th century to open layouts that encourage collaborative working.

Human beings like to **belong**.

Teams help to **generate a sense of place** and counter anomie.

None of us is as smart as all of us.

Organizations can be thought of as a **collection of teams**.

Successful teams **provide an environment** for new ideas.

W e might complain about routine and familiarity, but research shows that human beings have an innate need for some degree of stability. Without rules, norms, values, and expectations, people begin to feel anxious, rootless, and confused. This is termed "anomie," and it is the reason that humans often self-organize into groups. The routine and familiarity of belonging to a group helps people to avoid anomie, and find security and purpose.

The existence of groups serves two purposes. Organizations, and the groups within them, can be seen as an expression of the human desire to belong. As psychologist Abraham Maslow identified in his 1943 paper "A Theory of Human Motivation", groups give us a sense

See also: Creativity and invention 72–73 ▪ Organizing teams and talent 80–85 ▪ Make the most of your talent 86–87 ▪ Organizational culture 104–09 ▪ Avoid groupthink 114 ▪ The value of diversity 115

of belonging. Maslow believed that there is a hierarchy of human needs; once we have met the most basic of needs—the physiological ones, such as hunger and thirst—we progress to the next: security. When these needs are satisfied, we move to the third basic need: a sense of belonging. Once this is met, we will proceed toward increasing self-esteem through achievement, and ultimately toward self-actualization, by using our inner talents with creativity.

When Maslow's theory is applied to the workplace, working in groups and gaining a sense of belonging make employees more effective. With the need to belong already addressed, individuals are able to focus on other things, such as a desire for achievement and the practicing of inner talents. In this way, the movement through the stages of satisfying needs can benefit a company. Free from anomie, groups are places where human beings, and therefore ideas, can flourish. Teams that are carefully chosen and supervised

will increase an individual's security and encourage collaborative, creative, work—as US management expert Ken Blanchard said, "none of us is as smart as all of us." In turn, commitment toward a project creates ties that strengthen the bond between individuals and, ultimately, the company's communal purpose.

Places to belong

Great organizations recognize the value of teams and the importance of the working environment. Cisco Systems, the Internet infrastructure company, has created what it calls

Cisco Systems uses workspaces that can be transformed from small groups of work pods to large open spaces for conferences. Cisco aims to be flexible for connectivity and a sense of community.

the "Connected Workplace", which offers employees great flexibility in working practice and environment, while ensuring that they always feel part of the Cisco community.

Business success is rarely achieved through individual genius, and the greatest leaders are those who recognize the value of maximizing talent through teams. ▪

Abraham Maslow

The American psychologist Abraham Maslow was born in 1908. He grew up in Brooklyn, New York, and earned a degree, masters, and PhD in psychology from the University of Wisconsin. Maslow started his career as a teacher, working at Brooklyn College from 1937 to 1951, after which he became chair of the psychology department at Brandeis University, US. Here he met Kurt Goldstein, the originator of the idea of self-actualization, and Maslow became fascinated with the path of human development toward "being all

you can be." Contrary to many of his peers, Maslow focused on the positive side of mental health. The hierarchy of human needs, which Maslow outlined in "A Theory of Human Motivation", remains influential even today in fields as diverse as social work and management theory.

Key works

1943 "A Theory of Human Motivation"
1954 *Motivation and Personality*
1962 *Toward a Psychology of Being*

INNOVATION MUST BE INVASIVE AND PERPETUAL: EVERYONE, EVERYWHERE, ALL OF THE TIME
CREATIVITY AND INVENTION

IN CONTEXT

FOCUS
Creativity

KEY DATES
17th century Polish poet Maciej Kazimierz Sarbiewski applies the word "creativity" to human activity. For more than a century and a half, the idea of human creativity is resisted—"creation" is reserved for describing God's creative act.

1970s Influenced by the work of psychologists Abraham Maslow and Frederick Herzberg on the subject of motivation, businesses begin to design jobs that allow employees space for creative freedom.

2010 IBM lists creativity as the most sought-after trait in business leaders.

2013 Bruce Nussbaum's book *Creative Intelligence* states that creativity is the greatest source of economic value.

Our fondest childhood memories are often those that involve the freedom of play, and the unbridled use of imagination to create and live out fantasies. As human beings we never lose the inner joy of creativity, but it tends to be suppresed by the responsibilities of adult life—we trade the playground for the office.

Like the playgrounds of our childhoods though, companies that embrace creativity and innovation as "invasive and perpetual"—as consultant Stephen Shapiro puts it—are exciting places to be. Google, Facebook, and Procter & Gamble, for example, are renowned for hiring and nurturing creative people, and for rewarding

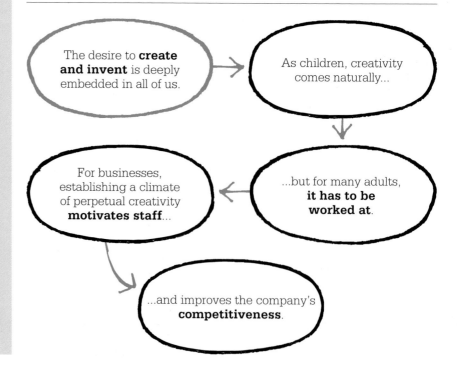

The desire to **create and invent** is deeply embedded in all of us.

As children, creativity comes naturally...

...but for many adults, **it has to be worked at**.

For businesses, establishing a climate of perpetual creativity **motivates staff**...

...and improves the company's **competitiveness**.

See also: Stand out in the market 28–31 ▪ Gaining an edge 32–39 ▪ Thinking outside the box 88–89 ▪ Changing the game 92–99

imagination and invention. They attract thousands of applicants as a result. Moreover, creativity is not only a potential source for ideas that can yield economic value, but is a vital asset for individuals and companies operating in increasingly changeable global markets.

Defining creativity

Creativity involves the generation of ideas, alternatives, or possibilities, and the consideration of situations or problems in novel ways. Invention is the practical application of creative thought. When successfully realized, creativity and invention are highly motivating. They allow us to combine our innate desire for autonomy, purpose, and mastery. They also produce a sense of achievement, which is a key element in what Abraham Maslow described as the "Higher Order Needs" of motivation—the factors that allow us to feel value and self-actualization.

For businesses, establishing a climate of creativity has the dual benefit of enhancing employee satisfaction and improving its competitiveness. Excited by the pursuit of invention, employees will

When you innovate, you've got to be prepared for everyone telling you you're nuts.
Larry Ellison
US co-founder, Oracle Corp. (1944–)

often work harder, longer, and more productively, yielding innovative solutions to problems, new cost-saving processes, or profitable new products.

So significant is the competitive edge that can be gained that a 2010 IBM survey listed creativity as the most sought-after trait in leaders. When it was announced that the Creative Director of Mulberry, Emma Hill—who was largely credited with the fashion label's renaissance—was stepping down in 2013, the company's shares fell by more than 9 percent. As Steve Jobs proved at Apple, "thinking differently" is not just cool or quirky—it matters to staff, to customers, and to investors.

Fostering creativity

The challenge is for companies to balance creativity with financial prudence. Unbridled creativity rarely leads to commercial success, yet businesses are required to make profits in order to survive.

For Mulberry, it was a clash of these values that resulted in Hill's departure. When the joined company in 2007, Hill was responsible for some of the label's biggest hits—notably its Alexa and Bayswater handbags—and presided over a period of significant innovation and growth. In 2013 though, with sales falling, the brand's management decided it needed a new creative direction— even the most creative brands feel the need for reinvention.

As creative organizations know, to the benefit of their staff and the bottom line, creativity and invention—by everyone, everywhere, and all of the time—are vital ingredients for business success. ▪

Emma Hill

UK-born fashion designer Emma Hill studied at the Wimbledon School of Art in 1989 before graduating from Ravensbourne College of Design and Communication in 1992. Starting her fashion career at luxury brand Burberry, Hill also worked for UK retailer Marks & Spencer, US fashion designer Marc Jacobs, and US retailer Gap, before moving to Mulberry— which has stores in Europe, US, Asia, and Australia—as Creative Director in 2007.

At Mulberry, Hill's creative talent for designing handbags carried by the likes of model Kate Moss and musician Lana Del Rey resulted in waiting lists for purchases. Thanks to her expansion of the brand into small leather goods (such as brightly colored card holders) in order to appeal to the more price-conscious end of the market, the brand enjoyed stellar growth. When she joined Mulberry the company's shares had stood at $1.78 (111 pence); at the time of her departure in 2013 they were worth nearly 10 times as much. In 2010, thanks to Emma Hill's work, Mulberry won the "Best Designer Brand" prize at the British Fashion Awards.

DISSENT ADDS SPICE, SPIRIT, AND AN INVIGORATING QUALITY
BEWARE THE YES-MEN

IN CONTEXT

FOCUS
Behavioral management

KEY DATES
1992 Indian economist Abhijit V Banerjee looks at how decision makers refer to the choices made by previous decision makers for guidance, in his book *A Simple Model of Herd Behavior.*

1993 US economist Canice Prendergast writes *A Theory of Yes Men*, identifying the tendency of subordinates to agree with their superiors as a "market failure."

1997 US psycholinguistics expert Suzette Elgin writes *How to Disagree without Being Disagreeable.*

2000s Leadership theory encourages leaders to embrace constructive conflict as a healthy, and necessary, part of the business environment.

If managers are only brought **good news**...

...they are forced to make decisions based on **incomplete or inaccurate** information.

Leaders should **beware "the yes-men"** and embrace constructive conflict in their companies.

Sometimes **"no"** is ultimately more **useful** than "yes."

For many employees, working within an organization means forever saying "yes." Fearful of losing their jobs, eager to please, and ambitious for promotion, subordinates are often happy to pass on good news, but reluctant to deliver bad news. This might be good for their manager's ego but it can be damaging for the business—if bad news is hidden, managers lack vital information and can make bad decisions as a consequence.

This can happen at the highest levels with catastrophic results. A Financial Services Report in 2012 on the Royal Bank of Scotland (RBS) suggested that the bank's failure in 2008 was, in part, due to "a lack of effective challenge by the board and senior managers to the CEO's proposals, resulting in risks being overlooked and strategic mistakes being made."

A tolerant business culture
Being an effective leader involves recognizing that it is impossible to be right all of the time. Seeking, and graciously accepting, critical feedback from trusted colleagues can help maintain a balanced perspective. The challenge for

See also: The value of teams 70–71 ▪ Hubris and nemesis 100–03 ▪ Effective leadership 78–79 ▪ Ignoring the herd 146–49 ▪ Learning from failure 164–65 ▪ Avoiding complacency 194–201 ▪ Creating an ethical culture 224–27

In an organization where innovation happens, very often people ignore orders.
Robert Sutton
US professor of management

leaders is to create an environment where bad news is tolerated, and even encouraged. If leaders react to unwelcome news without screaming or recrimination, staff is more likely to be confident about delivering it. Good leaders tend to address the problem, rather than simply apportioning blame, helping to prevent a repeat scenario.

An important way of preventing a yes-men culture is to create a culture of collective responsibility. Often, the most valuable employees are those who are courageous and caring enough to tell the truth, no matter how bad it might be.

For employees, delivering bad news is a skill in itself. It is better if the news comes with a proposed solution attached, and with causes of the problem acknowledged rather than ignored. The news should be delivered promptly; the sooner a problem is identified, the sooner it can be solved, and the better a manager's reaction is likely to be.

Testing your ideas

Jean Paul Getty, founder of the Getty Oil Company, recognized the value of outspoken employees, claiming that "dissent adds spice, spirit, and an invigorating quality."

Ken Olsen, founder of Digital Equipment Corporation, built dissent into company culture, using debate and conflict resolution as the primary ways of decision making. Jack Welch, CEO of General Electric (GE), encouraged no-holds-barred debates, saying, "if the idea can't survive a spirited argument, the marketplace will surely kill it."

Saying yes to every task and giving only good news to a leader might result in popularity, but will soon overload the employee and risks blinded decision making by the leader.

Management teams that can challenge each other's thinking develop a richer understanding of strategic options, and, ultimately, make better decisions. The best business leaders attempt to harness criticism and debate. If everybody is saying "yes," something is seriously wrong. ▪

Jean Paul Getty

Jean Paul Getty was born in Minneapolis in 1892. His father was a lawyer who moved into the oil business in 1903. Getty studied at universities in the US and UK before joining his father's business, The Minnehoma Oil Company. He set out to make a million dollars within his first two years, and did so by buying and selling oil leases.

Because Getty married five times, his disapproving father bequeathed him only $500,000 from his $10-million estate. Undeterred, Getty combined this with his own amassed earnings to buy several oil companies and build these into a pyramid of corporations, with the Getty Oil Company at the top. In 1949, he purchased a 60-year concession in a tract of land between Saudi Arabia and Kuwait that was thought to be barren of any oil. His company struck oil in massive quantities in 1953, making Getty a billionaire. He died in 1976 at the age of 83.

Key works

1953 *My Life and Fortunes*
1965 *How to be Rich*

NO GREAT MANAGER OR LEADER EVER FELL FROM HEAVEN
GODS OF MANAGEMENT

In his influential 1978 book *Gods of Management*, Charles Handy used the allegory of the gods of ancient Greece to describe the nature of organizations. Handy proposed that four management styles could be identified, a combination of which are likely to be present in every organization. Zeus represents the "club culture," in which relationships with the leader are more important than formal titles or positions. Apollo's "role culture" is defined by functions, divisions, rules, and rationality. In Athena's "task culture," power lies within teams who have the expertise to solve problems. In Dionysus's "existential culture," the organization exists to support the individual's needs.

Handy's typology provided an entirely new and original method for managers to analyze a company's dynamics, and to understand culturally embedded behaviors, biases, and beliefs. However, it soon became clear that because organizations are vast and diverse entities, and are seldom static, organizational behavior evolves over time. Under pressure externally and internally, most companies operate in a constant

---

Handy's Gods of Management reveals **different types of organizational dynamic**...

→ ...but **organizations are complex** at institutional and the individual level.

↓

Effective leadership requires God-like omniscience, but **no great leader ever fell from heaven.**

←

Therfore, **typologies can still be helpful** for understanding organizational and individual complexity.

See also: Leading well 68–69 ▪ Effective leadership 78–79 ▪ Organizational culture 104–09 ▪ Mintzberg's management roles 112–13

Zeus—
Club Culture
As the ruler of the Greek gods, Zeus was at the center of power and influence. Club cultures are built on affinity; proximity to the center of the club reflects an individual's standing within it. Investment banks often have dominant club cultures.

Apollo—
Role Culture
Apollo was the god of order and rules. Successful in times of stability, role cultures tend to flounder when rapid change is required. Insurance companies are among those typically led along Apollonian principles.

Charles Handy's Gods of Management

Athena—
Task Culture
Athena, the goddess of wisdom, was a problem-solver. Task cultures thrive where innovation is required, but struggle with routine. Advertising agencies and consultancies often display task cultures.

Dionysus—
Person Culture
Dionysus, the god of wine, stood for individual freedom. In person cultures, professional opinion is privileged and management is seen as an unnecessary burden. Professional service companies, such as legal firms, mirror Dionysian cultures.

Charles Handy

Professor Charles Handy, born in 1932, is Britain's best-known management guru. After graduating from Oxford University he joined the Massachusetts Institute of Technology in 1965, moving to the London Business School (LBS) in 1967 to run the only Sloan School of Management program outside the USA. Handy's challenging ideas, articulate style, and use of provocative imagery—such as his text *The Empty Raincoat*, a critique of the "impersonal mechanics of business organizations"—set him apart from his contemporaries. Handy sees himself as a social philosopher rather than management guru—his writings, he believes, are commentaries rather than manuals for success. His opinions have influenced business thinking for decades.

Key works

1976 *Understanding Organizations*
1978 *Gods of Management*
1994 *The Empty Raincoat*

---

state of flux—they adapt and change in unforeseen, unplanned, and unpredictable ways.

Accounting for complexity
Organizational complexity is often measured by the number of countries a company operates in, or the number of brands under a manager's control. Such institutional complexity is not insignificant; it pales though compared to individual complexity. For example, something novel that motivated a member of staff one

year may not motivate them the next. When a company consists of a staff of thousands, it is clear that people, and therefore organizations, are more complex than the stylistic Gods of Management suggest.

Handy later wrote of the Shamrock Organization—a flexible organization made of core employees, peripheral outsourced staff, and an external, flexible work force. Each category of worker has a different commitment to the organization, a different understanding of its vision, and their own motivations for work.

The job of leadership is to align these differences toward a common, organizational goal.

Organizational dynamics are important because people matter. Typologies only take a leader so far. Leaders must recognize that each employee perceives the company differently, and has unique drivers (and barriers) to effectiveness. As US businessman Tom Northup said, great leaders do not "fall from heaven," but God-like omniscience is a useful—albeit unreachable—goal to strive for. ■

A LEADER IS ONE WHO KNOWS THE WAY, GOES THE WAY, AND SHOWS THE WAY
EFFECTIVE LEADERSHIP

IN CONTEXT

FOCUS
Leadership

KEY DATES
1520s Italian diplomat Niccolò Macchiavelli's *The Prince* discusses the perils of leadership in political life.

1916 French executive Henri Fayol's work *General and Industrial Management* defines a leader as someone who "should possess and infuse into those around him courage to accept responsibility."

1950s and 60s The authoritative "Command and Control" school of management becomes popular. Charismatic leaders dominate organizations through force of personality.

1980s and 90s Leadership thinkers, such as US professor Warren Bennis, encourage a leadership style based on integrity, trust, and the ability to build an organization's capacity for change.

Effective leadership **builds capacity in others**.

A leader's charisma alone is not enough. **Effective leadership** requires the establishment of...

...**integrity, trust, empathy, and empowerment**.

Effective leadership requires **action from the leader**, not just brainpower.

For centuries scholars have attempted to determine the definitive styles, characteristics, and personality traits of great leaders. Yet, despite thousands of studies, effective leadership remains a subject of debate. However, one common theme is that effective leadership requires action, not just intellect.

Leaders cannot simply rely on charisma. While charismatic leadership has its place—for example, Henry Ford was renowned for his charismatic leadership style—there is a danger that rhetoric can exceed reality. Rather than empowering their employees, charismatic leaders often micromanage tasks and prevent their staff from gaining a sense of achievement from their work. Charismatic leaders are often heralded as champions of organizational success, but that charm can be a blessing and

See also: Leading well 68–69 ▪ Gods of management 76–77 ▪ Changing the game 92–99 ▪ Develop emotional intelligence 110–11 ▪ Mintzberg's management roles 112–13

Actively participating in business life, from the boardroom to the factory floor, is vital for effective leadership. Carlos Ghosn visited car assembly lines to build integrity and trust with staff.

a curse—the void created by the departure of a charismatic leader can be hard to fill. It may flatter the ego to be proclaimed a hero, but great leaders know that success involves building long-term organizational capacity that will outlast their own tenure.

Keys to effectiveness

To be effective, a leader must be confident and secure, and at the same time open and empathetic. Effective leadership involves the ability to create capacity in others through the process of interacting, informing, listening, developing, and trust-forming. Credibility of the leader is achieved through collaboration, not domination. Central to effective leadership is empowerment—the art of enabling other people to get things done.

One of the most effective contemporary business leaders is Carlos Ghosn, CEO of car makers

Renault and Nissan. Within a year of his appointment in 1999, Ghosn returned Nissan to profitability and was credited with saving the company from collapse. This proved to be one of the most dramatic turnarounds in modern business history.

Among the leadership traits that contribute to Ghosn's effectiveness is his belief that leadership is learned "by doing." On joining Nissan as CEO he walked around every factory, meeting and shaking hands with every employee. To this day he remains a common sight on factory floors. Integrity and trust, Ghosn believes, are built when leaders are seen to be willing to "get their hands dirty" and remain in touch with the factory floor of the business.

Empowering staff

Leaders must communicate a strong vision but, above all, they must empower staff to make decisions themselves. In large, diverse organizations a leader cannot, and should not, make all the decisions—helping others to understand the necessity for change, and giving them the tools to manage that change is key to the leader's role. The success of Nissan is also attributed to Ghosn's ability to manage cross-cultural teams. Leaders, Ghosn suggests, require the ability to listen and to empathize, not just with employees from their own countries, but also with people from different countries and cultures.

Ghosn's insights illustrate that effective leadership requires putting vision into action. Achieving this requires more than just rhetoric: effective leaders must "talk the talk" and "walk the walk." ∎

Carlos Ghosn

Born in 1954, Carlos Ghosn, a French-Lebanese Brazilian, started his career with Michelin, moved to Renault in 1996, and was appointed the CEO of Nissan in 1999 following Renault's purchase of a substantial stake in the ailing Japanese company. At the time, Nissan's debts had reached $20 billion and only three of its 48 car models were generating a profit. Promising to resign if the company did not reach profitability by the end of the year, he defied Japanese business etiquette, cut 21,000 jobs, and closed unprofitable domestic plants. Within three years Nissan became one of the most profitable automakers, with operating margins of higher than 9 percent—more than twice the industry average.

Having presided over what has been described as one of the greatest turnarounds in business history, Ghosn was named "the hardest-working man in the global car business" by *Forbes* magazine in 2011.

The universe rewards action, not thought.
Russell Bishop
US executive coach

TEAMWORK
IS THE FUEL THAT
ALLOWS COMMON PEOPLE
TO ATTAIN UNCOMMON
RESULTS

ORGANIZING TEAMS AND TALENT

IN CONTEXT

FOCUS
Teamwork

KEY DATES
1965 US professor Bruce Tuckman proposes that teams go through five stages: forming, storming, norming, performing, and adjourning.

1981 British management theorist Meredith Belbin writes *Management Teams: Why they succeed or fail*, describing nine distinct roles that are essential to team success.

1992 Peter Drucker describes three kinds of team in "There's more than one kind of team," published in *The Wall Street Journal*.

1993 Jon Katzenbach and Douglas Smith write *The Wisdom of Teams*, claiming that forming a team leads to greater success than individual efforts.

Effective teams are the key to great organizations. This is especially true in business, where teamwork merges individual talent into something greater than the sum of its parts, enabling "common people to attain uncommon results" in the words of US industrialist Andrew Carnegie.

Manufacturing companies in Europe and the US began to explore the idea of teamwork in the 1960s and 1970s, in response to the success of Japanese team-based working methods such as *kaizen* (staff are responsible for a company's continuous improvement) and "quality circles" (groups of staff tasked with improving quality). In the 1980s, as many companies adopted "total quality management" (organization-wide quality), teamwork began to spread beyond its genesis in manufacturing. Today, it would be rare to find an organization, of any type or size, that did not value teamwork.

The benefits of teamwork

Teamwork has been credited with bringing about substantial reductions in absenteeism, lower staff turnover, significant increases

Members of a team seek out certain roles and they perform most effectively in the ones that are most natural to them.
Meredith Belbin

in profit, and improved job satisfaction. In Honeywell's commercial flight division in Minneapolis, for example, teamwork was credited with achieving an 80 percent market share in flight and navigation systems—and for generating profits that were 200 percent higher than projections.

Teams succeed because they provide an environment where weaknesses can be balanced out and individual strengths multiplied. Teams also safeguard against individual shortcomings, such as underperformance and personal agendas. Projects are more likely to stay on track when peers support each other and review each other's and the team's work. Teams also create an environment that most people enjoy. The security of a group makes each individual feel less exposed and, in turn, more likely to take risks, be more creative, and therefore be better able to perform.

Storming and norming

Effective teams take time to develop. It is rare that a group of people can come together and begin to perform immediately; most teams go through a series of stages before effectiveness is achieved. Bruce Tuckman, a US professor of

Meredith Belbin

Meredith Belbin was born in Beckenham, UK, in 1926. He earned a degree in Classics at the University of Cambridge, and then a doctorate in psychology, during which he did research on the importance of teamwork. He then took a research fellowship at Cranfield—where he studied the benefits of ergonomics (designing tools and systems that fit best with people's needs) and improving efficiency in production lines—before becoming a management consultant. Belbin studied teamwork in the UK, US, and Australia, and in 1981 wrote *Management Teams: Why they succeed or fail*, which became one of the world's best-selling management books. Belbin has advised the US government, the European Union, companies and public service bodies.

Key works

1981 *Management Teams: Why they succeed or fail*
1993 *Team Roles At Work*
2000 *Beyond the Team*

See also: Leading well 68–69 ▪ The value of teams 70–71 ▪ Effective leadership 78–79 ▪ Make the most of your talent 86–87 ▪ Organizational culture 104–09 ▪ Avoid groupthink 114 ▪ The value of diversity 115 ▪ Kaizen 302–09

educational psychology, described these stages as forming, storming, norming, performing, and adjourning. During forming, the group comes together, and members get to know one other. It then moves into a storming stage, where members challenge each other for coveted group roles, and group processes begin to emerge through trial and error. The middle stage—norming—marks a period of calm, where agreement is reached on roles, processes, and group norms. By the fourth stage, members have become familiar with each other, with their roles, and with the processes involved. At this stage, team performance hits its most effective level. Once their work is done, the group moves to adjourning, or disbanding.

Businesses are eager for teams to move quickly through the early stages, reaching "performing" as soon as possible. This is why companies invest so much in team-building activities, where teams face and solve artificial challenges, often in a different environment. Many companies also use the architecture of their building to encourage team interaction. For example, at Pixar, the movie animation studio based in California, the cafeteria, meeting rooms, employee mail boxes, and bathrooms are located around a centralized atrium designed for collaborative working. The building design and layout encourages members of teams to meet and interact with one another, even when they are based in different departments within the company.

Research has shown that team-building activities and collaborative work spaces help to improve team work because the most effective teams are those where members trust one another, share a strong sense of group identity, and have confidence in their effectiveness as a team.

Effective team building
In 2005, US researchers Jon Katzenbach and Douglas Smith identified a series of factors that seem to be essential for effective teamwork. First, team members must be chosen for their skills, not their personality. The team then needs to get off to a good start; setting the right tone is essential. The tone should not be too casual—teams perform better when challenged, so a sense of urgency needs to be imparted.

The team should agree on clear rules for group behavior and norms, and meet often, both formally and informally. If possible, the team should be allowed to enjoy some early success; a few easy wins early on has been found to boost performance later. Likewise, the group—and its individual members—needs to be lavished with praise. Continuing motivation »

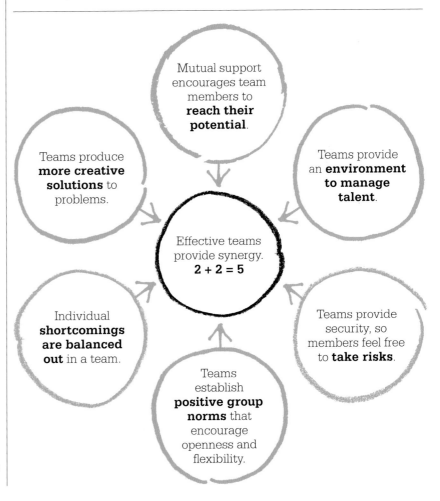

Mutual support encourages team members to **reach their potential**.

Teams produce **more creative solutions** to problems.

Teams provide an **environment to manage talent**.

Effective teams provide synergy. **2 + 2 = 5**

Individual **shortcomings are balanced out** in a team.

Teams provide security, so members feel free to **take risks**.

Teams establish **positive group norms** that encourage openness and flexibility.

Belbin Team Inventory

Team role	Talent	Weakness
Plant	Creative, unconventional thinker who excels at solving problems	Not good at managing (or communicating with) less creative people
Resource investigator	Communicative extrovert who develops contacts and explores opportunities	Loses interest once initial enthusiasm has passed
Coordinator	Mature, confident person who is able to clarify goals and promote decision making	Can be manipulative and appear aloof
Shaper	Dynamic, outgoing, highly strung person who will challenge, pressure, and find ways around obstacles	Prone to provocation and short-lived bursts of temper
Monitor/ evaluator	Sober, strategic, discerning person able to see and judge options objectively	Lacks drive and ability to inspire others
Teamworker	Social, mild, perceptive and accommodating, this teamworker averts friction	Indecisive in crunch situations
Implementer	Disciplined, reliable, conservative, efficient person who can turn ideas into practical actions	Somewhat inflexible, slow to respond to new possibilities
Completer/ finisher	Painstaking, conscientious person who is always able to meet deadlines	Inclined to worry unduly, reluctant to delegate
Specialist	Single-minded, dedicated self-starter who brings knowledge or technical skills that are in rare supply	Contributes only on a narrow front

is encouraged by new challenges, since they help to keep the work fresh and engaging.

Successful roles

Individuals offer different talents and attributes, and these need to be taken into account when putting together teams. UK management theorist Meredith Belbin claims there are nine distinct roles within a team that are essential to team success, and that the key to a well-organized team is balance. For example, Belbin found that teams without Plants (creative, unconventional thinkers) struggle to come up with ideas; but if there are too many Plants, idea generation starts to take precedence over action. Similarly, if there is no Shaper (a dynamic, driven person who pushes the group toward decisions), teams lack drive and direction. But in a team with too many Shapers, arguments occur frequently and will lower morale.

Now an established business tool, the Belbin Team Inventory is frequently used by companies to maximize team effectiveness. However, many companies make the mistake of using it after teams have been formed; to work successfully, it must be used before creating a team.

Managing talent

Sir Alex Ferguson, former manager of Manchester United, one of the world's best-known soccer teams, is a master of building winning teams over and again, and his methods can be applied to the business environment. His team was bonded by a strong sense of shared mission—a desire to win. Players were cohesive on the field, because Ferguson demanded cohesiveness off the field. An exceptional team culture ran through the veins of every player

> Teams develop direction, momentum, and commitment by working to shape a meaningful purpose.
> **Jon R. Katzenbach**
> **Douglas K. Smith**

and every staff member. Ferguson realized the value of positive group norms. He was, for example, one of the first managers to ban the consumption of alcohol. Moreover, alongside a host of team-building activities—quizzes on the team bus, for example—he demanded ferocious loyalty. Players could expect unfailing public support from Ferguson and the team. Equally, players were expected to observe a code of media silence in regard to teammates. Anyone breaching this team ethic was quickly ousted.

Team management often involves dealing with large egos and highly talented people. Ferguson recognized that it was folly to rein in significant talent—players Eric Cantona and Cristiano Ronaldo were both encouraged to express their soccer-playing flair—but he also transferred highly skilled players who felt themselves to be more important than the team. Talent management is a source of frustration for many executives,

Flying geese demonstrate the power of teamwork. By flying together, each one reduces air resistance for the ones behind. They rotate leadership and "talk" continuously by honking.

because talented people often resist being managed, and it can be difficult to find challenges that keep them sufficiently motivated, while at the same time aligned with organizational goals. However, teams provide an environment where talent can thrive. By giving talented staff teams to manage, or—although risky—grouping talent together in teams, it is possible to stretch even the most gifted member of staff. Teams provide a framework and value system to which all members, however skilled or talented, must adhere.

Collective products

Businesses, like sports teams, face performance challenges for which teams are a powerful solution. This is because teams are not simply a group of people who work together; they are judged not by individual performance, but by their "collective work products." These are the pieces of work—which might be products, surveys, or experiments—that come about as a result of joint

contributions. In *The Wisdom of Teams*, Jon Katzenbach and Douglas Smith defined a team as "a small number of people with complementary skills who are committed to a common purpose, set of performance goals, and approach, for which they hold themselves mutually accountable." No individual is responsible for success or failure, because no one acts alone. Teamwork encourages listening, responding constructively to the views of others, providing support, and recognizing the interests, skills, and achievements of the other team members.

Most successful teams are formed in response to a perceived threat or opportunity. When these arise, the role of senior leaders is to organize teams with clear purpose, balanced membership, disciplined procedures, and strong bonds, while giving them enough flexibility to develop their own timing and approach. By doing so, leaders create environments where individuals—and therefore the organization—are able to succeed and flourish. ∎

LEADERS ALLOW GREAT PEOPLE TO DO THE WORK THEY WERE BORN TO DO
MAKE THE MOST OF YOUR TALENT

IN CONTEXT

FOCUS
Work-force effectiveness

KEY DATES
1959 US psychologist Frederick Herzberg defines factors in job satisfaction in his study *The Motivation to Work*.

1960 In his book *The Human Side of Enterprise,* US academic Douglas McGregor proposes Theory Y, urging companies to adopt a participatory management style that motivates workers to strive to achieve their potential.

1989 US management guru Rosabeth Moss Kanter's *When Giants Learn to Dance* suggests that employees are most productive when empowered to make their own decisions.

Staff in many organizations reports feeling undervalued, overstretched, and forced to work in areas beyond its competence. Because of this they feel ineffective —they want to work better, but feel that the organization is constraining them. The best companies allow staff to build careers around what they excel at—in leadership expert Warren Bennis's words "to do the work they were born to do."

Contemporary organizations, faced with dynamic, fast-moving markets, favor employees who are flexible and multiskilled. Yet in a 2012 Global Work force Study only 35 percent of employees reported engagement with their jobs, revealing a disconnect with what employers want and what employees are willing to give. Studies have found engaged employees—those devoted to their jobs and committed to the company's values—are significantly more productive, provide better customer service, and outperform those who are less engaged. But many companies treat staff as little more than pieces on an organizational chessboard that can be moved around at will.

Effective people create **effective organizations**.

Great leaders allow great people to excel at what they do well.

They **value the factory floor** as much as the shareholders.

See also: Leading well 68–69 ▪ Creativity and invention 72–73 ▪ Effective leadership 78–79 ▪ Organizing teams and talent 80–85 ▪ Is money the motivator? 90–91

Google's innovative, dynamic culture, in which staff are encouraged to work to their strengths and explore projects that they are passionate about, is one of the reasons for the company's success.

In his two-factor theory, US psychologist and management thinker Frederick Herzberg identified a sense of achievement as being closely linked to motivation to work. Effectiveness is intrinsically rewarding; even the most generous salary cannot, over the long term, replace the satisfaction of a job well done. The same generous salary will not offset the dissatisfaction of underachievement. Consequently, equipping employees with the tools to develop effective habits can lead to more effective performance, happier, more productive staff, and, in turn, improve a company's results.

Working better, not harder

Google, borrowing from a practice introduced by US conglomerate 3M in 1948, encourages staff to spend 20 percent of their time on projects of their own choosing. Rather than distract from directed projects, Google found that their staff works better on all tasks—when people are passionate about their work, it does not feel like work. Such discretionary effort, the willingness of employees to "go the extra mile," can be the difference between good and great. Great businesses focus on getting the best out of people, not the most out of them. Gmail, one of Google's most popular products, is a result of the company's 20-percent time.

Enabling staff to work better, not harder, requires an enlightened leadership approach that looks down to the factory floor as well as up to the shareholders. Companies that value effectiveness over volume, and performance over presenteeism (when staff works despite illness, instead of taking sick leave) often find themselves at the top of best-employer lists. Leaders of these companies realize that shareholder value is driven by staff performance; allowing staff to build careers around what they excel at is good for employees and the bottom line. ▪

The man who does not work for the love of work, but only for money, is likely to neither make money nor find much fun in life.
Charles M. Schwab
US industrialist (1862–1939)

Warren Bennis

Born on March 8, 1925, Warren Bennis is an American scholar, organizational consultant, and management author. Enlisting in the US Army in 1943, Bennis was one of the youngest infantry officers to serve in World War II, and was awarded the Purple Heart and Bronze Star for service in action. After leaving the military, Bennis studied at Antioch College, Ohio, and later became a professor at the Massachusetts Institute of Technology's Sloan School of Management. Widely regarded as the pioneer of the contemporary field of leadership studies, Bennis was named one of the ten greatest influencers on business thinking by *BusinessWeek* magazine in 2007. The *Financial Times* lists his classic 1985 book *Leaders* as one of the top 50 business books of all time.

Key works

1985 *Leaders: Strategies for Taking Charge*
1997 *Why Leaders Can't Lead: The Unconscious Conspiracy Continues*
2009 *On Becoming a Leader*

THE WAY FORWARD MAY NOT BE TO GO FORWARD
THINKING OUTSIDE THE BOX

IN CONTEXT

FOCUS
Innovation

KEY DATES
1914 The nine-dots puzzle is published in Sam Loyd's *Cyclopedia of Puzzles*.

1967 Edward de Bono coins the term "lateral thinking" to describe the process of the "horizontal imagination," which has a broad sweep but is unconcerned with detail.

1970s There is a surge of management consultants encouraging creativity. Strategic thinking is said to embrace retrenchment and retreat.

2012 Jeff Bezos of Amazon claims that "if you're inventing and pioneering, you have to be willing to be misunderstood for long periods of time."

The competitive pressures that businesses face are constantly in flux: new ideas and disruptive technologies emerge, the economic power of countries shifts, and market dynamics change. Yet business history is littered with companies that ignored change and pushed forward with flawed strategies based on the old environment. To avoid this, the idea of "thinking outside the box" is used to challenge precepts and assumptions—to consider that sometimes, the way to move forward is not to move forward at all.

The idea of thinking outside the box emerged in the 1960s and is based on the nine-dots puzzle, a game that was used by management

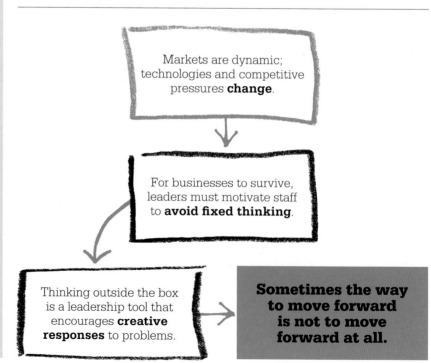

Markets are dynamic; technologies and competitive pressures **change**.

↓

For businesses to survive, leaders must motivate staff to **avoid fixed thinking**.

Thinking outside the box is a leadership tool that encourages **creative responses** to problems.

Sometimes the way to move forward is not to move forward at all.

See also: Gaining an edge 32–39 ▪ Keep evolving business practice 48–51 ▪ Creativity and invention 72–73 ▪ Changing the game 92–99 ▪ Forecasting 278–79 ▪ Feedback and innovation 312–13

Nintendo's Wii console is a product of lateral thinking. Rather than taking on their industry rivals head on, the Wii's designers redefined gaming as a family-friendly, social activity.

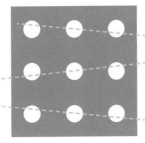

The nine-dots puzzle challenges players to connect the nine dots with four straight lines or less, without lifting pen from paper or tracing the same line twice. The solution involves drawing lines "outside the box."

consultants to encourage lateral thinking. Several of its solutions involved drawing lines that were literally outside the puzzle's box. The phrase was adopted to represent any kind of creative thinking that goes beyond the obvious. Today, thinking outside the box represents innovation, the need to be aware of market changes, and the need to avoid fixed ways of thinking.

The bold retreat
Linear thinking—the opposite of thinking outside the box—has been responsible for the downfall of many businesses. MySpace, a website that dominated the online social-media market in the early 2000s, is an example of a business that fell victim to strategic retrenchment—sticking to a failing strategy rather than adapting to new competition or a changing marketplace. Purchased by News Corp for $580 millon in 2005, the business was sold in 2011 for $35 million, having failed to match the creative vision of Mark

Zuckerburg's hugely successful Facebook. The future survival of MySpace depended on new thinking—it turned its business around by successfully refocusing on a core market of creative music professionals, leaving the social-media mass-market to Facebook.

Other companies have employed leaders with a more radical approach to guide them through fast-changing times. Nintendo's response to the technological superiority of the X-Box and Playstation, for example, was to think differently. Instead of competing on the usual grounds of

BT should have invented Skype. But they didn't because the concept of a free platform totally disrupts their business model.
Alan Moore
US systems expert

price and increasingly sophisticated games, the Nintendo Wii created a whole new market. Its unique player interface—with a range of handheld, wireless controllers—and focus on group-based gaming made it family-friendly; suddenly gaming was a social activity for gamers of all ages and experience levels. The console quickly outsold the competition in almost every territory.

Leaders taking this kind of "bold retreat" willingly cede technological advantage or market position to the dominant player, pursuing instead less vulnerable (and often more profitable) market positions.

Rethinking the box
Some business leaders believe that even creative thinkers may take certain things—such as organizational structure—for granted. They are therefore encouraging their staff to think literally "beyond the building" for new ideas. Procter & Gamble CEO A G Lafley sent employees to live temporarily in the homes of consumers to better understand their needs and identify product opportunities. The box itself, it seems, is perhaps a distraction. ▪

THE MORE A PERSON CAN DO, THE MORE YOU CAN MOTIVATE THEM
IS MONEY THE MOTIVATOR?

IN CONTEXT

FOCUS
Motivation

KEY DATES
1914 Henry Ford doubles wages at Ford Motor Company in an effort to reduce labor turnover. Thousands apply for jobs with the company.

1959 Fredrick Herzberg proposes his theory that "motivators" and "hygiene factors" lead to satisfaction or dissatisfaction at work. He stresses that pay demotivates, but it does not motivate.

2000s "Best Employer" lists reveal that the highest ranked companies are often not those offering the biggest salaries.

2012 *Fortune* magazine cites Google as the best organization to work for in the US, and it also tops the list of employers in developing countries, including India. High salaries and a range of perks contribute to staff satisfaction.

When present, **motivators**—such as recognition, professional growth, and responsibility—can contribute to job satisfaction.

If poorly managed, **hygiene factors**—such as pay, conditions, supervision, and security—can increase job dissatisfaction.

Money matters, but **workplace motivation** is much more complex than financial reward alone.

If you were paid more, would you work harder? The answer is probably partly yes, and partly no. Higher pay might encourage you to move to a new job or to work a little faster or harder, but this focus is soon eroded—or equally, magnified—by other factors, such as job satisfaction, respect from managers, and the challenge presented by the work itself.

Financial gain can move us to do things, but motivation is more complex than money alone. US psychologist Professor Frederick

Herzberg began to study workplace motivation in the 1950s while teaching at Case Western Reserve University, OH. In 1959 he proposed the "two-factor theory"—that a series of "motivators" encourage job satisfaction, while aspects of work termed "hygiene factors" contribute to dissatisfaction in the workplace if they are poorly managed.

Removing dissatisfaction
Hygiene factors include working conditions, job security, relationships with other workers, and salary.

See also: Leading well 68–69 ▪ The value of teams 70–71 ▪ Creativity and invention 72–73 ▪ Effective leadership 78–79 ▪ Make the most of your talent 86–87

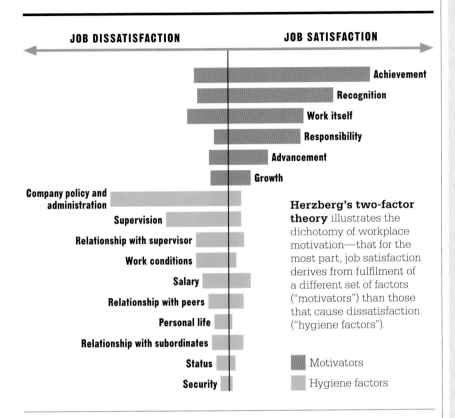

Herzberg's two-factor theory illustrates the dichotomy of workplace motivation—that for the most part, job satisfaction derives from fulfilment of a different set of factors ("motivators") than those that cause dissatisfaction ("hygiene factors").

Frederick Herzberg

US psychologist Frederick Herzberg was born on April 18, 1923. He attended City College of New York and later held a professorship at the University of Utah, USA. Herzberg's service in the US Army, in particular his observation of conditions at the Dachau concentration camp in Germany during World War II, is thought to have inspired his interest in motivational theory.

Challenging the notion that workers are driven only by money and other benefits, Herzberg suggested that achievement and recognition are powerful motivators. He believed that managers should create safe, happy workplaces and make tasks interesting, challenging, and rewarding. His work influenced a generation of managers.

Key works

1959 *The Motivation to Work*
1968 *One More Time: How do you Motivate Employees?*
1976 *The Managerial Choice: To Be Efficient and to Be Human*

Motivators include recognition, responsibility, the opportunity for advancement, a sense of personal achievement, and potential for growth—as Herzberg put it "the more a person can do," the more easily they can be motivated.

Herzberg argued that job dissatisfaction is as important as satisfaction. He believed that unless hygiene factors were well managed, no matter how good the motivators, staff would not be inclined to work hard. They would, he suggested, be so dissatisfied as to be demotivated. He also believed that hygiene factors do not, in themselves, motivate; but when fulfilled, they reduce dissatisfaction and provide a foundation for motivation. On the other hand, motivators have great potential to

increase job satisfaction, but when lacking, actually only result in low levels of employee dissatisfaction.

Motivators in practice

Herzberg's findings are significant for business leaders. The two-factor theory proposes that job design is crucial—it must create conditions in which employees can feel a sense of achievement, enjoy responsibility, and gain recognition for their work. Levels of pay may be important for recruitment and retention, but it is less important in encouraging staff to work effectively.

Every day, thousands of people around the world apply for jobs at fast-food outlet McDonald's. Frequently rated at the top of "best employer" lists, the chain is popular because of a friendly working

environment and flexible working policies. Initiatives such as the "friends and family contract"—in which employees from the same family or friendship group can cover each other's shifts—give staff a sense of shared responsibility, and enhance loyalty to the company.

The top-paying companies are rarely ranked as the best employers. Money matters, but job satisfaction, career advancement, management attitude, and personal relations are the workplace factors that most motivate us to work harder. ▪

BE AN ENZYME— A CATALYST FOR CHANGE

CHANGING THE GAME

IN CONTEXT

FOCUS
Innovation

KEY DATES
1997 US professor Clayton M. Christensen introduces the concept of "disruptive technologies"—major and unforeseen technological advances that cause companies to redefine how they operate.

2000s Global Positioning System (GPS) navigational technology emerges as a disruptive innovation in a range of industries, from travel and fitness to recreation and smartphone applications.

2014 US professor of business administration David McAdams writes *Game-Changer: Game Theory and the Art of Transforming Strategic Situations*. McAdams uggests that game-changers are those who are "determined enough to change the game to their own advantage."

The business people we remember are those who do things differently—people such as Facebook COO Sheryl Sandberg, US investor Warren Buffett, Hong Kong business magnate Stanley Ho, British entrepreneur Richard Branson, and US media giant Oprah Winfrey. Similarly, the companies we remember are those whose products and services stand out. Companies that shuffle along with the crowd, doing the same thing in the same old way, are soon forgotten; those that disrupt industries and change the game are celebrated, sometimes even idolized.

In today's global market, competition is fierce and every percentage point of market share is hard fought and precious. Operating in these markets is often a zero-sum game: competition drives prices down and costs up. Gaining a significant competitive advantage requires more than gradual improvement, it demands radical and disruptive shifts—if you cannot win the game, move the goalposts. Redefining the rules and boundaries of an industry is the essence of game-changing business strategy.

> I want to put a dent in the universe.
> **Steve Jobs**

Thinking one step ahead of customers and competitors disrupts the status quo in a business's favor.

Disruptive innovation
Harvard Business School scholar Clayton Christensen identified two types of technology that can influence businesses: "sustaining technologies," or advances in technology that help companies make gradual improvements to product performance; and "disruptive technologies," radical advances in technology that disrupt the industry and force companies to rethink their entire mode of being. Christensen later changed the term "disruptive technology" to

---

Steve Jobs

Entrepreneur and inventor Steven Paul Jobs was born on February 24, 1955 in San Francisco, California, US. In 1976, at the age of 21, he and Steve Wozniak started Apple Computers (from the garage in Jobs's home). The business went public in 1980, with a market value of $1.2 billion.

In 1985, after disagreements with the board, Jobs was fired by recently appointed CEO John Sculley. Jobs nevertheless went on to found NeXT Computer and invest in Pixar Animation Studios, which was to become hugely successful. In a twist of corporate fate, Apple bought NeXT in 1996 and Jobs returned to Apple later that year, becoming CEO in 1997. In 1998 Jobs launched the iconic iMac computer and went on to preside over one of the most famous corporate renaissances in history. Under his guidance, Apple led the way with innovative product design and technology to become one of the most valuable technology businesses in the world.

In 2010, Steve Jobs was 61st in *Time Magazine*'s "100 People who Changed the World." He died on October 5, 2011.

See also: Stand out in the market 28–31 ▪ Gaining an edge 32–39 ▪ Creativity and invention 72–73 ▪ Thinking outside the box 88–89 ▪ Leading the market 166–69 ▪ The value chain 216–17 ▪ Creating a brand 258–63

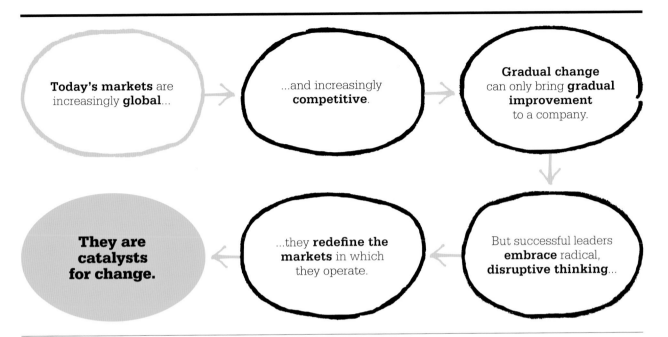

Today's markets are increasingly **global**…

…and increasingly **competitive**.

Gradual change can only bring **gradual improvement** to a company.

They are catalysts for change.

…they **redefine the markets** in which they operate.

But successful leaders **embrace** radical, **disruptive thinking**…

"disruptive innovation" to reflect the fact that it is not so much technology itself that is disruptive as how that technology is applied.

One such product that has changed the game by adapting technology for new purposes is GlowCap. A screw-on top that can be attached to prescription medicine containers, GlowCap contains a glowing LED and audio alert that signal when medication should be taken. It also connects via Wi-Fi to the user's smartphone, sending a text message or an email alert if a dose is missed. Like many game changers, it utilizes lateral thinking to present a solution to an existing problem, effectively meeting the consumer's needs. Disruptive innovation creates the

need for a product, even before customers realize such a need exists, and opens up new, untapped markets with significant first-mover advantages—not least of which is brand association

with the new market segment. The German company Siemens, for example, built the world's first electric elevator in 1880, and in 1881 provided power for the world's first electric street lights (in

The Crystal is one of the world's most sustainable buildings. Built in the UK by Siemens, it symbolizes the spirit of innovation that has been the hallmark of the company since the 1880s.

Disruptive innovation refers to an innovation that transforms the market. When an existing product boasts more features or services than customers require, it may become too complex or difficult to use. As the gap between the existing product's performance and customer requirement grows, it creates a gap in the market that can be exploited by a new, "disruptive" product. Over time, the new product can redefine the market.

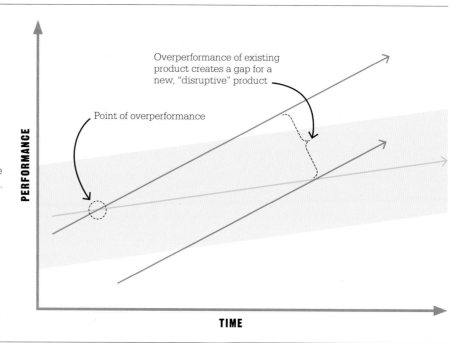

Performance demand of mainstream consumers

Mean performance demand

Existing company/ product

New "disruptive" company/product

Godalming, England). More recent game-changing products in lighting, energy, transportation, and healthcare have ensured that the Siemens name is associated with quality and innovation.

Leaders like the company's founder, Werner von Siemens—those with the vision and courage to pursue game-changing strategies—are, however, all too rare. It takes great courage to break from tradition; and charisma and conviction to lead individuals, organizations, and entire industries away from the status quo. Success is met with reward and celebration; failure with ridicule and scorn. For would-be game changers, the line between fame and infamy is often thin.

Rewriting the rules

Another company that has changed the game in its favor, on several occasions, is Apple. Under the guidance of its co-founder and CEO, Steve Jobs, the organization disrupted the desktop computer industry, the music industry, the cell-phone industry, and the tablet-computer industry.

Apple's iMac, with its focus on user-friendly design and software, made a significant impact on the personal computer industry. However, Apple's first major game changer was the iPod, first introduced in 2001. The product was met with scepticism—but this, according to Christensen, is a classic reaction to a game changer. A product that is accepted at first glance as a "winner" is

You cannot lead from the crowd.
Margaret Thatcher
UK former Prime Minister (1925–2013)

unlikely to have shifted the market very far—true game changers raise eyebrows and prompt questions.

Interfacing technologies

The iPod was a cross between the early crop of low-storage MP3 players and the large, hard-drive-based players that provided several gigabytes of storage. Amid a sea of bland competing products, the iPod stood out thanks to its stylish and distinctive design. It was small, easy to use, and came with the promise of "1,000 songs in your pocket."

The real disrupter, however, was the combined power of the iPod and its software interface, iTunes. Customers could now access a huge amount of music from one place, buy it, download it, and "sync" music from their computer to their devices with ease. The iPod could also be charged while syncing. The fact that we now take such features for granted demonstrates the extent to which Apple transformed the market for personal-music devices.

The iTunes Music Store (now the iTunes Store) redefined the music industry in 2003. At the time, digital music piracy was on the rise; record labels were fighting against digital distribution for fear of losing control and further damaging already declining revenues. Jobs exploited the record executives' nervousness to his advantage, offering people a way to purchase music legally but easily and instantly.

Apple's software changed the music industry's business model forever. In addition to changing the way we access and listen to music, iTunes enabled people to buy single tracks from albums. Artists no longer needed to slave for months on albums, but could release a steady stream of singles instead. Consumers no longer felt trapped into album purchases and felt less need to search for free, pirated downloads in place of legal versions.

The Apple logo has become a global emblem of the modern age—an indication of the extent to which the organization has revolutionized technology and product development.

The iTunes Store and the iPod system, quite simply, worked for consumers, who had been baffled by the many MP3 players and online methods of finding music. Apple simplified the process, and made its solution aesthetically appealing at the same time. By 2013, its strategy had brought sales of around 400 million iPods and more than 25 billion iTunes Store downloads.

Continually game-changing

Such radical disruption, if achieved only once, could be put down to good luck, but true game changers are those who persistently seek to separate themselves from the competition. Steve Jobs was not content merely to have changed the music industry: in 2007 he turned his attention to the cell-phone industry. Cell phones had been getting smarter for a while, but the iPhone was a giant leap forward. Offering users access to a suite of computer-like applications and, in particular, seamless Internet access, it was an instant hit. The real breakthrough was the iPhone's touch-screen technology. Jobs

It's kind of fun to do the impossible.
Walt Disney
US entrepreneur (1901–1966)

called the iPhone "a revolutionary product," claiming it was "five years' ahead of any other cell phone." His words were prophetic: for some years after, the iPhone remained the standard against which all other cell phones were assessed and defined.

Shortly before his death in 2011, Jobs did it again—this time with the iPad. Launched in April 2010, to confusion and some cynicism, the iPad came to (re)define the industry. It extended access to technology beyond its accepted business, educational, and »

> What today seems odd, unnecessary, offbeat—maybe even outrageous—may prove integral to solving tomorrow's problems.
> **Pierre Omidyar**

desktop-bound roots, in a format that few, at first, expected to be popular. The iPad ushered in a new era of computing, and remains, even in an increasingly crowded tablet-computer marketplace, the industry standard.

Corporate culture
Apple has changed the game so significantly that the brand has entered the cultural zeitgeist: its products are seen everywhere—from coffee shops and classrooms to television shows. Apple's technology has made its products ubiquitous and its customers fanatically brand loyal. With such a competitive edge, it is no surprise that the company's prices are able to sit well above industry averages.

But the challenge for any organization is to ensure that such game-changing mentality informs the spirit of the whole company. As French businessman Pierre Omidyar, founder of the online auction site eBay, suggests, a leader must be "a catalyst for

Pierre Omidyar, chairman and founder of the popular auction site eBay, has embedded the desire for innovation and dramatic change within his company's corporate culture.

change." But to be truly successful, and to outlive the tenure of a highly driven leader, the desire to disrupt must be pervasive. The energy, innovation, and courage required to repeatedly disrupt industries must be deeply ingrained in the corporate culture, which must also allow for flexibility to change.

In the case of eBay, Omidyar realized that the future was unpredictable and nonlinear, and decided to structure his new venture with the approach of a software engineer (his former job), "who has learned to strive for flexibility in design." While a software program might seem initially to provide more than its customers need, this is what gives it the flexibility to change and "prepare for the unexpected." Ebay's self-sustaining system required little intervention and was able to adapt and grow according to customer needs. Its design effectively embedded disruption within the core structure. The idea of allowing users to rate each other was both new and risky—as was a business model that required

> Problems cannot be solved at the same level of awareness that created them.
> **Albert Einstein**
> **German-born physicist (1879–1955)**

users to do most of the work. These features nevertheless ensured that eBay evolved not only around Omidyar's ideas and energy, but also around the requirements of the entire eBay community.

Embracing failure
However, such deeply embedded game-changing mentality is rare. Heroic leaders—game changers and risk takers—are difficult to find and even more difficult to replace. With fewer than one in ten new product ideas making it to market, people

are rarely brave enough, or confident and committed enough in their ideas, to stake their careers and reputations on risky game-changing innovations. The heroic leader's strength lies not just in their vision, but also in their willingness to stand in the spotlight when things go wrong.

Corporate history is littered with examples of failed products. Most businesses are therefore, by nature, risk averse. Even Apple has made mistakes—and, again, its example is instructive. Jobs may be best remembered for transforming the music, computer, and phone industries, but he'll also be remembered as the poster boy for embracing failure, and bouncing back from it. He has reigned over a long list of failures. The Pippen games console, for example, was unable to compete with the likes of Sony's Playstation, and was quickly dropped. The Apple III computer suffered major design faults, and the Lisa—a computer that would eventually provide the basis for the iMac—had poor sales. The Apple Newton, a forerunner of today's smartphones, was a flop.

These failures led to Jobs being fired in 1985. In a speech to students graduating from Stanford University in 2005, Jobs stated that the dismissal triggered him to change his own game: "The heaviness of being successful was replaced by the lightness of being a beginner again, less sure about everything. It freed me to enter one of the most creative periods of my life."

History is filled with examples of trailblazers who stumbled before finding success. KFC chicken, invented by Harland David Sanders, was rejected by more than 1,000 restaurants; R. C. Macy opened and closed many stores before founding the largest department store in the

Challenging the status quo

African-American businessman John H. Johnson had the acumen to recognize the untapped potential for publications aimed at the African-American market. Excelling at high school despite an impoverished upbringing, Johnson won a scholarship to the University of Chicago and supported himself with an office job at an insurance company. It was while at work that he came up with the idea for *Negro Digest* (later renamed *Black World*), a magazine that would feature African-American history, literature, arts, and culture. It was a rapid success, reaching a circulation of 50,000 in only six months. A second magazine, *Ebony*, was founded in 1945, and at its height reached a circulation of more than 2 million. Thanks to his willingness to challenge the status quo, Johnson built a publishing empire that included radio, television, and books. He was named in the *Forbes* 400 list of wealthy Americans in 1982.

world; Walt Disney's Laugh-O-Gram studio went bankrupt in 1923; and Henry Ford had three failed businesses before finding success. Game changers such as Albert Einstein (labeled "slow" by his teachers) and billionaire Oprah Winfrey (told she was not "fit to be on screen") seem to defy the future mapped out for them.

Long-term thinking

It is the ability to recover from failure, and maintain the courage and conviction to keep changing the game, that sets great leaders apart from the rest. From a strategic point of view, a focus on game-changing innovation encourages long-term thinking. Adopting such a strategy means that shareholders must be tolerant of risk and uncertainty, and patient with regard to returns; payback periods may be long, and rewards difficult to measure. But if allowed to flourish, this longer-term approach enables a business to build a stronger brand, invest in research and development, create better business processes, and avoid taking (possibly damaging) actions to boost short-term profits.

As Christensen's *The Innovator's Dilemma* suggests, game-changing leaders are not bound by incremental change and "me-too" thinking: they rewrite the terms of competition by embracing unique ideas, and recognize that in a corporate world characterized by the mantra "change or die," disrupting the status quo in your own favor puts you not just one step, but several steps ahead of the competition. In today's hypercompetitive markets, game-changing leaders do not simply outthink, outsmart, and outcompete their rivals—they move the goalposts and redefine the rules of the game. ∎

You have to be willing to be misunderstood.
Jeff Bezos
US entrepreneur (1964–)

THE WORST DISEASE THAT AFFLICTS EXECUTIVES IS EGOTISM

HUBRIS AND NEMESIS

IN CONTEXT

FOCUS
Success and failure

KEY DATES
c.500 BCE The ancient Greeks coin the term "hubris" to describe a form of pride that loses touch with reality and leads to "nemesis"—a fatal retribution or downfall.

2001 Kenneth Lay, CEO of Enron, sends employees an email saying "our performance has never been stronger." Four months later, Enron files for bankruptcy.

2002 US activist Herbert London claims that hubris is as great a danger in the 21st century as in ancient Greece.

2009 Jim Collins identifies five stages of corporate decline in *How the Mighty Fall*.

E ven iconic companies can falter, fail, and become irrelevant. History repeatedly shows that successful corporate goliaths—such as Swissair, Enron, and Lehman Brothers—can fall from greatness. The list of possible causes is long and includes management complacency, poor marketing, poor products, strategic blindness, a weak economic environment, or simply bad luck. However, in many cases, paradoxically, success is the catalyst for failure.

This is because success can lead to an overconfidence that blinds business owners and managers to the real state of affairs. Meanwhile, they also start to

See also: Reinventing and adapting 52–57 ▪ Beware the yes-men 74–75 ▪ Good and bad strategy 184–85 ▪ Avoiding complacency 194–201

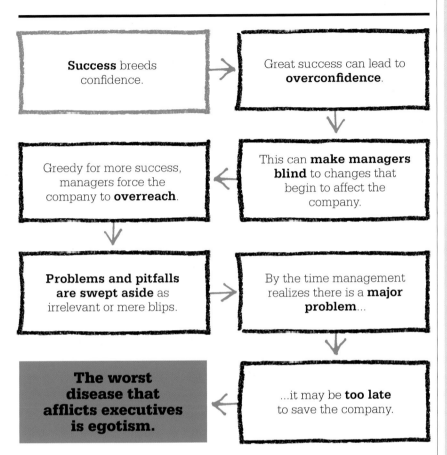

Success breeds confidence.

Great success can lead to **overconfidence**.

This can **make managers blind** to changes that begin to affect the company.

Greedy for more success, managers force the company to **overreach**.

Problems and pitfalls are swept aside as irrelevant or mere blips.

By the time management realizes there is a **major problem**…

…it may be **too late** to save the company.

The worst disease that afflicts executives is egotism.

Jim Collins

Business consultant, author, and self-titled "student of great companies" Jim Collins was born in the US in 1958.

Collins holds degrees in business administration and mathematical sciences from Stanford University, and several honorary doctoral degrees. He has worked alongside senior executives and CEOs at corporations of all types—from health care, education, and the arts, to religious organizations and government. His interest lies in the difference between good and great: how do companies attain such superior performance?

In 1995 he founded a management laboratory in Boulder, Colorado, to do further research into business excellence. His books have sold more than 10 million copies globally and have been translated into 35 languages.

Key works

1994 *Built to Last*
2001 *Good to Great: Why Some Companies Make the Leap … And Others Don't*
2009 *How the Mighty Fall: And Why Some Companies Never Give In*

believe their own hype. Internal warning signs may be present long before management—buoyed by seemingly unstoppable success—notices or chooses to do anything about them. Hubris, a kind of blind pride, can shield people from seeing that a company is already on the path to corporate catastrophe.

Five stages of decline

Jim Collins identified five stages of corporate decline. In stage 1, the business is doing well, perhaps exceptionally well. Press coverage is positive, finances are good, and morale is high. However, as a result of such success, during stage 1 the first warning sign appears—the company's directors and staff start to become overconfident. In highly successful companies there is a risk that staff members will become arrogant, and will begin to regard their success as a right or entitlement. Managers lose sight of the underlying factors that created success in the first place, overestimating their own strengths and those of the business.

If stage 1 is a feeling that "we're so great, we can do anything!" stage 2 is characterized by the feeling that "we should do more!" Collins calls this stage the "undisciplined pursuit of more": more sales, more stores, more growth, more of everything. »

Continued management arrogance breeds indiscipline; decisions are made out of greed and warning signs are ignored. Companies at stage 2 make indisciplined leaps into areas where they have little competitive advantage; diversify into areas in which they have no expertise; or undertake ill-conceived mergers and takeovers. The complacency of stage 1 turns into the overreaching of stage 2.

By stage 3, problems begin to mount, staff begins to question management decisions, and disturbing data suggest things might not be all that they seem. However, as Collins points out, it is possible to be in stage 3 of decline and not yet realize that it is happening. Anomalies in performance at this stage tend to be explained away; any problems are blamed on "difficult trading conditions." Management holds firm in the view that the company is strong and nothing is fundamentally wrong. They believe that once the

"Rogue trader" Jérôme Kerviel claimed his company, Société Générale bank, was aware of his dangerously large trades, but turned a blind eye because they were focused on profits.

markets pick up, their business brilliance will ensure that the company regains market leadership.

Now or never
Stage 3 represents the turning point. Many companies reach this stage but manage to avert collapse. If management listens to the views of its staff (especially from the front lines, such as sales staff), heeds shareholder concerns, and changes strategy in line with the changing reality, it is likely to recover. Andy Grove famously pulled Intel back into profitability by pursuing this strategy. However, the same cannot be said for Lehman Brothers. In 2007, with its stock price at a record high, the US investment bank ignored the early warning signs of collapse. Even as cracks in the US housing market became apparent, with subprime mortgage defaults rising to a seven-year high, Lehman continued to expose itself to mortgage-backed financial products. Management, particularly the chief executive, Richard Fuld, were blinded by hubris and deep in denial. They pressed on with ill-conceived strategies and quickly found themselves in stage 4.

Dealing with disaster
By stage 4 a company's difficulties become undeniable—even the most headstrong and arrogant manager has to acknowledge that there are problems. The question now is how to respond. Unfortunately, as the Lehman example shows, acknowledgment does not always result in appropriate action.

As the global credit crisis erupted in August 2007, Lehman's stock fell sharply. Having grown Lehman to become the fourth biggest bank on Wall Street, Fuld could not accept that it was time to adopt a new strategy. When uncertainty started to grip the

> The best leaders never presume they've reached ultimate understanding of all the factors that brought them success.
> **Jim Collins**

bank and journalists asked questions about its future, Fuld was reluctant to countenance any capital infusion. Selling parts of the bank was not an option he felt he could consider. Although Fuld eventually revoked this decision, it was too late: the bank declared bankruptcy on September 15, 2008.

The way in which management responds to a crisis brought about by success and accompanying hubris is critical. Inevitably, "band-aid" solutions that do not address the underlying problems rarely succeed. Quick fixes based on the same overconfidence that brought crisis in the first place—such as a bold but risky strategy, a hoped for blockbuster product, or a "market-changing" acquisition—usually result in the company moving to stage 5: capitulation to irrelevance, or death.

Capitulating to irrelevance
In stage 5, reality finally hits home. Expensive failed strategies erode financial strength and accumulated setbacks damage the individual spirits trying to repair the damage. Key managers generally leave the company at this stage, and the few customers that remain migrate to

US homeowners were prey to companies such as Lehman, which made big profits in mortgage-backed securities in the 2000s. Lehman's managers ignored warnings of unrepayable mortgages.

other brands. The once-mighty company has finally fallen. A management buy out, merger, or takeover may save the business and protect some jobs, but the company is unlikely to ever recapture its former glory. Most, having slipped this far, survive (if they survive at all) as niche brands trading on past history.

Return to glory

Decline is, of course, not inevitable for all successful companies. Those that reach the later stages of corporate decline do so because managers failed to heed the early warning signs of change or were irrationally sure of their ability to "beat the odds." However, it is possible to reach stage 4 and recover. According to Collins, this involves taking a calm, clear-headed approach and reaching not for savior strategies, but for the basic core values and disciplines that made the organization great in the first place.

Steve Jobs did just that at Apple. In the late 1980s and early 1990s, the company's management perceived Apple as vastly superior, ignored increasing competition from PC manufacturers, and expected customers to dismiss quality and compatibility issues as "quirks." After the 1995 release of Microsoft's Windows 95 operating system, Apple fell into decline. Sales, profits, and Apple's image tumbled. *BusinessWeek* called it "the fall of an American icon." The CEO, Gil Amelio, cut costs, reorganized the company, and added a new Internet Services

Group. By 1997, Apple was months from bankruptcy, as the business continued to spiral out of control. A new board assembled and called for the return of one of the cofounders—Steve Jobs—as CEO. Many expected him to respond with a slew of new products, but he did the opposite. He shrank the company to a size that reflected its niche position, and cut back the desktop computer models from 15 to one. He ended production of printers, cut software development, and moved production abroad. He redesigned the company around a

Success comprises in itself the seeds of its own decline.
Pierre de Coubertin
French educator (1863–1937)

simplified product line, sold through a limited number of outlets. He stabilized Apple and allowed a return to its core values—a focus on innovation and quality—that later brought iconic products such as the iMac, iPod, iPhone, and iPad.

The pursuit of less

Hubris is not the single cause of business failure. Even the most skilled management may fail when faced with turbulent markets, the collapse of a key supplier, or other factors beyond their control (the 2008 credit crunch, for example, was the final blow for an already struggling Woolworths). Hubris may occasionally be a factor in corporate decline, but failure may also result from poor business practice or simply from bad luck.

However, if overconfidence leads to an "undisciplined pursuit of more," the remedy seems to be the disciplined pursuit of less—a return to a company's strategic roots. Ego, though, is a powerful thing, and humility is too rarely the tool managers reach for when fighting for survival. ■

CULTURE
IS THE WAY IN WHICH A GROUP OF PEOPLE SOLVES PROBLEMS

ORGANIZATIONAL CULTURE

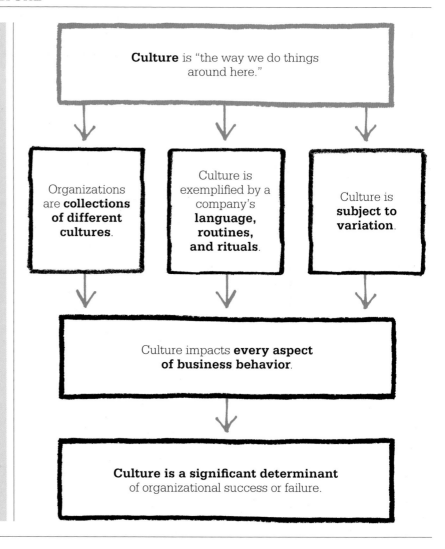

Culture is "the way we do things around here."

Organizations are **collections of different cultures**.

Culture is exemplified by a company's **language, routines, and rituals**.

Culture is **subject to variation**.

Culture impacts **every aspect of business behavior**.

Culture is a significant determinant of organizational success or failure.

O
rganizations build a sense of identity through tradition, history, and structure. This identity is kept alive through the organization's culture: its rituals, beliefs, legends, values, meanings, norms, and language. Corporate culture determines how "things are done around here."

Culture provides a shared view of what an organization is (the intangibles) and what it has (the tangibles). It is the "story" of the organization: a narrative reinforced through idiosyncratic languages and business-specific symbols. In the

1940s, human relations experts began to consider organizations from a cultural point of view, drawing inspiration from earlier sociological and anthropological work associated with groups and societies. However, the term "organizational culture" only became part of the business lexicon in the early 1980s, following the publication of *Culture's Consequences* by the Dutch cultural psychologist and management expert Geert Hofstede.

Looking closely at organizational structure for the first time, Hofstede observed that it is shaped by and

overlaps with societal culture. He identified five dimensions of culture that influence business behavior: power distance, individualism *vs.* collectivism, uncertainty avoidance, masculinity *vs.* femininity, and long- *vs.* short-term orientation.

Five cultural dimensions
The first of Hofstede's dimensions—power distance—refers to the distance in authority between manager and subordinates. Business cultures that have a high power distance tend to be rule-driven and hierarchical (everyone "knows their

See also: Creativity and invention 72–73 ▪ Gods of management 76–77 ▪ Hubris and nemesis 100–103 ▪ Avoid groupthink 114 ▪ Balancing long- versus short-termism 190–91 ▪ The learning organization 202–07 ▪ Creating an ethical culture 224–25

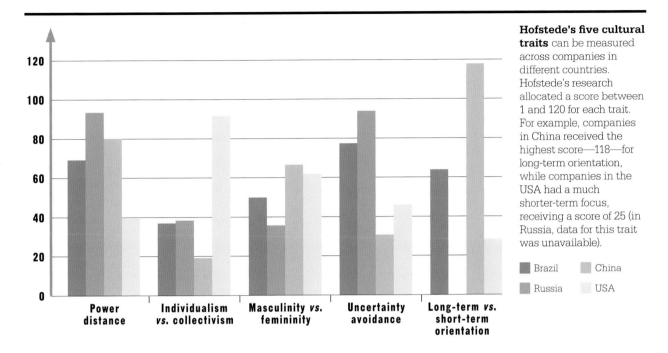

Hofstede's five cultural traits can be measured across companies in different countries. Hofstede's research allocated a score between 1 and 120 for each trait. For example, companies in China received the highest score—118—for long-term orientation, while companies in the USA had a much shorter-term focus, receiving a score of 25 (in Russia, data for this trait was unavailable).

■ Brazil ■ China
■ Russia ■ USA

place"). In Russia, for example, employees have little access to executives (power distance is high). Conversely, in low power-distance cultures, such as many companies in Australia, decision making is distributed more evenly throughout the organization.

Anthropologists have long theorized that collectivist cultures control members through external societal pressure (shame), whereas individualistic cultures control their members more through internal pressure (guilt). In his second dimension, Hofstede proposed that this tendency toward collectivism or individualism can be most clearly seen in the difference between Asian and US companies. When problem-solving, US businesses tend to look to the individual for a solution, whereas Asian companies prefer to pose the problem to a group.

Masculinity and femininity, Hofstede's third cultural dimension, are viewed differently from one organization to another. Some place great emphasis on masculine traits (such as status, assertiveness, and advancement), while others accord feminine traits (such as humanism, cooperation, collegiality, and nurturance) greater value. Italian organizations, for example, tend to have assertive, competitive cultures.

The fourth of Hofstede's dimensions is known as uncertainty avoidance. This is the extent to which workers feel threatened by ambiguous situations. The more uncomfortable people are with "not knowing" how to react in a certain scenario, the more rules and policies the company will need to introduce to reduce that uncertainty. Companies with a low degree of uncertainty avoidance are likely to thrive in

more uncertain and ambiguous situations. British organizations, for example, are considered fairly at ease with unstructured and unpredictable situations.

Hofstede's fifth dimension, long- vs. short-term orientation, is the extent to which organizations privilege the short-term (profit) over the long-term (value generation). »

The thing I have learned at IBM is that culture is everything.
Louis V Gerstner Jr
US businessman (1942–)

Japanese businesses, for example, think very much in the long-term: Toyota Motor Corporation has a 100-year business plan.

Why culture matters

Every organization's culture has varying degrees of these different dimensions. The best leaders know which cultures operate within different parts of their organization (and within different parts of the world), and adjust their leadership style to suit—valuing collective approaches, for example, when dealing with Asian subsidiaries.

Today, organizational culture is more important than ever before. Increasingly competitive markets, globalization, the prevalence of mergers, acquisitions, and alliances, and new modes of working (such as teleworking) require coordination across vast numbers of staff and huge geographic distances. Hofstede's observations highlight the difficulties that leaders face in maintaining unified business cultures, whether operating across multiple national or international cultures. The challenge is to balance the promotion of "one culture" within an organization against the influences of local cultures in the external world.

Companies with strong cultures, such as Nike and India's Tata Motors, are intensely aware of their history and image. At Nike it is not unusual for employees to have the company's "swoosh" logo tattooed on their body. At these businesses, culture encompasses an internalized sense of "who we are" and "what we stand for" to such an extent that many of the staff are able to recite corporate maxims from memory. Similarly, the UK smoothie company Innocent has worked hard to create a corporate culture based on communication. Dan Germain, the brand's Head of Creative, explains: "if people aren't involved in all decisions, big and small, then they start to feel unloved and removed from the business and its success."

Cultural benefits

Strong cultures give staff a sense of belonging, which in turn brings benefits, such as job satisfaction and staff retention. At Nike, staff are considered rookies if they have been at the company for less than a decade. Moreover, culture defines "the rules of the game," simplifying priorities. Decision making is faster and easier if everyone understands company values, beliefs, and vision. Deeply embedded cultures also improve the customer experience; if staff believes in the product, they will transfer this belief to customers.

Culture also protects an organization from the whims of charismatic leadership and the fickleness of fashion. A leader may influence corporate culture, but a successful culture should endure even when management changes.

Features of culture

Strong organizational cultures can suffer from problems of groupthink (everyone is too like-minded), insularity (too narrow a vision), and arrogance (a belief that everything the company does is right). Culture can become a source of power and resistance; necessary change may be resisted simply because "that's not the way we do things."

Terrence Deal and Allan Kennedy's 1982 publication *Corporate Cultures* outlined a range of cultural phenomena. The authors suggested that culture is composed of a framework of six interlocking elements: a company's history; its values and beliefs; its rituals and ceremonies; its stories; the heroic figures whose words and actions embody corporate values; and the cultural network.

Visible aspects of culture, such as an organization's rituals, stories and symbols, are only the tip of the iceberg. Its beliefs, values, attitudes, and basic assumptions are hidden but definitive.

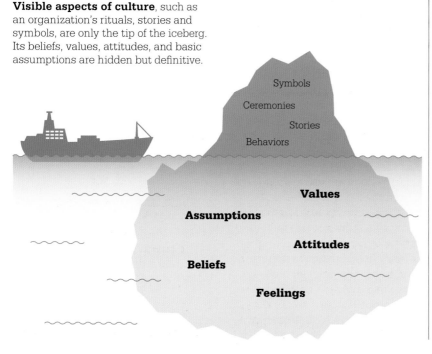

Symbols
Ceremonies
Stories
Behaviors

Values
Assumptions
Attitudes
Beliefs
Feelings

The cultural network, devised by Deal and Kennedy, refers to the informal channels in a company—storytellers, gossipers, and whisperers—through which culture is formed and passed on.

Deal and Kennedy also defined four types of organizational culture, which emerge from the interplay between a company's attitude to risk, and the speed of feedback and reward. In the tough-guy, "macho" culture, rapid feedback and reward are combined with a high tolerance of risk, as in the advertising industry. In the work-hard, play-hard culture —such as a sales company—risk is less prevalent, but rapid feedback and reward produce a high-pressure environment. In the "bet-your-company," high-stakes culture, the risk attached to decisions is high, but feedback on success or failure is slow. The oil industry is typical of the high-stakes culture. In a process culture, such as an insurance company or government agency, feedback is slow and risks are low.

Leadership and culture are interwoven and interdependent. If a leader does not protect or redefine the core values that made a company successful, culture can erode. In 2012, a Goldman Sachs employee bemoaned the investment bank's "toxic culture" in an open letter to *The New York Times*, claiming: "the culture was the secret sauce that made this place great and allowed us to earn our clients' trust for 143 years ... I look around today and see virtually no trace of [that] culture." The letter made headlines, and the company's shares fell by 3.4 percent.

Culture in practice

The desire by leaders for some sort of standardized culture—one that is fixed, visible, and stable—is understandable, but it likely to operate only in the imaginations of leaders than in the experiences of employees. Companies rarely have one culture; they are usually a combination of many, which overlap across departments, countries, and business units. The task for leaders is to ensure that these cultures do not diverge too far from core organizational values.

Organizational culture is not static. Every type of culture is dynamic and shifts, incrementally and constantly, in response to internal and external pressure. Managing culture, especially through periods of deliberate change, is one of the most difficult business tasks a leader can face.

The advice for leaders seeking to change culture is start small. Culture is slippery, and trying to change everything at once often results in failure. Bold new mission statements, big office redesigns, or exhortations that "working here is fun" rarely have the desired impact. Cultural change requires long-term investment in employees, not in buildings and branding. This is because culture may be led from the top, but it grows from the bottom; it requires patient nurturing over time. Leaders must understand the dynamic of an organization's culture so that they can usefully draw on its strengths, rather than be overcome by its constraints. ∎

Geert Hofstede

Born in 1928 in Haarlem, the Netherlands, Geert Hofstede went to technical college then gained an MSc in mechanical engineering from Delft Technical University. He spent two years in military service with the Dutch army, before going into industrial management and beginning a PhD. In 1965, while studying part-time, he joined IBM and founded a personnel research department. His years at IBM were to prove formative; the data and insight gleaned there formed his research base and his "bottom-up" view of organizations. Hofstede became a professor of management in 1973, and was named one of the world's most influential thinkers by the *Wall Street Journal* in 2008. The ideas in his 1980 book *Culture's Consequences* continue to inform global debates on organizational culture.

Key works

1980 *Culture's Consequences*
2010 *Cultures and Organizations: Software of the Mind*

Culture eats strategy for breakfast.
Peter Drucker
US management consultant
(1909–2005)

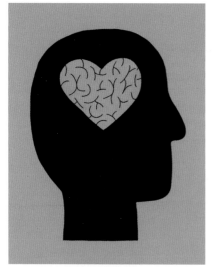

EMOTIONAL INTELLIGENCE IS THE INTERSECTION OF HEART AND HEAD

DEVELOP EMOTIONAL INTELLIGENCE

IN CONTEXT

FOCUS
Emotional intelligence

KEY DATES

c.400 BCE The philosopher Plato says that all learning has an emotional base.

1930s US psychologist Edward Thorndike describes the concept of "social intelligence"—the ability to get along with other people.

1983 US psychologist Howard Gardner suggests that people have multiple intelligences, including interpersonal, musical, spatial-visual, and linguistic.

1990 US psychologists Peter Salovey and John Mayer publish the first formal theory of emotional intelligence.

1995 Daniel Goleman publishes *Emotional Intelligence: Why It Can Matter More Than IQ*, which becomes a global best seller.

E motional intelligence (commonly abbreviated as "EQ", for emotional quotient) is the ability to perceive, control, and evaluate emotions, both in oneself and in others. The concept emerged from research into social intelligence in the 1930s, and from work in the 1970s on different forms of intelligence. In the 1990s, US psychologist Daniel Goleman published the highly influential *Emotional Intelligence: Why it Can Matter More Than IQ*. In the book he identified the five "domains" of emotional intelligence: knowing your emotions; managing your emotions; motivating yourself; recognizing and understanding other people's emotions; and managing relationships.

Goleman pinpoints high EQ as a common trait among effective business leaders. Without emotional intelligence, he argues, a leader can have limitless energy and ideas, a perceptive and logical mind, and impressive qualifications, but still be ineffective and uninspiring.

Goleman cites Bob Mulholland, head of client relations at Merrill Lynch during the 9/11 attacks, as a leader with high EQ. After his staff saw a plane hit the twin building opposite their own, they began to panic—some ran from window to window, and others were paralyzed with fear. His first response was to "unfreeze" their panic by addressing each of their concerns individually. He then calmly told them that they were all going to leave the building, via the stairs, and that they all had time to get out. He remained calm and decisive, but did not minimize people's emotional responses. All his staff escaped without injury. This was a rare and unusual context, but Mulholland's approach shows the value of EQ in managing staff in any form of volatile situation.

The most effective leaders are alike in one crucial way: they all have a high degree of emotional intelligence.
Daniel Goleman

See also: From entrepreneur to leader 46–47 ▪ Effective leadership 78–79 ▪ Organizing teams and talent 80–85 ▪ Avoiding complacency 194–201 ▪ The learning organization 202–07 ▪ Kaizen 302–09

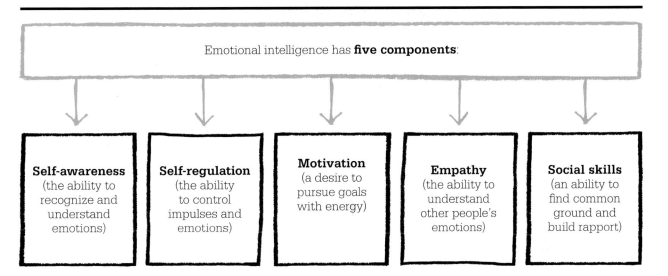

Emotional intelligence has **five components**:

| **Self-awareness** (the ability to recognize and understand emotions) | **Self-regulation** (the ability to control impulses and emotions) | **Motivation** (a desire to pursue goals with energy) | **Empathy** (the ability to understand other people's emotions) | **Social skills** (an ability to find common ground and build rapport) |

Goleman suggests that high EQ facilitates other essential leadership traits. For example, the ability to recognize accurately what another person is feeling (empathy) enables one to manage that feeling and any behaviors that arise from it.

What makes a good leader?

One persistent debate within the business world is whether leaders are born or made. Goleman suggests that the answer is both: inherent personality traits are important in leadership, but EQ—which grows with age, experience, and self-reflectiveness—is just as important.

Today, the development of EQ lies at the heart of leadership coaching. New and aspiring leaders are mentored by experienced ones; together, they discuss past and future scenarios, various possible responses, and what the emotional trigger points might be. This procedure seeks to increase emotional maturity. A 1999 study showed that partners in a multinational consulting company who scored highly on EQ delivered $1.2 million more profit than other partners. Other studies have shown similar correlations between EQ and effectiveness. Emotional balance, it seems, is a key factor in commercial success. ▪

Daniel Goleman

Psychologist Daniel Goleman was born in 1946 in California, US. His parents were both college professors, and Goleman was president of his high school before receiving a scholarship to study at Amherst College, MA. During the course, he transferred to the University of California, Berkeley, for a year, where he studied the rituals of social interaction under sociologist Erving Goffman.

Goleman then took a doctorate at Harvard University, where he studied under David McClelland, best known for his theories on the drive to achieve. After completing his PhD, he traveled widely in India and Sri Lanka, studying meditation and mindfulness. He taught briefly as a visiting lecturer at Harvard University before becoming a journalist and author. His bestselling book, *Emotional Intelligence*, has sold more than 5 million copies in 40 languages.

Key works

1995 *Emotional Intelligence*
1998 *What Makes a Leader?*
2011 *Leadership: The Power of Emotional Intelligence*

MANAGEMENT IS A PRACTICE WHERE ART, SCIENCE, AND CRAFT MEET
MINTZBERG'S MANAGEMENT ROLES

IN CONTEXT

FOCUS
Management roles

KEY DATES
1949 French engineer and business theorist Henri Fayol develops what becomes known as "the classical theory of management." This claims that managers have five key functions: planning, organizing, coordinating, commanding, and controlling.

1930s Australian psychologist Elton Mayo publishes the *Hawthorne Studies*, which ushers in an era of people-oriented management, rather than managing according to business objectives alone.

1973 In *The Nature of Managerial Work*, Henry Mintzberg dismisses Fayol's claims about the management process as "folklore."

Managers perform a **multitude of roles**, which can be divided into three categories...

...Informational:
Monitor
Disseminator
Spokesperson

...Interpersonal:
Figurehead
Leader
Liaison

...Decisional:
Entrepreneur
Disturbance handler
Resource allocator
Negotiator

Management is a blend of these often conflicting roles, where art, science, and craft meet.

The question "What do managers do?" has vexed experts, and many front-office staffs, since organizations came into existence. In his 1975 paper "The Manager's Job," business guru Henry Mintzberg argues that managers are not the reflective, systematic planners that people assume; instead, "their activities are characterized by brevity, variety, and discontinuity." He finds them to be strongly oriented to action, and disliking of reflection.

Mintzberg suggests that there are ten basic management roles, which fall into three categories: informational roles (managing through the use of information); interpersonal (the management of people); and decisional (managing decisions and action).

See also: From entrepreneur to leader 46–47 ▪ Leading well 68–69 ▪ Gods of management 76–77 ▪ Learning from failure 164–65 ▪ Crisis management 188–89 ▪ Simplify processes 296–99 ▪ Kaizen 302–09

The informational role is possible because, although managers do not know everything, they tend to know more than their subordinates. "Scanning the environment" and processing information is a key part of the manager's job. In this sense, Mintzberg claims, they are "the nerve center of the organizational unit." They monitor what is going on, disseminate it to others in the companies, and act as a spokesperson for the business in the world at large.

Information is easily available to the manager because the role connects him or her to many people. In this sense, the manager plays an interpersonal role, which also involves acting as a figurehead for the companies, providing leadership, and acting as a liaison point between a large group of people. The group may include subordinates, clients, business associates, suppliers and peers (managers of similar organizations).

The third role of management, is decision making. Managers must oversee financial, material, and personnel resources and decision making (be a "resource allocator"), encourage innovation (act as an entrepreneur); and seek conciliation or pacification when the company is unexpectedly upset or transformed (be a "negotiator" and "disturbance handler").

None of these roles is exclusive or privileged. Mintzberg claims that effective managers shift seamlessly between these different functions and know when each role is most appropriate for the given context.

Fact and fiction

The traditional view held that management was a science, where managers controlled a company's constituent parts—people and machinery—both of which acted in predictable and scientifically controllable ways. Mintzberg argues, however, that management is a practice in which art, science, and craft meet. It involves sorting and processing of information, organization of systems and, most importantly, highly subjective, nonscientific management of people.

Organizational effectiveness does not lie in that narrow-minded concept called rationality. It lies in the blend of clearheaded logic and powerful intuition.
Henry Mintzberg

Mintzberg argues that the answer to the question "what do managers do?" is not simple. He concludes that management is complex and contradictory in its demands, relying as much on intuition, judgment, and intellectual agility as on technical skill, planning, and scientific logic. All these come into play, he says, since a manager designs, monitors, and develops the ways in which things are done. ▪

Henry Mintzberg

Born on September 2, 1939 in Montreal, Canada, Henry Mintzberg's background was in mechanical engineering. After graduating in 1968 from the Massachusetts Institute of Technology (MIT), US, he moved to McGill University in Montreal, where he joined the faculty of management. He later took a joint appointment as professor of strategy and management at both McGill in Montreal and INSEAD, in Singapore and Fontainebleu, France.

Mintzberg is the author or co-author of 15 books and more than 150 articles, and is best known for his work on management and managers. His *Harvard Business Review* paper "The Manager's Job: Folklore and Fact" won a McKinsey award in 1975. In 1997 he was made an Officer of the Order of Canada and of l'Ordre national du Quebec; and in 2000 he was awarded Distinguished Scholar of the Year by the Academy of Management. In 2013, he was awarded the first honorary degree ever given by the Institut Mines-Télécom in France.

Although he has been teaching since 1968, Mintzberg's interest in organizations and managers emerged during his first degree, when he spent time at the Canadian National Railway. His memoirs describe the catastrophic result of two boxcars colliding as an excellent metaphor for corporate mergers.

Key works

1973 *The Nature of Managerial Work*
1975 "The Manager's Job"
2004 *Managers not MBAs*

A CAMEL IS A HORSE DESIGNED BY COMMITTEE

AVOID GROUPTHINK

IN CONTEXT

FOCUS
Group dynamics

KEY DATES
1948 US advertising guru Alex Osborn promotes the practice of "brainstorming"—generating ideas in groups, without criticism.

1972 US research psychologist Irving Janis publishes *Victims of Groupthink*.

2003 An investigation into the Columbia space-shuttle explosion cites a culture where it was "difficult for dissenting opinions to percolate up."

2005 Robert Baron publishes the academic paper "So Right it's Wrong," claiming that groupthink tendencies may be confined to the early stages of the formation of a group.

2006 Steve Wozniak, the inventor of the first Apple computer, advises creative thinkers: "Work alone. Not on a committee. Not on a team."

The desire to belong is a powerful human emotion. We want to be accepted and to be part of a group, which explains why individuals may set aside their opinions, remain silent in meetings, and nod in agreement even when they disagree. This deterioration of individual "mental efficiency, reality testing, and moral judgment" was outlined by US psychologist Irving Janis in 1972, and is known as "groupthink."

Groupthink is the idea that concurring with others is the sole overriding priority. It can become so strong that it precludes realistic assessment and analysis. Insulated from contrary perspectives, groups displaying groupthink self-justify their own conclusions. Irrational decisions may be made based on false or incomplete information.

Irving noted that groups displayed a series of characteristics when groupthink gains hold. The group begins to feel invulnerable, which encourages extreme risk taking. It collectively rationalizes decisions, fails to check the reality of assumptions, and ignores warnings. It begins to assume a position of moral superiority, and fails to consider the ethical consequences of its actions.

The challenge for managers is to recognize groupthink and take action to prevent it. Encouraging dissent, assembling groups with diverse demographics, and listening to others' opinions before airing their views are means of doing so. ∎

Swissair went into liquidation in 2001. Once labeled "the flying bank" due to its profitability, the airline's executive structure displayed groupthink traits, such as a sense of invulnerability.

See also: The value of teams 70–71 ▪ Beware the yes-men 74–75 ▪ Hubris and nemesis 100–03 ▪ Organizational culture 104–09

THE ART OF THINKING INDEPENDENTLY, TOGETHER
THE VALUE OF DIVERSITY

As with most clichés, it is also a truism that managers often tend to recruit in their own image—males, for example, have a tendency to employ males. If left unchallenged, such behavior can lead to companies staffed with homogenous clones—people from the same backgrounds and with the same view of how the business should be run.

In contrast, when organizations actively pursue diversity—by employing people from different cultures and socio-economic backgrounds, and of different genders and ages—the more dynamic and stimulating they are as places to work.

The case for diversity
Greater diversity means greater scope for creativity—the more varied are the sources of an organization's views, the more likely that out-of-the-box thinking and problem solving will occur. Studies have shown that diversity can also combat groupthink, a malaise in group dynamics that

Diversity management isn't merely nice to have, it's a business must.
Daimler company statement (2005)

can stifle innovation and growth. In diverse teams, opinions are less likely to go unchallenged.

Diversity is not confined to employee demographics. It might simply involve creating cross-functional teams that incorporate the views of people from across a company—the marketing team, for example, might benefit from the insight of operations or finance. But whatever the context, monochrome recruitment can lead to stasis—diversity fights against it. ∎

See also: The value of teams 70–71 ▪ Beware the yes-men 74–75 ▪ Thinking outside the box 88–89 ▪ Organizational culture 104–09

MAKING WORK

MANAGING FINANCES

MONEY

Finance has always been seen as having two distinct functions: recording what has happened (financial accounting) and helping businesses to make decisions about the future (management accounting). Today, it has a third function: financial strategy. This incorporates judgments about risk, which some companies (especially banks) have realized must play a larger part in financial decision-making.

Understanding risk

Fundamental to an understanding of financial strategy are the concepts of leverage and excess risk. "Leverage" is a measurement of the extent to which a business is dependent upon borrowings. The higher the leverage, the greater the level of risk. In good times, directors come under pressure to produce impressive profit growth, and one easy way to achieve it is to borrow money and invest in the most profitable parts of the business. However, if the economy turns downward, toward recession, heavy borrowings turn into an overwhelming burden. Leverage becomes toxic.

The risk level generated by leverage is worsened when businesses use off-balance-sheet finance, in other words, when they do not report loss-making investments on the company's balance sheet, thereby appearing to boost profits. This leads to an important question in relation to modern business: who bears the risk? Traditionally it was assumed that the risk taker was the shareholder, because it is the shareholders who collectively own the business. However, in Europe and the US especially, the desire to encourage entrepreneurship has led to generous rules that reduce the extent to which losses are borne by business owners. Since 2008, many business collapses have proved expensive for customers, staff, and suppliers, but less so for the

The bonus mania which caused the recession could never have happened without corrupted accounting rules.
Nicholas Jones
UK film maker, ex-accountant

business owners, particularly when the failing institution has been a bank. Some financial commentators wonder whether the balance has swung too far away from tradition.

Director involvement

When times are tough, directors have to make difficult decisions about investment and dividends. Usually the directors will have an agreed policy in place—perhaps that half the after-tax profit will be paid as dividends to shareholders, while the other half will be retained to invest in future growth. But during recessions it is wise to keep more cash within the business, so directors may decide that dividends should be cut. If the business also cuts its investment plans, it can keep more cash in its current account, providing the liquidity to survive difficult trading conditions.

So who is responsible when things go wrong? This depends on the systems of accountability and governance within each company. Ideally, the directors of the business should be sufficiently involved to know when things start to go wrong, and call for discussion of a change in strategy. If the directors are too hands-off, they may feel unable to hold the CEO fully accountable when things do go wrong. Alert,

hands-on directors should also spot when rewards for staff are so out-of-control as to threaten the profits being made for shareholders and for the future financial health of the business. "Profit before perks" should be the mindset.

Important to good governance is a willingness to ignore the herd. For example, if every US bank began to expand into South America, a smart South Korean bank would refuse to copy. However, in practice, this proves hard to do. Directors meet each other in the same clubs and conferences, and like to be part of the same pack. Nevertheless, US investment guru Warren Buffett has become one of the world's wealthiest men by ignoring the herd instinct among investors.

The mass market

Some modern boards of directors accept that if there is wisdom among crowds, there may be even greater wisdom among staff. Henry Ford was one of the first to realize that your workers are your customers, but it has taken a century for others to see the potential in this phrase. Not only is there value in drawing ideas from staff who care about the products they both produce and use, but there is also strategic value in

understanding the huge potential of the mass market. When looking at China today, the most exciting opportunities are for products that would appeal to the hundreds of millions of potential consumers who are workers, not managers.

Using money wisely

In management accounting, two factors are of particular importance: cash and costs. A management accountant works hard to provide accurate data on production costs, so that managers can make informed decisions about pricing, on outsourcing, and on which products to back with marketing spending. Activity-based costing, which provides the most complete data on costs per unit, is the best way to do this. When trading is poor, however, management accountants place their tightest focus not on costs but on cash flow, following the maxim that "cash is king." This arises because the worse the trading conditions, the more that companies try to hold onto the cash they have—making it much harder to get paid if they are your customers. The flow of cash dries up, so an early focus on cash flow makes sense: start your own cash hoard before others begin trying to create their own.

For financial accountants, the traditional stance has long been "playing by the rules." Integrity and adhering to accounting principles such as prudence and consistency were seen as most important. More recently, career opportunities have arisen for accountants who are willing to be more creative. This way of thinking stems from the scope for "making money from money," by lending the company's cash deposits to other companies at high rates of interest, or speculating on future trends in exchange rates or commodity markets. In a world where a quicker, bigger buck can be made from money than from manufacturing, playing by the rules may seem a poor choice. ∎

I am incredibly nervous that we will implode in a wave of accounting scandals.
Sherron Watkins
US executive, former vice president of Enron (1959–)

DO NOT LET YOURSELF BE INVOLVED IN A FRAUDULENT BUSINESS

PLAY BY THE RULES

IN CONTEXT

FOCUS
Governance and ethics

KEY DATES
1978 US scholars Ross Watts and Jerold Zimmerman write *Towards a Positive Theory of the Determination of Accounting Standards*.

1995 French professor Bernard Colasse claims that "there isn't any true result, but a result arranged using creative accounting techniques."

2001–02 Telecoms giant WorldCom overstates earnings by more than $3.8 billion.

2009 UK professor David Myddelton publishes *Margins of Error in Accounting*.

2012 Directors of US discount website Groupon identify a "weakness" in financial reporting, five months after becoming a public company.

Business accountants have two roles: to record profits and cash flow and to provide tightly estimated data about costs to help make strategic decisions. The accountant's instinct is to be cautious and prudent—costs and cash-outflow figures generally err on the high side, while revenues and cash inflows tend to be on the low side. Any surprises should be positive. For example, in January 2009, Honda Motor Company warned that dramatic falls in sales worldwide—due to the global downturn and the strong Yen—would force the company into a $3.7 billion loss in the fourth quarter of its financial year. However, the loss

See also: Hubris and nemesis 100–03 ▪ Profit before perks 124–25 ▪ Making money from money 128–29 ▪ Accountability and governance 130–31 ▪ Morality in business 222 ▪ Creating an ethical culture 224–27 ▪ The appeal of ethics 270

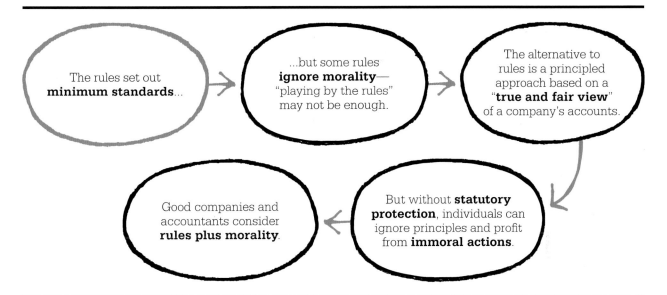

The rules set out **minimum standards**...

...but some rules **ignore morality**— "playing by the rules" may not be enough.

The alternative to rules is a principled approach based on a **"true and fair view"** of a company's accounts.

But without **statutory protection**, individuals can ignore principles and profit from **immoral actions**.

Good companies and accountants consider **rules plus morality**.

turned out to be $3.3 billion, demonstrating that the company had erred on the side of caution.

Accounting for profit

An accountant who follows safe practices sleeps well, but may struggle to climb the corporate ladder. When the stock market is full of optimism (a "bull market"), there are intense pressures within companies to push the stated profit level to the highest feasible point. This could be considered an odd statement, since profit might seem to be a simple matter of fact. However, the calculation of profit (which is effectively an estimation) is underpinned by a series of assumptions, and a company's stated profit is effectively a moveable figure. Different accounting teams may come

up with different figures, even though the underlying data that they are analyzing is the same.

In 1992, British banking analyst Terry Smith published a book called *Accounting for Growth*. This publication set out the remarkable array of opportunities for publicly traded companies to provide an artificial boost to their stated profit levels. The book had a huge impact, and influenced the

UK's newly formed Accounting Standards Board, which in turn developed new accounting rules in an attempt to minimize the scope for "creative accounting."

Today, most countries around the world follow the rules laid down by the International Financial Reporting Standards (IFRS). As a consequence, the income statements and balance sheets of companies in most countries follow the same format. **»**

Accountants must decide how cautious they are going to be when reporting a company's financial status, since they may be under pressure to boost the stated level of profits.

Mark-to-market accounting is a risky method of valuation, since it values a company's assets according to current market value. Historic cost valuation is a more reliable, and cautious, measure of value.

During a **stock-market boom**, valuing a company's assets and investments according to their **current market value** can lead to an **overinflated balance sheet**.

If the **stock market falls**, the value of the **balance sheet will shrink**, leaving the company in a **vulnerable position**.

Although the time frame for implementation is unclear, a widely supported plan is in place to merge the IFRS with the US's Generally Accepted Accounting Principles (GAAP) to provide globally recognized accounting rules.

Although the rules are becoming clearer, important areas for debate remain. These might be raised internally, in arguments between company accountants and directors; or the debate might be between independent auditors and the organization. When UK bank Halifax Bank of Scotland (HBOS) collapsed in 2008, the UK government bailed it with $32 (£20) billion, before the bank was acquired by Lloyds Bank. In 2008 the gap between the bank's loans and its deposits was $341 (£213) billion. The bank's auditor, KPMG, was heavily criticized over the HBOS collapse, although KPMG had consistently raised warnings over the risks involved. When the UK's regulator, the Financial Services Authority, published a report on HBOS in 2012 it noted that KPMG had "consistently

suggested that a more prudent approach would be to increase the level of provision" against bad debts. Ultimately, the directors of HBOS had decided to take an optimistic view of the bank's lending. They chose to play beyond the rules.

Cautious accounting

Professor David Myddelton, a UK management scholar, argues strongly against the expansion

of rules in accounting. He believes in traditional accounting principles, because these supply the required flexibility for accountancy across many different types of companies. He claims that the idea that there is a "single correct answer" when preparing a company's accounts is nonsense. Nevertheless, this idea lies behind the call for increased regulation. "People want it to seem as if we're doing something about scandals," he says; they think that greater regulation will make a difference, "but it never does." Myddelton also believes that directors should gain a "true and fair view" of their accounts, instead of being forced to rely on a picture produced by someone else's idea of the accountancy rules.

Some "creative accountancy" practices stretch the flexibility within the rules so far that they can produce potentially misleading accounts. "Mark to market" accounting, for example, values assets at their current market value. This means that when the stock market is booming, any investment (such as shares in another business) will also be booming. This boosts the value of the company's balance

Moral duty

Julian Dunkerton is the founder and major shareholder in the fashion business SuperGroup plc, whose leading brand is the popular street-wear label Superdry. Based in Britain, but with business and outlets worldwide, SuperGroup could easily follow the lead set by other organizations and manipulate accounts to minimize its tax liabilities.

Instead, the business plays by the spirit of the tax rules, paying about 30 percent of its profit to the tax authorities. Not that Dunkerton wants to claim the moral high ground—in its annual report, SuperGroup plc explains that "We recognize the commercial value, as well as the moral duty, of consistently operating with integrity, honesty, and a commitment to responsible and ethical business practices." Dunkerton has the wisdom to appreciate that acting responsibly can yield financial benefits, particularly in the long term.

Major accounting misconduct was unearthed by US company Caterpillar Inc. in a Chinese business it purchased in 2012. Irregularities included overstated profits and falsified stocks.

sheet and may encourage it to expand beyond its means. All it takes is a fall in the stock market for this valuable shareholding to become worth considerably less. Myddelton suggests that it is better to use "historic cost" accounting than "mark to market," since this provides a more stable set of figures; it values assets at their cost at time of purchase, minus any depreciation that has taken place, rather than at their current market value.

The argument of rigid rules *vs.* looser-based principles will be heard repeatedly when the merger talks between the US's rules-based GAAP system and the IFRS become serious. Even though the IFRS is far more rule-based than its predecessors, it retains a greater reliance on principles than the US's GAAP system.

Ethical conduct

Whether rules based or rooted in principles, no accounting methods can prevent a deliberate attempt by directors to mislead. In June 2012, for example, US construction-equipment giant Caterpillar Inc. completed a $650-million purchase of Chinese company ERA Mining Machinery Ltd. and its wholly owned subsidiary Zhengzhou Siwei Mechanical and Electrical Equipment Manufacturing Co. This was part of Caterpillar's long-standing strategy of growth in China. Unfortunately, a series of black holes in Siwei's accounts soon emerged, including the discovery in November 2012 that the company did not hold the stock levels it had claimed. In January

2013 Caterpillar said it was writing off $580 million from the value of ERA, thereby virtually admitting that the purchase was a complete waste of money. Caterpillar then accused the previous management at Siwei of deliberately creating misleading accounts, but let the matter drop in May 2013 when a financial settlement was reached.

In other circumstances, directors can find solace in the rules. Operating in South Africa, Canada, and Europe, short-term money-lender Wonga.com sets its annual percentage rate (APR) on "payday loans" as high as 5,800 percent. This is perfectly legal because the

Mark-to-market accounting is like crack. Don't do it.
Andrew Fastow
US former Enron executive (1961–)

countries in which it operates have no legislated cap on interest rates, so the directors are playing by the rules. However, a report by the UK Citizens' Advice Bureau in 2013 stated that three out of four "payday loan" customers struggle to repay. In contrast to the UK, countries such as France and the US have rules that set maximum interest levels for consumer credit loans.

Ultimately, no set of rules can substitute for ethical behavior nor safeguard the system from a determined attempt to manipulate accounting figures in a misleading way. In the hands of principled accountants, flexibility within the rules is useful; but if someone seeks to gain huge financial advantage no matter what, that flexibility will enable him or her to do so, even if this entails acting immorally.

Rules help to ensure that companies operate at an acceptable minimum standard. The argument revolves around where this standard lies, balanced as it is between useful standards and costly overregulation. Rules also encourage those with ethical principles to go further than the minimum. ■

EXECUTIVE OFFICERS MUST BE FREE FROM AVARICE
PROFIT BEFORE PERKS

IN CONTEXT

FOCUS
Equity and performance

KEY DATES
1776 Adam Smith says that managers will not watch over a business with the same vigilance as partners in a private company would watch over their own.

1932 US professor Adolf Berle and US economist Gardiner Means coin the phrase "the separation of ownership and control."

1967 Canadian-American economist J. K. Galbraith says that shareholders no longer control the organizations they legally own.

2012 Larry Ellison of US computing corporation Oracle Inc. becomes the world's highest-remunerated CEO, when he receives $96.5 million in pay, shares, and perks.

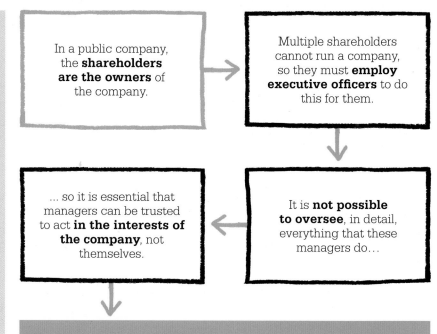

In a public company, the **shareholders are the owners** of the company.

Multiple shareholders cannot run a company, so they must **employ executive officers** to do this for them.

It is **not possible to oversee**, in detail, everything that these managers do…

… so it is essential that managers can be trusted to act **in the interests of the company**, not themselves.

Executive officers must be free from avarice.

In an ideal business, directors pursue the company's objectives without undue consideration for personal gain. Upon election to the board, they negotiate their salary and standard perks, and from then on, their focus is on the success of the business.

Yet there is a risk that bosses can be dazzled by the wealth generated around them, and work toward boosting personal gain instead of the profits due to shareholders.

This situation, known as "the divorce of ownership and control," first arose in the late 19th century,

See also: Beware the yes-men 74–75 ▪ Is money the motivator? 90–91 ▪ Organizational culture 104–109 ▪ Avoid groupthink 114 ▪ Play by the rules 120–23 ▪ Accountability and governance 130–31

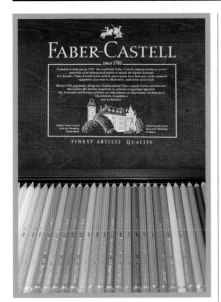

German *mittelstand* companies— such as Faber-Castell, a world-leading producer of pencils—are usually family-owned. Directors of such firms are more likely to focus on long-term performance.

with the creation of large, public limited companies (plcs) that allowed senior management more freedom to operate beyond effective shareholder scrutiny. As long as the company profits were satisfactory, directors were free to conduct their business functions as they saw fit. However, if a business enterprise comes to reflect the aims of its managers, will the business be focused on profit maximization (for its owners, the shareholders) or on increasing the status, financial rewards, and power of its managers?

Personal interests

Some directors act opportunistically; they seem to be more interested in personal gain than in the company's financial well-being. The banking crisis of 2008 led the shareholders of many companies to question corporate governance mechanisms and executive pay. The shareholders of Barclays Bank, for example, were stirred into taking action just before the bank's 2012 AGM. They had discovered that in the previous year, profits had fallen by 3 percent, shares had dropped by 26 percent, but chief executive Bob Diamond was due to receive a bonus of $4.2 (£2.7) million and total pay in excess of $10 (£6.3) million.

Restricted ownership

In private limited companies, the situation is simpler. Since share ownership is restricted (often within a single family), the directors and the shareholders are usually the same people. In any case, it is unusual for people to take advantage financially of those within their own circle of family and friends. For example, the problem of perks before profits is rarely an issue in Germany, where the *mittelstand* (medium-sized) companies—which are mainly family companies—are the dominant business model. A recent study of the different performances of family-owned and publicly owned companies in Spain found that family-owned companies performed better, in terms of financial equity, than nonfamily companies of the same size in the same industry. Countries such as the UK and US, however, have a larger proportion of plcs than many other countries. After decades of noninterference, shareholders are once again becoming interested in corporate governance and gain. ▪

Leadership is a privilege to better the lives of others. It is not an opportunity to satisfy personal greed.
Mwai Kibaki
Former President of Kenya (1931–)

Fewer perks, more profits

Several companies have taken positive steps to eliminate perks as part of a cost-cutting strategy. At the German company T-systems International, an ICT subsidiary of Deutsche Telekom AG, all workers must now fly in coach class, regardless of the traveler's position within the company, or the distance and duration of their journey. The change from business- to economy-class travel is thought to have saved T-systems $1.5 million annually. Executives were told that the choice was between a reduction in travel expenses, or a cut in their annual bonuses.

Since the 2008 financial downturn, there has been an increase in the trend of organizations tightening their purse strings. Even the mighty entertainment company Walt Disney is phasing out executive car allowances. Cost cutting and eliminating perks puts greater pressure on managers to boost their company's profitability.

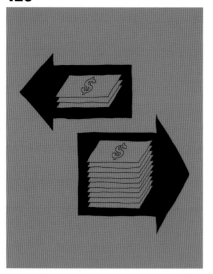

IF WEALTH IS PLACED WHERE IT BEARS INTEREST, IT COMES BACK TO YOU REDOUBLED
INVESTMENT AND DIVIDENDS

IN CONTEXT

FOCUS
Financial strategy

KEY DATES
1288 The first recorded share certificate is issued to the Bishop of Vasteras in Sweden by Stora Enso, a pulp and paper company.

17th century The Dutch East India Company issues shares, heralding the emergence of organized share trading.

1940 Peter Drucker writes on the need for businesses to balance short-term dividends and long-term reinvestment.

1961 Modigliani and Miller claim that paying or retaining dividends does not affect a business's long-term performance. Their seminal work is later disputed, with several studies showing that dividend increases boost a company's share price.

After calculating the year's profit, a company's directors can choose whether to pay a dividend to shareholders or reinvest the sum. A dividend is the annual payment to shareholders that most businesses manage each year. It might amount to a 3 percent return on the sum invested, which would make it comparable to the interest a saver might receive from a bank deposit.

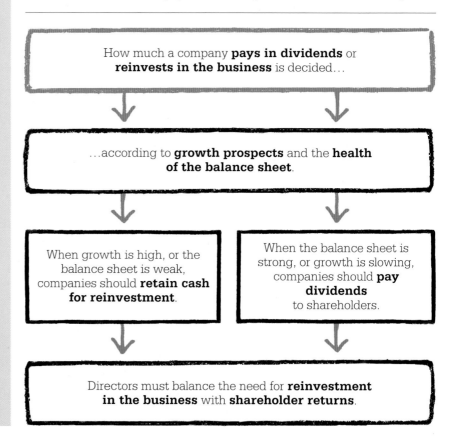

How much a company **pays in dividends** or **reinvests in the business** is decided…

…according to **growth prospects** and the **health of the balance sheet**.

When growth is high, or the balance sheet is weak, companies should **retain cash for reinvestment**.

When the balance sheet is strong, or growth is slowing, companies should **pay dividends** to shareholders.

Directors must balance the need for **reinvestment in the business** with **shareholder returns**.

See also: Accountability and governance 130–31 ▪ Who bears the risk? 138–45 ▪ Ignoring the herd 146–49 ▪ Profit versus cash flow 152–53

The Dutch East India Company was the first public company to offer shares. Investors put up money for voyages in return for a share of the profits made from successful trips.

In 2012, for example, Honda Motor Company of Japan paid out just under half its $2.7 million profit in dividends, leaving just over half to reinvest in the company.

The first dividend payments were made in the 17th century by the Dutch East India Company, which was the world's first company to issue shares in exchange for capital. To encourage investors to buy shares, a promise of an annual payment (called a dividend) was made. Between 1600 and 1800 the Dutch East India Company paid annual dividends worth around 18 percent of the value of the shares.

Invest or pay out?
Dividend payouts are entirely the gift of the directors. Their decision is simple: what proportion of after-tax profit should be paid in dividends, and what should be retained inside the company for reinvestment? The higher the company's growth prospects, the greater the incentive to keep money within the business. Slow-growing companies should therefore pay out a high proportion of profits in dividends, whereas booming organizations are more likely to keep the cash within the business. There is no safer source of capital than retained profit: it does not need to be repaid, nor does it require the payment of interest. Another factor to consider is the health of the company's finances. If they are weak, profits should be retained; only if the balance sheet is strong should generous dividends be paid to the shareholders.

Dividend payouts must be considered carefully. In 2006, the Royal Bank of Scotland (RBS) declared a 25 percent increase in dividends to shareholders. Market commentators praised the move, with one team of analysts issuing the note: "Thanks Fred [Goodwin, CEO of RBS], we love you." The dividend increase put money directly into the hands of the shareholders.

John Kay

Professor John Kay is a British economist born in 1948. Best known for his sceptical support for free-market business behavior, he is a visiting professor at the London School of Economics and regular contributor to the *Financial Times*. In 2012 he presented a detailed report to the UK government on the stock market, which emphasized that the normal purpose of stock markets is not speculation, but to provide companies with access to capital and to provide savers with an opportunity to share in economic growth. He also highlighted concern about excess dividend payouts.

Key works

1996 *The Business of Economics*
2003 *The Truth About Markets*
2006 *The Hare and the Tortoise*

Just two years later RBS was forced to ask shareholders to buy shares at 200p ($3.13) each, in order to raise £12 ($18) billion. Six months later, those shares were worth only 65p ($1.03); three months after that, just 11p (¢17). The company's generosity in 2006 cost its shareholders dearly.

In contrast, Apple did not pay dividends from its formation in 1977 until 2013. The directors, led by Steve Jobs, argued that shareholders would benefit in the long term by allowing Apple to reinvest profits. Only in 2013, with its growth rate beginning to fall, did the company announce dividend payouts, which it projected would average $30 billion a year until 2015. ▪

BORROW SHORT, LEND LONG

MAKING MONEY FROM MONEY

Companies with a good cash flow and **liquidity** can make money from money, by…

…**investing in financial products** such as derivatives and futures contracts.

…**borrowing short-term** and lending to customers long-term, like a bank.

But this can prove to be a **money-losing exercise** if there is a crash in markets or the economy.

Making money from money is a **risky, short-term strategy**.

Some companies opt to "make money from money." This means they use their cash assets not only to further the development of their products, but also to generate money through the financial markets. Some companies believe that by making hedges (bets) on the fluctuations of the currency markets, for example, they can gain access to a new source of profit. The two terms that exemplify the idea of making money from money are "treasury function" and "shadow banks."

Hedge betting

"Treasury function" is a term that emerged in the late 1970s in the wake of economic challenges, such

See also: Managing risk 40–41 ▪ Hubris and nemesis 100–03 ▪ Investment and dividends 126–27 ▪ Who bears the risk? 138–45 ▪ Leverage and excess risk 150–51

Many manufacturing companies, such as Brazilian paper company Aracruz (known as Fibria since 2009), used the treasury function to make money, not just manage it, from the 1980s onward.

as quadrupled oil prices and "stagflation" (where inflation and unemployment are both high at the same time). The idea emerged that the goal of a company's treasury function (the department responsible for stewarding its finances) should be to achieve the optimum balance between liquidity and income from the company's cash flows.

During the decades leading up to the 2007–08 financial crisis, large companies steadily added greater responsibilities to the treasury function. Often, these began as ways to minimize risk, but the opportunities for profitable trading became very tempting—to the point that some companies took out contracts on financial hedges that were worth more than all their export earnings. For example, in 2008, the Brazilian paper and pulp company Aracruz used cash assets to make bets on currency futures (the value of currencies at a future date). Specifically, it bet that the Brazilian currency would continue

to rise, but in fact it underwent a sharp devaluation and the company ended up losing $2.5 billion.

As a result, some companies now spell out their opposition to making money from money. Mining multinational Rio Tinto, for example, stated in its 2013 annual report that its treasury "operates as a service to the businesses of the Rio Tinto group and not as a profit center."

Shadow banks

Other companies, however, have extended the treasury function to become a major, or even majority, profit center for the business. Companies such as US conglomerate General Electric (GE) have developed this function into an effective "shadow bank." In 2007, GE's treasury function GE Capital held over $550 billon of assets, making it larger than some of America's top ten banks. It contributed 55 percent of GE's profits, mainly by borrowing money short-term to lend to customers over the long-term ("borrowing short and lending long"). GE was able to flourish as a member of the shadow banking system without having to bear the regulatory burdens of banks. By 2008, however, it was forced to ask to participate in the US government's banking sector bail-out program.

Making money from money carries serious risks, whether the bets go wrong or not. This is because the more profits a company's treasury generates, the less willing the board may be to invest in research and development for the future growth of the company. This way of making money from money is strongly correlated with short-termism in business. ▪

Treasury in focus

For the decade prior to the financial crisis of 2007–08, many companies began to use short-term financing to fund long-term capital expenditure. However, the financial crisis of 2007–08 changed conditions dramatically, as banks collapsed or came close to doing so. CEOs demanded to know where their company's cash was, and the real-time cash position. Not all treasurers were able to provide immediate answers, since some of their investments were in local, manually operated, less-than-transparent systems.

As a result, the treasury function has moved to the forefront for many companies, with an increased need for transparency and up-to-the-minute accountability. Boards expect treasurers to be prepared for the unexpected—such as by increasing cash reserves to reduce liquidity risk. However, this brings up a new problem for the treasury function: if more cash is kept in reserve, how can this surplus liquidity be used most effectively to fund growth?

The line separating investment and speculation is never bright and clear.
Warren Buffett
US investor (1930–)

THE INTERESTS OF THE SHAREHOLDERS ARE OUR OWN
ACCOUNTABILITY AND GOVERNANCE

IN CONTEXT

FOCUS
Executive control

KEY DATES
1981 Austrian-born US management consultant Peter Drucker suggests that chief executives "have not yet faced up to the fact that they represent power—and power has to be accountable."

1991 The Cadbury Committee is established in the UK to investigate scams, failures, and accountability in corporate governance. Its influential report, *Financial Aspects of Corporate Governance*, is published a year later.

2002 The US government's Sarbanes-Oxley Act sets out much stricter guidelines to govern accounting practices and the publication of previously confidential data (such as operational business risks).

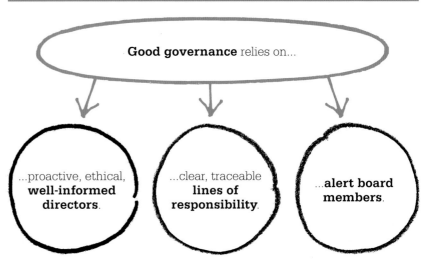

Good governance relies on...

...proactive, ethical, **well-informed directors**.

...clear, traceable **lines of responsibility**.

...**alert board members**.

Accountability is the obligation of an individual or organization to accept responsibility (be accountable) for their actions. In business, it is often used to trace chains of responsibility: staff may be held to account for their actions by those above them in the organization's hierarchy; or higher tiers of management may be held accountable for those below them. Ultimately, the way the company is governed is the responsibility of the directors; their governance should therefore be proactive and ethical.

Following a series of business disasters (from Enron through to Lehman Brothers and numerous banks), corporate governance has become a major issue worldwide. To achieve effective accountability, directors need to make sure that roles and lines of authority are clear. This makes it possible to trace the cause of a mistake to its source— and attribute responsibility to the right person or group. For governance to work well, board members must be well-informed, fully independent, and should work together for the long-term interests

See also: Profit before perks 124–25 ▪ Who bears the risk? 138–45 ▪ Profit versus cash flow 152–53 ▪ Balancing long- versus short-termism 190–91

Companies that bury their heads in the sand—like the proverbial ostrich—may be reluctant to be held accountable for actions and decisions, with damaging consequences for business ethics.

of the business and its owners—the shareholders. Nonexecutive directors have an important role to play in corporate governance: they are not company employees and should be able to quiz executives with impunity.

Board-level scrutiny
In 2011, consultants McKinsey & Company published findings from a survey of 1,597 board directors, providing fascinating insights into the proceedings of board meetings. The survey showed that in Asia, no more than a third of a board's meeting time was spent scrutinizing management actions and decisions; far longer was spent on strategic planning. Although this sounded sensible, it suggested that accountability and governance received less time. By contrast, in North America nearly two-thirds of board time was spent on scrutiny.

More surprisingly, the same sample showed a lack of satisfaction with fellow board members. Directors thought that more than 30 percent of their peers had

limited or no understanding of the risks their company faced. This suggested a flaw in the ability of the board to hold executives to account.

Most of the time, in most companies, executives make sound decisions that require minimum scrutiny. However, good governance ensures that the board is always alert—so it will be fully aware of what is happening when a mistake is made. Such a mistake might be related to strategy (an overpriced takeover bid, for example), or to the ethics of a particular situation. Independently minded nonexecutive directors should be in a prime position to question, for example, whether the company is right to be using very low-cost suppliers, or whether a contract has been won using questionable means.

When things go wrong
The importance of good governance was made clear in the case of Japan's mighty Olympus camera business in 2011. Newly appointed Chief Executive Michael Woodford found that a $1.7 billion cover-up of losses had been made when acquiring other companies. The Olympus directors had hidden these losses from the published accounts and therefore from public scrutiny. The board responded by firing Woodford. Only after a successful campaign by Woodford did the Japanese authorities charge key Olympus directors with fraud. Eventually the whole board resigned. The case demonstrated how ineffective Olympus's nonexecutive directors had been in holding the board to account, and how important good governance and accountability are to the well-being of every company. ▪

Jamsetji Tata

Born on March 3, 1839 in South Gujarat, India, Jamsetji Tata might have appeared an unlikely candidate to be the founder of a business that would grow to be one of the largest conglomerates in the world. Tata followed his father—who had broken the family tradition of being a Brahmin priest—into business at 14 and soon showed potential, graduating from Elphinstone College in Mumbai in 1858. After working for his father, Tata took on his first enterprise—a cotton mill—in 1868. One of his dreams was to found a steelworks, and although this business aim would not be achieved in his lifetime, Tata Iron and Steel Company was set up in 1907 by his son Dorabji. The steel industry went on to be the foundation for Tata Group's global success.

One of Jamsetji Tata's overriding principles was fairness, which permeated his entire business approach. In terms of accountability, his vision was simple: "We started on sound and straightforward business principles, considering the interests of the shareholders as our own."

Accountability breeds response-ability.
Stephen R. Covey
US management consultant (1932–2012)

MAKE THE BEST QUALITY OF GOODS AT THE LOWEST COST PAYING THE HIGHEST WAGES POSSIBLE

YOUR WORKERS ARE YOUR CUSTOMERS

IN CONTEXT

FOCUS
Market expansion

KEY DATES
1914 Henry Ford doubles his employees' wages to $5 a day.

1947 US psychologist Alfred J. Marrow finds that productivity increases when employees are involved in decision making, and introduces the concept of participative management.

1957 Douglas McGregor publishes *The Human Side of Enterprise*, claiming that organizations thrive best by trusting staff to apply their creativity and ingenuity to the enterprise in which they work.

1993 Ricardo Semler of Brazil's Semco writes *Maverick!*.

2011 Google is revealed to have the highest job satisfaction in the US high-tech sector; young "Googlers" are both employees and customers of the company.

Most economic models state that during the early stages of economic development, low-wage workers find themselves making products that are bought by middle- and upper-class consumers. The workers tend to eat simple food, such as potatoes, rice, or corn, and travel on foot or—if they are lucky—use a bicycle as a means of transportation. Meanwhile, their employers eat expensive meat-based meals, and travel in luxurious transportation—from the fine horse carriages of the 17th century to the sleek, "dream machine" automobiles of today.

However, economic growth takes a huge step forward when workers are able to buy the products that they make; when they, too, can afford to eat meat and purchase household and leisure goods. This is now starting to happen rapidly in China, where the sales of staple products—such as toilet paper and refrigerators—are growing quickly.

Building a market
Workers were recognized as potential customers by US car-making pioneer Henry Ford. Ford's

The Ford Motor Company quickly realized that its production line was efficient but made workers unhappy. By giving them a large pay rise, Ford created a market of staff-customers.

Model T automobile was priced at $825 in 1908, at a time when Ford workers earned less than $2 a day. In 1913, Ford introduced a system of conveyor-belt mass production, reducing the time taken to make a Model T from 750 to 93 minutes. With this improvement in efficiency, the company could afford to cut the price of one of its vehicles to $550.

One problem remained, however. The repetitive jobs required to run the Model T production line made

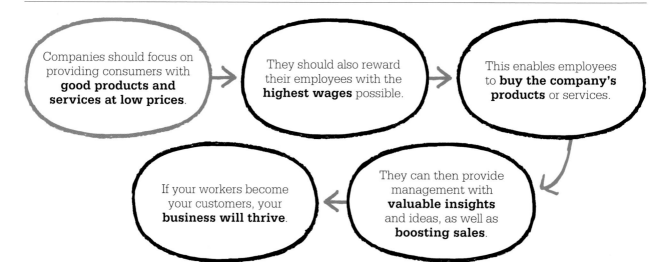

Companies should focus on providing consumers with **good products and services at low prices**.

They should also reward their employees with the **highest wages** possible.

This enables employees to **buy the company's products** or services.

They can then provide management with **valuable insights** and ideas, as well as **boosting sales**.

If your workers become your customers, your **business will thrive**.

See also: Changing the game 92–99 ▪ Organizational culture 104–09 ▪ Understanding the market 234–41 ▪ Focus on the future market 244–49 ▪ Make your customers love you 264–67 ▪ Maximize customer benefits 288–89

workers dissatisfied, and pushed labor turnover to higher than 370 percent—the average employee stayed for only three months before quitting. To counter this, Ford announced that wages at the company's factories would be more than doubled, to $5 a day. His actions made headlines around the world, and in the factory, labor turnover fell to 16 percent annually, helping the output per worker (a measure of overall productivity) to rise by around 40 percent.

By 1914, it took a Ford worker just three months to save enough money to purchase a Model T. By 1924, the price of a Model T fell again to $260, making it possible to buy a brand new car with a month's pay. By 1924, the Ford Motor Company sold more than 50 percent of the world's cars.

Learning from employees

Although Henry Ford generated excellent publicity by making his policy of paying high wages sound like altruism, his practical need to lower the labor turnover helped him

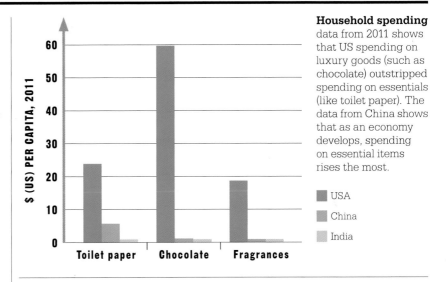

Household spending data from 2011 shows that US spending on luxury goods (such as chocolate) outstripped spending on essentials (like toilet paper). The data from China shows that as an economy develops, spending on essential items rises the most.

■ USA
■ China
■ India

stumble upon an important fact: when your workers earn enough to afford to be your customers, there can be huge benefits for the business. Along with increases in staff pride and commitment, managers are likely to be given valuable insights into the company's products and processes.

In Toyota City, Japan, more than half the work force owns a Toyota vehicle. This is a significant factor

in helping to generate the 400,000 work force suggestions per year on how the company might improve production efficiency and quality.

Emerging markets

In 1924, the US government published a report titled *Cost of Living in the USA*. It showed that the average family spent 38 percent of its $1,430 annual expenditure on food. This is interesting because, in the past five years, India's family spending pattern has slipped below this level, to 36 percent, indicating that the average wealth of Indian families is increasing. When China's proportion of spending on food fell toward 30 percent of income, households could afford to increase their wider spending on nonfood items, such as consumer goods. In the US today, just 7 percent of household income is spent on »

Farm wages in India increased by 17.5 percent annually from 2007 to 2012. Since farm labor is at the bottom of the economic pyramid in India, this signifies a very fast overall rise in wages.

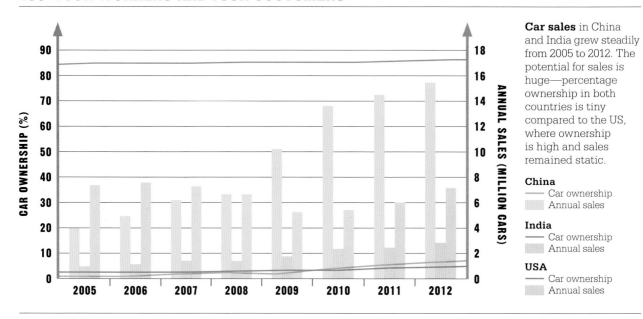

Car sales in China and India grew steadily from 2005 to 2012. The potential for sales is huge—percentage ownership in both countries is tiny compared to the US, where ownership is high and sales remained static.

China
— Car ownership
▨ Annual sales

India
— Car ownership
▨ Annual sales

USA
— Car ownership
▨ Annual sales

food, leaving the average family with a huge surplus with which to buy nonessential items that quickly become "necessities," such as cosmetics and gym membership. India is perhaps about to embark on this stage of economic development. If so, this will have an impact on the sales of a huge range of everyday items.

The significance of this trend lies in the numbers of people involved. If India, over the next

I will build a car for the great multitude … [that] will be so low in price that no man making a good salary will be unable to own one.
Henry Ford
US industrialist (1863–1947)

five years, boosts its spending on toilet paper to China's per-capita spending, the market growth in India will be $8.4 billion ($6.72 x 1.25 billion population). For China to catch up with the US would imply market growth of $24.3 billion ($17.98 x 1.35 billion population). And that's just the increase in market size—not the total market.

Exactly the same logic applies across the market for ordinary household goods throughout the developing world. Already, China is the world's biggest market for luxury items, such as Swiss watches, jewelry, and cars. Over the coming decades, China is also likely to dominate sales of ordinary items (such as toothpaste), and services (such as insurance). The potential sales volumes involved are huge. Today, China is the world's largest car market, even though fewer than 10 percent of households own a car.

In touch with reality
The television show *Undercover Boss* sends senior executives into low-level jobs in their own companies, under alias and

disguise, to find out what the business looks like from that perspective. The show clearly illustrates how those in charge of a business are often unaware of the opinions, insights, and feelings of their customers and staff. Despite a world of online praise and blame, some companies are able to remain in a bubble of self-delusion.

However, this is unlikely to be true of an organization in which the worker is also the customer. These employees care about the product or service because they experience it themselves and realize that their job security relies on customer satisfaction and the company's commercial success. If a customer waiting room becomes messy and dirty, for example, staff-customers will quickly draw attention to it.

In Europe, fashion retailer Primark enjoys huge success in the mainstream market. The company turns runway fashion speedily into low-priced garments with a target market of 15–35-year-olds. However, its growth was instigated by an unusually elderly senior management team. By

Clothing retailer Primark has built a reputation for low-cost fashion in the European ready-to-wear market. Its success is due in no small part to the opinions of its workers.

his engineers to start a special new business division. This became the nucleus of a new Semco, developing new ideas that soon generated 66 percent of the company's business.

Semler's leadership approach is to encourage his work force to manage themselves in terms of time-keeping, work-scheduling, and career development. By doing so, he believes that workers will truly care about what they do; this means that they will inevitably be taking care of not just the business, but its customers too.

Semler describes his methods in his book *Maverick!* (1993) and outlines how much companies can benefit from the staff engagement that results. This approach has become known as participative management. It holds that people are naturally capable of self-direction if they are committed to corporate goals. And when your workers are your customers, the two sets of goals become perfectly aligned. ∎

the time Primark had reached its strongest phase of growth in the 2000s, its senior executives were in their 60s and 70s. It was critical, therefore, for directors to listen to the young work force, who could give insights into customer views.

Democratic management

Ricardo Semler, head of Brazil's Semco Group, is perhaps the world's most radical employer. He believes that bosses need to move beyond empowerment toward worker fulfilment, even delight. Born in 1959, Semler took over the business from his father at the age of 21. Between 1982 and 2003, he drove Semco's sales turnover from $4 million to $200 million. On his first day in the office, he fired nearly two-thirds of the senior management team, who he believed were too rooted in his father's autocratic management style. In the late 1980s, he backed a proposal by three of

Work should be a pleasure, not an obligation …
We believed that people working with pleasure could be much more productive.
Clóvis da Silva Bojikian
Brazilian former HR officer of Semco (1934–)

Arthur Ryan

Born in Ireland in 1935, Arthur Ryan is the founder of Primark. After leaving school, Ryan worked at a department store and then a fashion wholesaler in London before returning to Dublin, where he worked for retailer Dunnes Stores. In 1969, Garfield Weston, CEO of Associated British Foods (ABF), hired Ryan to set up a discount clothing chain with a seed fund of $80,000 (£50,000). The first store, Penneys, opened later that year in Dublin, but Ryan changed the name to Primark for the business model that he was to use in the UK, the Netherlands, and Spain. From 1973 until his retirement in 2009, Ryan built up the business to change it from being a "bargain" store to an inexpensive, on-trend fashion retailer. In 2013, Primark employed more than 43,000 staff in stores in Ireland, Spain, the UK, Austria, Belgium, Portugal, Germany, and the Netherlands. ABF is still its parent company. In the recessionary year of 2009, Primark's like-for-like sales grew by more than 7 percent.

UTILIZE OPM OTHER PEOPLE'S MONEY

WHO BEARS THE RISK?

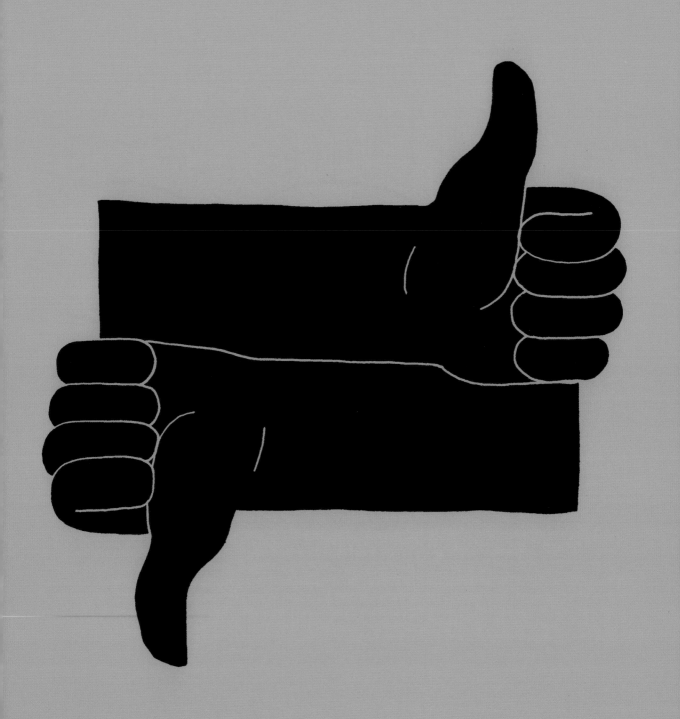

IN CONTEXT

FOCUS
Financial risk

KEY DATES
1950s US economist Harry
Markowitz advocates
gathering a portfolio of
investments to protect against
losses due to financial risk.

1990s Research on types of
financial risk identifies ways
of measuring and managing
different kinds of risk, including
market risk (changes in the
value of equity, interest rates,
currency, and commodities)
and credit risk (the risk of
nonpayment of debts).

1999 UK conglomerate General
Electric Company (GEC) is
renamed Marconi plc, and its
traditional businesses are
sold off. The directors' gamble
on this change in strategy
fails—the business collapses
in 2001 and shares are
suspended. Nearly 25 percent
of staff is laid off.

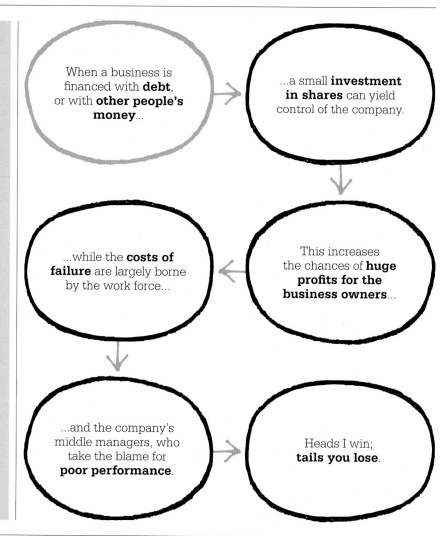

When a business is financed with **debt**, or with **other people's money**...

...a small **investment in shares** can yield control of the company.

This increases the chances of **huge profits for the business owners**...

...while the **costs of failure** are largely borne by the work force...

...and the company's middle managers, who take the blame for **poor performance**.

Heads I win; **tails you lose**.

The degree of financial risk borne by a company has profound implications for the long-term viability and success of the business, its employees, and its shareholders. A business structured in a traditional manner would put the most risk on the shareholders, since they stand to lose their investment if the venture fails. But the proliferation of increasingly complex financial mechanisms and means of accounting have, to a degree, insulated a business's owners from the worst effects of failure.

Greek shipping magnate Aristotle Onassis built a business empire that stretched across the world and incorporated dozens of industries, and was underpinned by complex financial arrangements. Onassis recommended utilizing "other people's money," and while this approach might yield financial success, it may end with others bearing the costs of failure.

Traditional risk
In theory, the risk takers in a market economy are the shareholders, who effectively "own" the business. The shareholders' capital finances the business start-up, and remains at risk until it is repaid in full. If the business liquidates, the holder of "ordinary" shares (as opposed to "preferred" shares, which are higher in ranking and yield dividends before ordinary shares) is the last in the line to be paid. The ordinary shareholder is therefore the least likely to recover his or her investment. Because of the risks they take, entrepreneurs are held in high esteem. So are early-stage, venture-capital investors, who invest in start-ups in return for equity.

See also: Managing risk 40–41 ▪ Play by the rules 120–23 ▪ Accountability and governance 130–31 ▪ Leverage and excess risk 150–51 ▪ Off-balance-sheet risk 154 ▪ Balancing long- versus short-termism 190–91 ▪ Morality in business 222

Venture capitalists, such as Indian-born Vinod Khosla of Sun Microsystems, invest in companies at an early stage and risk bearing the brunt of failure. But returns can be high with success.

The association of risk with the shareholder is beneficial in many respects. A risk-bearing shareholder in a large, multinational bank would be inclined to discourage senior management from taking large risks with the bank's capital or reputation. Calculated risks may be considered, but not risks that threaten the existence of the business. The shareholder can play a significant part in the business process, acting as a natural check on the company's propensity to take risks. This view of business has been held since the foundations of modern capitalism in the 18th century.

Suppliers and creditors

The traditional view may be threatened due to effects of new rules and practices. In an attempt to encourage entrepreneurship, Chapter 11 of the US bankruptcy

The burden of risk associated with a business is spread wider as its financial affairs grow more complex. Executives and staff stand to lose financially and perhaps even punitively—with prison sentences possible—if the company fails. Creditors and shareholders can lose financially, while in the worst-case scenario taxpayers may bear the heaviest burden of all—in the form of high taxation and low economic growth—if their government chooses to rescue the business.

Shareholders

Creditors

Business

Executives

Staff

Taxpayers

$ Risk of financial loss

🏛 Risk of criminal prosecution

code gives a struggling business substantial protection from those to whom it owes money (its creditors, such as suppliers of raw materials, ingredients, or subsidiary services). This protection is intended to allow a company to rethink its business plan and perhaps find a more profitable business model.

In the UK, a struggling company can choose to enter a phase of "pre-pack administration," in which the business's assets are sold after it has entered bankruptcy. The assets and operating model are sold to new owners, leaving the original business entity behind. Suppliers and other creditors may receive no more than a token payment, such as 10 percent of the value of their claims on the business. The new shareholders then have a debt-free business with all the assets of the old company, but with none of the »

Suppliers are among the last to receive compensation for their goods or services if a business goes bankrupt. If, in the UK, it enters "pre-pack administration," suppliers might receive nothing at all.

liabilities. This method can be especially controversial, since it can allow the owners of the original business to sell the "pre-packaged" new entity and still be involved in the business. In August 2008 the London-based restaurant business of Michelin-starred chef Tom Aikens went into administration. It was bought by TA Holdco Ltd., of which Aikens was appointed partner and shareholder. Around 160 suppliers were left nursing losses that would never be recovered. However, by early 2010 Tom Aikens' business achieved a financial turnaround, and opened three new ventures in London.

When pre-pack administration is utilized, suppliers are revealed to be in a much more vulnerable position than might otherwise be expected. The financial losses incurred by Aikens's restaurants were effectively absorbed by suppliers, not shareholders. In a world of pre-pack administration and Chapter 11 bankruptcy

protection, the creditors can find themselves in a riskier position than the shareholders.

Employees at risk

Staff employed by a business is also at risk when a company fails. When US energy company Enron collapsed in 2001, an extraordinary feature of the unfolding story was the plight of many employees. Unlike the senior executives, rank-and-file staff had been part inspired and part browbeaten into "showing faith in Enron" by investing

personal pension funds in Enron shares. When the business was liquidated, employees not only lost their jobs, but also their pensions. When the collapse of the business was becoming clear, Enron froze its pension fund, preventing employees switching their pension holdings out of Enron shares.

Employees can also be vulnerable due to the predations of the investment market. If a company is bought through private equity, employees can find themselves worse off if the business fails. A private-equity purchase is when a publicly traded company is bought by a "private-equity group," often through a leveraged buy out, where the assets of the purchased company are used as security to borrow funds with which to finance the purchase. In so doing, the burden of risk is on the business (and its employees), not on the owners.

The UK franchise of Canadian underwear business La Senza collapsed in 2012, with 1,100 employees losing jobs. In cases like this, the staff has little to gain when things go well, but everything to lose when they go wrong. Suppliers

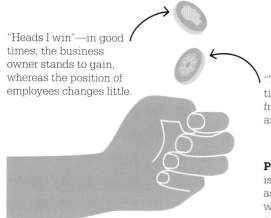

"Heads I win"—in good times, the business owner stands to gain, whereas the position of employees changes little.

"Tails you lose"—in bad times, the owner is protected from losses, but the business and its employees suffer.

Private-equity ownership is typically structured in an asymmetric way. If things go well the private-equity owner gains, and if things go badly the subsidiary business loses.

are in the same position. Only the private-equity shareholders are protected—by limited liability.

When publicly traded soccer team Manchester United was purchased by US businessman Malcolm Glazer and his family in 2005, the transaction was effectively a private-equity deal. The Glazers followed standard practice, buying the publicly-listed company for $ 1.3 billion, then put the debts onto the balance sheet of the new Manchester United Ltd. Private-equity owners suggest that debt is an effective means of forcing employees to work efficiently to make a profit and meet interest payments. More plausibly, though, it is a way of transferring risk from the private-equity owner to a limited liability subsidiary. If Manchester United Ltd. were to enter financial trouble, the liability of the Glazers would be minimal due to the protection of "limited liability," which limits the owners' liability to the value of their investment, not the total debts of the business.

Research published in 2013 compared the performance of 105 companies purchased through private equity and 105 "control" companies in the same industries.

We have corporate CEOs who raise their pay 20 percent or more in years when they lay off thousands of people. It's obscene.
Charles Handy
UK management expert (1932–)

They were investigated over a ten-year period—the six years leading up to the buy out, and the four years after it. The researchers found that in the year following the buy out, 59 percent of the private-equity owned businesses cut their staffing levels, compared with 32 percent in the control group. In the following years, private-equity ownership was associated with falling average wage levels among staff. In the short term employees appear to lose out—and in the medium to long term their chances of losing their jobs are higher due to the greater level of debt of the companies they work for.

Private-equity iniquity

Not everyone loses out under private equity. In 2003 the British retailer Debenhams was purchased by three private-equity companies. The businesses paid themselves a dividend of $1.9 (£1.2) billion before floating the publicly traded Debenhams onto the stock market in 2006—laden with debt. Years later, in its 2012 annual accounts, the financial strain still showed. The degree of "gearing" (debt as a percentage of capital employed in the business) at Debenhams was a high 51.5 percent, and its liquidity (as measured by the "acid test ratio," which determines whether a company has enough short-term assets to cover its immediate liabilities) was a very weak 0.175. Yet for the private-equity owners, the deal was highly profitable— they made $1.9 (£1.2) billion very quickly and still retained shares in Debenhams (a stake that was sold in the years that followed). Their overall profits exceeded 200 percent.

For the bosses of private-equity companies, the rewards can also be impressive. Bernard Schwarzman of US private-equity investment

There is a simple way of avoiding excess risk taking by the managers of our financial institutions. It is to make it a crime.
Paul Collier
UK economist (1949–)

company Blackstone Group earns $130 million a year. He is closely followed by the bosses of Carlyle Group, Apollo Global, and KKR— who each earn in excess of $100 million a year. Remarkably, all these bosses enjoy favorable tax treatment in both the US and the UK. This became an important issue in the 2012 US presidential election, when Republican candidate Mitt Romney (a former private-equity boss) had to admit that his income tax rate, at 14 percent, was lower than that of average, working Americans.

Executives on the hot seat

In the world of public limited companies and corporations, the CEO might be in the riskiest position of all. They may have the most to gain from their business's success, but also the most to lose from its failure. These risks may be partly financial, but even more they are reputational. Richard Fuld, chief executive of Lehman Brothers at the time of its 2008 bankruptcy, went from being an award-winning CEO to a nominee for a range of "worst ever..." awards. From being a director of the Federal Reserve Bank of New York, he became a pariah. »

Italian food giant Parmalat's 2004 $1.6-billion accounting cover-up was primarily due to fraud. The effects were sharply felt by shareholders and the many employees who lost their jobs.

In the UK, a similar fate awaited figures such as Fred Goodwin (CEO of Royal Bank of Scotland when it collapsed in 2008) and James Crosby (CEO of Halifax Bank of Scotland until 2006). Both were blamed for the dramatic collapses of their banks in 2008, and for their part in the subsequent economic turmoil.

Is it fair that a company's bosses should have to take the blame for failure so personally? After all, it is inconceivable that the CEO is the only one to blame for the failure of a business. Objectively, the answer is clear, because business failure is certainly the responsibility of more than just the CEO. Yet high-profile executives often strive to associate themselves so closely with the company— making it seem as though they personally are the business—and are so eager to back this up with massive remuneration packages, that it can be no surprise when the public and the media turn on them.

Taxpayers to the rescue
In mature, developed economies, businesses are supposed to take risks in pursuit of reward. Failure should, on this basis, lead to the death of the business. Austrian-American economist Joseph Schumpeter, in his classic 1942 book *Capitalism, Socialism, and Democracy*, made the famous statement: "The process of Creative Destruction is the essential fact about capitalism." Schumpeter, like many others, viewed recessions as a cleansing mechanism, allowing the weak to fall back and new, stronger companies to emerge.

Yet modern governments seem to see things differently, certainly in relation to large businesses. The term "too big to fail" illustrates that business risks have been transferred to the taxpayer. Faced with the bankruptcy of General Motors and Chrysler in 2009, the US government —in other words, US taxpayers— took on billions of dollars' of debt to give the companies a fresh start. In the UK and Europe, bank bailouts in 2008 and 2009 saved the private sector from huge losses. In Europe, what was put forward as a Eurozone government problem was in fact a private-sector problem, as banks faced nonrepayment of loans to businesses within Greece, Portugal, or Italy. The bailouts were arranged and financed by governments, meaning that taxpayers turned out to be the risk takers, even though nobody asked their opinion. American economist Nouriel Roubini summed this up by saying: "This is again a case of privatizing the gains and socializing the losses; a bailout and socialism for the rich, the well-connected, and Wall Street."

This issue has stretched far wider than the US and Europe, influencing the economic situation in both Japan and China in recent decades. From the start of its 20-year depression in 1990, land prices in Japan fell by more than 80 percent, and today remain far below the levels reached in 1988 before the recession began. In effect, almost every bank in Japan was insolvent as a result of vast portfolios of nonperforming loans—loans that were made to companies that could neither repay the debt, nor pay the interest on that debt. Only the support of the Japanese central

Risk comes from not knowing what you are doing.
Warren Buffett
US investor (1930–)

bank kept these commercial banks alive. The taxpayer took on the risks that are supposed to be taken by the private sector. Many analysts suggest that the same is true in China at present, although the opacity of the Chinese banking system makes this hard to verify.

Who bears the risk?

Roubini's statement that losses are "socialized" (borne by the public) while profits remain in the private sector appears to be true. Income inequality has widened considerably around the world in recent decades, in countries including the US, UK, China, and India. For instance, between 1979 and 2007 in the US, the income of the top 1 percent of earners rose by 266 percent, while that of the bottom 20 percent rose

Greek citizens protest in Athens against austerity measures in 2011. Rescue loans from the European Union to Greek banks mean that the country faces years of economic hardship.

by only 37 percent. Government bailouts for big business effectively mean that taxpayers are providing support for those who benefit most from today's economic system. In the long run, businesses may enjoy substantial profits, and accept the rewards as recompense for the risks they take. But if the risks (and losses) are borne by the taxpayer, it is fair to question why only shareholders gain the profits in the good times.

Often, employees and suppliers bear higher levels of risk than seems fair—shareholders, who enjoy the rewards of success, should bear the primary risk of failure. Even trade-union protection for workers has been eroded in recent decades—in the US and many countries around the world, unions account for no more than 10 percent of private-sector employees, which leaves workers unprotected when things go wrong. Although labor flexibility has its merits, imbalance between "my risk" and "your reward" has perhaps gone too far. ∎

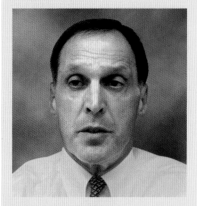

Richard Fuld

Richard "Dick" Fuld was born in 1946 in New York City, NY. He graduated from the University of Colorado in 1969, and received an MBA from the Stern School of Business in 1973. He was CEO of Lehman Brothers investment bank from 1994 to the day of its collapse in 2008, and during that time, he received more than $500 million. Known as the "Gorilla of Wall Street," Fuld was the domineering boss who pushed the company into the subprime mortgage business. For many critics, the decision that illustrated his hubris was his refusal of bailout funds from investor Warren Buffett and the Korea Development Bank, even though Lehman Brothers was in the throes of being toppled by the 2008 credit crunch. His reasoning was that the offers of cash did not match his own valuation of Lehman Brothers. Following the company's bankruptcy in September 2008, *Time Magazine* named Fuld as one of the "25 People to Blame for the Financial Crisis," and *Condé Nast Portfolio* magazine ranked him number one on its list of "Worst American CEOs of All Time."

SWIM UPSTREAM. GO THE OTHER WAY. IGNORE THE CONVENTIONAL WISDOM

IGNORING THE HERD

IN CONTEXT

FOCUS
Business behavior

KEY DATES
1841 Scottish journalist Charles MacKay documents herd behavior in his book, *Extraordinary Popular Delusions and the Madness of Crowds.*

1992 Indian economist Abhijit V. Banerjee publishes *A Simple Model of Herd Behaviour.*

1995 In "Herd Behaviour, Bubbles and Crashes," German professor Thomas Lux claims prices and sentiment affect one another, so feelings of the herd affect prices (for example, faith in the housing market pushes up prices).

2001–06 The housing bubble in the US and parts of Europe gathers pace before collapsing in the 2007–08 financial crisis.

The herd instinct is clear in nature and just as clear in business. Most people feel more comfortable following what others are doing than standing out as a "loner" or maverick. Ignoring the herd takes great psychological strength. When stock markets rise steeply, new—perhaps first-time—investors get sucked in by the apparently easy pickings. These latecomers to a booming "bull market" cause share prices to propel upward for a last time before they slump back toward their previous value. By following the herd in this way, most first timers invest when share prices are near the top and usually sell when they find that their

See also: Stand out in the market 28–31 ▪ Gaining an edge 32–39 ▪ Beware the yes-men 74–75 ▪ Thinking outside the box 88–89 ▪ Avoid groupthink 114 ▪ Protect the core business 170–71 ▪ Forecasting 278–79

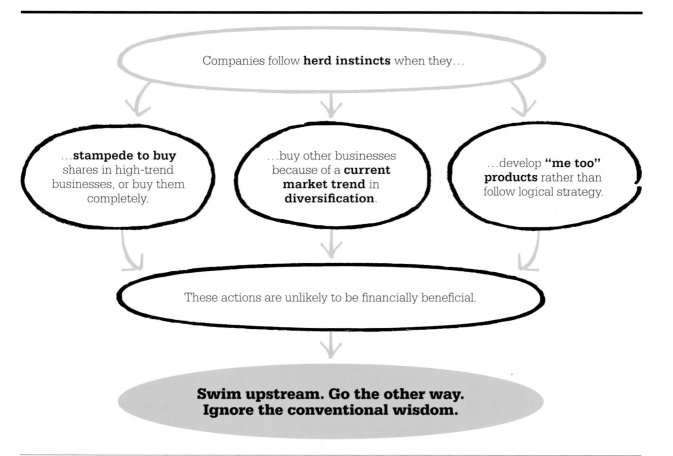

Companies follow **herd instincts** when they…

…**stampede to buy** shares in high-trend businesses, or buy them completely.

…buy other businesses because of a **current market trend** in **diversification**.

…develop **"me too" products** rather than follow logical strategy.

These actions are unlikely to be financially beneficial.

Swim upstream. Go the other way. Ignore the conventional wisdom.

assets have dropped in value. They often suffer serious losses. A contrarian investor—or a savvy company that holds a portfolio of investments—does the opposite. When share prices rise and new investors are attracted into the market, they sell, and if the market slumps, they buy. However, few investors show the foresight required to know when a boom is turning to bust. Warren Buffet, a legendary investor, says: "We simply attempt to be fearful when others are greedy and to be greedy only when others are fearful." Between 1965 and 2013, Buffet's investment company gave investors a capital gain of more than 900,000 percent.

An example of the risks of following the herd came with the dot-com bubble, between 1998 and 1999. Among numerous examples of extraordinary share-price gains followed by equally huge losses, was the business eToys.com, which was opened in 1997. In May 1999 it was launched onto the New York Stock Exchange at $20 per share, raising $166 million. Buyers piled in, pushing the price up to $76 by the end of the first day. By fall 1999, the share price was $84, giving the business a higher market value than the retail giant Toys R Us. As the market turned downward, the experts started to sell, leaving the herd with the

shares. And by February 2001, the share price had fallen to 9 cents. A little later the business was declared bankrupt. »

The herd instinct among forecasters makes sheep look like independent thinkers.
Edgar R. Fielder
US economist (1930–2003)

Global market shares of smartphones in 2009–13 varied greatly: Apple stayed relatively stable; Nokia and RIM, who had responded with herd instincts to the iPhone's success, saw huge losses; Samsung's shares soared, reflecting its development of products that would stand the test of time.

— Nokia
— Samsung
— Apple
— RIM

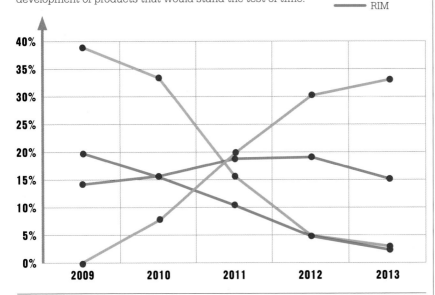

It makes sense for the share-buying public not to follow mass trends, but is the same true for business leaders? In 2008, US mass-media corporation AOL, noticing the growth in social network sites, bought the social-networking site Bebo for $850 million. It joined the herd and lost out badly. In 2013, it sold the same business back to its founders for $1 million.

Following trends

Business leaders, then, must be as cautious as anyone else about treading the same path as the majority. There are three main types of herd to ignore. The first, as mentioned, is the occasional stampede to make takeover bids. In this case, business leaders worry that if they do not buy a rival, someone else will and perhaps create a bigger, more difficult competitor. At such times, there is much talk of synergies (the sum being worth more than the parts)

but little mention of long-standing research, which suggests that 60 to 66 percent of all takeovers destroy shareholder value for the winning company. In other words, most takeover bids prove to be a disappointment.

The second herd behavior to ignore is the strategic clash between focus and diversification, and the way the market tends to concentrate on one of these two at any one time. When "focus" is the market mantra, share prices rise in companies that sell off peripheral assets or divisions of the business. This is what happened to British Aerospace (BAe) when it sold its 20 percent stake in the Airbus aircraft business in 2006. At the time, the stock market liked its $2.99 (£1.87) billion sale of the largely civilian aircraft maker, since it focused BAe on the defense and military sector. By 2013, this view looked absurd, as Airbus powered ahead but governments—especially the US—cut back on

military spending. A worried BAe then approached the owner of Airbus, suggesting a merger and implying that a mix of civilian and military businesses was a preferable focus. Could things really have changed that much between 2006 and 2013, or was BAe responding to the trend for diversification? Strong business leaders look to the long-term and ignore fads and fashions among stock-market analysts and management consultants.

Following the leader

The third herd behavior to avoid is "followership." This occurs when companies develop "me-too" products to imitate market innovators. Of course, if a business already has a genuinely differentiated offering, it is wise to follow a new trend. Often, though, businesses rush out copycat products to demonstrate that they are staying competitive in a sector. When the iPhone was launched in 2007, Nokia could boast more than 40 percent of the global smartphone market. Despite a series of new product launches by the company,

Those entrapped by the herd instinct are drowned in the deluges of history. But there are always the few who observe, reason, and take precautions, and thus escape the flood.
Anthony C. Sutton
UK economist (1925–2002)

We find that whole communities suddenly fix their minds upon one object, and go mad in its pursuit.
Charles MacKay

its share of smartphone sales collapsed to around 3 percent in the first quarter of 2013. Throughout this period, Nokia was desperately trying to catch up with Apple's iPhone—but doing no more than throwing new products at the problem, instead of taking a deep strategic breath and deciding what innovations might earn it a stake of the market.

The contrast between Nokia's behavior and that of Apple's could not be greater. In 2008 and 2009 the big trend in mobile computing was away from laptops and toward "netbooks." In 2009, global netbook sales rose by 72 percent. The herd instinct of businesses such as Dell was to produce their own netbook. At Apple, by contrast, boss Steve Jobs announced that "the problem with netbooks is that they're not better than anything." He worked to develop a superior alternative to netbooks—the iPad. By mid 2013 the iPad had sold more than 145 million units and the original makers of netbooks (Taiwan's Asus) had halted production completely.

Those who ignore the herd can apply cool logic to their situation and think ahead to possible future scenarios. The herd tends to think that tomorrow will mean more and more of today. Those who ignore the herd can identify fundamentals that persist over time, while looking toward what might be different tomorrow. As US entrepreneur Sam Walton advised, it often makes sense to "swim upstream." ∎

The success of the iPad reflected Apple's resolve to develop a superior alternative to the "netbook." Companies like Apple and Samsung need to be ahead of the herd, not behind it.

Warren Buffett

Generally considered the most successful investor of the 20th century, Warren Edward Buffett was born on August 30 in 1930 in Omaha, NE. He demonstrated an early ability with mathematics and was able to add large columns of numbers in his head. His father was a stockbroker and congressman.

Buffett began investing at the age of 11. He started several small businesses while still a teenager, before going to the universities of Pennsylvania, Nebraska, and Columbia to study business. In 1956 he formed the company Buffett Partnership, where his investment successes led to his nickname, "the Oracle of Omaha." In 2006 he announced that he would be giving his entire fortune to charity. In 2012 his net worth was estimated at $44 billion.

Key works

2001 *The Essays of Warren Buffett: Lessons for Corporate America* (with Lawrence A Cunningham)
2013 *The Essays of Warren Buffett: Lessons for Corporate America, Third Edition* (with Lawrence A Cunningham)

DEBT IS THE WORST POVERTY
LEVERAGE AND EXCESS RISK

IN CONTEXT

FOCUS
Managing risk

KEY DATES
1970–2008 Banks in developed countries double the ratio of loans that they issue compared to the value of money they hold.

2002 The Global Executive Forum report on the collapse of the Enron corporation says that "the genius of Enron was infinite leverage."

2007–08 Increasing numbers of people access credit to finance mortgages, but later default on their loans. Global financial markets collapse.

2013 The UK government forces banks to publish their leverage ratios. Among the highest leveraged is Barclays, which has loans worth 35 times its (equity) capital base.

In 2012, US theoretical physicist Mark Buchanan wrote *Forecast*, a book detailing his investigations into the workings of the economy. In assessing the variables that affect economic growth and decline, he noted the importance that central banks (and governments) place on inflation, interest rates, exchange rates, and consumer confidence. He was puzzled by the absence of one variable that had proved a central factor in past extremes of boom and

Increasing leverage allows companies to...	**Decreasing leverage** allows companies to...
↓	↓
...focus on **growth** and convert **short-term debt into long-term loans**...	...focus on **increasing profit** through minimizing costs and **repay** long-term loans...
↓	↓
...and pay **increased dividends** to shareholders.	...and issue **more shares**.
↓	↓
However, it can leave businesses **vulnerable to cash-flow problems**.	However, the company may **fall behind rivals** who can boost growth through higher leverage.

See also: Who bears the risk? 138–45 ▪ Profit versus cash flow 152–53 ▪ Maximize return on equity 155 ▪ The private equity model 156–57

Borrowing on credit cards can lead to financial ruin. In 2007–08 many homeowners borrowed on credit to pay their mortgages, but had insufficient income to meet loan repayments.

bust—leverage. This is a measure of indebtedness, or the extent to which people or companies finance their future by borrowing money. Society and business had ignored the warning of UK historian Thomas Fuller: "debt is the worst poverty."

When high leverage is widespread in the economy—as occurs when lots of people borrow large amounts of money—the degree of debt can create a short-term boom. But this often comes at the cost of a subsequent bust.

Taking risks
The financial crisis of 2007–08 was largely caused by high leverage. Individuals borrowed large amounts on credit cards and took out 100 percent mortgages, both against inadequate levels of income. When the debts could not be met and house prices fell, huge numbers of people defaulted on their debts. The equally highly leveraged banks stumbled; their problems were made worse by the large-scale

use of complex financial products (also based around leveraging), and the financial system crashed.

Leverage carries similar risks for businesses. During good times, when demand is rising and profit margins are high, borrowing capital to finance extra growth may seem an attractive means to boost profits. But leaders often ignore the increase in risk that accompanies an increase in borrowings. Paying back debt is not optional (unlike the payment of dividends, for example). Highly leveraged businesses can suddenly find that their high levels of debt are no longer serviced by sales. The borrowings that had driven profits can begin, instead, to drive the company into severe cash-flow problems.

Broadly speaking, it is wise to restrict borrowings to around 25 to 35 percent of the total long-term capital employed in the business. Any higher than 50 percent is regarded as carrying too high a risk level for a normal business. After all, while the directors need to aim for maximum profits, they are also responsible for the long-term health of the business, together with the welfare and security of staff, customers, and suppliers. ▪

The leveraged buy-out

In a leveraged buy-out, a business is acquired by a company or group of individuals using a large amount of borrowed money, most often from bank loans or bonds (interest-bearing loans that are used to raise capital). Typically, the buy-out may be paid for with a ratio of around 90 percent debt to 10 percent equity, and the assets for the loans are those of the company being acquired. In other words, the theory is that the debt is later repaid by money raised from the acquired business. Leveraged buy-out investment companies are today known as private-equity companies.

In the 1980s, leveraged buy-outs became notorious, as some acquirers used a borrowing ratio level of 100 percent, and the interest levels on debt repayment were so large that cash flows crashed and companies went bankrupt. More recently, a $2.85 billion leveraged buy-out and subsequent restructure was used to rescue struggling US film-production giant Metro-Goldwyn-Mayer (MGM).

When you combine ignorance and leverage, you get some pretty interesting results.
Warren Buffett
US investor (1930–)

CASH IS KING
PROFIT VERSUS CASH FLOW

For new businesses, fast-growing companies, and in times of recession, cash is king. In other words, profit takes a back seat, while cash flow becomes the critical factor. In accounting, profit is an abstract concept based on matching costs to the revenues generated within a period of trading. This sounds fine, but in practice it can lead to a huge cash shortfall. For example, if a construction business links its costs to the time when the finished houses are ready for purchase, it has ignored the huge cash outflows that are incurred during the building process, and might run out of cash before the houses are sold. When times are good, a

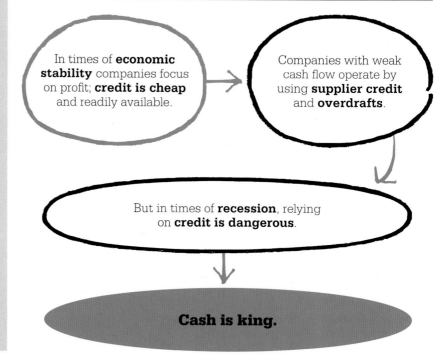

In times of **economic stability** companies focus on profit; **credit is cheap** and readily available.

Companies with weak cash flow operate by using **supplier credit** and **overdrafts**.

But in times of **recession**, relying on **credit is dangerous**.

Cash is king.

See also: How fast to grow 44–45 ▪ Investment and dividends 126–27 ▪ Making money from money 128–29 ▪ Leverage and excess risk 150–51 ▪ Maximize return on equity 155 ▪ Balancing long- versus short-termism 190–91

company may rely on dipping into an overdraft to make up for a cash shortfall. But when times are tough, a reliance on the bank may be too risky. A business needs to manage its finances well enough to avoid periods of negative cash flow.

How good companies fail

Cash is a constant pressure for every new business. Even if the company keeps to its start-up budget, it takes time for trading to reach a high enough level to generate positive cash flows. For example, a sports' equipment store may take three years to build up the regular clientele that will enable it to start making money. Until then, the business faces negative cash flow. So it is crucial for new businesses to prioritize cash flow from the beginning. This may mean leasing equipment, or buying it secondhand rather than new, and choosing suppliers that provide the same credit period as the store gives to its customers, even if these suppliers cost a little more. Cash-

A business receives a $24,000 order, and has to plough cash into making the goods. By week six, $20,000 has been spent by the company; the customer is invoiced, but is not required to pay until week 13. This means the company faces serious negative cash flow for 12 to 13 weeks.

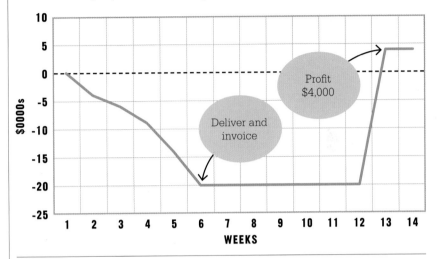

flow problems can also cause well-established companies to stumble and even collapse. In 1998, South Korea's Daewoo Group encountered growing problems because of "increasing difficulties in arranging working capital and investment funds." The group had been aggressively expanding, and admitted that its overall financial stability had been seriously undermined by a new reliance on borrowings, but insisted that it was a brief moment of crisis. Despite being one of the largest conglomerates in the world, the group collapsed the following year due to massive cash shortfalls. ▪

Money scams

US investment advisor and financier Bernard Madoff was sentenced to 150 years in prison in 2009 following a money scam that is believed to have led to about $18 billion of losses to investors. Although hailed as a distinguished and expert financier, capable of generating very high returns for investors, Madoff was in fact responsible for running a "Ponzi scheme," in which cash from new investors is used to pay generous returns to earlier investors. The delight of these early customers led them to recommend the scheme, which then continued to pay earlier investors with the cash put into the company by subsequent investors.

This type of financial pyramid is able to stay afloat as long as sufficient numbers of new savers put cash into the scheme. If the flow of funds dries up, the scheme collapses. Madoff's scam collapsed due to a loss of investor confidence following the 2008 financial crisis.

Farmers buying livestock at market must—like many business owners— pay up front. Costs, such as feed and storage, will mount before they see a return on their investment.

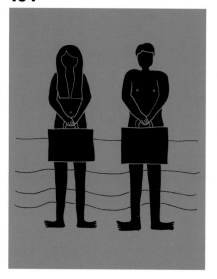

ONLY WHEN THE TIDE GOES OUT DO YOU DISCOVER WHO'S BEEN SWIMMING NAKED

OFF-BALANCE-SHEET RISK

IN CONTEXT

FOCUS
Financial risk

KEY DATES
1992 Terry Smith publishes *Accounting for Growth*, an insider exposé of accounting practices in big businesses.

2001 The spectacular collapse of Enron shows that practices such as off-balance-sheet accounting are not just obscure talking points.

2010 Lehman Brothers bank is revealed to have used "Repo 105" and "Repo 108" repurchase transactions to temporarily remove some loans and investments from its balance sheet for 7 to 10 days, creating a misleading picture of its activities and value.

2011 UK care provider Southern Cross collapses due to off-balance-sheet debts to the value of $8 (£5) billion.

The balance sheet is a snapshot of a company's assets and liabilities and should show any financial risks that a company is facing. Yet in reality, not all of the company's liabilities appear there. This means that when calculating the debts of a business, it may not be possible to account for everything. This was the case when Enron failed in 2001, and it was also true for the Western retailers and banks that struggled from 2007–08.

Operating off balance sheet was at the heart of the 2011 scandal at Japanese camera company Olympus. To hide poor management decisions, such as overpaying in takeover bids, the board set up unconsolidated subsidiaries to hold the transactions that were causing losses. As unconsolidated losses, the figures did not have to appear in the its annual accounts. Analysts and auditors should have spotted that something was wrong when profits appeared "healthy" while cash was draining out of the business. But nothing was spotted until new CEO Michael Woodford blew the whistle.

Enron used off-balance-sheet accounting to hide overvalued assets in subsidiary businesses. Its financial records continued to look perfect even as it spiraled toward bankruptcy.

Off-balance-sheet finance has been increasingly used by governments in recent decades. In China, the National Audit Office has warned that local government may have as much as three times its official debt of $600 billion in off-balance-sheet unofficial debt. This will add greatly to future interest charges—and may carry significant risk if China experiences a credit crunch similar to that in the US and Europe from 2007–08 onwards. ∎

See also: Play by the rules 120–23 ▪ Accountability and governance 130–31 ▪ Who bears the risk? 138–45 ▪ Leverage and excess risk 150–51

RETURN ON EQUITY IS A FINANCIAL GOAL THAT CAN BECOME AN OWN GOAL
MAXIMIZE RETURN ON EQUITY

IN CONTEXT

FOCUS
Business goals and risks

KEY DATES
1978 Legendary investor Warren Buffett claims that ROE is not likely to stray from a level of 12 percent for very long.

1995: *The Warren Buffett Way* by Robert Hagstrom introduces the public to Buffett's approach to investment, including the importance he places on ROE.

1997 The US's S&P (Standard and Poor) index of industrial companies reveals an average ROE of 22 percent.

2012 Among international clothing retailers, ROE varies from 40 percent at Gap and 39 percent at H&M, to -139 percent at American Apparel. Based on its ROE alone, American Apparel should no longer exist in its current form.

Many stockmarket analysts regard "return on equity" (ROE) as a vital measure of business success. ROE measures profit as a percentage of the shareholder's equity on the balance sheet. This "equity" is comprised of share capital (capital raised from selling shares) and reserves (the company's accumulated, retained profit).

ROE is affected by trading conditions. Still recovering from a tsunami and floods, Toyota achieved an ROE of 3.9 percent in 2012. Rival General Motors (GM), unaffected by the natural disasters, managed 16.7 percent. Based on its ROE, GM appeared to be four to five times better at generating profit from shareholders' investment.

A misleading measure

As an indicator of investment potential, ROE can be problematic. The percentage outcome is a function of two things: how high the profit is, and how low the shareholders' equity is. Toyota and GM both made a similar pretax profit in 2012, but the amount of shareholders' equity in the two companies creates a misleading picture. Toyota has a huge balance sheet with high shareholder equity, bolstered by decades of high profits. GM's bankruptcy in 2009 had wiped out its reserves, leaving it with a small equity base. GM's high ROE was largely due to its collapse and US government bailout.

In the 2000s, many banks cut their balance sheets through "share buybacks." Cash was used to buy shares back from shareholders, reducing the equity at the bottom of the formula. This increased the ROE, but led to a risky capital structure. By maximizing ROE, the banks left too little cash to deal with the 2007–08 financial crash. ∎

ROE is calculated by dividing profit by average shareholder equity. The higher the figure, the more efficient the company is at generating shareholder returns.

$$\text{ROE (\%)} = \frac{\text{Profit}}{\text{Average shareholder equity}} \times 100$$

See also: Investment and dividends 126–27 ∎ Accountability and governance 130–31 ∎ Who bears the risk? 138–45 ∎ Ignoring the herd 146–49

AS THE ROLE OF PRIVATE EQUITY HAS GROWN, SO HAVE THE RISKS IT POSES

THE PRIVATE EQUITY MODEL

IN CONTEXT

FOCUS
Profit and risk

KEY DATES
1959 Fairchild Semiconductors, the first venture-capital-funded start-up, is created.

1978 US investment group KKR pays $380 million to take manufacturer Houdaille Industries Inc. private; this is probably the first private-equity transaction.

1988 KKR buys conglomorate RJR Nabisco for $25 billion in the biggest private-equity purchase the world has yet seen.

2006–07 A peak year for private equity—in the US alone, private equity companies buy 654 companies for a total of around $375 billion.

At first, private equity came only from **large investors** wanting long-term gains.

⬇

But in the 1980s, smaller investors used **leveraging and debt** to buy companies.

⬇

This type of private equity requires high **short-term profit** (to service debts).

⬇

Long-term opportunities are likely to be overlooked in favor of short-term profit.

⬇

As the role of private equity has grown, so have the risks it poses.

Some economists believe that "private equity" is misnamed, since it is a model based on debt, not equity (the value of assets owned outright by an individual or company). Private equity involves "leveraging" a balance sheet by loading debt onto the business. This is similar to the controversial practice of "leveraged buy-outs" (LBO), in which a company is acquired using a high percentage of borrowed funds, loading it with a high level of debt.

Such levels of debt pose inherent risk, as US politician Jack Reed highlighted. Pressure on managers increases—good profits are necessary in order to minimize interest charges on the company's debt. The theory is that this forces managers to perform better, but critics claim that a company run on the private-equity model is likely to maximize short-term profit at the cost of long-term business growth.

Less pressure, more focus
To its supporters, the main strength of the private-equity model is in what it removes. First, it removes the regular profit pressure from shareholders that is faced by bosses of a publicly traded company. For

See also: Beating the odds at start-up 20–21 ▪ Who bears the risk? 138–45 ▪ Leverage and excess risk 150–51 ▪ Balancing long- versus short-termism 190–91

example, in 2012, the US department-store chain JC Penney was given a facelift and a new, more upmarket strategy. A sharp downturn in sales forced a quick rethink, including firing the recently hired CEO. Short-term underperformance is unacceptable to a public company, and can even attract the attention of private-equity investors seeking new acquisitions.

The second strength of the private-equity model is said to be the focus it provides. The boards of publicly traded companies often direct a diverse range of businesses. For example, in 2012, the Sumitomo Corporation of Japan sold a 50 percent stake in its Jupiter Shopping Channel subsidiary to US private-equity group Bain Capital. This effectively separated Jupiter from Sumitomo, ensuring that the Jupiter directors could focus on just one area of business. This enabled them to play a more hands-on role in

Jupiter Shopping Channel is Japan's most popular television shopping company. Now 50 percent privately owned, it benefits from an increased focus on call-center efficiency.

decisions and strategy. In the long term, there are two critical questions about private equity: does it produce a better profit performance? And is it better for the long-term success of the business, taking into account innovation, staff commitment, and customer satisfaction?

In 2013, a combined study by three UK universities found that a company's performance falls after being subject to a private-equity buyout, based on profits and employment levels. The research showed that four years after a private-equity purchase, revenue per employee rose from $190,000 to $252,000, while in a control group it increased from $190,000 to $295,000. However, other studies have suggested the opposite—that private equity boosts profits—so the research is inconclusive.

It might seem that when "private equity" is used as a term to describe debt-fueled growth, years of success can be followed by spectacular losses. However, the majority of companies making private-equity purchases are institutional investors, who want to invest large sums of money over long periods. ▪

Alec Gores

Perhaps the richest private-equity businessman in the world, Alec Gores's personal fortune was estimated at $1.9 billion in 2013. Gores was born in Israel in 1953 to a Greek father and Lebanese mother. He emigrated to the US in 1968, where he attended high school in Michigan.

After earning a degree in computer studies from Western Michigan University, he founded a computer retail business (Executive Business Systems) selling computers from his basement in 1978. Within seven years, he employed more than 200 people. Gores sold the company for $2 million at the age of 33 and used the capital to start the Gores Group in 1987.

The Gores Group private-equity fund specialized in acquiring and operating undervalued and under-performing noncore businesses from major corporations, and turning them into profitable concerns. These included loss-making divisions from large companies, including Mattel and Hewlett-Packard. Since its founding, the company has acquired more than 80 businesses.

ASSIGN COSTS ACCORDING TO THE RESOURCES CONSUMED
ACTIVITY-BASED COSTING

IN CONTEXT

FOCUS
Costs and efficiency

KEY DATES
1911 F. W. Taylor—one of the first management "gurus"—writes *The Principles of Scientific Management*. In it, he suggests methods for creating an accurate costing model.

1971 US professor George Staubus writes *Activity Costing and Input-Output Accounting*. His book encourages interest in activity-based costing among US manufacturers.

1987 US business experts Robert Kaplan and Robin Cooper define activity-based costing in their book, *Accounting and Management*.

C ost accounting seeks to determine a company's costs of production by measuring direct costs (such as raw materials) and adding an estimate of overhead or fixed costs (such as utilities). According to Professor David Myddelton of Cranfield School of Management in the UK, the inherent inaccuracy of this method often means that companies know far less than they

Activity-based accounting calculates the **actual overhead cost** of products and services.

⬇

These are exact, so the company is able to calculate **accurate unit costs**.

⬇

This accuracy allows the company to make **good decisions** about how best to use resources.

⬇

Assign costs according to the resources consumed.

See also: Play by the rules 120–23 ▪ Profit versus cash flow 152–53 ▪ Good and bad strategy 184–85 ▪ The value chain 216–17 ▪ Product portfolio 250–55 ▪ Benefitting from "big data" 316–17

should about their costs. They may be relatively clear about direct costs, but vague about the overhead costs that should be attributed to specific products. The commercial consequence of this is that a business may allocate marketing spending to a product that is not very profitable. In the long run, a business that makes wrong decisions like this will struggle to keep up with its rivals.

Activity-based accounting

Ideally, an accounting system measures every aspect of every transaction and decision related to a particular product or service. The most effective way of achieving this is through activity-based costing. Whereas traditional accounting systems estimate the overheads (perhaps by assuming that every unit produced at a factory should have the same share of the total overhead bill), activity-based costing is much more precise: it breaks down the overhead costs to find out which activities create which costs. This allows the company to realize

that the cost of making a chocolate product, for example, is not "about 65 cents," but exactly "59 cents."

This level of accuracy tends to be especially important when considering nonstandard products, such as the completion of a special order of merchandise for the Brazil Olympics in 2016. Activity-based costing might show that the costs associated with this special order are higher than they would be for standard products. This would help the business to set the right prices for the Olympic items.

To perform effective activity-based costing, a company needs to: first, identify all the direct and indirect activities and resources; second, determine the costs per indirect activity; and third, identify the "cost drivers" for each activity. A cost driver is a factor that influences or creates costs. For example, a bank teller has many activities—when measuring the cost driver of an activity such as handling incoming checks, the bank should figure out how long the teller spends on this task alone. From these three

> Keeping of costs with a reasonable degree of accuracy can be made a matter of very great profit to the company.
> **F. W. Taylor**

calculations, a company can calculate the total direct and indirect costs for a product or service. By dividing these costs by the quantity produced, an accurate unit cost can be obtained. The company can then establish reliable break-even points, identify the products with the profit margins that make them worth backing (with advertising support, perhaps), and allow clear comparisons for making sound investment decisions. ■

Frederick Winslow Taylor

Born in 1856 in Philadelphia, PA, F. W. Taylor trained as a mechanical engineer. He later became famous for his study of "Scientific Management," which was based on the idea that effective management is a science with clearly defined laws. Taylor was also known as the "father" of cost accounting.

In the late 19th century, he established new accounting systems involving the "monthly determination of unit costs." He highlighted the value of cost data as information that managers could use to set prices and decide what to produce. His belief was that if accounting information is to be valuable, it must be useful, timely, and formed into comparable statements, so that progress (or decline) can be identified quickly. F. W. Taylor died of pneumonia in 1915 at 59.

Key works

1911 *The Principles of Scientific Management*
1919 *Two Papers on Scientific Management: A Piece-rate System and Notes on Belting*

WORKI A VISION
STRATEGY AND OPERATIONS

G WITH

In Lewis Carroll's *Alice in Wonderland* the Cheshire cat tells Alice that if you don't know where you are going, "it doesn't matter which way you go." This is a trap that businesses must avoid—the starting point for any new venture is having a goal and there must be a clear strategy as to how to get there. It is also essential to have a vision of what success will be like once that goal has been reached. This vision must be shared and understood by everyone so that the company has a common objective.

Following a vision

Making decisions about a good business strategy starts with critical analysis, such as SWOT analysis,

Determine that the thing can and shall be done, and then we shall find the way.
Abraham Lincoln
US former president (1809–65)

but it should also involve identifying which actions not to take. Strategy is also vital for companies who want to lead the market—most do so by offering a product or service that is either the cheapest or the best. There are numerous business models and theories that can be followed to devise a successful strategy. Leading US strategist Michael Porter, for example, has provided organizations with ideas to help them analyze their market, understand the competitive forces at play, and position themselves for competitive advantage.

Once the board of a company has agreed a strategic direction, it must be prepared to change course if the need arises—but always keeping the original vision in mind. In addition, business leaders should be on continual alert for changes in the external environment. Avoiding complacency is crucial, since the pace of business and change is constantly increasing. Competition is fierce, and companies must innovate if they want to stay at the top and avoid being overtaken or becoming outdated. There are many examples of companies who failed to do this, such as Research in Motion (now known as BlackBerry Ltd), the Canadian technology company whose business suffered

when sales of its BlackBerry smartphones fell sharply—bosses had failed to anticipate Apple's more advanced iPhone.

Keeping a balance

Companies should always balance long- and short-term objectives. The board must keep the long-term vision in sight, but in the short term they need to make decisions that allow them to create enough profit to stay in business—a precarious balancing act, particularly in an uncertain world. It is impossible to predict what the future will bring, so executives often use scenario planning by asking "what if?" questions. Assessing the likelihood of unwanted events does not remove uncertainty, but it does help to avoid complete surprises.

The trend of diversification into unrelated businesses has declined recently, and companies now focus on the core business. Management experts C. K. Prahalad and Gary Hamel argued that a company's ability to consolidate its strengths into core competencies can provide a competitive edge over rivals.

Flexibility

Globalization, technology, and a changing world order have made business far more complex.

  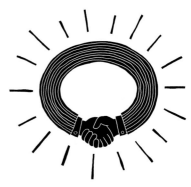

Hierarchical structures tend to be inflexible, so the emphasis today is on nonhierarchical structures, empowering people, and teamwork. Flexible businesses ensure that everyone is involved and can adapt swiftly to change. Such organizations collaborate with external partners, rather than merely transact with them, thus encouraging shared learning. US scholar Peter Senge introduced the concept of the "Learning Organization," whereby a company facilitates the learning of its employees and is able to transform itself on a continual basis. Control by management is replaced by leadership and direction.

Organizations with a learning culture and a shared vision enable people with different functions to work together to develop ideas, make decisions, and create new products and services more quickly. Staff act as a group of entrepreneurs rather than as paid employees. Being able to learn from failure requires a culture in which people are not criticized for mistakes, since this impairs initiative and new ideas.

Companies have to learn not just to deal with chaos but to thrive. In the ever-changing environment of the 21st-century's digital economy, companies have to manage chaos and use it as an opportunity to grow and refresh the business.

Business today

Business may be complex in the modern world, but it has never been more interesting or exciting. Physical size no longer equates with success. The Internet changed everything—now small can be beautiful. Businesses that spring up offering customized products in niche markets are often able to compete effectively in the global economy. Some of today's most successful businesses started with just one person, often in a garage

You have to have vision. It's got to be a vision you articulate clearly and forcefully on every occasion. You can't blow an uncertain trumpet.
Father Theodore Hesburgh
US priest and scholar (1917–2015)

or at a kitchen table. The important thing is that companies should not only offer what people want, but also make it easy for consumers to reach them online.

In addition to this is the overall importance of ethics. "Profit at any cost" is no longer an acceptable maxim. There is growing regulation on financial reporting and on issues such as bribery. Today's consumers are increasingly demanding and discerning: they want to know how raw materials are sourced, how products are made, and how the company impacts the environment. Some companies have policies and procedures in place to help create an ethical culture. In this way, employees know what standards are expected. And yet there are still numerous cases of corporate tax avoidance, price-fixing through collusion, and excessive risk taking. These issues persist because individuals are often motivated by personal gain. High-profile cases include the 2008 collapse of the US financial-services organization Lehman Brothers early in the global economic crisis.

However, many of the examples in this chapter suggest that companies who hold a clear vision and do the right thing, in the right way, are most likely to succeed. ∎

TURN EVERY DISASTER INTO AN OPPORTUNITY

LEARNING FROM FAILURE

IN CONTEXT

FOCUS
Management thinking

KEY DATES
c.560 BCE Chinese philosopher Lao Tzu says that failure is the foundation of success and the means by which it is achieved.

1960s Soichiro Honda, founder of the Honda Motor Company, says that "success can only be achieved through repeated failure and introspection."

1983 Apple Computer Inc. releases the Lisa computer. It is a commercial failure, but plays a vital role in the development of the Apple Mac.

1992 US management professor Sim Sitkin introduces the idea of "intelligent failure" in *Learning Through Failure: The Strategy of Small Losses*.

When a company performs an activity, it **gains experience**.

The experience gained provides **useful feedback**, whether the activity succeeded or not.

The company must analyze the feedback to find out what could be done **differently and better**.

The company implements these **better methods and approaches** in new projects.

Every disaster is an opportunity for learning.

There are many stories of success built on failure: the US inventor Thomas Edison failed to register patents for his ticker tape machine so felt compelled to continue inventing, eventually perfecting the incandescent light bulb. British inventor James Dyson produced more than 5,000 prototypes before he came up with a successful bagless vacuum cleaner. Success for entrepreneurs always involves trial and error, and resilience. US industrialist J. D. Rockefeller, the world's first dollar-billionaire, looked

See also: Managing risk 40–41 ▪ Luck (and how to get lucky) 42 ▪ Reinventing and adapting 52–57 ▪ Creativity and invention 72–73 ▪ Beware the yes-men 74–75 ▪ Thinking outside the box 88–89 ▪ The learning organization 202–07

to "turn every disaster into an opportunity." As the world turned to electric lighting from kerosene oil lamps, his business was threatened. However, he quickly saw the potential of Ford's automobile and realized that oil could just as easily be converted to gasoline as kerosene. His fortune rocketed.

Constant learning

Personal experience is recognized as the way individuals learn, and it is much the same for organizations; they gain knowledge and capability from corporate experience. The pace of change in the global market means that constant improvement has become the norm. The greatest challenge, however, is for companies to recognize failure and learn from it. In order to do this, an organization needs to build a culture in which people are not criticized or penalized for mistakes, but are actively encouraged to gain useful insights from them.

Some companies recognize that it is only through failure that success can be found, and build this principle into their culture. US corporation 3M, for example, allows technical staff to allocate 15 percent of their time to experimenting with ideas, understanding that there will be occasional winners (such as the Post-it Note) along with the repeated failures.

Recognizing error, cutting losses, spotting new opportunities, and changing course is a test of leadership and also sends out a positive message to those who work in the organization. It requires rational, unemotional thought that focuses on the costs and benefits of changing direction.

In the mid-1980s, the Coca-Cola Company decided to replace its original formula with a sweeter product: New Coke. In the US, this prompted consumer protests. The company learned that US consumers were protective of Coca-Cola and felt unhappy about any tampering with the recipe. The CEO quickly reintroduced the original formula as Coke Classic. By responding quickly, he grasped an opportunity for significant publicity; sales soared.

> I have not failed.
> I've just found 10,000 ways that won't work.
> **Thomas A. Edison**
> **US inventor (1847–1931)**

The world's third-largest retailer, Tesco, opened its Fresh & Easy stores in the US in 2007. After six years and $2.27 billion in costs, it admitted failure and pulled out. The stores were unsuccessful because Tesco misjudged the shopping habits of its target customers. Chairman Richard Broadbent said they had learned the value of remaining open-minded about projects. Flexibility, feedback, and fast response are key to finding a new path via failure. ▪

J. D. Rockefeller

John Davidson Rockefeller was born in 1839 in Richford, NY. At age 16, he took a job as an assistant bookkeeper with a commission-merchants business. Just four years later, he set up his own, similar company with a partner: it grossed $450,000 in the first year. He then opened his first oil refinery in 1863, founding Standard Oil.

Rockefeller's business interests made him the richest person in the world at the time, but his practices were unpopular. Realizing the value of effective distribution, he arranged an exclusive deal with the railroad company to transport his oil, putting all his competitors out of business. Standard Oil gained a monopoly position first in Cleveland and then in the US. In 1902 his monopoly in refining, transporting, and marketing oil made headline news and the company was broken up by the US Supreme Court in 1911.

Rockefeller then became the world's greatest philanthropist, giving away around $350 million, and setting up many charitable institutes. He died in 1937, at 97 years old.

IF I HAD ASKED PEOPLE WHAT THEY WANTED, THEY WOULD HAVE SAID FASTER HORSES

LEADING THE MARKET

IN CONTEXT

FOCUS
Market leaders

KEY DATES
1780s British inventor Richard Arkwright devises a complete mechanized system for the production of yarn on an industrialized scale.

1860s US general Nathan Bedford Forrest claims the key to military success is "to get there first with the most men."

1989 Dutch businessman Arie de Geus suggests that a company's only sustainable competitive advantage is its ability to learn faster than its competitors.

1994 Al Ries and Jack Trout publish *The 22 Immutable Laws of Marketing*, in which they outline the advantages of being first to market.

Business logic often dictates: hold back; let someone else go first, incur the costs, and make mistakes. But there are many examples of significant advantages for companies first off the mark.

A company that leads the way into a new market gains a competitive advantage, which might enable it to dominate over the long term. Richard Arkwright, the inventor of the modern factory system, is an example. He devised the first complete mechanized system for the spinning of cotton yarn in the 18th century in Britain. His patents were overturned just five years after they were filed, but his head start ensured that he

See also: Stand out in the market 28–31 ▪ Gaining an edge 32–39 ▪
Balancing long- versus short-termism 190–91 ▪ The value chain 216–17

Consumers do not innovate—they are **happy with a better version** of an existing product.

When a company introduces a **totally new concept**, it creates a new market and is "first" in consumers' minds.

Even if competition arrives, consumers **continue to associate** the first company with the concept.

The company gains the **competitive advantage** of being first to market.

A company that leads the way can **dominate the market**.

Henry Ford

Henry Ford was born in Michigan, US, in 1863. He was always fascinated by machines, and as a child built rudimentary steam engines. He left school at 15 to work on his father's farm, but in 1879 he moved to Detroit to work as an apprentice at the Michigan Car Company, which made railroad cars. He moved home for a while, and did several engineering jobs, before returning to Detroit to work as an engineer for the Edison Illuminating Company.

At the same time, Ford began to make a gasoline-driven car, Thin Lizzie, in his garden shed. He persuaded a group of businessmen to back him, but a lack of experience led to business failure—twice. His third business—the Ford Motor Company—was formed in 1903. Its first car, the Model A, was followed by several other models until the company struck gold with the Model T: "a motorcar for the multitude." By 1925 Ford was producing 10,000 cars every 24 hours, producing 60 percent of the US's total output of cars. His last great innovation—at the age of 69—was the V8 engine. He died in 1947.

continued to dominate the market. The knowledge he had gained enabled him to improve his water-powered spinning frame.

Moving ahead

Henry Ford did not invent the automobile, but he did develop the first affordable car for middle-class Americans at the beginning of the 20th century. Most people had never aspired to owning a car because they were seen as a luxury item for the wealthy, and, as Ford said at the time, most people would have been happier with "a faster horse."

Ford, like Arkwright, succeeded because of a technical edge. His idea was that of mass production, using a moving assembly line to reduce production costs. By 1918, Ford Motor Company was the clear leader in the US automobile market —the Model T made up half of all cars in the US. Ford continued to lead the market until the mid-1930s.

Moving ahead of others in a market involves risk. By taking the initiative—with an innovative product, new technology, lower prices, better distribution, promotional offers, or forceful advertising campaigns—a company creates an opportunity to seize the leadership position. Organizations may seek such an advantage because their strategy and approach is always to lead into »

a new market, such as Gillette, the men's grooming business, with its long-held policy to be the "first to get it right." Some companies choose not to do this; Samsung, for example, aims to be a fast follower, having learned from competitors.

First-mover advantage

Being first to market gives a company "first-mover advantage," which can be long-lasting or short-lived. Long-term advantage brings durable benefits, either by creating an entirely new market, or by improving a company's market share over a long period. Companies that succeed in building long-term advantage often dominate their product categories for many years. Hoover and Post-it Notes, for example, were so successful in their market sectors that their brand names have become generic terms.

Short-term advantage typically occurs because it is based on new technology. Today, innovation is exceptionally fast in many sectors, with increasingly shorter gaps between new introductions and

superior products. Sony is one example of a technology company that led the market for around 20 years, until competition from new technology arrived.

Sony's corporate philosophy is built on "doing things that no one else is willing to do." The business was set up in the ruins of Tokyo after World War II, and the founder Ibuka Masaru was determined to develop leading-edge products and get them to market faster than the competition. This idea became a personal obsession for Ibuka and his successor, Morita Akio.

> It's not the consumers' job to know what they want.
> **Steve Jobs**
> **US former CEO of Apple (1955–2011)**

Yarn spinning was the first activity to become entirely mechanized. The British government restricted export of this technology, maintaining its first-mover advantage for as long as possible.

In 1979 Sony introduced the Sony Walkman, the first portable music-listening device. Just as Ford had changed the way people traveled, Sony changed music-listening habits—and lifestyles. Its launch coincided with the aerobics craze, and millions used the Walkman to add music to their exercise workouts. Between 1987 and 1997, the height of the Walkman's popularity, the number of people starting to walk as exercise increased by 30 percent, according to *Time* magazine. Sony sold 200 million of their portable cassette players, and by 1986 the word "Walkman" had entered the Oxford English Dictionary.

The Walkman evolved from cassette to CD technology, and consumers were happy with their portable music players until 2001, when Apple CEO Steve Jobs said: "The coolest thing about the iPod is that your whole music library fits in your pocket." So began a new industry, based on portable digital music, and dominated by market-leader Apple.

Being first is everything

Leading the way often depends on the product being embraced by "early adopters"—consumers who are willing to pay a price premium to be the first to own something. This happened with the launch of Apple's iPhone in the summer of 2007. Even though the price was reduced a few months after launch, those who had bought at the higher launch price did not resent it due to the cachet of being at the forefront of the latest trends and fashion.

As long as products remain the only one of their kind available, the company that is first to market has a monopoly position; this means it can set the price, establish loyalty, and build a reputation before competitors catch up. When competition does arrive, the first-mover still has the advantage, because it has established itself. This is generally the case even when subsequent products are better than the first.

It's all in the mind

Al Ries and Jack Trout, authors of *The 22 Immutable Laws of Marketing,* developed a theory of why the first company to market can continue to dominate. They proposed that the customer's perception of where a product or service sits in the market is of utmost importance, claiming that "it is better to be first than it is to be better." It is easier to get into the consumers' minds first than to dislodge a product or service from their minds and convince them that your company has a better product. Ries and Trout argued that most marketing stems from the assumption that companies are fighting a product battle rooted in reality. But consumers are not concerned with reality; they make purchases based on perception. "Being first in the mind is everything in marketing. Being first into the marketplace is important only to the extent that it allows you to get into the mind first," say Ries and Trout.

The car in front

Japanese car manufacturer Toyota tries to be first to market, and imparts this message in the minds of consumers with the slogan: "The car in front is a Toyota." Toyota was the first company to introduce a hybrid car—with an engine drawing power from both gas and electricity —to market. Its Prius went on sale in Japan in 1997. Several manufacturers were considering the concept of a hybrid car in the 1980s, but combining an internal combustion engine and an electric motor required significant investment. Despite this, Toyota knew that if they could lead the way, there would be a number of advantages for the company. First, Toyota would gain early-adopter consumers who were looking for an environmentally friendly driving option. Second, creating a hybrid car would increase access to new and existing markets, such as the US, where emissions legislation would favor a hybrid car. Third, it would enhance Toyota's image, because of its clear message of the company's commitment to environmental protection, while at the same time generating excitement about Toyota's new products and the company's innovative capabilities.

The Prius went on sale worldwide in 2001, and more than ten years later Toyota continued to lead the hybrid market. The Prius was the top-selling car in California in 2012, giving Toyota a 21.1 percent market share, compared to closest rival Honda's 12.5 percent. Although other companies, such as Ford and Nissan, have now developed their own hybrid models, Toyota's first move into the market continues to yield benefits in an ever-growing market. ∎

> The key to success for Sony, and to everything in business … is never to follow the others.
> **Ibuka Masaru**
> **Japanese co-founder of Sony**
> **(1908–99)**

The Prius gas-electric hybrid has won a sizable share of the low-emissions market for Toyota. The company was willing to invest significant development funds in return for a market-leading position.

THE MAIN THING TO REMEMBER IS, THE MAIN THING IS THE MAIN THING

PROTECT THE CORE BUSINESS

IN CONTEXT

FOCUS
Business strategy

KEY DATES
1900s–1950s Growth of large, vertically integrated corporations that control and own their assets, requiring complex and multilayered management structures.

1950s–1990s Organizations begin to expand by acquiring unrelated businesses.

1990 Business experts C. K. Prahalad and Gary Hamel introduce the idea of "core competencies" in their *Harvard Business Review* article "The Core Competence of the Corporation".

1995 US companies start to outsource functions to companies "offshore," such as businesses located in India.

2000s Companies begin to sell off unrelated businesses to refocus on their core.

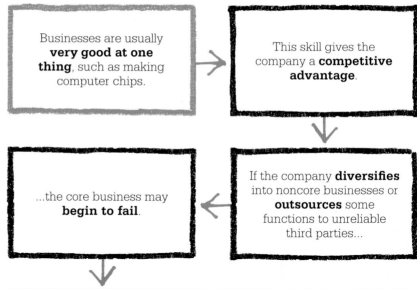

Businesses are usually **very good at one thing**, such as making computer chips.

This skill gives the company a **competitive advantage**.

If the company **diversifies** into noncore businesses or **outsources** some functions to unreliable third parties...

...the core business may **begin to fail**.

The main thing to remember is, the main thing is the main thing.

The expression "Jack of all trades" refers to someone who can do many things, but is not particularly good at any one thing. Unless a company is able to maximize its competitive advantage over its competitors, the same can also be true in the world of business. Success usually relies on using that advantage rather than branching out with something new. The core business is the "main thing" at the heart of a company's operation, and organizations must remember that "the main thing is the main thing," according to Brigadier General Gary Huffman of the US Army. When a company

See also: Study the competition 24–27 ▪ Stand out in the market 28–31 ▪ Gaining an edge 32–39 ▪ Porter's generic strategies 178–83 ▪ Why takeovers disappoint 186–87 ▪ The MABA matrix 192–93

is struggling to win sales for its core product, it may be tempting to consider diversifying, but this often ends up being a distraction.

During the second half of the 20th century, there was a trend for companies to acquire unrelated businesses. Gillette, a leader in razors, bought PaperMate pens; Dalgety, which made Homepride Flour, acquired a pig-breeding company; and Cadbury, best known for candy, took control of Schweppes beverage business. The trend began to turn in 2003, when McDonald's began to sell off diverse restaurant chains it had acquired, including a pizza brand purchased during the 1990s. This was because it wanted to focus on its core business: McDonald's. Other companies soon began to divest unrelated businesses to protect the core.

Understanding the core

The theory behind selling secondary interests is that the business should focus its energy and resources on what it is good at. This idea was taken further during the 1990s, when some companies decided to "outsource"—contracting a business activity to an outside company—peripheral activities that they had previously performed internally. The trend of outsourcing gathered momentum as companies realized they could cut their business back to the core and achieve leaner, more efficient, cost-effective operations.

For example, a company that manufactures refrigerators may decide that its core business is simply the design, manufacture, and marketing of those refrigerators. It might outsource delivery (which it sees as not adding value), and its information technology (IT) needs (which it views as a specialized function). In the short term, handing over these activities to a third party would seem to make sense. But in the long term, it could be a mistake. Delivery might be an important part of customers' perceptions of the product, and the business could suffer if the outsourced delivery company is unreliable. Similarly, IT is increasingly integral to the success of a business, both for

McDonald's acquired several food chains, such as Donatos Pizzeria, during the 1990s in an attempt to enter new market sectors. In 2003, it sold them to refocus on its core business—burgers.

internal functions and customer interaction. Outsourcing is useful for lesser functions, but only as long as it works well—if it fails, it can adversely affect the core business.

Whenever companies outsource or acquire a separate business to take over a peripheral function, it is vital that management take steps to protect the "main thing." Any secondary units or third parties must be fully aligned with the vision and values of the organization. ▪

If you cannot be the best in the world at your core business, then your core business absolutely cannot form the basis of a great company.
Jim Collins
US business expert (1958–)

Core competencies

An organization has a particular set of diverse production skills and individual technologies. These are its core competencies, according to business experts C. K. Prahalad and Gary Hamel. Unlike physical assets, which inevitably deteriorate over time, competencies become enhanced, because they are applied and shared. They are strengthened by involvement, communication, and a shared commitment to working across an organization's boundaries.

Prahalad and Hamel describe the corporation as a tree. Its roots are its unique competencies, and from these roots grow the organization's core products, which in turn nourish separate business units. From these business units come the end products. The idea of core competencies can be used to identify those things within an organization that are not "at the core," which might be a distraction, consuming a company's valuable resources.

YOU DON'T NEED A HUGE COMPANY JUST A COMPUTER AND A PART-TIME PERSON

SMALL IS BEAUTIFUL

IN CONTEXT

FOCUS
Internet business

KEY DATES
1974 US computer scientists Vent Cerf and Bob Kahn design the first Transmission Control Program, enabling computers to talk to each other.

1977 The first electronic mail ("email") is sent, via the US Department of Defense's ARPANET.

1991 The World Wide Web (WWW), the first widely accessible system to share data files via the Internet, is released by Tim Berners-Lee.

1993 Netscape launches Mosaic, the first commercial Internet browser.

2013 More than two million third-party sellers use Amazon to reach their customers.

When British computer scientist Tim Berners-Lee harnessed the Internet to develop the World Wide Web, he was simply creating a way of sharing information. It was not viewed as a money-making exercise. However, the Internet's disruptive power soon became clear: it would change business and our way of life, enabling commerce to be conducted by a profusion of individuals and organizations.

Early search engines were invented as an increasing amount of information became available on the web. Larry Page and Sergey Brin, two US computer science students, designed a search engine that could quickly search all the available documents and generate highly relevant results. In September 1998 they set up a work space in a friend's garage and opened a bank account in the name of Google Inc. The soon-to-be giant company began, as Page said, with no more than "a computer and a part-time person."

Within a year Google had 40 employees, and in June 2000 announced its first billion-URL index, making it officially the world's largest search engine. By 2013, Google employed 30,000 people worldwide, of whom around 53 percent worked in research and development, which may explain the company's phenomenal growth.

Doing business on the web

As two-way communication over the Internet became a reality during the 1990s, organizations began to see the potential offered by the new e-commerce platform. The first books were sold online in 1992, and in 1994 Pizza Hut in Santa Cruz, California enabled people to order a pizza delivery via the Internet.

The idea of online selling took off in 1995 when Jeff Bezos dispatched the first book sold by Amazon.com, then located in his Seattle garage. Around the same time, software programmer Pierre Omidyar was starting a simple website called AuctionWeb from his San Jose living room. The first product he posted for sale was a broken laser pointer. It sold for $14.83. Omidyar recognized the Internet's power to reach individual customers, anywhere in the world, when he checked whether the buyer

Larry Page

Born in 1973 in Michigan, Lawrence (Larry) Page was exposed to computer technology at an early age; his father was a pioneer in computer science and his mother taught computer programming. Page studied engineering at the University of Michigan and then completed a Masters in computer engineering at Stanford University.

On his first visit to the campus, Page was shown around by fellow postgraduate student Sergey Brin, who would later be the co-founder of Google. During a research project in 1997, Page and Brin

created a search engine called BackRub, which operated on Stanford servers until it outgrew their capacity. The pair worked together on a bigger and better version, which they named Google after the mathematical term "Googol"—the number 1 followed by 100 zeros. Page and Brin were jointly awarded the Marconi Prize in 2004, and Page was elected to the US National Academy of Engineering in 2004. Today Google is the world's most popular search engine, handling more than 5 billion search queries every day.

See also: Beating the odds at start-up 20–21 ▪ How fast to grow 44–45 ▪ The weightless start-up 62–63 ▪ Creativity and invention 72–73 ▪ The long tail 212–13 ▪ M-commerce 276–77 ▪ Feedback and innovation 312–13

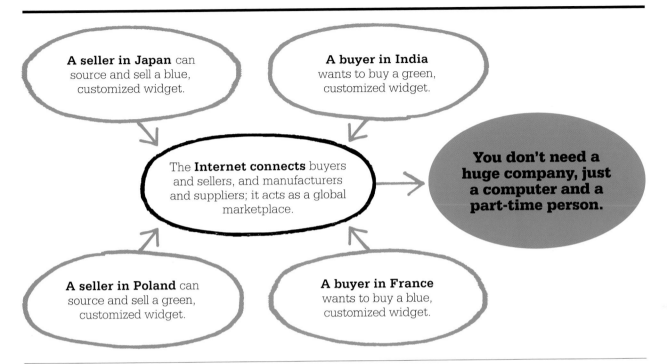

A seller in Japan can source and sell a blue, customized widget.

A buyer in India wants to buy a green, customized widget.

The **Internet connects** buyers and sellers, and manufacturers and suppliers; it acts as a global marketplace.

You don't need a huge company, just a computer and a part-time person.

A seller in Poland can source and sell a green, customized widget.

A buyer in France wants to buy a blue, customized widget.

understood that the pointer was broken. The buyer assured him that he was a collector of broken laser pointers. One year later, with two full-time employees, the soon-to-be-renamed eBay sold goods to the value of $7.2 million. By acting as an auction service, eBay sees itself as in the business of linking users, not selling them things.

Starting small

Both eBay and Amazon started small, and their platforms have empowered countless other small businesses around the world. Their pioneering use of the Internet changed the way that businesses and consumers interact, putting buyers and sellers in touch with one another in a way that had not been possible before. Amazon and eBay demonstrate the power of the idea that "small is beautiful." Anyone can sell products from their platforms, from individuals selling unique items to "power sellers" who set up virtual stores, either within the platform or linked to it. In the online marketplace the same opportunities exist for every business, whether large or small.

Before the existence of the Internet, if someone wanted to sell their products, a physical presence was necessary: a store, market stall, or going door-to-door. Generally, the bigger the presence, the more successful the business. Success »

In the pre-Internet age, vast numbers of people were often necessary for administration. The combined power of computing and the Internet changed organizational structures forever.

A business succeeds not because it is long established or because it is big, but because there are men and women in it who live it, sleep it, dream it.
J. W. Marriott
US businessman (1932–)

In the digital, networked economy, people can work anywhere, at any time. This shift in working habits is changing the face of business environments and staff distribution.

in retail, for example, traditionally relied on a prominent store on a town's main street, where the retailer could attract the largest number of customers through the door. Companies often depended on a large sales force, who visited customers to build relationships. Businesses held significant amounts of stock in warehouses, and had a large office staff to take phone calls and handle paperwork. That has all changed.

Consumers can now find retailers large or small via the Internet from a laptop, smartphone, or tablet. The physical scale of a business no longer correlates with success. Many businesses no longer need large offices. Paperwork has diminished, while online communication—email, instant messaging, and social media —allows sole-traders and employed people alike to work remotely, from home, anywhere in the world.

Large companies used to be more competitive than small companies because they had better economies of scale (the cost advantages that enterprises obtain due to size). When computers were first developed, this continued to be true, because large, costly servers were required for file storage.

Today, however, the Internet is free and technology prices are relatively inexpensive. Cloud computing— whereby organizations share virtual infrastructure, software, and storage —has enabled small businesses to have access to the power of integrated networks and computing at a very low cost, and with no use of physical space.

Just as scale is no barrier to success, neither is geography. A small business can now reach customers all over the world just as effectively as a large one. It is possible to live on one side of the globe and sell items from an entirely different continent. The introduction of PayPal in 2000 allowed simple payment and money transfers in a wide range of currencies via the Internet, furthering opportunities for small companies to operate as global e-commerce businesses.

Competing with giants

With an increasing choice of goods and services available online for consumers, small businesses must offer something more than the giants in order to compete. Price is critical because consumers can easily compare prices online. But it is not the only factor that affects an online

purchase; cost and speed of delivery are critical too. Free shipping and free returns are attractive incentives to purchase. Time of delivery is also important: retailers who can offer one-hour time slots and deliver beyond the traditional working day gain a competitive edge. Customer service is more important than ever.

Feedback is king

Whatever the goods being sold, they must be of the quality stated, because feedback on the Internet can have a powerful effect on the market. For hotels and restaurants, feedback and ratings by customers are now the norm, and many consumers base their purchasing decisions on other people's comments. A well-run, small, family-owned hotel, which focuses on excellent service and delighting its guests, can build a reputation as the number one place to stay in a particular town—ahead of a big chain hotel—because of review websites such as Trip Advisor.

The Internet is really about highly specialized information, highly specialized targeting.
Eric Schmidt
US former CEO of Google
(1955–)

> The Web does not just connect machines, it connects people.

Sir Tim Berners-Lee
UK inventor of the World
Wide Web (1955–)

Organizations recognize the power of feedback and often encourage customers to post comments online. Fashion retailers, furniture manufacturers, and retail stores—even dental and medical practices—invite customers to comment on and share their experiences. Small companies benefit from this trend, since their personal service is more likely to generate positive reviews.

A more personal service

The Internet has removed the "middle man" from many areas of business. The travel industry is one example, since travelers can now book direct with airlines. Another example is the book industry, where authors can self-publish via the Internet, taking their fiction straight to readers without the need for literary agents or big publishing houses. The runaway success *Fifty Shades of Grey* by E.L. James began life as a free ebook on the Internet.

Previously, mass production and limited space in brick-and-mortar stores dictated the range of goods a business could stock. Now, small businesses selling niche products or services can thrive because the Internet connects them to consumers looking for exactly these

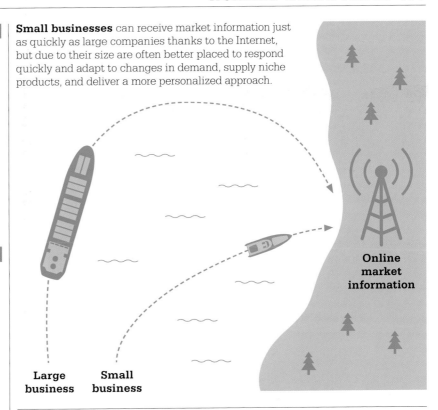

Small businesses can receive market information just as quickly as large companies thanks to the Internet, but due to their size are often better placed to respond quickly and adapt to changes in demand, supply niche products, and deliver a more personalized approach.

Large business
Small business
Online market information

offerings. People wanting to buy a spare part for an old car, or a rare edition of a book, can search and buy from anywhere in the world.

Small companies can also thrive through customization. Digital methods of production and online retailing enable narrowly targeted goods and services to be profitable. Customized production of a single item is possible—from personalized books, mugs, and clothing to customized cars, furniture, and even houses, which can be designed and tailored online.

Customers can get exactly the item they want, delivered at the right time and at a price they are willing to pay. Websites offering personalized printed items are small businesses with software that allows consumers to approve the final design and send it straight to print, so employees are only needed for packing and shipping.

Although small businesses can thrive on the Internet through their own websites, many now use portal websites as a "store window" to reach a wider audience. The British company Not on the High Street is one such portal. Started by two working mothers as a marketplace for personalized creative items, it launched in 2006 with 100 small businesses (many of them women working at home). In 2013, the business had grown to include 1,600 partners and had a turnover of more than $23 million.

Not on the High Street is successful because it combines the idea of personalized products with an awareness of the producer, giving buyers the chance to select a local maker. Although it promotes global trade, the Internet can enable a very personal form of communication between buyer and seller, regardless of size or scale. ∎

DON'T GET CAUGHT IN THE MIDDLE

PORTER'S GENERIC STRATEGIES

IN CONTEXT

FOCUS
Business strategy

KEY DATES
1776 UK economist Adam Smith introduces the concept of comparative advantage, where one party has the ability to produce a particular good or service at a lower marginal cost than another.

1960 US economist Theodore Levitt says that rather than finding a customer for their existing product, businesses should find out what customers want, and produce it for them.

1985 Michael Porter publishes *Competitive Advantage*.

2005 Professors W. Chan Kim and Renée Mauborgne recommend a "blue ocean" strategy for generating growth and profits, in which new demand is created in an uncontested market space.

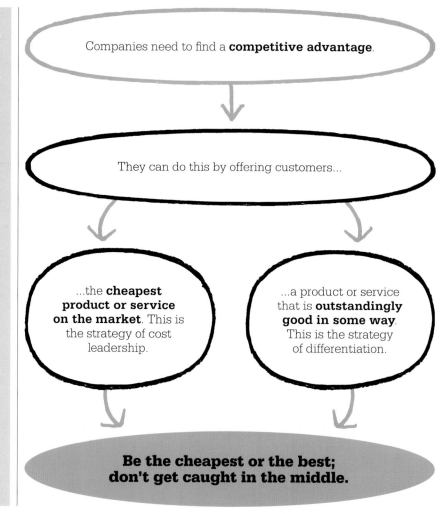

Companies need to find a **competitive advantage**.

They can do this by offering customers...

...the **cheapest product or service on the market**. This is the strategy of cost leadership.

...a product or service that is **outstandingly good in some way**. This is the strategy of differentiation.

Be the cheapest or the best; don't get caught in the middle.

Consumers have choice. And different consumers will choose differently—some like to pay the most for the luxurious option, while others will always opt for the cheapest. Companies recognize this and pitch their business at a particular group of consumers. This is because it is never wise for a company to be caught between groups of customers.

Harvard Business School professor Michael Porter proposed "generic strategies" for gaining competitive advantage, explaining his idea in *Competitive Advantage: Creating and Sustaining Superior Performance* (1985). Porter used a four-celled matrix to represent the four different generic strategies in his theory.

Companies generally choose between two generic strategies: either "cost leadership," where they aim to be the cheapest in the market; or "differentiation," where they create unique products or services. However, there is another element that can be added to these two generic strategies: a company might choose to pursue a "focus strategy," offering a specialized service in a niche market. This position can be applied to both of the initial generic strategies, resulting in a cost-focus strategy (where the company aims to be cheapest within a niche market) or a differentiation-focus strategy (where the company offers unique products or services within a niche market).

Cost-leadership strategy
Companies pursuing a cost-leadership strategy have two options. They can choose to sell products at average industry prices

See also: Gaining an edge 32–39 ▪ Leading the market 166–69 ▪ Good and bad strategy 184–85 ▪ The MABA matrix 192–93 ▪ Porter's five forces 212–15 ▪ The value chain 216–17

> Once stuck in the middle, it usually takes time and sustained effort to extricate the company from this unenviable position.
> **Michael Porter**

to earn a greater margin than competitors; or sell at below industry prices to gain more market share. Some supermarkets, such as German retailer Aldi and UK company Tesco, take the low-price approach to cost leadership. They achieve this by purchasing large volumes from close-relationship suppliers, and offer the customer "deep discounts." Their slogans— Tesco's "Every little helps" and Aldi's "Like brands, only cheaper"—convey their drive to pass savings on to the consumer.

Porter suggests that to pursue a cost-leadership strategy, a company has to be the leader in terms of cost in their industry or market, rather than be among a group of low-cost producers, because this makes them vulnerable. With fierce competition there is always the chance for other low-cost producers to reduce prices, and so take market share. Companies that choose cost

Bose Systems is an audio specialist that pursues a differentiation strategy. It distinguishes itself from competitors through research and development, which results in innovative technology.

leadership have to be confident that they can both achieve the number one position, and also maintain it. Several requirements must be met to achieve this, including: a low cost base (across labor, materials, and facilities); efficient technology; efficient purchasing; well-organized and cost-effective distribution; and access to capital for any required investment, to keep costs down.

These low-cost principles are not exclusive to any one company, however, and the risk is that they are easily replicated. Companies pursuing a cost-leadership strategy have to build in continuous improvement in all their processes to ensure the company can keep costs below those of other competitors.

Differentiation strategy

A company that pursues a differentiation strategy has to make markedly different products or services from competitors, so they have greater appeal to consumers.

This strategy is more appropriate in markets where products are not price sensitive, and customers' needs are typically underserved. It also means being able to satisfy those needs in ways that are difficult to copy.

Bose Systems is a company that pursues a differentiation strategy. A privately owned US audio electronics company, it consistently reinvests profits to fund innovation. Customer-focused research has led to Bose's dominant position; their noise-canceling headphones and stylish speakers have become aspirational items.

The approach to differentiation will vary according to the products and services, and the nature of the particular industry, but typically involves additional features and functionality, enhanced durability, and better customer service. Companies that choose to pursue this strategy require certain fundamentals in place, including »

good research and development, an innovative culture, and the ability to deliver consistently high-quality products or services. This needs to be supported by effective marketing, so that the differentiation is positioned and communicated to customers. Brand image is integral, and is often strengthened by the nature of the differentiation.

Focus strategy

Companies pursuing a focus strategy choose a particular niche market. They have to understand the dynamics of that market and the unique needs of customers within it, and then develop either low-cost or well-specified products or services. They also tend to serve their customers well, and so build strong brand loyalty. This makes their particular market segment less attractive to potential new entrants.

Ferrari is an example of a company in a niche market that has chosen to differentiate itself. The company targets the limited high-performance sports-car segment, and its cars are differentiated through high-spec design, high-performance, and the company's Grand Prix association.

Whichever focus a company chooses, it must do so on the basis that it can successfully compete on the strength of a particular ability or competence that will help it in its chosen market niche. If the company aims for cost leadership in a niche market, for example, it has to be based on distinctive relationships that have been developed with specialized suppliers. If the company goes for differentiation in a niche market, on the other hand, it has to be on the strength of a deep understanding of customer needs. However, a company that chooses to focus on a small market segment because it is too small to serve the larger market risks being sidelined by bigger companies with distinctive abilities, which enable them to better position their offerings.

Airline strategies

The airline industry illustrates Porter's idea. Consumers have a choice when they book an airline ticket. They can choose between a no-frills airline or a more expensive operator offering better service, quality, and comfort. There may also be a third option: a small airline that

Every company competing in an industry has a competitive strategy, whether explicit or implicit.
Michael Porter

offers only a few routes. Airlines tend to focus on a particular group of travelers as an effective way of achieving competitive advantage in a crowded market, for example by offering discounted travel or a more luxurious traveling experience.

Low-cost, Ireland-based airline Ryanair has championed the idea of cost leadership, and describes itself as "Europe's only ultralow cost carrier." The notion of a low-cost airline was pioneered by Texas-based Southwest Airlines, and Ryanair followed with similar principles: use a single plane type to keep costs down, constantly review overheads, turn aircraft around as quickly as possible, and do not offer a loyalty plan.

Ryanair bought 100 Boeing 737-800 passenger jets at a significant discount in 2002. Starting with newer, more fuel-efficient planes than many rivals, Ryanair could afford to fill its planes with passengers buying low-price tickets. However, Ryanair could make a profit because passengers would also spend money on areas such as on-board food and hotel reservations.

Ryanair is able to increase profits year after year since it continually looks for ways to keep costs down and charge customers for extras.

		Lowest cost	Markedly different
COMPETITIVE SCOPE	**Large markets**	Cost leadership	Differentiation
	Niche markets	Cost focus	Differentiation focus

SOURCE OF COMPETITIVE ADVANTAGE

Porter's generic business strategies fall within two basic categories: lowest cost or marked differentiation. Companies can choose between these approaches whether they are small or large, and whether they are operating in broad target markets, or niche ones.

Singapore Airlines' customer service ethic is personified by "The Singapore Girl," who portrays the idea of Asian hospitality. Her image has become a successful brand icon.

These include being the first airline to implement baggage charges; working to eliminate the need for check-in desks (by offering online check-in facilities); and charging for options such as seat reservation and priority boarding. This consistent search for new ways to transform costs is the essence of the cost-leadership strategy. In the 12 months ending March 31, 2013, Ryanair transported nearly 80 million passengers and announced record profits of $753 million, despite a rise in fuel costs.

Singapore Airlines (SIA) by contrast, pursues a differentiation strategy. The brand's major drivers are groundbreaking technology, innovation, quality, and excellent customer service. It maintains the youngest fleet of aircraft among major air carriers, and keeps to a stringent policy of replacing older aircraft with newer, better models. SIA has always been first to take delivery of new aircraft types.

Singapore Airlines recognizes that innovation is short-lived in the airline industry. New features and ideas can easily be copied by other airlines, so it continues to invest heavily in innovation and technology as an integral part of achieving its differentiation strategy. The airline runs a comprehensive and rigorous training program for cabin- and flight-crew to ensure the customer's in-flight experience is consistently excellent. The success of its brand strategy and its entire positioning around service excellence mean that customers are more than happy to pay a premium price.

Porter's generic business strategies can be used by any company to achieve a competitive advantage. However, the competitive environment consists of more than just present rivals; changes in the industry and environment add to a constantly changing business context. For this reason, strategy choice must be regularly reviewed and checked. ∎

Ben & Jerry's ice cream is now part of the Unilever brand, but continues to use the differentiation strategy it adopted to become a market leader.

Ice cream with a difference

Quirky flavor names—such as Imagine Whirled Peace, Chubby Hubby, and Brownie Chew Gooder—set Ben & Jerry's ice creams apart. Ben Cohen and Jerry Greenfield started the company in 1978 and wanted it to be alternative. According to Jerry, "if it's not fun, why do it?" Ben claims to have no sense of taste, so he relied on texture (what he called "mouth feel")—big chunks of added ingredients such as fruit, chocolate, or cookies therefore became the brand's signature.

Consumers are prepared to pay a premium price because of the ice cream's all-natural, high-quality ingredients and innovative flavors—months of research go into perfecting the taste. The company's strategy to differentiate itself from the competition extends beyond the product. The organization is active in social campaigns such as gay marriage, buys only from fair-trade suppliers, and considers environmental aspects in production and delivery.

THE ESSENCE OF STRATEGY IS CHOOSING WHAT NOT TO DO
GOOD AND BAD STRATEGY

IN CONTEXT

FOCUS
Strategic thinking

KEY DATES
1960s Strategic planning grows in popularity, and is enthusiastically adopted in the new field of management consultancy.

1962 Alfred Chandler's *Strategy and Structure* sets out a model in which a company's structure matches its strategy, not vice versa.

1985 Michael Porter's *Competitive Advantage* redefines business thinking on competition, repopularizing the ailing field of strategic thinking in the process.

1990s/2000s Strategy is increasingly practiced as a continuous process by all in a business, not just by those at boardroom level. Nokia says that strategy should be "a daily part of a manager's activity."

Strategy is a concept with its roots in military history, when army generals planned campaigns of war. Today, it is an overused and often misunderstood word in business theory. Put simply, strategy is the way a business gets from where it is to where it wants to be; it involves identifying the choices that must be made to overcome the obstacles that lie in the way. Often, choosing what not to do is as important as what to do. Strategy guru Michael Porter first drew attention to this in 1985, then specifically explored it in his 1996 article "What is Strategy?"

For businesses, it is just as possible to follow bad strategy as good. Richard Rumelt's *Good Strategy/Bad Strategy* (2012) explained that good strategy should emerge out of an analysis of the company itself, and its goals. SWOT analysis (strengths, weaknesses, opportunities, and threats) is one of the most popular systems for such audits, and to be effective it should be conducted among middle managers and people across the organization, not just those at the top. Good strategy requires analysis of the competition and any threats to the organization,

Kodak failed to recognize that film-based photography was effectively "what not to do." Choosing to move away from this area could have made Kodak a market leader in digital technology.

and may involve painful decisions. It should result in a strategy based on clear goals that capitalizes on the company's strengths and can be flexible if external factors change.

Bad strategy often goes hand in hand with setting a simplistic goal or vision. Leaders in organizations may use powerful rhetoric about "winning" to motivate staff, but empty goals are easy to set—formulating the strategy required to achieve them is much more difficult. Executives bent on pursuing a bad strategy will ignore problems and

See also: Protect the core business 170–71 ▪ Avoiding complacency 194–201 ▪ Porter's five forces 212–15 ▪ The value chain 216–17

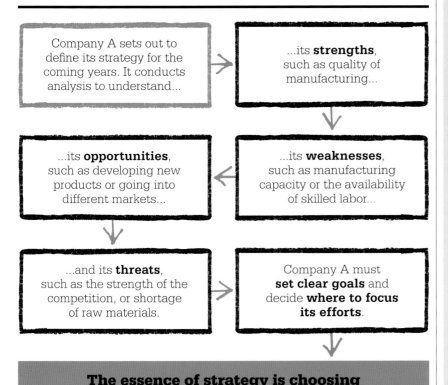

Company A sets out to define its strategy for the coming years. It conducts analysis to understand...

...its **strengths**, such as quality of manufacturing...

...its **weaknesses**, such as manufacturing capacity or the availability of skilled labor...

...its **opportunities**, such as developing new products or going into different markets...

...and its **threats**, such as the strength of the competition, or shortage of raw materials.

Company A must **set clear goals** and decide **where to focus its efforts**.

The essence of strategy is choosing what not to do.

Richard Rumelt

Professor Richard Rumelt (1942–) studied electrical engineering at the University of California, Berkeley, before going on to receive a doctorate in business administration from Harvard Business School in 1972. He worked as a systems engineer at NASA's Jet Propulsion Laboratories while also serving on the faculty of Harvard Business School. In 1976 he joined the Anderson School of Management at the University of California, where he has remained ever since, rising to become Professor of Business and Society. From 1993 to 1996 he taught at INSEAD, the leading French business school at Fontainebleau, near Paris. Rumelt also works as a consultant to several companies and governments.

Key works

1982 *Diversity and Profitability*
1991 *How Much Does Industry Matter?*
2012 *Good Strategy/Bad Strategy*

be blinded to the choices available. Rather than making tough decisions, they will try to accommodate a multitude of conflicting demands and interests to stick to a plan. Managers in these circumstances risk following old ideas and paths that no longer work, rather than leading with new ones.

Film is dead

The demise of Kodak is a prime example of a company following bad strategy. Founded in 1890, by the 1970s Kodak was the US market leader in the photographic sector, with nearly 90 percent of the film and camera market. It was rated as one of the world's top brands. In 1975 Kodak engineers invented the digital camera, but the senior management of Kodak ignored the opportunity presented by this new technology. They believed they were in the chemistry-based film business and were not prepared to "kill the golden goose." Executives failed to see that digital photography would make film redundant and challenge their near-monopoly business. Japanese company Fujifilm, however, recognized the threat and diversified successfully. Kodak began its shift to digital cameras too late, as smartphones and tablets replaced cameras. The senior executives' inability to make the tough decision to change course led to the company being declared bankrupt in 2012. ▪

Good strategy honestly acknowledges the challenges being faced and provides an approach to overcoming them.
Richard Rumelt

SYNERGY AND OTHER LIES
WHY TAKEOVERS DISAPPOINT

Companies have to grow in order to survive. One way to make an organization bigger is to buy (acquire) another and make it part of the original company. Alternatively, two businesses can agree to merge, forming another organization with an entirely new identity. The purpose of an acquisition or merger is often to increase shareholder value beyond the sum of the two companies. These benefits are known as "synergy"; the concept being that one plus one equals three.

The reasons for two businesses joining together might seem compelling. The new, combined company increases sales, market share, and revenue. It should also be a more efficient operation. Bigger companies also enjoy economies of scale: overhead costs are shared and money can be saved from increased buying power. Fixed costs can also be reduced because the combined business needs less staff in functions such as finance, human resources, and marketing, than the two separate entities. Companies' also buy businesses to acquire new technology, reach new markets, or increase distribution.

Corporate divorce
In practice, takeovers and mergers are rarely marriages made in heaven, a fact underlined by Harold Geneen in the books he co-authored in 1997 and 1999 on the pretence of synergy. Mergers can fail to deliver the value promised, with one plus one often equaling less than two. There are many reasons for failure. Hidden

Synergy is the additional value that is created when two business units are joined. A holy grail in business circles, academics Campbell and Goold concluded that "synergy initiatives often fall short of management's expectations".

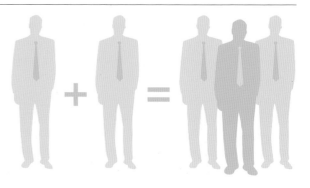

See also: The Greiner curve 58–61 ▪ Organizing teams and talent 80–85 ▪ Organizational culture 104–09 ▪ Protect the core business 170–71

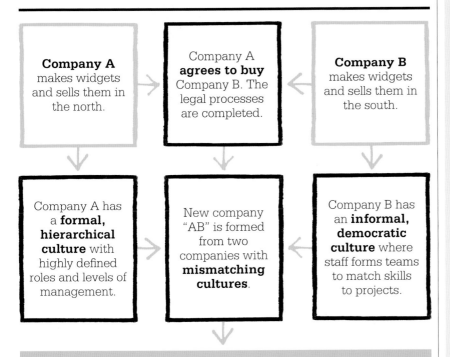

Company A makes widgets and sells them in the north.

Company A agrees to buy Company B. The legal processes are completed.

Company B makes widgets and sells them in the south.

Company A has a **formal, hierarchical culture** with highly defined roles and levels of management.

New company "AB" is formed from two companies with **mismatching cultures**.

Company B has an **informal, democratic culture** where staff forms teams to match skills to projects.

The new company does not deliver synergy. Takeovers disappoint.

Harold Geneen

Harold Geneen was born in Dorset, UK, in 1910, but his parents emigrated soon after his birth and he was raised in the US. He studied accounting at NYU (New York University) and went on to become a highly successful businessman in the US. He is best known as the father of the conglomerate concept, where a large corporation is created from seemingly unrelated businesses. In 1959 he became president and CEO of International Telephone and Telegraph Corporation (ITT), and grew the company from a medium-sized business to a multinational conglomerate. His 18-year tenure included 350 acquisitions and mergers in more than 80 different countries, including Sheraton Hotels in the US, and telecommunications companies in Europe and Brazil. Despite his success and wealth, he was known for his no-nonsense values and plain talking. He died in 1997.

Key works

1997 *The Synergy Myth* (with Brent Bowers)
1999 *Synergy and Other Lies* (with Brent Bowers)

problems might be discovered after the deal is done because of the limitations on sharing commercially sensitive information prior to common ownership. The focus at the time of the deal is often on the event of joining together rather than planning what will happen next. Effective integration requires quick, courageous decision making so that time and momentum are not lost. However, the most common reason for failure is that the two organizations have different approaches and lack synergy.

In 1998, German car producer Daimler-Benz bought US automotive business Chrysler for $38 billion. The logic seemed obvious: create a trans-Atlantic powerhouse that would dominate motor markets. The new company, DaimlerChrysler, was dubbed a "merger of equals." But the reality was a classic culture clash. Daimler was a formal, hierarchical organization, while Chrysler favored a more team-oriented approach. Chrysler operated in a market where low price and catchy design were important; high-end Daimler was focused on quality and luxury.

Chrysler executives felt undermined in the new alliance because Daimler tried to dictate the terms on which the new business should work and to place its people in key positions. The result was a costly corporate divorce with Daimler-Benz selling Chrysler to a private-equity firm for a mere $7 billion in 2007. ▪

THE CHINESE WORD "CRISIS" IS COMPOSED OF TWO CHARACTERS: "DANGER" AND "OPPORTUNITY"

CRISIS MANAGEMENT

IN CONTEXT

FOCUS
Business crises

KEY DATES
1987 Ian Mitroff, Paul Shrivastava, and Firdaus Udwadia publish the paper "Effective Crisis Management."

1988 Shrivastava, Mitroff, Danny Miller, and Anil Miglani say that organizational crisis requires an interdisciplinary approach, using psychological, technological-structural and social-political perspectives.

1995 A. Gonzalez-Herrero and C. Pratt suggest a model for crisis management: diagnosis of impending trouble; decision and actions; implementation of change; and monitoring.

2000s Business continuity planning is introduced to deal with terrorism and major technology failure.

2010s Social media allows a crisis to be publicized rapidly, often to a company's detriment.

Mankind has faced crises throughout history, from natural disasters to man-made calamities. Businesses face similar crises—internal or external events can pose major threats to the organization. Unpredictable in nature, they require quick decision making and action from leaders.

Globalization has increased the complexity of the business world, so an event in one country can affect businesses across the world. Digital, 24/7 communication means that news travels far and fast. The result is that crises may seem to be more prevalent than they were during the predigital age.

Responding to crisis
The random nature of crises means that they can strike anywhere. Typical crises include technological failure; employee actions, from

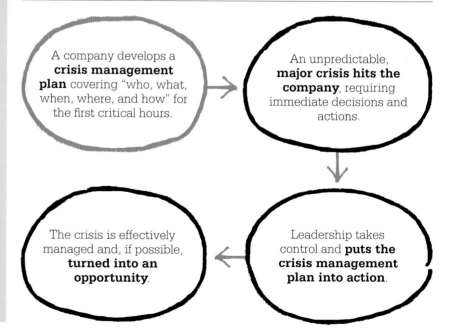

A company develops a **crisis management plan** covering "who, what, when, where, and how" for the first critical hours.

An unpredictable, **major crisis hits the company**, requiring immediate decisions and actions.

Leadership takes control and **puts the crisis management plan into action**.

The crisis is effectively managed and, if possible, **turned into an opportunity**.

See also: Managing risk 40–41 ▪ Hubris and nemesis 100–03 ▪ Learning from failure 164–65 ▪ Contingency planning 210 ▪ Coping with chaos 220–21

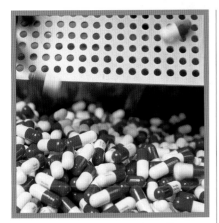

Tylenol was the top pain reliever in the US when it was hit by a crisis: lethally contaminated capsules. Over 30 million bottles were recalled at huge cost, but consumer faith was retained.

walkouts to fraud; sudden supplier loss or rising prices in raw materials; and environmental disasters. Every crisis has the potential to damage a company's profits and reputation. The extent to which it is able to withstand a crisis and limit the damage is determined by its ability to respond fast and appropriately.

Planning and decisions

Effective crisis management involves careful planning, so that if a crisis strikes it can be addressed in a calm, professional way. This involves quickly establishing the "who, what, when, where, and how" of the crisis within the critical first few hours. Any crisis—no matter how small—is newsworthy, so a company's public response must be fast. Public perception affects consumer trust.

Leadership during a crisis is particularly important, since swift, effective decision making is critical. Every company recognizes that if it handles a crisis well, damage can

be minimized and its reputation even enhanced. As president John F Kennedy said, "in Chinese, the word 'crisis' is composed of two characters—one represents danger and one represents opportunity."

Handling a crisis

In 1982, Johnson & Johnson reacted to a crisis effectively when Tylenol pain-relief capsules sold in the Chicago, IL, area had been laced with cyanide. The company recalled the product, stopped advertising, and reintroduced Tylenol in a triple-seal, tamper-resistant package. The public felt reassured by the move, and once again trusted the product.

At around the same time, another US company tried to contain a similar crisis using a very different approach. A woman returned a jar of Gerber Product's baby food to her local supermarket, saying that it contained a shard of glass. Gerber ran laboratory tests and found nothing; the store had lost the shard, and the company decided there was no problem on its production line. However, customers in 30 different states then said they too had found glass in the baby food. The company could find no evidence to support these claims, so announced that they were "being had" by people wanting to file false liability claims. They did not recall any products. Public confidence in the company fell; some states demanded other Gerber products be removed from stores. Although the company's position was evidence-based, it seemed callously indifferent to the welfare of babies. It lost sight of the essential rule in any crisis: always show commitment to the safety and well-being of your consumers. ▪

Effective crisis management is a never-ending process, not an event with a beginning and an end.
**Ian Mitroff,
Paul Shrivastava,
Firdaus Udwadia**

YOU CAN'T GROW LONG-TERM IF YOU CAN'T EAT SHORT-TERM

BALANCING LONG- VERSUS SHORT-TERMISM

IN CONTEXT

FOCUS
Managing objectives

KEY DATES
1938 US author F. Scott Fitzgerald writes that "intelligence is the ability to hold two opposed ideas in the mind at the same time, and still retain the ability to function."

1994 US business experts James Collins and Jerry Porras publish *Built To Last: Successful Habits of Visionary Companies*.

2009 In *The Opposable Mind*, Canadian business professor Roger Martin claims that great business leaders are able to use "integrative thinking" to creatively resolve the tension in opposing ideas and models.

If a company only thinks **short-term**...

...about **immediate issues** with customers, wages, suppliers, and staff...

...it becomes outdated and creates **no new opportunities for growth**.

If a company only thinks **long-term**...

...about new products, new markets, **innovation, and growth**...

...it **runs out of capital** to fund investment.

Successful companies have to balance short-term and long-term thinking.

A successful business has to balance two different time horizons: short-term and long-term. In the short term, a company needs cash to pay its wages and bills. But if it focuses too much on the immediate present, it risks missing opportunities. Conversely, if a company's sole focus is on new prospects, it will soon become unprofitable. As Jack Welch, CEO of GE, said: "You can't grow long-term if you can't eat short-term. Anybody can manage short. Anybody can manage long. Balancing those two things is what management is."

See also: Take the second step 43 ▪ How fast to grow 44–45 ▪ Effective leadership 78–79 ▪
Investment and dividends 126–27 ▪ Accountability and governance 130–31 ▪ Profit versus cash flow 152–53

In 1994, James Collins and Jerry Porras studied companies such as General Electric, Marriott, and 3M that had been in business for more than a century and that consistently outperformed the stock market. They used the Chinese yin-yang sign—symbolizing complementary opposites—to explain how successful businesses maintain control of both the short- and long-term. The organizations they studied were able to manage contradictory ideas at the same time, by focusing on "both … and …" rather than "either … or …" They also demonstrated the concept by performing well both in the short-term and in the long-term.

Public and private

In a private limited company (Ltd), managers can plan for different time horizons without scrutiny from shareholders. Sir Anthony Bamford, for example, runs JCB, a privately owned British company. JCB was started by his father, Joseph Cyril Bamford, who began making agricultural tipping trailers in 1945.

Today JCB is the third-largest manufacturer of earth-moving machinery in the world, with 22 factories in Europe, Asia, and North and South America. Bamford can invest when and where he chooses. He decided to invest in India by opening a factory in 1978, a long-term prospect that paid off; JCB is now market leader there. In 2012, JCB opened a factory in Brazil.

Unlike many CEOs, who hold a post for a few years then move on, Bamford saw that balancing the short- and long-term is critical. His dual focus has paid off: despite the worldwide recession, JCB sales grew 40 percent in 2011 and topped £2.75 ($4.3) billion in 2012.

In contrast, a typical public limited company (plc), owned by shareholders and quoted on a stock exchange, is under greater scrutiny. These investors look for returns, in the form of dividends, on an annual basis. This can become a strategic issue, since institutional shareholders may put pressure on directors of limited companies to return cash, rather than to reinvest

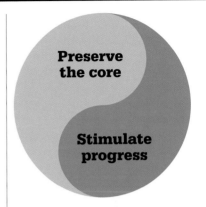

The yin-yang symbol reflects the dual nature of visionary companies, according to Collins and Porras. They suggest replacing the "tyranny of the 'OR'" with the "genius of the 'AND.'"

in the business, without regard to the impact on long-term prospects. This happened in 2013 at Apple.

To ensure the right balance between short- and long-term, companies often split planning responsibility between different management teams. This allows the organization to manage the immediate operation, while looking ahead for growth and innovation. ▪

Jack Welch

Born in 1935, John F. Welch studied chemical engineering at the University of Massachusetts, then gained an MSc and PhD in chemical engineering from the University of Illinois. In 1960, he joined General Electric (GE), rising to become the company's chairman and CEO from 1981 until his retirement in 2001. During this time, Welch increased the value of the business from $13 billion to several-hundred billion. His management skills became legendary; he had little time for bureaucracy and managers were given free reign as long as they followed the GE ethic of constant change and striving to do better. In 1999, *Fortune* magazine named him Manager of the Century, and the *Financial Times* claimed he was one of the three most admired business leaders in the world. He founded the Jack Welch Management Institute at Strayer University, US, in 2009.

Key works

2001 *Jack: Straight from the Gut* (with John A Byrne)
2005 *Winning*

MARKET ATTRACTIVENESS, BUSINESS ATTRACTIVENESS
THE MABA MATRIX

IN CONTEXT

FOCUS
Business strategy

KEY DATES
Early 1970s The Boston Consulting Group develops the Growth-share matrix to help companies decide how to allocate resources to products or business units on the basis of their relative market shares and growth rates.

1970s McKinsey & Company consultants develops the MABA matrix.

1979 Michael Porter develops the Five Forces model to enable companies to analyze the structure of their industry and develop a more profitable position.

2000 The Market-Activated Corporate Strategy (MACS) framework is introduced by McKinsey to measure each business unit's stand-alone value within the corporation and health for sale.

An organization must **allocate capital** between its different business units, or to different products.

A consistent method for a company to **identify where to invest, and where to cut back,** is to analyze...

...**Market Attractiveness** (the size of the market, its growth potential, and pricing), and...

...**Business Attractiveness** (the competitive strength of the unit or product in that market).

Using the MABA matrix can help a company **plot the relative profitability of its business units or products.**

Until the mid-20th century, many businesses were simple companies selling one product. However, from around 1950, large corporations emerged, which were divided into business units. It was difficult to manage these different units profitably, so management consultants began to develop frameworks to address the new complexity. One such model to arise during the early 1970s was MABA—the market attractiveness/business attractiveness framework. It is also known as the GE-McKinsey nine-box framework and the GE-McKinsey Matrix, because it was developed by consulting

See also: Study the competition 24–27 ▪ Protect the core business 170–71 ▪ Good and bad strategy 184–85 ▪ Porter's five forces 212–15 ▪ The value chain 216–17 ▪ Product portfolio 250–55 ▪ Ansoff's matrix 256–57

company McKinsey & Company for conglomerate General Electric, which had 150 business units.

The MABA matrix is a systematic, consistent method for a decentralized corporation to decide how to share its capital among the various business units by assessing each unit's profitability and market position. Past methods of budget allocation relied on each business unit's forecasts for growth and profitability, which were subject to error. Although designed for large companies, the matrix can also be used by smaller companies to assess the strength of a product line or brands, rather than business units.

Using the matrix
The matrix allows a company to judge each business unit on two factors to determine its future success: the attractiveness of its industry or market, and the business unit's competitive strength within that industry. Market attractiveness is rated according to the market size, growth rate, profitability, and level of competition. Business attractiveness is rated according to the unit or product's current and growth level of market share, its brand strength, and its profit margins relative to rivals.

By plotting the attractiveness of an industry on one axis and the competitive position of a business unit in that industry along the other, large corporations can compare the strengths of diverse business units. The matrix condenses the value-creation potential of multiple business units into a single, digestible chart.

Each business unit or product must be evaluated, using data analysis, and placed within the

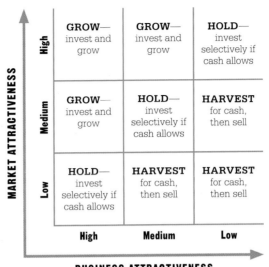

The MABA matrix provides a means of identifying which business units should be grown, held at their current level, or sold. Those at the top left of the matrix have a high business and market attractiveness, and should be grown. Those in the center have medium ratings for both factors, and may warrant selective investment. Those at the bottom right have low scores for both factors, and should be harvested for cash, and sold or liquidated.

matrix according to their market and business attractiveness. This sorts units into three categories: those that should be "grown" through investment, "held" (invested in selectively), and "harvested" for cash and either sold or liquidated.

Sorting units into these three categories provides a starting point for strategic analysis, and for determining where to invest to yield the highest growth. Over the years, the criteria for assessing industry attractiveness and competitive strength have grown more sophisticated. But even today, most large organizations with a formal approach to modeling their businesses use the MABA matrix or one of its derivatives. ▪

Why Kraft gobbled up Cadbury

When Illinois-based Kraft Foods bought British chocolate manufacturer Cadbury for more than $19 billion in 2010, it was because it saw Cadbury's competitive strength in an attractive industry. Cadbury would be positioned at the top left of the MABA matrix. Kraft was already the world's second-biggest food business with strong brands of its own, but it was generating 80 percent of its sales from the US and it was eager to capitalize on the potential for growth elsewhere in the world. In the first half of 2009 alone, 69 percent of Cadbury's sales growth came from emerging markets. The British company offered Kraft greater access to these markets, including the BRIC economies—Brazil, Russia, India, and China. Cadbury also had some of the world's leading chocolate, candy, and chewing gum brands. Cadbury's Chocolate, for example, was already a leading brand in India.

ONLY
THE PARANOID
SURVIVE
AVOIDING COMPLACENCY

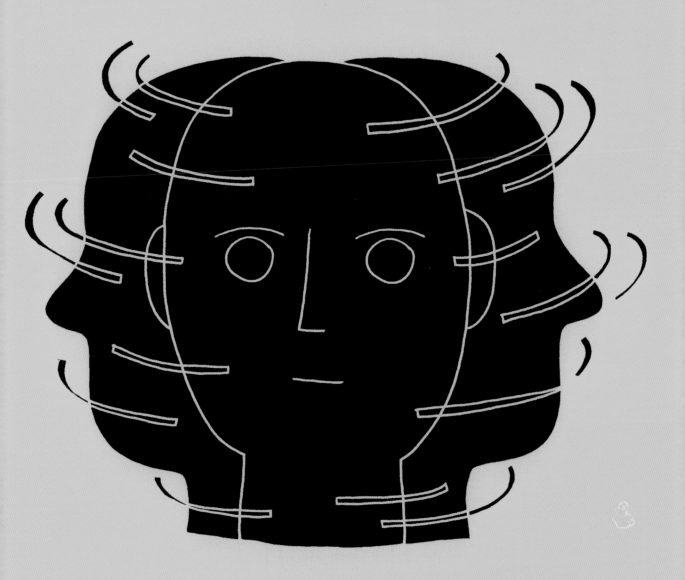

IN CONTEXT

FOCUS
Business change

KEY DATES
1979 Michael Porter writes *How Competitive Forces Shape Strategy*, saying that managers must always be aware of what the competition is doing.

1994 In *The Empty Raincoat: Making Sense of the Future*, Charles Handy uses a graph to illustrate how organizations have to be alert and respond to threats.

1996 Andy Grove writes *Only the Paranoid Survive*.

2010 In *The Black Swan: The Impact of the Highly Improbable,* Nassim Nicholas Taleb explains that we cannot predict the future from the past, so must expect (and prepare for) the unexpected.

I t is often easier for people outside a company to spot complacency than it is for those inside; executives are sometimes blind to it until their company plunges into a downward spiral. Research in Motion (RIM), manufacturer of the once-iconic BlackBerry, developed the idea of sending and receiving emails on mobile phones, and their innovation helped them to become the market leader. However, RIM rested on its success instead of continuing to innovate, and did not notice or foresee the direction in which Apple's products were developing. The rival technology company's iPhone delivered mobile emails and a range of other features. RIM quickly went from being the market leader into a period of decline, because it had become complacent instead of remaining alert to technological change, or threats from competitors.

It is human nature to relax when things are going well, but history shows this is the very moment to be wary. Former CEO of Intel, Andy Grove, believes that "Success breeds complacency. Complacency breeds failure. Only the paranoid survive." The latter phrase was

> A strategic inflection point is a time in the life of a business when its fundamentals are about to change.
> **Andy Grove**

framed by five questions (see below), and became the title of one of Grove's books. Grove had fled the communist regime in Hungary, and learned from a young age that paranoia could be a useful survival skill. Many years later, when he joined Intel, he transferred the skills of watching out for himself to monitoring the company, steering it safely through a series of threats.

Strategic inflection point
Every business faces change. Occasionally change can be massive, and positions once taken for granted can shift dramatically. Grove calls

Grove's Five Questions

| Do you think your **competition has changed**? | Is your old rival **no longer the biggest threat**? | Are you **relying on a complementary company** to make your company attractive? | Is everyone **talking about someone new**? | Where would you **point a gun** if you had one? |

↓ ↓ ↓ ↓ ↓

Only the paranoid survive.

See also: Reinventing and adapting 52–57 ▪ Changing the game 92–99 ▪ Hubris and nemesis 100–03 ▪ Learning from failure 164–65 ▪ Porter's five forces 212–15 ▪ Coping with chaos 220–21 ▪ Forecasting 278–79 ▪ Feedback and innovation 312–13

such a moment a "strategic inflection point." This is not necessarily a single point in time, but it is usually accompanied by a noticeable period of unrest within the organization. It may be initiated by changes in the external environment, or by new competition, and senior managers are often among the last to notice what is happening.

Intel's first strategic inflection point came when Japanese companies began to produce better-quality, lower-cost memory chips than US companies in the 1980s. It took Grove three years and huge losses to realize that only through rethinking and repositioning could Intel again become a market leader.

10X change

In the 1970s, US professor Michael Porter summarized five competitive forces that face companies: competition, substitute products, new entrants, suppliers, and buyers. Grove added a sixth force: complementary products. This is the impact of other businesses that sell a product or service that

A strategic inflection point is the point at which a major change (such as the arrival of the Internet) takes place in the competitive environment. If the company recognizes it and adjusts, the company may soar; if it ignores the change, the company will decline.

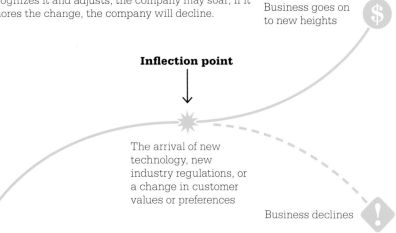

Business goes on to new heights

Inflection point

The arrival of new technology, new industry regulations, or a change in customer values or preferences

Business declines

complement a company's own product or service by adding value to mutual customers; for example, software products complement those produced by computer hardware manufacturers.

Grove describes all these forces as "a steady wind," but if one force becomes ten times stronger it acts more like a typhoon. Leaders have

to be alert to such major change—a "10X" change—because it requires a fundamental change in strategy. Depending on the actions leaders take at this point, the change can either take the organization to new heights or send it spiraling down into oblivion. The important thing for leaders is to discern between expected change and profound change, when the balance of forces shifts from old to new.

In his book, Grove uses the example of the growth of the Internet. The Internet was a "10X" change for every company, but some failed to recognize its force or were complacent and did not take action to exploit it. Many companies in the book industry were guilty of these failures—even those who had been extremely »

The Intel Corporation in California, US, became the world's largest computer-chip maker under Andy Grove's leadership. He encouraged employees to bring him bad news.

> It is not the strongest
> of the species that survive,
> nor the most intelligent,
> but the one most
> responsive to change.
> **Leon C. Megginson**
> **US management professor (1921–2010)**

proactive. In 1974, US company Barnes & Noble was the first bookseller to advertise on television, in 1975 it was the first to discount books, and in 1989 it opened a "book superstore." Its innovations helped it to hold a large share of the retail market. By 1995 it had 358 book superstores—but by 1996, the Internet had changed everything. Amazon—a master at Internet selling—suddenly outstripped it in sales and market valuation.

Staying alert

Points of sizable change are hard to spot, so executives must constantly scan the horizon, like a ship's watchmen looking for an iceberg that could sink the business. Companies today use many different approaches to monitor the competition and market. Typically, a large organization employs a team of people to scrutinize the company's sales, compare them to the competition, and analyze market

Black swans are rare but they do exist, which comes as something of a surprise to people who have only seen white ones. This demonstrates the error of basing predictions on past experiences.

trends. They may also have a team responsible for risk management, which covers far more than operational risks (such as safety). In recent times, such teams tend to monitor far-reaching global concerns, including weather extremes resulting from climate change, political change, and human-rights issues.

Successful negotiation of change relies not just on scanning the environment, but also making sense of the incoming information. Senior executives need to be particularly wary of understanding events and making decisions based solely on data or past events. In *The Black Swan: The Impact of the Highly Improbable*, Nassim Nicholas Taleb explains how individuals, businesses, and governments place too much weight on the odds that past events will be repeated. Forecasting the future from the past ignores the fact that the future holds different possibilities, as yet unseen. For example, if you have only ever seen white swans, you might assume that all swans are

white; unless you traveled to Australia and chanced upon a black swan. Taleb used the metaphor of the black swan to discuss major scientific discoveries and historical events. These "black swan events" combine low predictability and high impact. Examples include the 9/11 terrorist attacks in the US and the stock market crash of 1987. Taleb states that companies can never predict black swan events, but they do need to build robustness against potential negative eventualities, and be ready to exploit positive ones.

Listening to the front line

Grove claimed that business data (like white swans) is relevant only to the company's past, and cannot be used to predict the future. He suggests that when searching for clues about how to deal with the future, executives should look elsewhere, such as scrutinizing any misalignment between the company's strategy statements and its strategy actions. What is the difference between what the company says it is planning to do,

and what it is actually doing? Actions are driven by the stark reality of having to win business in the marketplace against the competition; a company's front-line personnel are likely to see and adapt to a new reality first. They are the people best positioned to identify critical issues.

This means that leaders in the organization have to be prepared to listen to people dealing with customers and suppliers—who often tend to be at the lower level of a company's hierarchy—and absorb what they are saying. It helps to have an organizational culture that encourages this and ensures that people are not afraid to speak out.

For the same reasons, it is just as important for senior management to listen to the kind of information being exchanged in corridor conversations, networking functions, and the general office grapevine as it is for them to use competitive analysis and modeling.

The "5-why" technique

To ensure they understand what is driving or impacting a company's performance, and what is happening in the market and the wider world, senior executives have to constantly ask questions. They also need to understand not just "what" is happening, but "why." One method to achieve this is the "5-why" technique, invented in the 1930s by the father of Kiichiro Toyoda, the founder of Toyota, and used by Toyota during the 1970s. By asking "why?" five times, you can move from the symptoms to the root cause of a problem. For example, the first question might be "why did we miss the deadline?" to which the answer might be "it took longer to complete the project than we thought it would." Why? "Because we underestimated the complexity of the task." Why? "Because we did a quick time estimate, without going through the project requirements in detail." Why? "Because we were

It is extremely important to be able to listen to the people who bring you bad news.
Andy Grove

already running behind on four projects." Why? "Because we are not allowing enough lead time when quoting." The technique can be used to interrogate internally and externally caused problems.

It is also important to ask the right questions. Management guru Peter Drucker claims that "the most serious mistakes are not made as a result of wrong answers. The truly dangerous thing is asking the wrong question."

Which questions to ask

Questioning goes beyond looking at the competitive environment. Sales bring in revenue, but companies also have to look at costs, because profit lies in the gap between these two. Managers must question their processes, to see where they can drive efficiencies, reduce costs, and so improve their profit margins.

Managers also need to constantly question whether there might be a better way to do something. For example, perhaps nonessential functions could be outsourced. Managers have to be restless, not complacent, and look for every opportunity to increase the profit margin and improve the business.

Managers have to use their knowledge and experience to connect all the information they gather, and try to anticipate what the world will look like in five or ten years' time. What changes might take place in that new world? They then have to position the company to take advantage. This requires thinking through several different scenarios and being able to think "outside the box." »

Victorinox's business model relied on the sales of its Swiss Pocket Knives, but a strategic inflection point—the prohibition of knives on planes—forced it to add luxury products to its range.

The impact of the 9/11 terrorist attacks on the US in September 2001 was felt across the world; for some businesses it proved to be a strategic inflection point. One such company was Victorinox, manufacturer of the ubiquitous Swiss Pocket Knife. The company had been producing pen knives since 1884, but it was hit by new airline safety regulations that prohibited knives to be carried on board aircraft following the 9/11 attacks. This had a drastic effect on Victorinox, because purchases of its products at airports around the world accounted for a significant portion of its annual sales.

Corporate sales also tumbled. By the beginning of 2002, pocket-tool sales had fallen 30 percent in just a few months. The company recognized that this could represent the start of a long decline, and that to survive, action would

have to be taken. The development of other products—including watches, travel gear, fragrances, and fashion—that could be sold at airports was accelerated. The company also began to explore new market opportunities, such as selling in China, India, and Russia.

Victorinox also took action to preserve one of its core strengths—a skilled and loyal Swiss work force. Layoffs were prevented by taking crisis measures such as reducing shift times, canceling overtime, encouraging planned vacations, and temporarily lending workers to other Swiss companies. Victorinox not only survived, but thanks to its new products, was able to enhance its high-quality brand image. More than 60 percent of the company's turnover now comes from items other than pocket knives.

Averting catastrophe

To detect the approach of a strategic inflection point, the CEO of a company, in conjunction with the board, must analyze all the available hard data, listen to the softer information, and then take decisive

action. British Petroleum (BP), once owned by the British government, became publicly owned in 1987. Its new CEO was John Browne, a nonexecutive director of Intel, who was influenced by Andy Groves's thinking on the importance of paranoia. Browne was concerned about something far bigger than rival companies—something that could harm the business of not just BP, but the entire oil industry.

Browne reviewed the available data on climate change, listened to experts in the field, and considered the impact on the business of BP. He recognized climate change as a slow-manifesting issue, but realized it could impact the oil industry. In 1997 he gave a seminal speech at Stanford University, CA, publicly acknowledging climate change as a reality and committing BP to do something about it.

This was a bold move for an oil company at a time when rival companies were trying to ignore the issue. BP pursued a strategy of investing in alternative energy, and it was the first oil company to set targets for reducing its own greenhouse gas emissions. Employees were asked to find ways

Real sustainability is about simultaneously being profitable and responding to the reality and the concerns of the world in which you operate.
John Browne
UK former CEO of BP (1948–)

to help meet targets. Browne caused more of a stir when BP launched a new brand identity in 2000. The bright green Helios logo, named after the sun god of ancient Greece, was accompanied by the slogan: "Beyond Petroleum". It represented the company's acknowledgement that it needed to provide more, and smarter, types of energy. It also sent a clear message that the company was not complacent; it was prepared to confront and adapt to difficult issues.

However, after Browne left BP in 2007, the new CEO pursued a different strategy, and the alternative energy business was closed down. Any environmental credibility the company had built was lost when an oil well exploded in the Gulf of Mexico in 2010.

Conquering complacency

In the late 1990s, UK retailer Marks & Spencer (M&S) took almost the opposite stance to John Browne at BP. Board members largely ignored the changing UK and global retail environments, and chose to focus on internal issues. The company was hierarchical and employees were expected to follow orders. In *The Rise and Fall of Marks & Spencer*,

BP's Helios logo demonstrated its commitment to finding new types of energy sources. Company responses to 10X changes, such as climate change, need to be communicated to the market.

author Judi Bevan describes a traditional business environment with carpeted executive offices, waiters with white gloves, and staff rules governing punctuality, efficiency, and politeness. M&S did not have a marketing department and its executives believed it did not need to advertise. Stores did not accept credit cards, and payment was possible only with cash or M&S's own charge card.

When rival retailers appeared with a more modern vision and fresh, contemporary designs, M&S's

clothes and stores began to look old-fashioned. Consumers started to shop elsewhere, but still M&S did not change course, despite a sudden drop in sales and profits. UK profits continued to tumble from a record high of $1.6 (£1) billion in 1997 to $232 (£146) million four years later, and the share price dropped by two-thirds. It was not until the emergency appointment of CEO Stuart Rose in 2004 to fend off a takeover that the dramatic decline was halted.

However, the recovery did not last: M&S once again risked complacency with a run of eight successive quarters of falling clothing sales to 2013. In response, the company announced it would invest in store revamps, logistics, and IT, and unveiled plans to turn M&S into an international, multichannel retailer, connecting with customers through stores, the Internet, and mobile devices.

This is the challenge for all organizations. Businesses must contend with accelerated change in a highly competitive, multichannel, global market, and guard against complacency—or risk losing out to competitors who are able to stay one step ahead. ∎

Andy Grove

Andrew ("Andy") Stephen Grove was born in 1936 to a Jewish family in Budapest, Hungary, as András István Gróf. He hid from the Nazis during their occupation of Hungary, survived the Siege of Budapest by the Soviet Red Army, then fled to the US during the uprising of 1956. Once there, he took the name Andrew Grove, graduated first in his engineering class at college and then studied for a PhD in chemical engineering at the University of California, Berkeley. He relocated his parents to San Francisco, and worked at Fairchild Semiconductor (1963–67),

before helping to found the Intel Corporation in 1968. He became its president in 1979, CEO in 1987, and was Chairman from 1998 to 2005. He is credited with the company's success; during his tenure as CEO, Intel's stock value rose by 2,400 percent, making it one of the world's most valuable companies.

A dedicated philanthropist, Grove has donated millions of dollars to cancer and neuro-degenerative disease research. He also serves on the board of overseers of the International Rescue Committee.

TO EXCEL
TAP INTO PEOPLE'S
CAPACITY TO
LEARN

THE LEARNING ORGANIZATION

FOCUS
The personal approach

KEY DATES
1920s Charles Allen develops a training program for shipbuilders in the US, which involves personal teaching intended to develop loyalty.

1950s Job training becomes individualized, replacing the teacher with programed materials that employees work through at their own pace.

1984 Professor Richard Freeman proposes that workers are "stakeholders" and are vital to the survival of the organization.

1990 Peter Senge publishes *The Fifth Discipline*, advocating "the learning organization."

When a company is devoted to the development and education of its employees it will be able to reinvent itself constantly, adapting to the market due to the intellectual skills and commitment of its employees. If the key to success in a rapidly changing marketplace is adaptability and foresight, then it makes sense to train and foster talented individuals as a means of marshaling an entire organization.

This is the essence of what management authority Peter Senge called "the learning organization," a place "where people continually expand their capacity to create the results they truly desire, where new and expansive patterns of thinking are nurtured, where collective aspiration is set free, and where people are continually learning how to learn together." To reach this ideal a company should adopt a collective, community-minded approach so that employees feel part of a worthwhile enterprise that will nurture them, and in return those employees will show commitment to the business. Senge proposed his vision for a corporate utopia in *The Fifth Discipline* (1990). In this book he set out the five disciplines to which an organization should aspire in order to succeed in the long term: personal mastery; mental models; shared vision; team learning; and systems thinking—the fifth discipline, which incorporates the preceding four.

The five disciplines
The first two disciplines are individual. By personal mastery, Senge means that individuals should use their own interest and curiosity to improve their capabilities. Mental models refers to ingrained ways of thinking, which should be challenged so that individuals become aware of why they think in a particular way, and of the effect this has on behavior. Senge encouraged employees to analyze their own subtle mental filters and to be prepared to question and change them in order to adapt to the future.

The remaining three disciplines are collective. The goal of shared vision involves the members of an organization deciding together what they want to create and agreeing on targets and processes

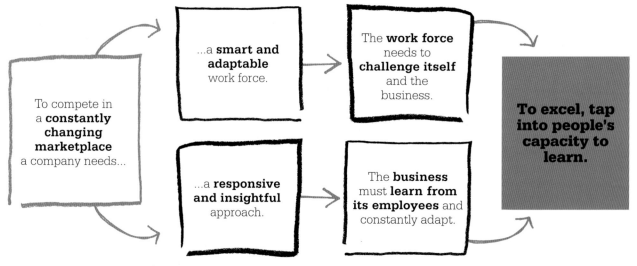

To compete in a **constantly changing marketplace** a company needs...

...a **smart and adaptable** work force.

The **work force** needs to **challenge itself** and the business.

...a **responsive and insightful** approach.

The **business** must **learn from its employees** and constantly adapt.

To excel, tap into people's capacity to learn.

See also: The value of teams 70–71 ▪ Creativity and invention 72–73 ▪ Effective leadership 78–79 ▪ Organizing teams and talent 80–85 ▪ Make the most of your talent 86–87 ▪ Organizational culture 104–09 ▪ Develop emotional intelligence 110–11

The five disciplines defined by Peter Senge enable organizations to change and develop through both individual and collective learning.

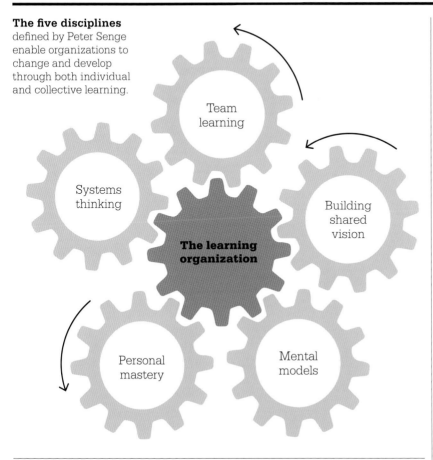

to help them get there. In this way, employees will work toward a goal because they want to, not because they are told to. Team learning is the process of employees learning together through discussion and dialogue so that they become more effective as a team than they would be individually.

The fifth discipline is the ability to see the organization as a whole, with its own behavior patterns. This capability is crucial in order for people to recognize potentially counterproductive behaviors that have come about simply through repetition and have remained unchallenged over the years.

Employee turnover

It is pertinent that Senge's proposal appeared against a backdrop of corporate brain drain. According to a 2004 paper by Arie C. Glebbeek and Erik H. Bax from Groningen University, the Netherlands, published in the *Academy of Management Journal*, when the labor market tightened and labor scarcity grew during the 1990s, businesses became concerned with the detrimental effects of turnover.

Turnover of personnel is one of the great blights of modern corporations and nations alike. A desire for further learning and development motivates talented individuals to move in search of a better environment with more opportunity for advancement. It is estimated that the cost of replacing an employee is between 10 percent and 175 percent of the departing employee's salary, depending on the field of skill. Data from the OECD (Organization for Economic Cooperation and Development) showed an increase in skilled labor migration around the world starting in the early 1990s. Much of this drain was from developing countries, and became gain for host countries in North America, Australasia, and Europe. But even in advanced economies, brain drain was a feature of corporate life.

During the 1990s, the highest voluntary staff turnover rates in Asia were in Singapore. The Singapore hotel industry, for example, had an average annual turnover rate of 57.6 percent in 1997, while average annual turnover rates in the retail industry ranged from 74.4 percent to 80.4 percent between 1995 and 1997. One study by Singapore's Nanyang Business School in conjunction with the UK's Cardiff Business »

Productivity … comes from challenged, empowered, rewarded teams of people.
Jack Welch
US former CEO, General Electric
(1935–)

School concluded that poor management practices were the major reason for employee turnover. The problem of high turnover in lower-paid jobs is still an issue. In the January 2012 edition of the *Harvard Business Review*, Harvard Business School professor Zeynep Ton wrote about companies that had found a way to invest in their staff while keeping product costs low: "Highly successful retail chains ... not only invest heavily in store employees but also have the lowest prices in their industries, solid financial performance, and better customer service than their competitors. They have demonstrated that, even in the lowest-price segment of retail, bad jobs are not a cost-driven necessity but a choice. And they have proven that the key to breaking the trade-off is a combination of investment in the work force and operational practices that benefit employees, customers, and the company."

Learning by listening
Peter Senge's theory about corporate learning went beyond just minimizing labor turnover. He intended it to be a model by which companies could maximize their success by actively fostering the education of all employees in order to innovate and adapt. In this respect, Japan's Honda Motor Company is often cited in case studies as a perfect example of a "learning organization."

In the 1980s, while professor of business studies at Stanford University, Richard Pascale analyzed the management style of Japanese companies, Honda in particular. He concluded that "organizational agility" was the reason for Honda's success. As evidence he cited the entry of the Japanese company into the US market in 1959.

Honda had been preparing to launch its larger 250 cc and 350 cc motorcycles in Los Angeles, but the advance sales team soon realized that the big Japanese bikes were inadequate for road conditions and the vast distances traveled in the US. The team reluctantly sent the models back to Japan for testing. Meanwhile, the three Japanese salespeople had been zipping around Los Angeles on the 50 cc Super Cub, a best seller at home but considered inappropriate for the power-hungry American biker. Nevertheless, US interest in the Super Cub grew and Sears

There is no organizational learning without individual learning.
Chris Argyris, Donald Schön

department store approached the Honda team to ask if it could sell the smaller bikes. The sales team reported back to head office and advised that instead of launching the larger bikes, the Super Cub should be the focus of Honda's debut in the US. Instead of dismissing the underlings, the managers took notice and agreed to go with the advice of the sales team. The result for Honda was phenomenal success in the US market. In Peter Senge's model, Honda is an example of how "every level of an organization should feel included and valued."

Questioning precedents
In essence, Senge's "learning organization" draws on earlier ideas, including those of Harvard's Chris Argyris. In 1977 Argyris published his theory of "double loop learning," showing that companies and their employees can assess and modify underlying ways of thinking to improve their capacity to learn and perform effectively. The following year

The Honda Super Cub became enormously successful in the US, thanks to managers who listened to their sales staff and broke away from the standard "macho biker" approach.

Organizational learning involves both single-loop learning, where errors are identified and corrected, and double-loop learning, in which the assumptions that underlie specific actions are questioned and improved.

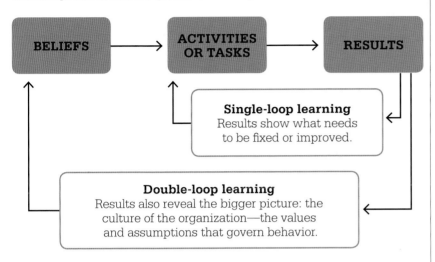

BELIEFS → ACTIVITIES OR TASKS → RESULTS

Single-loop learning
Results show what needs to be fixed or improved.

Double-loop learning
Results also reveal the bigger picture: the culture of the organization—the values and assumptions that govern behavior.

Argyris joined forces with MIT professor Donald Schön to write the highly influential book *Organizational Learning: A Theory of Action Perspective*, which explored theories such as double-loop learning.

Going further back, the first scientific studies of learning within an organization were conducted in the mid-20th century. Two theories in particular emerged to dominate thinking in this area. The first, from Yale professor Charles Lindblom in 1959, was that action taken in organizations is based on historical precedent rather than on anticipating the future. The second was set out by Richard Cyert and James March, who in 1963 published their observation that behavior in organizations is based on routines: the procedures, conventions, or technologies through which companies operate. These perceived negatives became the focus of scholars such as Argyris and Senge. Interest in the concept of the learning organization grew in the 1990s, as business conditions became more uncertain and companies more dependent on technology.

In 1993 management innovation expert Mark Dodgson, then senior fellow at the Science Policy Unit of the University of Sussex, UK, linked economic uncertainty and rapid technological change to an increased need for learning at all levels in a company, citing the view of psychologists that learning is the highest form of adaptation. Dodgson, like other scholars, made a distinction between "organizational learning"—when organizations learn a lesson from a particular event—and "the learning organization," which embraces a continual process of education and implements strategies to initiate that process. In Senge's opinion, organizations focused on continued learning will gain a competitive advantage in the marketplace. ∎

Peter Senge

A world-renowned expert on management and organizational learning, Peter Senge was born in Stanford, CA, in 1947 and studied aerospace engineering at Stanford University. He went on to obtain an MA in social systems and a PhD in management at MIT, and is now a senior lecturer at MIT's Sloan School of Management. He is also the founding chair of the global Society for Organizational Learning (SoL).

Senge pioneered the concept of "the learning organization"—an organization structured in a way that is conducive to new ideas, reflection, and engaging its employees. As he said on one occasion, a learning organization "is continually expanding its capacity to create its future."

In 1999, the *Journal of Business Strategy* named Peter Senge a "Strategist of the Century"—one of the 24 people who had had the greatest influence on business strategy in the 20th century.

Key works

1990 *The Fifth Discipline*
1999 *The Dance of Change*

THE FUTURE OF BUSINESS IS SELLING LESS OF MORE
THE LONG TAIL

IN CONTEXT

FOCUS
Internet business

KEY DATES
1838 French mathematician Antoine Augustin Cournot produces a graph to represent supply and demand.

1890 British economist Alfred Marshall introduces the concept of demand curves in his book *Principles of Economics*.

20th century Most companies sell a limited number of goods, with the bulk of sales and profits coming from their top-selling items.

1990s The introduction of the Internet proves to be a disruptive technology that changes economic and social traditions.

2004 Chris Anderson coins the term "Long Tail" to describe the concept that a larger proportion of sales is likely to come from the tail, rather than the head, of the demand curve.

Today, companies are **no longer constrained** by physical space or costs of reaching their market.

They can now **offer a large number of niche products** to many individual customers.

Consumers have **increasing choice** and want to express their **individuality**...

...by buying **niche items from online sellers**.

The future of business is selling less of more.

The "Long Tail" theory challenges basic principles of economics. In the past, successful businesses often sold high volumes of a limited number of products. Now, according to author Chris Anderson, the future of business is in selling less of more —low volumes of an increasingly large number of products.

A primary factor in today's global economy is the Internet, which is shifting the focus from mainstream products and markets—represented by the "head" of the demand curve—toward a large number of niche or low-volume products and markets, as seen in the "tail" of the curve. A conventional demand curve is drawn with price on the vertical axis, and quantity on the horizontal axis, and demonstrates that people buy more as the price falls. Anderson represents sales on the vertical axis and the number of products on the horizontal axis, showing that growth in many industries will come from the niche end of demand—the Long Tail.

Removing barriers
Supply was once constrained by factors such as cost of production, physical space for storage, and cost of distribution. Digital processing, online ordering, and electronic distribution have removed many of these barriers. Selling smaller numbers of a greater range of items can result in higher overall sales and profit than selling common items.

Books, music, and movies are classic examples of the Long Tail theory. A traditional bookstore can only stock books that are likely to sell. Amazon, however, can list every book, even though some may never be sold. Less popular titles that are not stored in its vast warehouses can be shipped direct

SALES ← **Head**

Long Tail
↓

PRODUCTS

The Long Tail is based on a representation of a demand curve of the future marketplace (sales are shown vertically, products horizontally). Author Chris Anderson suggests that overall sales of niche products at the thin "tail" of the curve may be greater than more popular products at the "head."

from a publisher to meet individual demand. Combined sales of one-of-a-kind books may be larger than that of bestsellers, and so may equal more profit. Similarly, iTunes can offer a longer list of music than any physical store, and Netflix can stream almost any film into your living room. When offered almost limitless choice, consumers exert their preferences and spend money.

Asia is a large and growing market, but it is fragmented by many different cultures. Individual countries offer numerous niche opportunities for companies that

can tailor products and services by language and ethnicity, rather than offering to the mass market. Start-ups are recognizing the Long Tail benefits and using the region's diversity to their advantage. One example is Brandtology, an online company that analyzes social media and online chat, in local languages, for clients in Singapore and Hong Kong. Native speakers of languages such as Mandarin, Japanese, and Korean offer social-media analysis to provide localized insights and interpretation of key issues within a particular culture. ▪

Chris Anderson

Author and entrepreneur Chris Anderson was born in London in 1961 and moved with his family to the US at five. He studied physics at George Washington University, then quantum mechanics and science journalism at the University of California, Berkeley; he later was a researcher at Los Alamos National Laboratory. After working on two leading scientific journals, *Nature* and *Science*, he joined *The Economist*, holding various positions (in London, Hong Kong, and New York), from technology editor to US business editor. Chris Anderson joined *Wired* magazine in 2001, where he was editor-in-chief until 2012. He currently lives in Berkeley, California, and is the CEO of 3D Robotics, a drone manufacturing company.

Key works

2004 "The Long Tail" (published in *Wired* magazine)
2006 *The Long Tail: Why the Future of Business is Selling Less of More*
2012 *Makers: The New Industrial Revolution*

TO BE AN OPTIMIST... HAVE A CONTINGENCY PLAN FOR WHEN ALL HELL BREAKS LOOSE
CONTINGENCY PLANNING

IN CONTEXT

FOCUS
Operational risk

KEY DATES
1947–1991 Governments and multinational businesses develop contingency plans for potential nuclear attack during the Cold War.

Late 1990s Countries around the world put contingency plans in place for the Y2K or "millennium bug"—an anticipated computer failure due to the millennial date change (from 1999 to 2000).

2010 A lack of contingency planning leads to closure of northern European air space for the first time, following the eruption of a volcano in Iceland. Businesses lose revenue due to the transportation restrictions.

2012 Due to the ongoing financial crisis, businesses around the world draw up contingency plans for the breakup of the Eurozone.

I n business, things rarely go as planned. Companies have to prepare for sudden changes to markets or the environment to ensure that day-to-day business can continue "when all hell breaks loose," as US professor Randy Pausch put it.

Contingency planning sets a course of action to deal with a crisis, whether this is industrial (such as the financial collapse of a key supplier), human, natural, or technical in nature. It requires identifying possible disasters, assessing the likelihood of occurrence, and developing a course of action to minimize the impact. Having a plan enables a company to manage the crisis and recover quickly.

Identify key tasks

A contingency plan has to be based on critical business activities. A utility company that relies on a call-center team to manage customer inquiries should identify alternative premises in case of flood. A marketing company planning for the same incident may need to allow staff to work remotely.

He who fails to plan is planning to fail.
Winston Churchill
UK former Prime Minister (1874–1965)

In 2011, a devastating earthquake struck Japan's east coast, followed minutes later by a large tsunami. The Japanese government's contingency plans for earthquakes—from earthquake-resistant buildings to an early-warning system and rapid-response coordination—saved countless lives. Many companies, such as NEC, were able to restore operations within minutes thanks to their prepared emergency plans. Even natural disasters as large as earthquakes can be managed with good contingency planning. ∎

See also: Managing risk 40–41 ▪ Learning from failure 164–65 ▪ Avoiding complacency 194–201 ▪ Scenario planning 211 ▪ Coping with chaos 220–21

PLANS ARE USELESS, BUT PLANNING IS INDISPENSABLE
SCENARIO PLANNING

I n addition to contingency planning, which involves preparing for sudden disaster, companies also need to prepare for the many alternative futures they face. This is known as scenario planning. It has its roots in military planning, and companies start the process by asking: "what if...?"

What is likely to happen in the next two, five, or ten years? Companies have to consider local, national, and international events, and must try to identify underlying trends. They have to determine the probability of future scenarios, how they might be affected, and how they can prepare to mitigate the effects, or even to reap the benefits. Scenario planning does not remove uncertainty, but it can help a company adapt to change.

Prepared for change

Oil company Royal Dutch Shell has used scenario planning for nearly half a century. Its early work was based on intuition, but it has now developed sophisticated techniques to create scenarios, which it shares publicly. However, it never comments on the scenarios it discloses, since this might guide other companies' or governments' decisions.

Shell's scenario planning allowed it to minimize the impact of an oil embargo on Western countries in October 1973. Within weeks, the price of crude oil had soared and stock markets tumbled. Although Shell was hit by these events, it had already begun to diversify into other energy sources, allowing it to recover more quickly than competitors. ∎

During the OPEC oil embargo of 1973, Shell's scenario planning meant it had already decided what it would do in the case of price hikes, allowing its executives to act fast and effectively.

See also: Managing risk 40–41 ▪ Learning from failure 164–65 ▪ Avoiding complacency 194–201 ▪ Contingency planning 210 ▪ Coping with chaos 220–21

THE STRONGEST COMPETITIVE FORCES DETERMINE THE PROFITABILITY OF AN INDUSTRY

PORTER'S FIVE FORCES

IN CONTEXT

FOCUS
Competitive strategy

KEY DATES
1921 US economist and statistician Harold Hotelling says that as long as there are profits to be had in a market, more and more vendors will arrive to serve it, until it reaches saturation point.

1979 Michael Porter's "How Competitive Forces Shape Strategy" is published in *Harvard Business Review*.

2005 W. Chan Kim and Renée Mauborgne publish *Blue Ocean Strategy*, suggesting that companies should aim for uncontested markets rather than compete with each other in existing markets.

2008 Michael Porter writes *The Five Competitive Forces That Shape Strategy*.

I n order to survive, companies have to understand and respond to competition. So it is natural to look at immediate competitors and established rivals to develop a strategy. However, this can restrict thinking, define competition too narrowly, and ignore other strategic forces. In the 1970s, economist and strategist Michael Porter changed people's thinking on strategy.

Porter's 1979 article "How Competitive Forces Shape Strategy" showed that awareness of wider competitive forces—those beyond the obvious competing companies—can help an organization understand the structure of its

See also: Study the competition 24–27 ▪ Gaining an edge 32–39 ▪ Leading the market 166–69 ▪ Porter's generic strategies 178–83 ▪ Good and bad strategy 184–85 ▪ The value chain 216–17

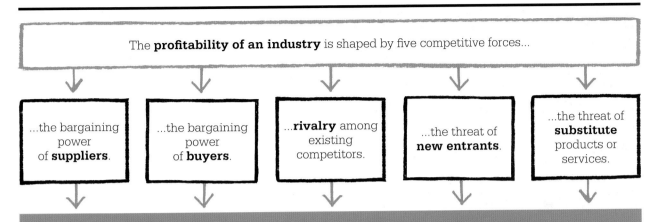

The **profitability of an industry** is shaped by five competitive forces...

...the bargaining power of **suppliers**.

...the bargaining power of **buyers**.

...**rivalry** among existing competitors.

...the threat of **new entrants**.

...the threat of **substitute** products or services.

The strongest competitive force—which varies according to the industry—determines the overall profitability of the industry.

industry and develop a position that is more profitable and less vulnerable to attack. According to Porter, there are five competitive forces that collectively define an industry's structure, shape the nature of competitive interaction within an industry, and ultimately determine profitability. Now referred to as Porter's Five Forces, this model places existing competitors at the center, surrounded by four other forces: customers, suppliers, potential entrants, and substitute products.

Using Porter's model

Porter used commercial aviation as an example to explain the model in action, because the strength of all five forces makes the airline business one of the least profitable industries of all. At the center are established rivals (such as Qatar Airways, Virgin, and Qantas), who all compete intensely on price. Customers can search easily for the best deal. Suppliers—in this case aircraft and engine manufacturers

and unionized labor forces—take the lion's share of profits. New players enter the industry on a regular basis. Substitutes are available in other forms of transportation, such as trains, buses, and cars.

Where the forces are much weaker—for example in the software, soft drinks, and toiletries industries—companies can make a bigger profit. In all industries, profit can be affected by weather or cyclical change in the short term, but in the medium and long term, it is the structure of the industry that drives competition and profitability. Porter is adamant that other factors—such as the type of product or service, the maturity of the market, regulation, or level of technical complexity—are not defining factors for profitability.

The force of "rivalry"

Of the five forces, rivalry among existing competitors is the major determinant of competitiveness and profitability within an industry. In a very competitive industry,

market share is tough to win and so profits are harder to make. Intense competitor rivalry occurs when there are many competitors, growth in the industry is slow, products are not differentiated and can be easily substituted, competitors are of equal size, customer loyalty is low, and it is difficult and costly to exit the industry.

The hotel business is just such an industry. In a city such as New York, there are many hotels. Guest numbers are relatively static, so »

The first one gets the oyster, the second gets the shell.
Andrew Carnegie
US industrialist (1835–1919)

> Industry structure,
> as manifested in the strength
> of the five competitive forces,
> determines the industry's
> long-run profit potential.
> **Michael Porter**

similar growth is slow; within a specific star-rating the hotels are all fairly similar, as are the sizes of the big hotel chains. Customers can choose to go to any hotel, and have good access to prices. Exit from the industry is difficult because of the upfront investment. Many large hotel groups have introduced loyalty programs as part of their strategy to differentiate their brand.

Substitutes

The most significant of the five forces is not always the most obvious one. For example, even though rivalry is often fierce in commodity industries, that may not be the factor that ultimately limits profitability. The "threat of substitutes" force is surprisingly important here—buyers in these markets can easily find substitute raw materials or products that have attractive prices or are higher quality. What's more, buyers can switch from one product or service to another with little cost. For example, it costs relatively little for a consumer to switch from tea to coffee, unlike switching from traveling by bicycle to car.

In some industries, companies try to limit the threat of potential substitutes by ensuring wider product accessibility. For example, soft-drink manufacturers have achieved this by introducing branded vending machines, so competitors are unable to offer their products at that particular place.

Buyer power

Buyers can demand lower prices or higher product quality from producers when their bargaining power is strong. Both scenarios result in lower profits for producers, because lower prices mean lower revenues, and higher-quality products usually incur higher production costs. Buyers exert strong bargaining power when there are few of them; they buy in large quantities; they are price sensitive; they control distribution to the final customer; there are many subsitites; and switching to another supplier can be done at low cost. Buyers may also be able to produce the product themselves—so may use this as a threat.

Buyers for big supermarkets have huge bargaining power in the food and drink industry. Fresh milk is often at the heart of supermarket price wars, because the big chains have significant buying power over suppliers. UK farmers have claimed that they are so pressured to reduce prices that they often make a loss on each bottle of milk produced.

Supplier power

When the bargaining power of suppliers is strong, it allows them to sell higher priced or lower quality raw materials. This directly affects the profits of the company that is buying, because it has to pay more for its raw materials. Suppliers have strong bargaining power when there are few of them (but many buyers); they hold scarce resources; the cost of switching raw materials is high; and when there are few substitute raw materials or suppliers. Their power is increased if they are large and can threaten to step in and produce themselves.

Oil is an example of a scarce resource that is controlled by a few countries. OPEC (Organization of the Petroleum Exporting Countries) represented the political power of oil-exporting countries in 1973 when it placed an oil embargo on the US. OPEC's action disrupted supply and forced up the price of oil four-fold.

New entrants

If an industry is profitable and there are few barriers to entry, Porter says that competition will increase and profits will fall. Typically, existing organizations try to create ways to deter new entrants. The threat of new entrants is high when the cost of entering the market is low; there is little government regulation; customer loyalty is low; existing businesses can do little to retaliate; and economies of scale can be easily achieved. Risk is increased if existing companies have not established brand reputation and do not possess patents, and when

Buyer power is high in the food and beverage industry because consumers can easily find a substitute that may be cheaper or differentiated, such as by offering increased nutritional benefits.

The hotel industry is characterized by intense competitor rivalry. Some hotel chains have introduced loyalty schemes to try to increase customer preference and encourage return visits.

products are nearly identical. An example of a market with a low threat of new entrants is the software market for personal computers. Microsoft came to dominate the market with its Windows 95 operating system. New entrants found it hard to break in because programs such as Excel, PowerPoint, and Word are universally used.

Choosing a position

Porter used the US heavy-truck manufacturer Paccar to illustrate the principles of choosing how to position a company within a given industry structure. In a crowded market, Paccar wanted to find a space where competitive forces were weak, and where it could avoid buyer power and price-based rivalry.

In the heavy-truck industry, where large fleet buyers dominate, it is hard to create a niche based on differentiation. Paccar, based in Washington state, chose to focus on one group of customers: owner-

operators. Personal pride in their own trucks and the fact that they were economically dependent on their vehicles made them less price-sensitive as purchasers. Paccar therefore decided to invest in developing an array of features with owner-operators in mind, such as luxurious sleeper cabins, leather seats, noise-insulated cabins, and sleek exterior styling. They offered thousands of options for owners to put their personal signature on their trucks, by simply inputting them on computers at network dealers. They also offered roadside assistance and fuel-efficient, aerodynamic designs. As a result, Paccar has been profitable for more than 68 years in succession, and delivers better-than-average returns.

No matter how different industries appear on the surface, Porter's model offers any company a way of assessing profitability through analyzing five easily calculated, competitive forces. In revealing an industry's underlying structure, Porter's model simplifies a mass of information, providing managers with a clear process for making sense of industry data and using it to form effective strategy. ∎

Michael Porter

Born in 1947 in Michigan, Michael E. Porter was the son of a US Army officer, and lived in different places around the world as a child. Porter served in the US Army Reserve following graduation. He received a BSE with high honors in aerospace and mechanical engineering from Princeton University, in 1969, an MBA in 1971 from Harvard Business School, and a PhD in business economics from Harvard University in 1973. The author of 18 books and more than 125 articles in the fields of competitiveness and management, Porter's academic studies encompass competitiveness in national, regional, social, and health-care arenas. He has served as an advisor to governments, corporations, nonprofit organizations, and academics across the globe.

Key works

1980 *Competitive Strategy*
1985 *Competitive Advantage*
1990 *The Competitive Advantage of Nations*

Defending against the competitive forces and shaping them in a company's favor are crucial to strategy.
Michael Porter

IF YOU DON'T HAVE A COMPETITIVE ADVANTAGE, DON'T COMPETE

THE VALUE CHAIN

The interconnected activities through which a company delivers products or services can be viewed as a **"value chain."**

↓

The chain consists of **primary and secondary value activities**.

↓

Primary value activities include inbound logistics, manufacturing, outbound logistics, marketing and sales, and after-sales service.

Secondary value activities include procurement, HR, technology, and infrastructure.

↓

Through analysis of its value chain, a company can identify where to achieve **cost or differentiation advantage** on its products.

The goal of every company is to create and sustain a competitive advantage so that it can sell more products and generate higher profits than its rivals. As Jack Welch, CEO of US multinational General Electric and celebrated business guru, advised: "If you don't have a competitive advantage, don't compete."

US professor Michael Porter's "generic strategies" consist of two types of competitive advantage: cost advantage and differentiation

See also: Leading the market 166–69 ▪ Porter's generic strategies 178–83 ▪ Good and bad strategy 184–85 ▪ Porter's five forces 212–15

advantage. Porter identified a set of activities that businesses can use to better understand how to achieve these forms of differentiation. These interrelated activities—dubbed the "value chain" by Porter—describe the flow of a product from its initial supply to the final customer. A company can add value to the product at each stage of the chain, through product-related activities—its inbound logistics (supply of parts or materials), manufacturing, and after-sales service—and market-related activities: outbound logistics (the delivery of products to the end user), and marketing and selling the product.

Gaining the advantage

To achieve competitive advantage, a company cannot focus on one activity alone, but needs to consider each of the activities in the chain. For example, Mercedes-Benz pursues a differentiation strategy, first through producing a high-end product, but also through providing outstanding after-sales service. Analyzing the value chain can also help companies to identify what areas of their business might be suitable for outsourcing, which can help the company to achieve a cost advantage.

Primary value-chain activities in a company are supported by a series of secondary activities, which can also be used to achieve competitive advantage. These activities vary by industry, but typically include: purchasing (procurement); human resource (HR) management; technology development, including research and development (R&D); and infrastructure functions, such as finance and legal. Although support activities may be viewed

> When you've got only single-digit market share—and you're competing with the big boys—you either differentiate or die.
> **Michael Dell**
> **US founder of Dell Computers** (1965–)

as "overheads," secondary value can be generated, for example, through better use of technology.

In addition to their horizontal activities, companies operate in a "value system" of vertical activities, such as a manufacturer who buys parts from suppliers and outsources its distribution. Competitive advantage relies not only on the company's value chain, but on the value system of which it is a part.

Reinventing value

Porter's theories on competitive advantage were highly influential, and have been built upon by other business theorists. Management scholars Richard Norman and Rafael Ramirez argued in 1993 that the market complexity of the 1990s required companies to "reinvent" the notion of value beyond the linear thinking of the "chain." In 1995, US executives Jeffrey Rayport and John Sviokla drew parallels with the emerging world of the Internet, suggesting that value could be added to online activities and products in a "virtual" value chain. ∎

Red, yellow, or purple?

Fashion retailer Benetton, launched by the Benetton family in Italy in the 1960s, pursues a differentiation strategy with its bold brand image. To achieve this, the company has focused on every aspect of its value chain, from supply to satisfying the latest consumer fashions. To ensure Benetton garments are up-to-the-minute, the company manufactures many of its clothes in gray, then dyes them to meet the demand for whatever colors are in fashion. Although this is costly in production, it minimizes stock, reduces wastage, and enables the company to respond quickly to changing consumer tastes. Benetton stores are run by agents, and garments are shipped directly to the stores and immediately placed on the shelves. This creates a strong value system, keeps costs lower, and allows each part of the chain to absorb fluctuations in demand. Benetton has more than 6,500 stores in more than 120 countries, and its turnover exceeds $3.2 (€2) billion a year.

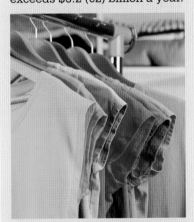

Benetton's value chain boosts its differentiation advantage. Clothes can be dyed in fashionable colors to match customer taste.

IF YOU DON'T KNOW WHERE YOU ARE, A MAP WON'T HELP

THE CAPABILITY MATURITY MODEL

IN CONTEXT

FOCUS
Business processes

KEY DATES
1899 US engineer and management consultant Henry Gantt develops the Gantt chart to illustrate a project schedule.

1970s Data-flow diagrams are developed to allow structured analysis of how data moves from one process to another.

1979 Philip B. Crosby develops a quality-management maturity grid in his book *Quality is Free*.

1988 The Capability Maturity Model (CMM) is described by Watts S. Humphrey in an article published in the journal *IEEE Software*.

2003 In *Business Process Management is a Team Sport*, Andrew Spanyi claims that strategy should drive business process design, which, in turn, should drive organizational design.

In level 1 of the Capability Maturity Model, **initial processes are ad hoc** and poorly controlled.

↓

In level 2, processes **start to be applied to projects** and are repeatable.

↓

In level 3, processes become **defined and can be proactively implemented**.

↓

In level 4, processes are measurable and **can be managed**.

↓

By the time level 5 is reached, processes can be **optimized through careful monitoring**.

Business processes are a series of actions taken to achieve an outcome. The objective might be to produce a product, to pay an invoice, or to serve a customer, for example. Adam Smith was one of the first people to describe business processes, when he dissected the many manufacturing processes used in an 18th-century pin factory. From describing the different actions, he developed the idea of division of labor, where work can be divided into a set of simple tasks performed by specialized workers, in sequence.

Continuous improvement
The sequence of steps in a process can often be visualized as a flow chart. As Watts Humphrey, inventor of the capability maturity model (CMM), pointed out, it is always "good to know where you are" in the process. Humphrey developed the idea that continuous process improvement is based on many small evolutionary steps, rather than large, revolutionary innovations. His CMM provides a framework for organizing these evolutionary steps into five levels of development, each of which prepares the way for the next. The CMM was developed

See also: Keep evolving business practice 48–51 ▪ Reinventing and adapting 52–57 ▪ Simplify processes 296–99 ▪ Kaizen 302–09 ▪ Critical path analysis 328–29 ▪ Benchmarking 330–31

Adam Smith observed workers making pins in a pin factory and realized that if the process were split into separate, specialized steps, productivity would increase by 240 to 4,800 times.

with funding from the US Air Force, and was used as a model for the military to evaluate software subcontractors. The model's original goal was to improve software-development processes, but it is now applied as a general model of the maturity of processes. It is often used in evaluating IT service management, for example, or more widely across organizational systems.

The CMM describes five levels of increasing maturity through which an organization or team manages its processes: in the first level, work is conducted in a chaotic and ill-defined way; in the second level, processes are put in place and adhered to with some discipline, and previous successes can be repeated; in the third level, processes are defined, standardized, and can be proactively implemented; in the fourth level, they are managed and monitored; and in the fifth level, they undergo regular improvement through monitoring and feedback.

Comparing industries

The CMM can be used to compare different organizations in similar industries. For example, two companies could be compared on the basis of their software-development processes. Increasingly, IT projects, which involve complex software development and new system implementation, can impact a company's operation and profitability, as they affect all of the company's departments.

The strength of CMM is its effective measurement of the standardization of an organization's processes. This is why the model moved from being used to assess software development, to applications in project management, risk management, personnel management, and systems engineering. It provides a starting point for managers looking to improve a company's processes and a framework for prioritizing actions. It also offers a way of defining what "improvement" might really mean. ▪

The whole idea was to motivate people to think about how they're working, and how to improve it.
Watts S. Humphrey

Watts S. Humphrey

Software engineer Watts S. Humphrey, known as the "father of software quality," was born in 1927 in Michigan, US. He credited his father with his approach to problem solving. After high school, where he struggled with dyslexia, he joined the US Navy to serve during World War II.

Humphrey then studied for a BSc and MSc in physics before completing an MBA in manufacturing at the University of Chicago Graduate School of Business. After graduating, he joined the Software Engineering Institute (SEI) at Carnegie Mellon University, Pennsylvania, where he founded the Software Process Program, which focused on understanding and managing the software engineering process. This work resulted in the development of the Capability Maturity Model (CMM), for which he is best known, and inspired the subsequent development of the Personal Software Process (PSP) and the Team Software Process (TSP), which was later adopted by IT companies Adobe, Intuit, and Oracle. Humphrey was awarded a National Medal of Technology in 2003 for his work in software engineering. With his wife, Barbara, he had seven children, and died at his home in Florida on October 28, 2010, at 83.

Key works

1995 *A Discipline for Software Engineering*
1999 *Introduction to the Team Software Process*
2005 *PSP, A Self-Improvement Process for Software Engineers*

CHAOS BRINGS UNEASINESS, BUT IT ALSO ALLOWS FOR CREATIVITY AND GROWTH
COPING WITH CHAOS

IN CONTEXT

FOCUS
Change and uncertainty

KEY DATES
1992 M. Mitchell Waldrop writes *Complexity*, which explains the theory of the science of complex systems.

1997 Researcher Shona Brown says that the edge of chaos has a structure that allows companies to be malleable enough to change but not fall apart.

1999 In *Surfing the Edge of Chaos*, Richard Pascale, Mark Millemann, and Linda Gioja say a too-rigid management system can have nothing original or innovative emerge from it.

2000 The dot-com bubble bursts, causing turmoil in financial markets.

September 2001 The 9/11 terror attacks in the US have far-reaching financial and business impacts around the world.

The top-down, hierarchical organization of businesses dates back to the industrial revolution, when management was all about control. Today's companies need a radically different approach.

The first decade of the 21st century saw many disruptive events across the world. These, combined with accelerated technological developments, the rise of developing nations, and a changing world order, make living with uncertainty a reality for business today. This means that companies now need a flatter structure, incorporating flexibility instead of direct control. Rather than being overwhelmed by

chaos, chaos can be managed and even embraced. US politician Tom Barrett acknowedged the value of working in an unstable world, noting that "chaos brings uneasiness, but it also allows for creativity and growth."

Managing chaos

Scientific chaos theory, which investigates the patterns in complex systems such as the weather, can be related to organizations. Effective leadership, clear vision, open communication, and strong values are necessary to deal with such complexity. Leaders need to set clear boundaries, then allow individuals and teams enough space to self-organize, self-regulate, and make their own decisions. Creativity and growth are enabled because employees have a higher level of responsibility and accountability for their work, as well as a bigger investment in the outcome.

A company also has to revisit its strategy continually, with the focus on delivering increased value to the customer, to ensure that it remains relevant in the changing external environment. A more flexible company helps to ensure that staff is involved and can adapt

Chaos theory proposes that complex systems are highly sensitive to initial conditions. A butterfly's flapping wings in Japan might start a chain of reactions that leads to a hurricane in the US.

See also: Managing risk 40–41 ▪ Reinventing and adapting 52–57 ▪ Creativity and invention 72–73 ▪ Avoiding complacency 194–201

Economic, social, and political events **create chaos**.

New technology **adds uncertainty**.

Rigid control no longer works—businesses need to be **flexible**.

If employees are given more information and involvement, they become **more creative**, helping the company to be flexible and change.

Chaos brings uneasiness, but it also allows for creativity and growth.

swiftly to change. Such companies collaborate more readily with external partners, rather than merely transacting with them, to encourage adaptability and shared learning.

Creativity from chaos

A potential source of chaos is internal change and reorganization of a company. Involving and engaging the employees is the answer to managing this. In the most complex financial services integration ever to occur in Europe, Halifax Bank of Scotland (HBOS) was acquired by Lloyds TSB following the financial crisis of 2008. External chaos (unprecedented economic turbulence) was mirrored by internal chaos—6,000 branches and 30 million customers had to be brought together to form the biggest

retail bank in the UK. The new company had to create one new identity, one new way of doing things, and streamline its IT systems and differing organizational cultures. It also needed ways of communicating positively to customers.

But the biggest challenge of all was common to many situations of business chaos—motivating employees who were harassed by customers and worried about their own jobs. Through constant communication (including daily team briefings on internal changes), workshops on team problem solving and vision building, and measures for gathering ideas from staff and customers, the combined companies showed that chaos can not only be managed, but may be a rich source of growth for a business in flux. ▪

Thriving on chaos

Thriving on Chaos, written by US business expert Tom Peters, was published on "Black Monday" (October 19, 1987), when stock markets around the world crashed. His timing could not have been better. In the book Peters laid out a future of change, stating that everything known "for sure" about management would be challenged—and that 100-year-old traditions of mass production and mass markets would be threatened. His forecast was correct. What had been a fairly predictable business environment disappeared; organizations and managers had to embrace change, or face collapse.

Peters correctly predicted that the business winners of the future would deal proactively with chaos, seeing it as a source of market advantage. Successful companies would be those who could create and add quality and value continually to their products and services in response to the ever-shifting desires of their customers. He described this as "a revolution."

There is no sense in pining for the past—the stability we took for granted for so long will never return.
Tom Peters

ALWAYS DO WHAT IS RIGHT. IT WILL GRATIFY HALF OF MANKIND AND ASTONISH THE OTHER
MORALITY IN BUSINESS

The US author Mark Twain said we should "always do what is right," but this has not always been the case in business. High-profile scandals such as Enron and Lehman Brothers in the 2000s have led to a collapse of public trust in companies.

Individuals are often tempted to use immoral means to further their aims. J. D. Rockefeller controlled the US oil industry in the 19th century because of underhanded methods to put competitors out of business. Today, some corporate companies are, in essence, a collection of individuals who want their company to get ahead of the competition, but are also alert to opportunities for personal gain. They may even go as far as illegal phone hacking or price collusion. For example, in 2013 Dow Chemicals was ordered to pay $1.2 billion for price-fixing.

Executives may be tempted to break the law because of pressure from shareholders for results or for performance-related bonuses. Gains from share prices and the value of the business overall pose additional temptations. In the 1980s, for example, the price of Guinness shares was inflated to assist the company's takeover bid for Distillers, a leading Scotch whisky company.

Businesses worldwide are under greater scrutiny to be ethical in their practices. In 2011–13 several multinational companies came under fire for shifting profits between countries, thereby avoiding large tax liabilities. Though not illegal, many regard it as immoral, and consumer perception can affect profit. ∎

In 2013, several oil companies came under investigation by the EU antitrust authority for preventing other companies from entering the price assessment process, thereby distorting oil prices.

See also: Play by the rules 120–23 ▪ Profit before perks 124–25 ▪ Collusion 223 ▪ Creating an ethical culture 224–27

THERE IS NO SUCH THING AS A MINOR LAPSE IN INTEGRITY
COLLUSION

IN CONTEXT

FOCUS
Ethics of competition

KEY DATES

11th century Legislation in England outlaws monopolies and restrictive practices.

13th century King Wenceslaus II of Bohemia passes a law to prohibit iron-ore traders from working together to increase prices.

1790s After the French Revolution, agreements by members of the same trade to fix prices are declared void, unconstitutional, and "hostile to liberty."

1890s The Sherman Act in the US makes it illegal for large companies to cooperate with rivals to fix their outputs, prices, or market shares.

2000s The Treaty of Lisbon prohibits anticompetitive agreements, including price-fixing, in the European Union.

I n a market economy, companies are in commercial competition with one another. It is illegal for them to "collude" to fix prices or make secret trade agreements. However, collusion and collaboration are close relatives, and sometimes companies argue that the way in which they "work together" does not constitute collusion. Rival companies have been known to "collaborate" in order to gain advantage over other competitors, or to increase profit. They might do this by sharing restricted information, limiting the supply of goods to influence the price, or fixing prices. Two airlines hit the media in 2007 when they were accused of price-fixing. Staff at British Airways had tipped off staff at competitor Virgin Atlantic over fuel surcharges. British Airways admitted to collusion, and was fined $195.5 (£121.5) million.

Accountability
Individuals in large organizations sometimes consider themselves infallible. In the mid-1990s, five

We have always known that heedless self-interest was bad morals; we now know that it is bad economics.
Franklin D. Roosevelt
US former President (1882–45)

businesses in the US, Korea, and Japan secretly colluded to raise the price of lysine (an ingredient in animal feed) above its average price in the international market. Within nine months the illegal cartel had raised prices by 70 percent. Gains for the companies and individuals would have been significant if they had not been caught. Several executives went to prison and US company, Archer Daniels paid the largest antitrust fine in US history. ■

See also: Play by the rules 120–23 ▪ Profit before perks 124–25 ▪ Morality in business 222 ▪ Creating an ethical culture 224–27

MAKE IT EASIER TO DO THE RIGHT THING AND MUCH HARDER TO DO THE WRONG THING

CREATING AN ETHICAL CULTURE

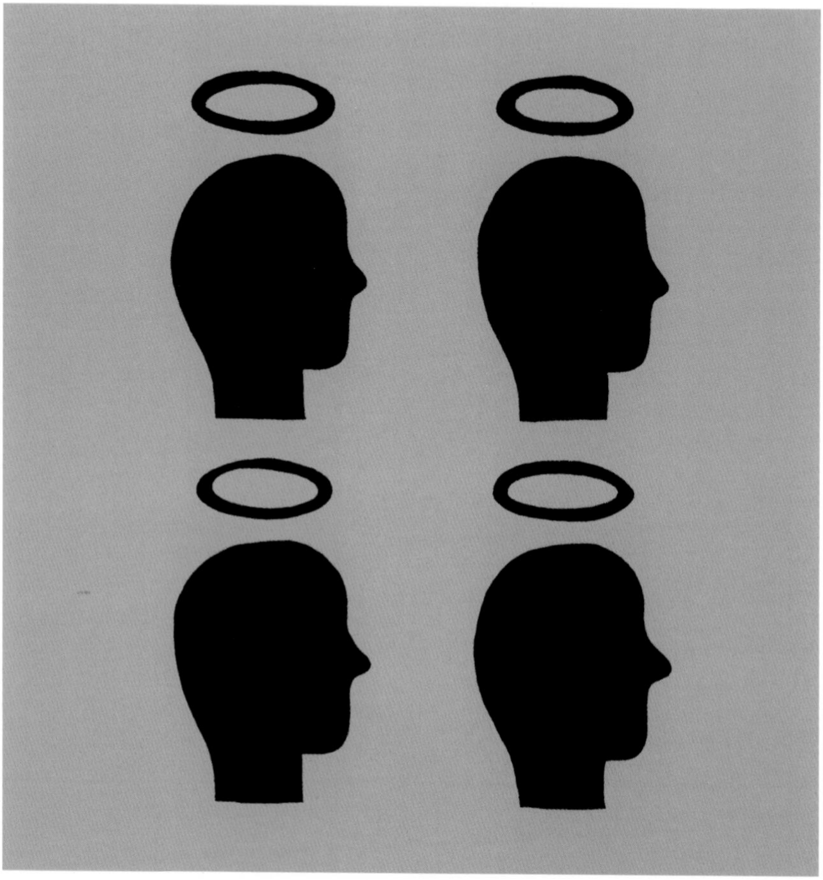

IN CONTEXT

FOCUS
Business ethics

KEY DATES
44 BCE Roman lawyer Marcus Tullius Cicero writes *De Officiis*, discussing ideals of public behavior.

1200s Italian philosopher and theologian Thomas Aquinas argues that price has a strong moral aspect.

Early 1900s US president Theodore Roosevelt declares that businesses should "act for the interests of the community as a whole."

1987 "Ethical Managers Make Their Own Rules," a *Harvard Business Review* article by Adrian Cadbury, highlights the conflict between ethical and commercial considerations, and the increasingly close scrutiny of corporate decisions.

The fundamental assertion of business is that it exists to make a profit. However, the way that companies make a profit has come under intense scrutiny, particularly in the global economy.

The first recorded reference to moral principles was Cicero's *De Officiis*, written in 44 BCE, which stated that "right is based, not upon men's opinions, but upon Nature." In the 13th century, the philosopher and theologian Thomas Aquinas defined the principle of natural law, saying that as a reflection of God's rational plan, our idea of what is naturally right is also rational: an action is ethical if it is judged to be rational, or reasonable. This is still

See also: Leading well 68–69 ▪ Effective leadership 78–79 ▪ Organizational culture 104–09 ▪ Avoid groupthink 114 ▪ Profit before perks 124–25 ▪ Morality in business 222 ▪ The appeal of ethics 268

The company's **leader demonstrates ethical behavior**.	The company **recruits new people for their values** as well as their skills.	The company **orients new people to its ethical culture**.	The company publishes and communicates its **code of conduct**.	The company **recognizes and rewards** ethical behavior.

A company must be proactive across its entire operation in order to make it easier to do the right thing and harder to do the wrong thing.

the basis for ethical conduct today. Aquinas also asserted the first principles for the marketplace, pointing out that the price set for a product is a moral issue.

A more moral world

The notion of what is acceptable in the business world today has changed radically from earlier centuries. Slave labor was the norm for cotton and sugar plantations in the US until the mid-19th century. At the same time, workers (including children) were exploited during the industrial revolution in Europe, being forced to work long hours, at low wages, in unhealthy conditions. A pioneer in showing that business could make a profit while pursuing an ethical path was Welsh social reformer Robert Owen, whose New Lanark Mill, near Glasgow, Scotland, became world famous for its moral rather than commercial values.

Today, companies have to consider every aspect of their operation—from sourcing ingredients to marketing policies—in order to be judged ethical by their consumers. Employment policies are very important. The Institute for Ethical Leadership, based in Canada, defines an ethical business as "a community of people working together in an environment of mutual respect, where they grow personally, feel fulfilled, contribute to a common good, and share in the personal, emotional, and financial rewards of a job well done." There is a shared understanding that success depends on a myriad of relationships —both internal and external—not all of which are under the organization's control, but which it can influence through the ethical way it operates.

An ethical business that employs people from diverse backgrounds starts by agreeing and documenting its own principles or standards, which are often termed the company's "charter" or "code of conduct." These standards become the reference point for decision making in the working environment, particularly when employees are faced with difficult decisions.

However, it takes more than a written pledge to ensure an ethical business. Organizations have to foster a culture in which it is far easier for people "to do the right thing and much harder to do the »

Stephen Covey

Born in Salt Lake City, Utah, in 1932, Dr. Stephen Covey was an internationally respected leadership authority, teacher, organizational consultant, and author. He grew up on a farm in Utah and was bound for an athletic career, but in his late teens he was struck by a degenerative disease that led him to require crutches while walking for several years. He studied business administration at the University of Utah, then spent two years as a Mormon missionary in Britain before earning an MBA at Harvard and then a PhD at Brigham Young University. In 1983 he opened the Covey Leadership Center in Provo, Utah, which later became the Franklin Covey Company. Covey died in 2012, at 79.

Key works

1989 *The 7 Habits of Highly Effective People*
1991 *Principle-Centered Leadership*

Fashion businesses use materials and labor from all around the world. Consumers increasingly demand transparency about goods and policies, so they can buy with a clear conscience.

wrong thing," according to US leadership expert Stephen Covey. Faced with daily decisions about the right way to behave, employees have to know what "doing the right thing" actually means. A company's policies covering everything from safety to accepting gifts from suppliers exist to ensure that people understand how they are expected to conduct business appropriately.

Driven from the top

Companies that prioritize an ethical culture often select employees for their values as much as their skills, and ensure that new employees are made aware of their role and responsibilities, and also how things are done in the organization. Such companies are eager to ensure that new staff both hears the company's values and sees them affirmed in the actions of people around them. Such a culture has to be driven from the top. US economist Milton Friedman famously said that the social responsibility of business is to increase its profits "subject to

We're pioneers and we want to show that this model works, that it can become self-sustaining.
Ali Hewson
Irish ethical businesswoman (1961–)

the limits of law" and "rules of the game" that ensure "open and free competition without deception or fraud." However, the 2007–08 financial crisis showed clearly that codes, laws, and regulations are not enough to maintain ethical business standards. Leaders with personal integrity are vital to enact and encourage ethical behavior throughout an organization. By espousing the company's principles at every opportunity and at every level, leaders can continually demonstrate their importance within organizational culture.

In *Principle-Centered Leadership*, Stephen Covey describes trust, respect, integrity, honesty, fairness, equity, justice, and compassion as the "laws of the universe," classing them as essential values for ethical leaders. Covey is best known for his book *The 7 Habits of Highly Effective People*, in which he proposed that ineffective people try to manage their time around priorities, whereas effective people lead their lives and manage their relationships according to principles. These natural laws and governing values are universally valid.

Ethical leadership

Typically, leaders in ethical organizations are not domineering. They are likely to have an open, engaging style and to be good listeners, able to tune in to issues across the business. The company they create will have a clear structure with well-defined roles and responsibilities, be transparent, with promotion based on merit, and a well-communicated strategy, so that employees know what they have to do and where they fit in.

Leaders with personal integrity are a powerful influence on others. Numerous studies have shown that good people can make bad decisions when acting in groups, particularly in stressful situations. To avoid the risk of unethical "groupthink," the CEO has to set the right tone for everyone in the organization. Effective governance is critical, and relies on good teamwork and communication between the board and the CEO. A board that has a defined structure and a healthy culture of debate will be more likely to recognize emerging problems and take timely, appropriate action.

This was not the case at Enron, a company that has become one of the most infamous examples of unethical leadership. The Enron Corporation started as a small gas-pipeline business in the US and grew to become the nation's seventh-largest publicly held corporation. CEO Jeffery Skilling actively cultivated a culture that would push limits; his mantra was "do it right, do it now, and do it better." But despite a clear set of values for employees to espouse, executives manipulated accounting rules and disguised enormous losses and liabilities. Enron collapsed in 2001; Skilling and chairman Ken Lay were tried together on 46 counts, including money laundering, bank fraud, insider trading, and conspiracy.

Doing the right thing
British fashion brand Ted Baker began life as a shirt specialist in Glasgow, Scotland, in 1988, and now has stores in the Americas, Europe, Asia, and the Middle East. The company is known for its irreverent designs, but in contrast to its styling, it strives to be an exemplar in the way it runs its business. To make this a reality rather than just a statement on its website, Ted Baker strives to ensure that environmental, social, and ethical matters are integral to its business operations, so that employees are always in tune with its high standards.

Ted Baker has set targets to continuously improve the overall sustainability of its collections, so employees know what they have to achieve. It is also committed to measuring and publishing its progress against sustainability targets and has a full-time "green guardian" to focus on improvement. The company also has a "Conscience Team," made up of people from across the organization, which is responsible for addressing social, environmental, and ethical issues.

Ethical companies often demonstrate ethical commitment by partnering with organizations that can help them to improve their standards. Ted Baker is a member of Made-by, a European not-for-profit organization that strives to improve social and environmental conditions in the fashion industry and to make sustainable fashion common practice. Any company partnering with Made-by must analyze the ethics of every aspect of operations, from the fibers used in products to factory conditions for workers. Companies can also inspire customers to act in a socially conscious way: some garments carry a symbol of a crossed-out trash can, encouraging consumers to recycle them.

Ethical business is also good business. Customers are attracted to companies they can feel good about, more talented staff is attracted and stays longer, and shareholders are shielded from the type of share-price falls that overtook Enron. ∎

Ethical trading depends on more than internal business practices and culture: a company's materials, suppliers, and business partners must also be ethically sound. To aid transparency, some companies and organizations publish data on aspects of their business, such as production locations, energy mix, recycling levels, and diversity among employees.

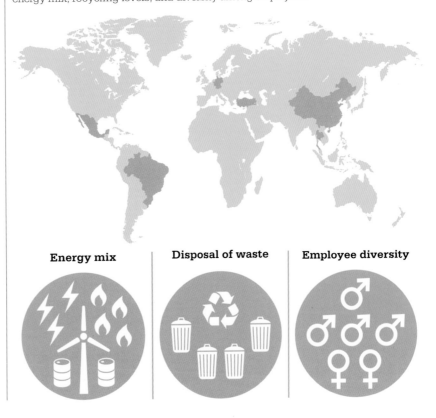

Energy mix　　**Disposal of waste**　　**Employee diversity**

SUCCES
SELLING
MARKETING
MANAGEMENT

SFUL

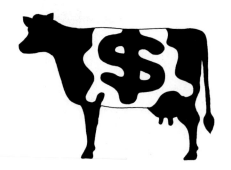

By definition, marketing is the field of management devoted to selling. It is the link between production and profit, providing the expertise for taking a product or service through the most appropriate channels to find the people most likely to buy it. To fulfil this goal, it is crucial to become adept at understanding the market. This means closely studying the behavior and lifestyle of the customer so that a product or service can be developed to be irresistible in every way, from the purpose, function, quality, and look of it, to the speed at which it is delivered, the places it is sold, its price, and the level of customer service support offered.

Knowing the customer

That is the theory. In practice, making your customers love you by always putting them first and fulfilling their needs and desires is the biggest challenge of marketing. Collecting data about the purchase history of customers is a starting point. Combined with analyzing any available demographic and lifestyle statistics, such data can be used to build a marketing model—essentially a mathematical formula that indicates potential purchase rates for a given set of variables.

Naturally there are dangers inherent in trying to predict the future using this type of forecasting. The marketer must also be aware of changing tastes, technology, politics, and economic conditions, so that the business can adapt quickly, avoiding what management scholar Theodore Levitt famously called "marketing myopia." For example, as consumers have become increasingly reliant on mobile phones and tablets, businesses with foresight have developed mobile-commerce channels and reaped the benefits.

In the quest to anticipate customer needs and wants, some of the most progressive companies gather data and examine it on a daily basis so that key elements

Marketing takes a day to learn. Unfortunately it takes a lifetime to master.
Philip Kotler
US marketing expert (1931–)

of the "marketing mix"—such as the product or service itself, the places where it is sold, its price, and any promotional offers—can be adjusted accordingly. Japanese camera company Konica Minolta, for example, uses specialized technology to monitor sales data, competitor activity, and market trends in real time so that it can respond effectively.

Marketing strategies

Arguably the product or service offered is the most critical component of the marketing mix. For most companies, each product or service in its product portfolio has its own cycle of growth, and can be managed to maximize profit by prioritizing the marketing spend. For example, for food group Mars, its best-selling namesake chocolate bar has been a long-standing source of profits, funding the corporation's expansion into other areas, such as ice cream and pet food.

To help decisions about diversifying into such new markets, companies can use a diagrammatic tool such as Ansoff's Matrix, which plots existing and potential products or services according to the risk factors involved. If a business decides to develop and

market something new, how it presents the offering and gets the message to consumers is an important consideration. In planning a launch, another valuable tool, the AIDA Model, provides clear-cut criteria for defining the features of any new product or service: how it grabs consumers' attention, holds their interest, generates desire, and is perceived to be attractive.

Concurrent with developing a specific product or service for a particular market, creating a brand is equally important. The goal should be to make the brand synonymous with a set of unique product qualities. In the words of marketing expert Seth Godin: "A brand is the set of expectations, memories, stories, and relationships that, taken together, account for a consumer's decision to choose one product or service over another. If the consumer … doesn't pay a premium, make a selection, or spread the word, then no brand value exists for that consumer."

Promoting the product

Once the optimal product or service has been developed in conjunction with brand identity, there is the question of how to get the word out to potential customers. Promotions and incentives—such as special offers, sweepstakes, and price discounting—can be deployed in the short term to garner initial interest. They can be especially effective for product launches in areas where many rivals fight for shelf space, such as household cleaning and candy.

One of the oldest strategies for communicating with customers is word of mouth. In the age of social media, generating buzz about a new product or service increasingly relies on reaching specific groups through Facebook, Twitter, YouTube, and other online means, and encouraging them to spread the word. When a branded video goes viral, the potential global reach runs into tens of millions. If relatively low-cost communications methods like this are effective, it can lead marketers to ask, why advertise? But for long-term image building, and for reinforcing brand values, advertising still has a role to play. For example, a sustained advertising plan can take an audience from children to adults with recognizable slogans, jingles, and formats.

Staying on message

Businesses must carefully consider the messages that they send to customers and their rivals, since the marketplace can judge them harshly. Companies found to have acted dishonestly or conveyed partial truths about their eco-credentials can be accused of "greenwashing," and will find it hard to win back public opinion. In fact, no matter how appealing a company's sales proposition, consumers increasingly want the people they buy from to have a social conscience. For this reason, it is vital for management to consider the role of ethics within the organization, and to develop the company's code of behavior toward suppliers, employees, consumers, and the community. Although shareholders may see corporate responsibility as the least important commercial priority, it is now an integral part of the marketer's strategy for successful selling. ∎

Don't find customers for your products, find products for your customers.
Seth Godin
US entrepreneur (1960–)

MARKETING IS FAR TOO IMPORTANT TO LEAVE TO THE MARKETING DEPARTMENT
THE MARKETING MODEL

IN CONTEXT

FOCUS
Marketing models

KEY DATES
1961 The Marketing Science Institute is founded.

1969 US academic Frank Bass publishes a seminal marketing model that can be used to predict demand.

1970s Complex measurement models and decision-making models are developed.

1980 The launch of in-store scanners at checkouts gives marketers new data and prompts the development of sophisticated new models.

1982 The journal *Marketing Science* launches, focusing on mathematical models for marketing purposes.

1990s Intelligent marketing-information systems computerize many routine modeling functions, providing daily updates and projections.

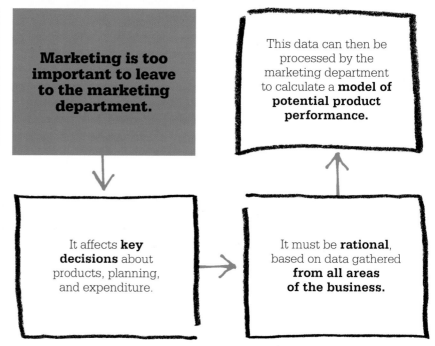

Marketing is too important to leave to the marketing department.

It affects **key decisions** about products, planning, and expenditure.

It must be **rational**, based on data gathered **from all areas of the business.**

This data can then be processed by the marketing department to calculate a **model of potential product performance.**

Companies need to study their customers' buying habits carefully in order to plan business marketing strategies. Using a mathematical model to plan product strategies and aid decision making is an integral part of any modern marketing practice. Marketing computer programs use sets of numerical data about the buying patterns of consumers, along with other variables relating to the product. These are entered into a mathematical model or equation programmed to make a customized calculation. The results will help to quantify the potential performance of products in different channels aimed at various market segments. By examining the data,

See also: Managing risk 40–41 ▪ How fast to grow 44–45 ▪ Organizational culture 104–09 ▪ Avoid groupthink 114 ▪ Good and bad strategy 184–85 ▪ Forecasting 278–79 ▪ Marketing mix 280–83 ▪ Benefitting from "big data" 316–17

> Marketing is inherently about producing results.
> **Geoff Smith**
> **VantagePoint Marketing (1962–)**

marketers and others in an organization can measure projected product growth, or return on investment, and make informed decisions on how to optimize the combination of factors most likely to generate market success.

Gathering the required data for modeling is crucial. Information is needed from all areas of the business so that every step in the process of getting the product from the drawing board to the customer is factored in. When David Packard, the co-founder of Hewlett-Packard, said that "marketing is far too important to leave to the marketing department," he was implying that the plans made by marketers can come to nothing if the rest of the organization is not fully engaged. In addition to getting approval on plans and budgets, marketers should communicate with all departments to gather data and share it once decisions have been made.

Using the data, the marketer can simulate product tests and input variations using different assumptions about elements of the marketing mix, such as market conditions and consumer behavior. The greater the amount of relevant

data and the longer the historical period it covers, the more accurate the results will be. Models reassure members of the business that every scenario has been investigated. Marketers can choose from different models or design their own, but the key to making the model work is data.

Gathering and using data

Consumer goods maker Procter & Gamble (P&G) has invested heavily in data gathering and modeling, implementing digital processes from the factory to the shelf in order to capture data and feed it back. The data can be used to make immediate adjustments to product planning and distribution, as well as added to a massive database for future use. According to CEO Robert McDonald in 2011, "Data modeling, simulation, and other digital tools are reshaping how we innovate."

P&G focuses on internal data-gathering processes and also relies heavily on market information from external partners. The leadership

team around the world confers once a week to examine data and make decisions in response to buying behavior. As McDonald says, "it's the data sources that help create the brand and keep it dynamic." ▪

Market research is valuable, but it can be very time consuming to gather data that is representative of the age, gender, and background of consumers. Computer models do the work faster.

The origin of marketing models

Models of consumer behavior date from the 1960s. They grew out of a need to make marketing more scientific and less driven by instinct or unproven ideas.

In the 1960s US scholar Robert Ferber advocated the use of mathematical simulation techniques and models. These became known as measurement models because they were devised to measure demand for a product as a function of various independent variables—for example, if the selling price

is raised by one percent how might this affect demand? Then in 1969 Stanford University's Frank Bass devised his Bass model, which is still used to predict how fast new products will be adopted and spread through a market.

Decision Support Systems (DSS) use measurement models to project the outcome of new decisions, adding variables—such as previous outcomes in similar contexts—to help marketers make optimal choices.

KNOW THE CUSTOMER SO WELL THAT THE PRODUCT FITS THEM AND SELLS ITSELF

UNDERSTANDING THE MARKET

IN CONTEXT

FOCUS
Focused marketing

KEY DATES
1920s The concept of market research emerges in the US.

1941 Robert K. Merton invents the idea of the focus group.

1953 Peter Drucker says the first step for any business is to ask: "Who is the customer?"

1970 US economist Milton Friedman puts forward the business model of shareholder maximization.

1998 Marketing professor Robert V. Kozinets coins the term "netnography" to refer to the theory of ethnography as applied to Internet users.

1990 US professor Gerald Zaltman develops the first neuromarketing technology, ZMET, to analyze consumers' subconscious reactions to advertising imagery.

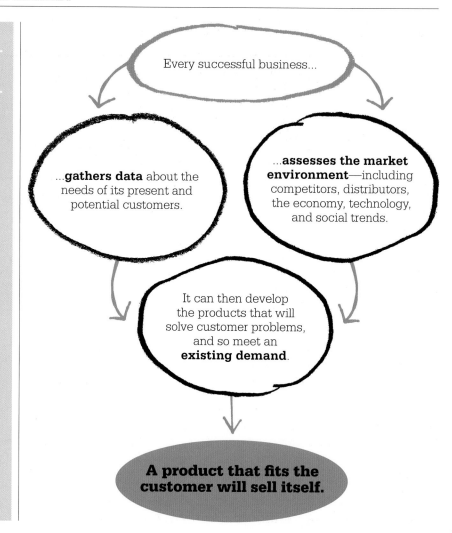

To be successful in a market, an enterprise needs to understand both the environment in which it wants to do business, and the way consumers in that environment think and act. The marketing environment is the world beyond the confines of the organization—the world that its customers live in—and includes the state of the economy, government regulations, social attitudes, current issues, competing companies, distribution infrastructure and partnerships, and technological changes. At the core of this market is the prospective customer, who will be influenced by many of those environmental factors, but will also be driven by individual needs and preferences, which will affect what products and services he or she buys.

This means that to understand the market, a company must make sense of the "broad brush" of the external environment and, at the same time, fathom the psychological profile and personality of the consumer. The end purpose of these investigations is to identify the biggest problems that consumers are struggling with. Once these are identified, a business needs to respond innovatively, to deliver the products and services that will be seen as perfect solutions.

Gathering data
This analysis may sound simple, but given that any particular market might number thousands or millions of individuals, how does a marketer go about understanding how those people think and behave—let alone what problems or unfulfilled wants they have, both

See also: Stand out in the market 28–31 ▪ Focus on the future market 244–49 ▪ Make your customers love you 266–69 ▪ Forecasting 278–79 ▪ Marketing mix 280–83 ▪ Maximize customer benefits 288–89

individually and collectively? The starting point is to fully explore the world in which the customer lives. What are the basic motives that drive buying decisions? What value does the customer place on price, quality, and design? Among all the social, cultural, financial, and technological forces in the environment, which ones particularly affect the customer? A marketer wants to know the practical details of the customer's daily life. How does that person live on a day-to-day basis? Does he or she have tasks that could be made easier? What other kinds of problems could the company potentially solve? The goal of all this research, according to influential management thinker Peter Drucker, "is to make selling unnecessary."

Beating the recession

In 1973, Drucker advised business leaders to "know and understand the customer so well the product or service fits him and sells itself." At that time, the corporate world was in turmoil as recession took hold across

Being customer driven … is about building a deep awareness of how the customer uses your product.
Ranjay Gulati
Harvard business professor

all of the major economies of the West, bringing to an end the upward growth that had, with the exception of a few slow years, persisted since the end of World War II. Everyone in business was thinking about how to survive the lean times ahead.

Recession struck in the very same year that Drucker published the work that would later be hailed as a masterpiece, *Management: Tasks, Responsibilities and Practices* (1973), in which he

advised that a business centered on the customer was the only sure way to realize growth. "There is only one valid definition of business purpose," he wrote, and that is "to create a customer." By this he meant that a customer's willingness to pay for goods or services is the catalyst that propels businesses to turn raw materials and resources into products for sale. Without the customer's desire or need, there is no impetus for commercial activity; and conversely, without commerce, nothing can be produced to meet the customer's demand.

Drucker suggested that when customers buy something, they are not thinking about the product or service itself, but about the usefulness of it to themselves. For them, value lies in the problem-solving ability of the purchase.

Although Drucker's idea is now at the core of most modern marketing theory and practice, at the time it was a counter to the prevailing management approach of the 1970s, which advocated the maximization of shareholder value. **»**

Peter Drucker

One of the most quoted experts in management and marketing, Peter Drucker was exposed to big ideas during his childhood years in Vienna, Austria. Born in 1909, his father was an economist and lawyer, and his mother was one of the first women in Austria to study medicine. The couple regularly held salons in their home and the young Drucker was encouraged to sit in on these discussion evenings, which were regularly attended by prominent professionals.

Armed with a degree in Law from Hamburg University, and with a budding journalistic career

unfolding, he moved to England as the Nazis rose to power, before settling in Los Angeles, where he became a professor of politics, and later a professor of management. Drucker wrote 39 books on the subjects of economics, leadership, and management. He died in 2005.

Key works

1946 *The Concept of the Corporation*
1954 *The Practice of Management*
1973 *Management*

Skaterboarders are a niche market, and have a specific set of requirements from equipment and fashion brands. Micromarketing can help businesses reach niche markets such as this one.

This theory placed the wealth of the corporation, rather than the needs and wants of the customer, at the core of a business. It held that business should be run solely to increase profits, which would boost the value of stock prices and allow the company to return value to the shareholders—who, after all, own the business. This way of thinking had been introduced by economist Milton Friedman in an article he wrote for *The New York Times* in 1970, and it was later developed further by business professors Michael Jensen and William Meckling in their paper, "Theory of the Company." As the title implies, Jensen and Meckling's thesis was not generally concerned with the world beyond the company—it focused on the relationship between upper management and shareholders, rather than the relationship between management and the market.

21st-century thinking
The concept of shareholder maximization was a dominant force in the last few decades of the 20th century, but the importance of understanding the market and of customer-centered management has gradually gained favor, partly

because the corporate-centered strategy has proved no guarantee of longevity. Business in the 21st century has become more people-centered with a number of huge success stories helping to sway management further toward customer-oriented strategies.

In 2010, business professor Richard Martin wrote an article for the *Harvard Business Review*, heralding "The Age of Consumer Capitalism." He claimed that we are now living in an era in which shareholder value is no longer the primary goal. "For three decades, executives have made maximizing shareholder value their top priority," he wrote. "But evidence suggests that shareholders actually do better when firms put the customer first."

An example of a serious failure to prioritize the customer is that of the British jewelry company, Ratners. By the late 1980s, Ratners was the world's biggest jeweler, with 2,000 stores on two continents. The stores sold jewelry at low prices and were very popular—until the disastrous speech by the company's chief executive, Gerald Ratner, at the Institute of Directors in 1991. In his talk, supposedly about the company's success, he instead

insulted one of his own products, joking that its low price was possible due to its poor quality. Offended customers abandoned the store and $800 (£500) million was wiped off the value of the company, which nearly went under. This notorious example shows how businesses who treat customers with contempt can pay a very high price.

Knowing the market
Since Drucker's initial proposition that a business must get to know the customer intimately, the market place has matured, making the task of understanding the consumer, customer groups, and the market as a whole, far more complex. One of the reasons is fragmentation, meaning that consumers are now divided among many small markets that are constantly in flux, and may suddenly emerge from nowhere. These micromarkets are defined by the common aspirations, likes, or needs of the consumers within them. Each consumer is subject to

Whether it's Google or Apple or free software, we've got some fantastic competitors and it keeps us on our toes.
Bill Gates
CEO of Microsoft (1955–)

> Research is formalized curiosity. It is poking and prying with a purpose.
> **Zora Neale Hurston**
> **US anthropologist (1891–1960)**

a wide spectrum of external factors, so it is crucial to understand these to get to their hearts and minds.

Price cutting by competitors, for example, can divide the customer's attention, providing enticement but also potentially damaging a brand's value in the eyes of the consumer. A business therefore needs to know how sensitive their existing and potential customers are to price.

The distribution system, which determines how products and services get to potential buyers, is also a vital aspect to consider. A business should figure out how to deliver products and services in a way that best suits purchasers. The Internet has transformed how this happens, and customers now expect sellers to understand where, when, and how they want to buy.

Types of research

The state of the economy, level of interest rates, regulatory law, and technological change can sway customers, while social and cultural forces are arguably the

Focus groups were used extensively in the late 20th century to gather informal comments and opinions on products, as shown here in a scene from the TV show, *Mad Men*.

most important in the marketing environment. These encompass gender, life stage, income, trends, current issues, and the influence of key individuals in the public eye.

The challenge for the marketer is finding out how all of these things influence customers and, consequently, what motivates them to buy. The obvious starting point is to ask questions. This basic premise developed during the 1960s and 1970s into a formal process of question-and-answer known as market research. Researchers gathered both quantitative evidence (from simple questions directed toward a large audience) and qualitative evidence (through direct observation or in-depth discussion with a small sample of individuals). Qualitative research is usually regarded as the more valuable of the two in getting a grasp of why a customer accepts or rejects a product, and in understanding the realities of customers' lives.

Personalized marketing

Since the 1990s, business has forged a direct path of communication with the customer via the Internet.

Marketers have developed new strategies for online information gathering, such as personalized, or one-on-one, marketing, in which a single consumer's interests and wants can be recorded and compiled to create a detailed profile.

Psychographic profiling is one way that marketers attempt to make sense of diverse consumer interests, by corralling individuals with shared interests and motivations into groups that can be targeted. Whereas businesses used to define their customers demographically, for example as Baby Boomers or Generation X, a psychographic profile is much more detailed. It is put together by using information about a consumer's daily habits; favorite brands, music, and athletic personalities; media habits; leisure activities; vacation destinations; and much more.

Social media and online communities have encouraged people to define themselves by an ever-more specific set of characteristics, likes and dislikes. At the same time, the Internet has allowed businesses to glean »

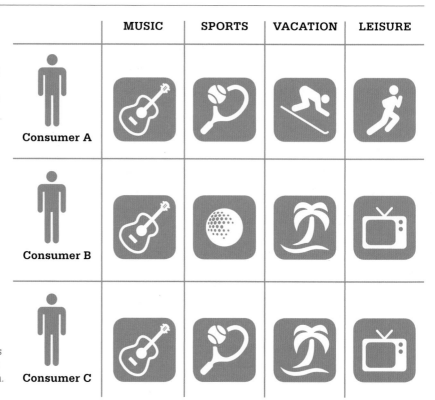

	MUSIC	SPORTS	VACATION	LEISURE
Consumer A				
Consumer B				
Consumer C				

Personalized marketing makes use of information gathered from social media and other platforms to create tailor-made advertising. Consumer A is an active, athletic individual, and would respond to marketing that speaks to this lifestyle.

Customer relationship marketing makes use of historical data to produce individual marketing. Consumer B is an avid TV watcher; an online retailer could make recommendations for DVDs based on previous purchase history.

Psychographic profiling allows marketers to find common ground among a diverse group of individuals. A canny marketer aiming for consumers A, B, and C could use their shared taste in music as a way forward for a campaign.

access to much of this information, providing companies with copious amounts of data for marketing purposes. Software that tracks and analyzes customer preferences via their online and mobile activities has enabled companies to engage in what is called customer relationship marketing (CRM)— using the data extracted about customers and their preferences to sell more products and services to them. Amazon, for example, uses a customer's shopping history to recommend similar products and to show online browsers what other customers with the same interests have recently bought.

Real-time data

Telephone customer service sits at the other end of the spectrum from social media. Pioneered in the 1980s, it began to prove even more

useful in the 1990s with the increase in call centers. Management can divert calls from customer service—or listen in—to learn what issues consumers may be having, what could be improved, and what problems they have that need to be solved. Marketers have dubbed this "customer experience management"

People are unlikely to know that they need a product which does not exist.
John Harvey Jones
UK industrialist (1924–2008)

(CEM), because it captures the customer's immediate interaction with the seller, whereas CRM uses a customer's history.

The field of neuroscience has taken the idea of customer understanding to the next level, advancing Drucker's premise that businesses needed to drill down into the customer psyche and discover how decisions are made. Several studies by branding guru Martin Lindstrom have caused a sensation by proposing that, no matter how consumers may answer in face-to-face research, the only way to know what subconsciously motivates them to buy is to measure changes to their brainwaves when exposed to certain images, sounds, and smells. According to Peter Drucker, "the main objective of neuromarketing is decoding the process that take place in the customers' mind, in order to discover the desires, wishes, and the hidden causes of their options, so that there is a possibility to get them what they want."

Neuromarketing is one way of understanding the customer, and it is actively used by companies such as Google and Disney to test consumer impressions. However, it is not in itself a solution to knowing what customers want to buy. A broader perspective is needed to truly understand a market and the elements that shape it. In some cases it is pure innovation, driven by a desire to transform the way people live through technology, that gives customers something they didn't realize they wanted, though the need for it was there. Apple's iPad is an example of how forward thinking about what customers lives could be like can lead to market success.

Innovative solutions

When the iPad was unveiled in 2010, investors and the press were sceptical, wondering who would want one, given that a laptop computer had more functions and was only slightly bigger. The iPad was a sellout because customers loved using it—it was fun and fast, and allowed them to do all the things they enjoyed on their iPod touch but with a bigger screen and a keyboard that was easier to use.

Apple CEO Steve Jobs claimed in an interview with *Fortune* magazine never to have done consumer research. "It isn't the consumer's job to know what they want," he reportedly said. "That

> Did Alexander Graham Bell do any market research before he invented the telephone?
> **Steve Jobs**

doesn't mean we don't listen to customers, but it's hard for them to tell you what they want when they've never seen anything remotely like it."

Steve Jobs instinctively understood what the consumer wanted because he had the same problem: the lack of a well-designed, portable device that would make communication and information-gathering fun and easy.

Although Peter Drucker emphasized the importance of knowing the customer, he did not narrow this to just asking the customer what they want; he intended that business should also think ahead and find ways to innovate. "The "want" a business satisfies may have been felt by the customer before he was offered the means of satisfying it," he reasoned. "It remained a potential "want" until the action of businessmen converted it into effective demand. Only then is there a customer and a market."

Professor Ranjay Gulati maintains that the first step in understanding the new, highly competitive market of the 21st century is asking customers the right questions; the most important ones being what problems and issues they are dealing with. But he says that a business must make a creative leap to figure out the innovations that will serve those customer needs, if they want to survive in the market place. ∎

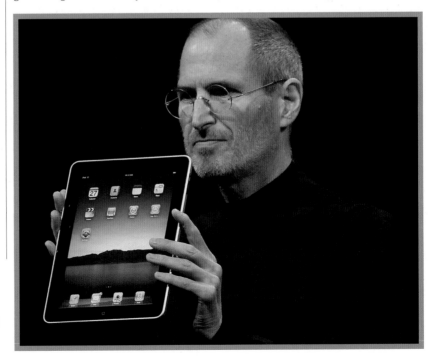

Steve Jobs of Apple encouraged the company to consider the changing technological world and people's existing daily habits to provide an innovative solution to an unfelt need: the iPad.

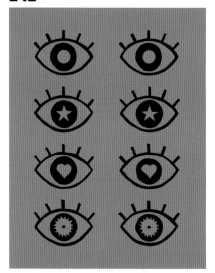

ATTENTION, INTEREST, DESIRE, ACTION
THE AIDA MODEL

IN CONTEXT

FOCUS
Marketing models

KEY DATES
1898 E. St. Elmo Lewis describes the principle that would become AIDA.

1925 US psychologist Edward Kellogg Strong Jr. refers to AIDA in *The Psychology of Selling and Advertising*.

1949 US marketing executive Arthur F. Peterson expresses AIDA as a sales funnel, in *Pharmaceutical Selling, Detailing and Sales Training*.

1967 US professors Charles Sanclage and Vernon Fryburger propose the EPIA model: Exposure, Perception, Integration, Action.

1979 US academics Robert L. Anderson and Thomas E. Barry propose adding brand loyalty to the various hierarchy of effects models based on AIDA.

The AIDA model is the foundation of modern marketing and advertising practice. It outlines the four basic steps that can be used to persuade potential customers to make a purchase. The first three steps lie in creating attention (A), developing interest (I), and building desire (D) for the product, before the fourth step—the "call to action" (A)—tells them exactly how and where to buy.

AIDA is often expressed as a funnel, because it channels the customer's feelings through each stage of the communication process toward reaching a sale.

AIDA in practice

Attracting the customer's attention is the first challenge, and this may be achieved by using an arresting catchphrase, offering a discount or something for free, or demonstrating how a problem can be solved. Once someone's attention has been seized, it must be turned into genuine interest. This is best done by providing a succinct assessment of the product's benefits to the consumer, rather than simply listing the product's main features. Problem-solving claims, results-based advice, or testimonials can be used to create desire, before finally laying out a simple way for that desire to be met—the means to buy. On website advertising, this might be a direct link; on TV, print, or billboards it may be a website, store name, or telephone number.

Commercial potential

In the movie industry, the stages of AIDA are used to great effect. Movie studios often begin their marketing campaigns months in advance with giant billboard posters to attract attention to the new movie. Short "teaser" trailers follow, which provoke interest by offering a tantalizing glimpse of the movie without giving too much away. Desire is instilled by the release of the full trailer, which is carefully crafted to show the highlights of the movie, from big explosions and special effects to witty lines of dialogue. On the opening weekend, advertisements in newspapers and on television spotlight the movie's release, provoking action by inviting the consumer to go and buy a ticket.

One of the movie hits of 1999, *The Blair Witch Project*, had an innovative approach to AIDA that made use of new viral marketing techniques. Before the movie's first showing, the filmmakers created a website that offered an intriguing insight into the background to the movie. It presented snippets of movie as "found film footage," and left viewers wondering whether the story of the movie was fiction or reality. The website grabbed attention, and continued to gain interest as more video clips and audio files were added. The buzz around the "myth" of the Blair Witch grew, creating further desire to see the movie. The call to action came in the form of a very limited release; moviegoers were urged to buy tickets before those few showings sold out. The movie cost just $35,000 to make, but generated revenues of more than $280 million worldwide.

E-marketing and AIDA

The advent of e-commerce prompted award-winning UK copywriter Ian Moore to suggest NEWAIDA as a more relevant model for e-marketing: AIDA preceded by navigation, ease, and wording. It seems that as markets have become more complex, marketers require ever-clearer ways of perceiving the customer journey. ■

Who invented AIDA?

Management expert Philip Kotler references Edward Kellogg Strong Jr.'s book *The Psychology of Selling and Advertising* (1925) as the source of AIDA. However, Strong's book gives credit for the idea to advertising pioneer Elias St. Elmo Lewis (1872–1948), maintaining that Lewis formulated the slogan "Attract attention, maintain interest, create desire" in 1898 and that he later added the fourth term "get action."

The first use of the AIDA acronym is commonly attributed to C. P. Russell's article "How to Write a Sales-Marketing Letter," published in the US advertising trade magazine *Printers' Ink* in 1921—Russell was also one of its editorial staff. He outlined the basis of the four-step process and pointed out that "reading downward, the first letters of these words spell the opera *Aida*." He advised, "When you start a letter ... say 'AIDA' to yourself and you won't go far wrong ..."

The AIDA model

ATTENTION
Make the customer aware of the product or service using an eye-catching advertisement or an arresting offer.

INTEREST
Hold the customer's interest by providing infomation about the advantages of the product or service and its benefits to the customer.

DESIRE
Generate the customer's desire to buy by convincing them that the service or product will meet their needs.

ACTION
Make it as easy as possible for the customer to make the purchase.

SALE

In practice, few messages take the consumer all the way from awareness to purchase, but the AIDA framework suggests the qualities of a good message.
Philip Kotler
US marketing guru (1931–)

MARKETING MYOPIA

FOCUS ON THE FUTURE MARKET

IN CONTEXT

FOCUS
Customer service

KEY DATES
1874 French mathematical economist Leon Walrus recognizes that small changes in consumer preferences have a big impact on business.

1913–1914 Henry Ford, US industrialist, installs the first production line, and informs companies that cheaper per-unit costs are the key to their sustained growth.

1957 US marketing theorist Wroe Alderson stresses that a business needs to grow and adapt to changes in order to survive and thrive.

1981 US marketing thinkers Philip Kotler and Ravi Singh coin the term "marketing hyperopia" to describe the problem of businesses having a clear view of distant issues but not of close ones.

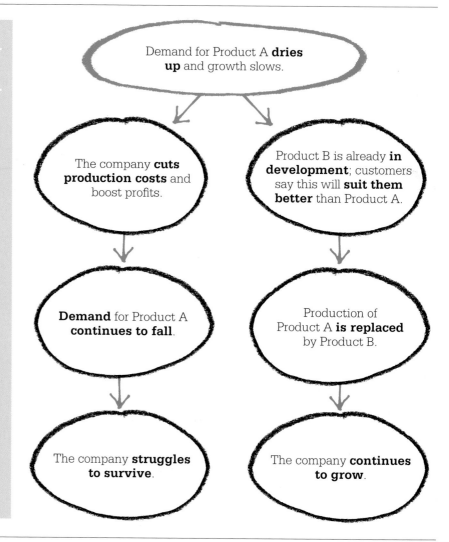

When a company has a fixed idea of what products or services it wants to sell, and a narrow idea of who it is selling to, it runs the risk of failure because it is not easily able to adapt to changes in market conditions. It will miss opportunities to expand and conquer new market areas. Harvard Business School professor Theodore Levitt dubbed this lack of foresight "marketing myopia," a term he first used in an article of the same name, published in the *Harvard Business Review* in 1960. He stressed that a company needs to look ahead and constantly evaluate new openings in the market. If it does not, growth will stagnate and, ultimately, decline.

In Levitt's view, when a business is concentrating on how to sell its products and is blind to the changing circumstances and desires of customers, it will not be prepared for shifts in the market. For example, a sudden change in the economy or government policy, a new technology, or a social crisis can have an almost immediate effect on the buying public. If a company is prepared for such changes, and flexible enough to adjust, it can find ways to tempt customers and prosper. The astute approach, Levitt said, is to build a business around the customer, rather than around the company. He proposed that "an industry is a customer-satisfying process, not a goods-producing process."

Grow or die
Underlying Levitt's idea is the inevitable growth pattern of a business. At first a business enters the market with a product or service and may enjoy rapid

See also: Finding a profitable niche 22–23 ▪ Make your customers love you 264–67 ▪ Maximize customer benefits 288–89 ▪ Feedback and innovation 312–13

growth. But all growth eventually tapers off because the market has already bought enough of the product or service, or develops different priorities. The company with marketing myopia turns inward to see how it can trim the costs of manufacturing or make other internal cost-saving measures. These tactics may offset a decline in profits for a while, but eventually they will not be enough to save the business from failing. Levitt, however, reasoned that an industry can continue to grow long after the obvious marketing strategies have been used, if the management is totally focused on the customer.

Levitt asked the corporate heads of America in 1960, "What business are you in?", demanding that they shift their focus from manufacturing to customer satisfaction. This concept is taken for granted in the current age geared to customer analysis and niche marketing, but given that the US economy had boomed in the 1950s, enjoying its most prosperous

Selling is not marketing.... the entire business process [is] a tightly integrated effort to discover, create, arouse, and satisfy customer needs.
Theodore Levitt

era for several decades, Levitt's idea may not have seemed very relevant at the time. Still, he cited convincing examples in US industry to support his case. In particular, he accused automobile manufacturers of marketing myopia.

The automobile industry
On the surface, the US auto industry appeared unstoppable. By 1960 the "Big Three" in the city of

Detroit (General Motors, Ford, and Chrysler) dominated the domestic and global markets. They produced 93 percent of the automobiles sold in the US, and controlled 48 percent of world sales. One-sixth of the US work force was employed directly or indirectly by the industry. Nevertheless, cracks were beginning to show.

In 1955, the Big Three had enjoyed a record year. However, demand fell dramatically in 1956 and 1957 because so many consumers had already bought cars. This sales slump was partly responsible for the recession of 1958, during which manufacturing as a whole declined. This was the first economic downturn in the US since the Great Depression. Meanwhile, car manufacturers in Germany, the UK, France, and Japan were threatening the dominance of the Big Three.

"Detroit never really researched the customer's wants," alleged Levitt. "It only researched the kinds of things which it had already decided to offer." By the time US carmakers realized what had happened, they found it difficult to adjust. After a series of dud models and marketing failures, they finally rebounded in 1965 with the ubiquitous "muscle" cars such as the Ford Mustang—but they would never again have such an iron grip on the market.

Before Theodore Levitt's groundbreaking article in 1960, marketing was not considered a **»**

Abandoned automobile factories in Detroit are a reminder of the US economic downturn in the late 1950s. Theodore Levitt argued that carmakers failed to adapt to their customer's needs.

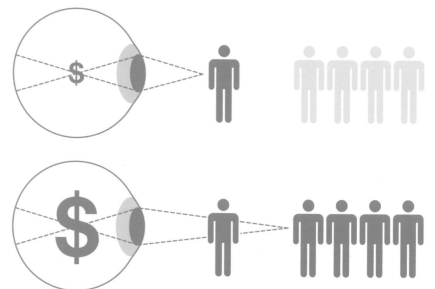

Shortsighted marketing focuses on current customers and their needs but overlooks potential new markets, leading to missed opportunities and more modest profits.

Farsighted marketing is adaptable, allowing businesses to shift their focus to reach a wider range of consumers with a broader product offering. Returns can then be much greater.

serious endeavor worthy of management attention; instead it was a formulaic task left to the sales or production departments. But "Marketing Myopia" prompted both the corporate and academic worlds to start thinking differently.

Taking marketing seriously

Around the same time that Levitt was writing that pivotal article, he inspired a student, Philip Kotler, who would take his proposition further to cement a fundamental change in the way managers approached business. Kotler studied at Harvard in 1960 for his postdoctoral work in mathematics, having already completed a PhD in economics at the Massachusetts Institute of Technology (MIT). Exposed firsthand to the ideas of Levitt and other marketing professors, he began to develop a rigorous outline for the role of marketing in any organization. The result was published in 1964, and *Marketing Management* is still regarded as the seminal textbook on the subject. It is credited with being

the first book to take a scholarly and scientific approach to marketing. Kotler's key teachings are that the customer should be at the center of any business, and that profit is derived not merely from selling but from delivering satisfaction to customers: thinking which is still at the core of most MBA programs.

The effect of Levitt and Kotler's ideas on the corporate world was almost immediate. In 1962, executive Robert Townsend had just been lured from American

The entire corporation must be viewed as a customer-creating and customer-satisfying organism.
Theodore Levitt

Express to take up the position of CEO at struggling car rental company Avis. He rebuilt the business by focusing on two interdependent principles: put customers first; and create a working environment in which employees love what they do. For the first time the business began to make a profit.

Customer service

By 1964 Avis was expanding. The man appointed as manager of operations in Europe, Africa, and the Middle East, Colin Marshall, was another believer in Levitt's customer-centered approach, and deployed it with great success. Within ten years he was running the entire company from New York, overseeing innovations that gave customers better service, and making Avis the market leader. In 1981, when he was recruited to help save British Airways (BA), he turned around the fortunes of the airline in a tough environment, creating a successful model of service-oriented business. His tactic was not to cut air fares but to offer better customer service. Marshall saw that the customer experience went beyond check-in, in-flight, touchdown, and passport control, and he introduced the world's first arrivals lounges.

Customer experience

Other full-service airlines have adapted the BA model. Most airlines now rely on optimizing customer relationships in order to gain a long-term, competitive advantage. United Airlines, for example, has implemented a system that lets staff identify high-value frequent flyers and proactively offer them special services if their flight is canceled. American Airlines has promoted its use of technology to make the flight experience more appealing for customers, becoming the first with permission from the Federal Aviation Administration (FAA) to allow flight attendants to use tablets to help them manage the onboard experience more efficiently. It was the first major commercial airline to provide branded tablets to First Class and Business passengers

Airport arrivals lounges were offered to BA passengers to enhance their experience of traveling with the airline. Rather than cutting prices, BA chose to focus on customer service.

Marketing is not the art of finding clever ways to dispose of what you make. It is the art of creating genuine customer value.
Philip Kotler

for inflight use. Enhancing a customer experience through internet access and applications on iPads, tablets, and cell phones is now a vital consideration in many sectors of industry, something on which Google has capitalized.

In 2005, Google purchased a little-known company called Android Inc., which was developing a smartphone platform. Two years later Apple released its iPhone and rapidly dominated the market; customers loved it since they could replicate the world of the Internet on a handheld device. Online search giant, Google, saw that it risked becoming beholden to Apple for access to sell its applications so, with other cell-phone makers, it developed an alternative—an open-source operating system that would work on all mobile devices. Google now had a platform through which it could generate profit with sales of applications and in-app advertising.

Kotler cites Google as a model of innovation, always seeking new ways to solve customers' problems and help them manage vast amounts of information. Levitt would have agreed with the first line of Google's corporate philosophy: "Focus on the user and all else will follow." ∎

Theodore Levitt

Acknowledged as one of the most original management thinkers of the modern age, Theodore "Ted" Levitt was born in Vollmerz, Germany but emigrated to the US with his family at ten. He served in the US Army during World War II, returning to enroll at Ohio University. With his PhD in Economics, he joined the faculty of Harvard Business School in 1959, writing his famous article "Marketing Myopia" just a year later. For the next 30 years he taught at Harvard, contributing 26 articles to the *Harvard Business Review*, of which he was chief editor from 1985 to 1989. In its 2004 edition, the journal cited marketing myopia as the most influential marketing idea of the past 50 years. Levitt created a similar stir in 1983 with another article, "The Globalization of Markets," which led to him being credited with popularizing the term "globalization."

Key works

1960 "Marketing Myopia," *Harvard Business Review*
1983 *The Marketing Imagination*

THE CASH COW IS THE BEATING HEART OF THE ORGANIZATION

PRODUCT PORTFOLIO

The term "cash cow" refers to an investment or area of business that provides a dependable source of revenue. In a corporate context, the cash cow is the product or service that buoys profits year in, year out and provides funds so the business can grow. It brings cash in, which becomes the lifeblood: contributing most of the operating expenses; paying for development, launch, and support of new products; and propping up it's less profitable ventures.

Cash generator

The cash cow is typically a product that has reached maturity in its life cycle. Like its real-life counterpart, its initial cost has been paid off, it needs little maintenance, and it can be "milked" for the rest of its life. Although such products may no longer be growing, they still generate substantial revenue because they have good market share and no longer require much capital outlay to keep them going.

Management veteran Peter Drucker is said to have first used the "cash cow" metaphor in the mid-1960s; he certainly referred to it throughout his career to describe

As entrepreneurs, we adore shiny new things. But don't forget to give some love to the (cash) cows that keep the business going.
John Warrillow
UK entrepreneur (1971–)

a product that is an easy cash generator. He was drawing on the history of commerce in his analogy: livestock such as cows, goats, and camels served as currency from around 9,000 BCE. While Drucker understood the value of the cash cow, at the same time he cautioned against overreliance on it. He advocated a strategy of planned abandonment when the cash cow is challenged by another product, potentially a rival within the company's portfolio, which is growing faster.

The Boston Consulting Group

In 1875, the Boston Safe Deposit and Trust Company was set up in its home port in New England to offer safekeeping services to local merchants and ship owners. Run by several generations of the prominent Bostonian family, the Lowells, the company had grown by the 20th century to become a prominent financial institution.

In 1963, a chance meeting between the Boston Safe Deposit and Trust Company CEO John Lowell and one of the US's brightest management thinkers Bruce Henderson (1915–1992) led to the founding of the Boston Consulting Group (BCG). This management consultancy was essentially a one-man band with Henderson at the helm.

Henderson had been a Bible salesman before completing an engineering degree at Vanderbilt University, Nashville, and going on to study at Harvard Business School. He joined Westinghouse Corporation before graduating, becoming one of the youngest vice-presidents in the history of the company. Initially finding it difficult to land clients and compete against larger consultancies, Henderson came up with the idea of offering "business strategy" as a unique service. A few years later, with a team of 36, Henderson devised the now-famous growth-share matrix (1968). His company, BCG, has since grown to become a significant global management consultancy employing more than 2,000 staff in 75 offices around the world.

See also: Managing risk 40–41 ▪ How fast to grow 44–45 ▪ The Greiner curve 58–61 ▪ Profit versus cash flow 152–53 ▪ Leading the market 166–69 ▪ The MABA matrix 192–93 ▪ The marketing model 232–33 ▪ Marketing mix 280–83

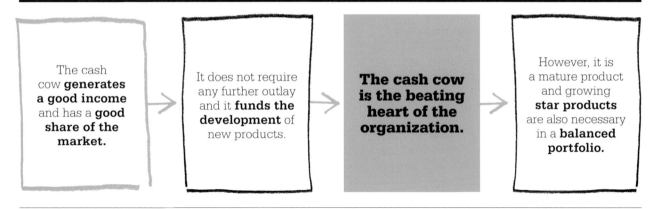

The cash cow **generates a good income** and has a **good share of the market.**

→ It does not require any further outlay and it **funds the development** of new products.

→ **The cash cow is the beating heart of the organization.**

→ However, it is a mature product and growing **star products** are also necessary in a **balanced portfolio.**

Peter Drucker cited the case of IBM in the mid-1970s. The mainframe computer was its cash cow, but the newly launched PC was its fastest-growing product; in fact, IBM dominated the PC market at first. However, the company deliberately restricted sales of PCs for fear of jeopardizing its cash cow, and in doing so, allowed time for clones to flood the market. In fact, IBM lost so much ground that its PC business never recovered. IBM's product portfolio continued to be subordinate to its cash cow. With investors in mind, they avoided the risks that come with innovation and developing new, leading-edge products and ended up being unable to compete amid the rapid technological and marketplace changes of the 1990s.

Drucker may have been the first to use the term in a business context, but the Boston Consulting Group (BCG), founded by Bruce Henderson, first incorporated the cash cow into a business model in 1968. Referred to as the BCG matrix, Boston Box, or growth-share matrix, this model graphically depicts the relationship between market growth and market share. It quickly became a popular business tool for making decisions about which products to wind down and which ones to invest in.

The product portfolio
The starting point for the BCG matrix is the concept of a product portfolio—the total mix of products offered by an organization. These can be categorized according to their share of the market, revenues, and growth potential. Each one can also be assessed by its position in the "product life cycle," which tracks the path of a product from initial growth to maturity and then decline. When making decisions about which products it should continue to manufacture, an organization needs to consider the life cycle of each product and the balance or synergy between all the products in their portfolio.

The BCG matrix provides an analytical tool for assessing the effectiveness of the product mix and its profitability. A business »

A company should have a portfolio of products with different growth rates and different market shares. The portfolio is a function of the balance between cash flows.
Bruce Henderson

IBM launched its PC in 1981 and it sold well. However, the company failed to capitalize on its success, focusing instead on its mainframe computers.

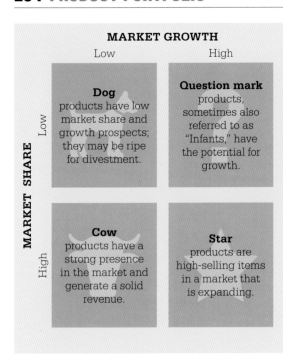

MARKET GROWTH

Low · High

MARKET SHARE

Low · High

Dog
products have low market share and growth prospects; they may be ripe for divestment.

Question mark
products, sometimes also referred to as "Infants," have the potential for growth.

Cow
products have a strong presence in the market and generate a solid revenue.

Star
products are high-selling items in a market that is expanding.

The BCG matrix
can be used to categorize products in terms of growth and market share, so companies can check that they have a well-balanced product portfolio. Products with a high market share are plotted into cells on the left-hand column, and those with low market share on the right. The top row is home to products with high potential for growth, while those in the bottom row are in declining markets.

"Stars" are products that have a large market share in a growing market. These require investment to maintain their position and help them grow into the dominant product in the market. They have the potential to be a future cow.

"Cows" are products that were once stars. They continue to hold a large market share, but they are mature products in an established market that has little potential for growth. They no longer need much investment, because they have reached their growth potential, and as market leaders they sell in large numbers of units, giving them the advantage of economies of scale. This means they generate cash while costing very little.

The matrix in practice
Nestlé is often cited by management theorists as a textbook example of how a company might arrange its product portfolio according to the BCG matrix. The world's largest food company, with some 8,000 brands, Nestlé has developed a strategy of building its long-term cows and keeping them as fresh as possible, devoting capital to product areas that have a prospect of high returns, and shedding

can use this information to make sure it has a mix of products that will satisfy its short- and long-term needs, and to think about the priority and resources they should allocate to each product. The matrix assesses products on two levels: first, the potential growth in the market for that product; second, the market share held by each product.

Using the Boston matrix
By using the matrix, managers can see where their products fall among four categories: dogs, question marks, stars, and cows. "Dogs" are products that have low growth prospects and a low market share. These products may be making a loss, barely breaking even, or possibly generating a tiny amount of profit. Because they are in a slow-growing market, there is little chance that performance will improve under current conditions. Products that fall into this cell of the matrix are candidates for

culling from the product portfolio. However, before the dog is sold off or disposed of, management must consider if it is worth keeping for strategic reasons. For example, if it is blocking a competitor product or the market for that industry is likely to pick up in the future, it might be worth retaining. Or it may play an important role in complementing another product in the portfolio and providing customers with a stepping stone to that product.

Like the dog, the "question mark" product also has a low share of the market, but it is in a high-growth industry. Products in this box can create a dilemma for the company. If it is new, does the product need more time to prove itself, and more investment in manufacturing or marketing? Or does it need more market share, which could be arranged by buying up competitors? Perhaps it needs repositioning in the market. Or should it be dropped entirely?

High-growth products require cash inputs to grow. Low-growth products should generate excess cash. Both are needed simultaneously.
Bruce Henderson

products with limited potential. The coffee brand Nescafé has continued to perform well since its 1938 launch, thanks in part to the company's strategy of investing in and expanding the range. At different times in the company's history it has been a cow and a star product. Instant coffee is now a reliable cow, funding expansion in other areas. However, the company's organic food range has suffered low market share in a growing market, making it a question mark. Nestlé's large share of the food seasonings sector, a low-growth area, could be seen as a cow.

Through a series of acquisitions, Nestlé has become the leading pet-food maker in a globally high-

Nescafé coffee is Nestlé's largest brand, a cash cow valued at $17.4 billion. Growing since World War II, the product generated sales of $10 billion in 2012.

growth market, elevating food products for real dogs and cats into star products.

Portfolio management

Other models have evolved from the BCG. In the 1970s, General Electric consulted with business advisors McKinsey & Company to develop an alternative known as the GE–McKinsey matrix. This nine-cell model enables a more complex analysis of the product portfolio, and allows companies to plot market attractiveness and

competitive strength. In 1982, H. C. Barksdale and C. E. Harris proposed two new product classifications to add to the original BCG matrix: "warhorses" and "dodos." Warhorses lead the market but are threatened by a negative market growth, so a business must gauge whether to ride out the storm in the belief that it will pick up, or work the horse as long as possible with minimal outlay. Dodos are about to become extinct, with low share in a negative growth market.

Using the matrices

A 1981 study by management professors Richard Bettis and W. K. Hall, and supported by P. Haspeslagh in 1982, found the BCG matrix was used by 45 percent of companies ranked in the *Fortune* 500.

However, the BCG matrix has attracted criticism for being overly simplistic and basing judgements on cash flow rather than return on investment. A study by Colorado State University in 1992 discovered that companies using the BCG matrix and similar models had lower shareholder returns than companies not using such models. Despite its detractors, the BCG provides an easy way to make sense of the product portfolio and the strategies involved in managing it successfully. ∎

Barksdale and Harris created a matrix that added two new classifications known as warhorses and dodos, both of which were expected to decline.

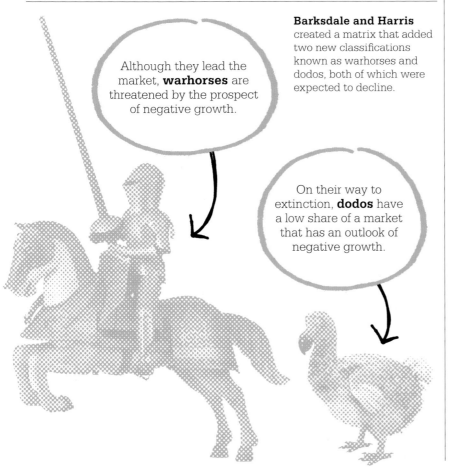

Although they lead the market, **warhorses** are threatened by the prospect of negative growth.

On their way to extinction, **dodos** have a low share of a market that has an outlook of negative growth.

EXPANDING AWAY FROM YOUR CORE HAS RISKS; DIVERSIFICATION DOUBLES THEM
ANSOFF'S MATRIX

IN CONTEXT

FOCUS
Strategic planning

KEY DATES
500 BCE The concept of "strategic planning" is first used in military campaigns in ancient Greece.

1920s Harvard Business School develops the Harvard Policy Model, one of the first strategic planning approaches to private businesses.

1965 Igor Ansoff's *Corporate strategy: an analytic approach to business policy for growth and expansion* is the first book on corporate strategy.

1980 Michael Porter introduces his theory of competitive strategy.

1989–90 Concepts of core competence and strategic intent are developed by Gary Hamel and C. K. Prahalad.

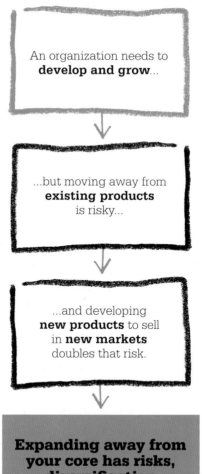

An organization needs to **develop and grow**…

…but moving away from **existing products** is risky…

…and developing **new products** to sell in **new markets** doubles that risk.

Expanding away from your core has risks, diversification doubles them.

First published in 1957 in the *Harvard Business Review*, Ansoff's matrix is a marketing tool for planning the strategic growth of an organization. Created by mathematician Igor Ansoff, it is intended for businesses that are ready to expand and have the resources to fund growth. The matrix offers four possible strategies that a company might adopt, depending on the status of its product and the conditions of the market: market penetration, market development, product development, and diversification. In addition to presenting these four strategic options, the matrix also attaches an inherent risk factor to each one. It is crucial for decision makers to take the risk factor into consideration, lest it gamble too heavily with the company's existing resources.

The four strategies
Each approach is differentiated by whether products or services are unchanged or new, and whether they remain in the existing market or are entering a new one. The least risky of the four strategies is "market penetration"—maximizing sales of an existing product in an existing market. In this approach,

See also: Managing risk 40–41 ▪ Take the second step 43 ▪ How fast to grow 44–45 ▪ Protect the core business 170–71 ▪ The MABA matrix 192–93

Ansoff's matrix is expressed as a square divided into four equal cells, each of which represents different marketing strategies, with different combinations of product status and market conditions. Market penetration is clearly the least risky, while the quadrant of diversification presents the highest risk.

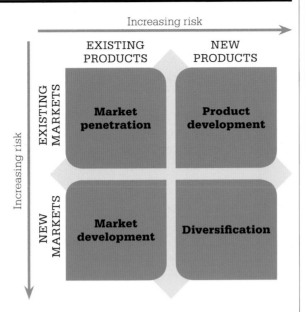

Increasing risk

Increasing risk

	EXISTING PRODUCTS	NEW PRODUCTS
EXISTING MARKETS	**Market penetration**	**Product development**
NEW MARKETS	**Market development**	**Diversification**

greater sales might be achieved through competitive pricing, advertising, loyalty programs, or by driving out competitors.

"Market development" entails selling the same product in different markets. Additional spending may be unnecessary unless localization is required, but the cost of setting up distribution channels in the new market poses some risk. In this model, different geographic or demographic markets, or alternative sales channels—such as online or direct—might be tapped.

"Product development" strategy is the sale of new or significantly improved products to an existing market. Here, the cost of product development, associated distribution, and marketing support poses a risk. Companies adopting this strategy might offer variants of the product, or develop related goods.

The final, and riskiest strategy, is that of "diversification"—moving into new product areas and new

markets. This strategy reduces risk in the long term by alleviating a company's reliance on core products. However, a company can risk a great deal, depending on the initial outlay, and needs to have plenty of resources if the strategy fails.

A risky venture

UK supermarket Tesco's venture into the US shows the risks of diversification. After 10 years' preparation, it launched its Fresh & Easy stores in 2007, but misread the market. Positioning itself in the middle, it was neither upscale nor discount, with most of its outlets in working-class suburbs where consumers looked for bargains. Critically, Tesco's small-scale, walk-in stores did not suit the average car-dependent US shopper. The investment did not pay off, costing Tesco over $1.9 (£1.2) billion. The outcome may not have been forecast by Ansoff's matrix, but the risk would have been clear. ▪

Is Ansoff's matrix still relevant?

Igor Ansoff (1918–2002) is remembered as the father of modern marketing strategy. His matrix has generated many variations over the decades and became one of the foundation stones of business strategy, underpinning ideas such as core competence and competitive strategy.

In the 1970s Ansoff recognized the problem of "paralysis by analysis"—the overthinking of a problem and subsequent failure to act. He advocated a more flexible approach, based on local conditions and a company's individual circumstances.

Ansoff's matrix has limitations. Because it focuses on market potential and strategies for growth, it is not able to support other factors and scenarios, such as the resources available, or if a company's priority is survival rather than growth. However, used with other marketing tools, it remains valuable and is still used to gauge actual and expected growth.

As companies became increasingly skillful strategy formulators, the translation of strategy into results ... created paralysis by analysis.
Igor Ansoff

IF YOU'RE DIFFERENT YOU WILL STAND OUT

CREATING A BRAND

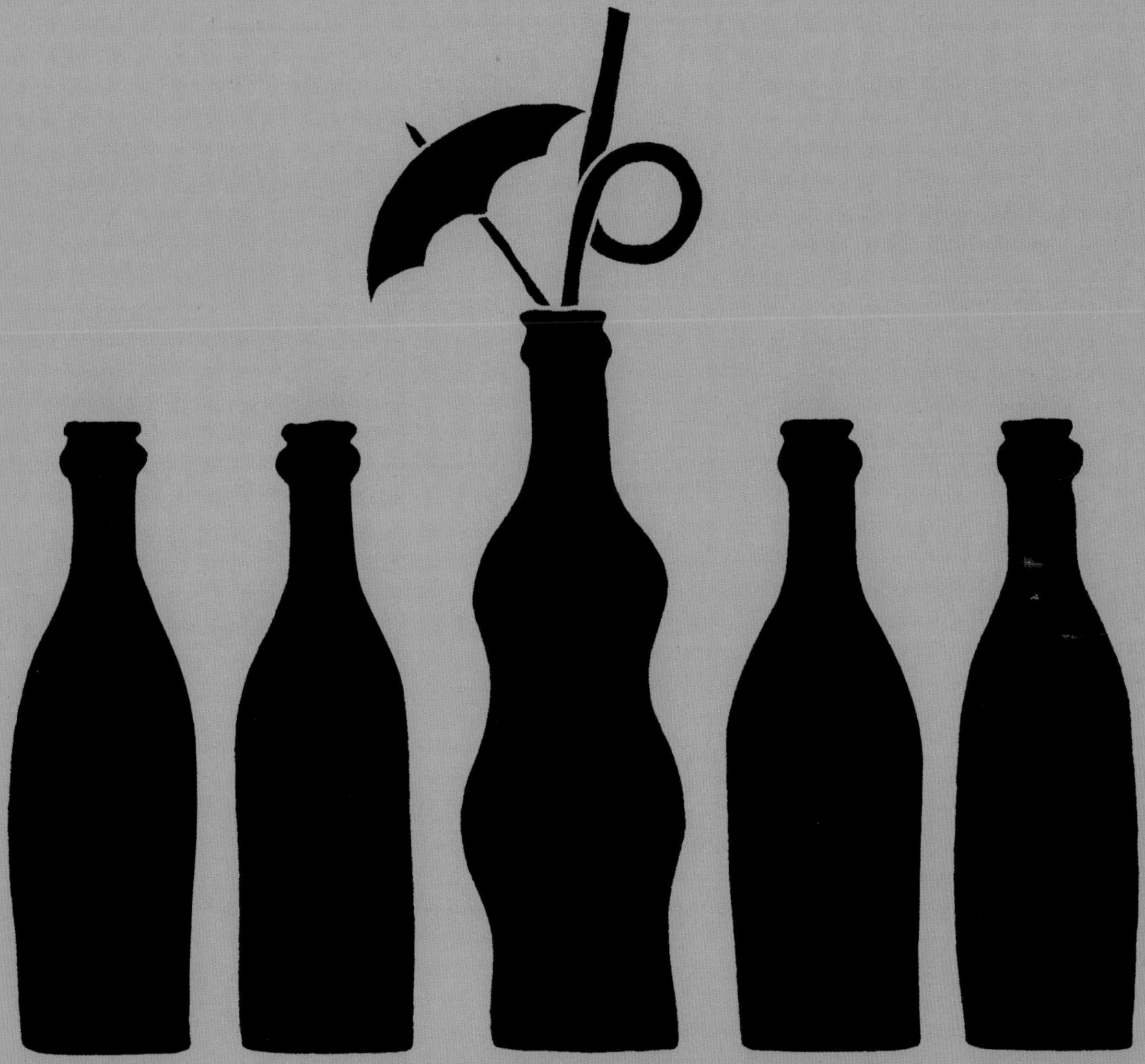

IN CONTEXT

FOCUS
Brand creation

KEY DATES
1850s During the industrial revolution products are mass-produced for the first time, so supply outstrips demand.

1880s and 90s In the US and Europe, brand names—including Coca-Cola, Kelloggs, and Kodak—become popular for promoting products.

1950s TVs become popular in the home, providing a new way for companies to send sales messages to the mass market.

2002 The average number of brands in a US supermarket is 32,000, compared to 20,000 in 1990.

2013 Brand advocates—members of the public who recommend products or services online—are estimated to number 60 million in the US alone.

Brands are how organizations make their product or service stand out from the competition. In ancient times, cattle and slaves were branded to show ownership, and in the Middle Ages paper manufacturers could be identified by a watermark in the paper. However, our modern idea of the brand—which includes every part of the perceived identity of a company, from logo to affiliations— did not emerge until the mid-to-late 19th century.

The increasing number of middle-class, literate consumers in Western societies were able for the first time to choose from a range of items rather than buy from necessity. In the US and Europe, as the supply of packaged goods continued to grow, manufacturers saw the importance of differentiating their products. Coca-Cola launched in 1886 with its name in a distinctive script, backing up the brand 30 years later with a now-famous contoured bottle. Quaker Oats used a man in Quaker clothing on its 1896 advertisment, holding a package of oats in one hand, and a scroll saying "Pure" in the other. Clothing manufacturers

Products are made
in the factory, but brands
are created in the mind.
Walter Landor
German brand expert
(1913–95)

such as Levi's began to stamp their name on products. These companies were seeking to build a direct relationship with the customer.

The dawn of advertising

Brands took off in the 1950s, when there was a postwar boom in mass production and televisions became a common item in homes. Businesses such as Unilever and Procter & Gamble began to create identities for otherwise indistinguishable soaps and laundry detergents. They needed to package their product so that consumers would reach for it

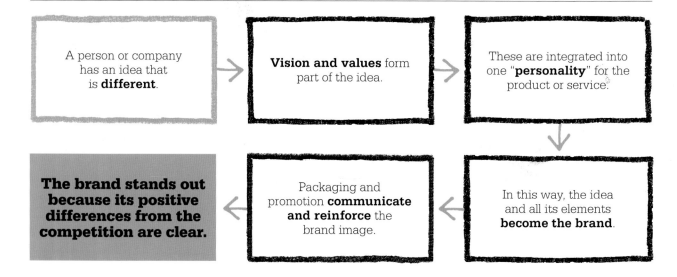

A person or company has an idea that is **different**.

Vision and values form part of the idea.

These are integrated into one "**personality**" for the product or service.

In this way, the idea and all its elements **become the brand**.

Packaging and promotion **communicate and reinforce** the brand image.

The brand stands out because its positive differences from the competition are clear.

See also: Finding a profitable niche 22–23 ▪ Stand out in the market 28–31 ▪ Understanding the market 234–41 ▪ Make your customers love you 264–267 ▪ Generating buzz 274–75 ▪ Feedback and innovation 312–13

The "easy" brand began as an airline, but its brand essence—"more value for less!"—has been successfully applied to more than a dozen businesses, from pizza delivery to office-space rental.

first. With the rise in self-service stores and supermarkets, brands had to catch the consumer's eye on the shelf and also appeal on an emotional level. Persil, for example, played on a housewife's pride in the whiteness of her laundry with the slogan: "Get your whites right."

Creating a brand

Today, a brand is more than just a logo or attractive packaging. Brand creation has to start with an idea, and the idea is more likely to be successful if it is different than the competition's. Typically, it starts with the customer and what they want or need. It might also be based on the way the new company or product is fulfilling a gap in the market. Pret A Manger, for example, launched its healthy fast-food cafés as an alternative to the ubiquitous burger chains. The brand revolves around the concept of fresh, additive-free food prepared daily at every branch. Alternatively, a new product might be something that improves on the existing technology through new and innovative design, such as Dyson's bagless vacuum cleaners. Or the idea might be something that no one has thought of before, and did not even know they wanted, like the iPad, which has become indispensible to millions.

One of the key things about a successful brand, such as Apple or Dyson, is that they build an affiliated community—people who like iPads or prefer Dysons, and are happy to be identified with the other members of that group. The most powerful brands even have identifiable "nonbelievers"—think Coke *vs*. Pepsi, or Mac *vs*. PC. The sense of belonging to a group that seems to share your own values is a key part of consumer loyalty.

Translatable brands

It is often hard to tell whether the product makes the brand, or the brand makes the product. EasyJet,

A product can be quickly outdated; a successful brand is timeless.
Stephen King
UK advertising executive
(1931–2006)

for example, was a simple idea. Company founder Sir Stelios Haji-Ioannou wanted to make air travel easy, cheap, and different than the large airline approach. The "easy" brand, which started in the UK with the launch of an airline in 1995, is now used by more than a dozen different businesses all over the world. The "easy" idea had many different elements that brought it to life—from the way people book their tickets online to the no-frills service onboard—but the essential idea of selling a basic service at an affordable price was translatable to many other forms of business.

Vision and values

The different elements that make up a company's vision and values are integrated to create a brand's personality. Companies look to this "personality" to provide the Unique Selling Proposition (USP) that will make their product or service stand out from the competition, while » the individual values and vision take the brand from an idea on a piece of paper to a commercial reality. The vision for the company reflects where the founders or directors want to take the idea. The vision of the furniture store IKEA, for example, is to create "a better everyday life for the many people." The business idea that supports this vision is to offer good-quality furniture at affordable prices. IKEA has become a global brand because all aspects of their business support this idea, from the unique layout of the shopping environment—such as family-oriented restaurants and children's play areas—to advertising. Today IKEA is the world's largest furniture retailer.

What kind of brand?

Values are another subtle element of the brand, and summarize what the brand stands for. It is important that companies don't just state their values; they should be reflected in the way the company operates.

The three founders of the fruit-smoothie company Innocent, which started life at a British music festival in 1999, decided they wanted one of the key values

> A brand that captures your mind gains behavior. A brand that captures your heart gains commitment.
> **Scott Talgo**
> US brand strategist

of their innovative company to be openness. Each fruit drink carries a label inviting customers to "call the bananaphone" with their views, or to drop in to the company headquarters, Fruit Towers, at any time. The Innocent website also invites visitors to join the Innocent "family" and make suggestions for what the company should do next, "as we sometimes get confused." Their chatty, informal approach suggests that the company prioritizes openness and dialogue with customers, whose values and opinions it respects. The tone of

language, informal website, and quirky offices at Fruit Towers also help create Innocent's personality, conveying a bold, irreverent brand.

The third place

Howard Schultz, who built Starbucks into a global brand, had the idea of a coffee company with a distinctive personality that could create a sense of connection. When Schultz joined in 1982, Starbucks was a single store in Seattle selling fresh-roasted, whole-bean coffees. The name, taken from a character in Melville's *Moby Dick*, evoked the seafaring tradition of early coffee traders. Schultz traveled to Italy the following year and observed that in Italian coffee bars, coffee was more than just a hot drink: it was an experience that sparked daily exchanges. He decided to bring the Italian coffeehouse tradition back to the US, where he had seen limited casual social interaction.

The concept of the "third place" was born—a place between work and home where you can enjoy conversation and a sense of community. This idea became an essential part of the brand and was carried through in the café design:

Anita Roddick

Born to an Italian immigrant couple in an English seaside town in 1942, Anita Roddick described herself as a "natural outsider." She started The Body Shop, a retail cosmetics and beauty business, in 1976, with one store in Brighton. Drawing on her own diverse experience and travels in Europe, Africa, and the South Pacific, she created natural cosmetic products in recyclable bottles. The Body Shop went on to shape ethical consumerism because of Roddick's personal drive and the campaigns that were promoted within her stores. Roddick's firm belief was that businesses have the power to do good, and she pioneered the prohibition of animal testing for cosmetic products, pushed the adoption of fair trade, and lent business support to political causes such as Greenpeace and Amnesty International.

In 2000 she published her autobiography *Business as Unusual,* followed by a series of activist publications. She was made Dame Commander of the Order of the British Empire in 2004. In 2006 The Body Shop was purchased by US giant L'Oreal. Roddick died in 2007.

REVENUE POTENTIAL

Bonding
This is definitely my kind of brand.

Advantage
I can see how this brand fits me better than others.

Performance
How well does it compare
with other brands?

Relevance
Does this brand fit my
needs and budget?

Presence
I have noticed
the brand.

LOYALTY

The brand pyramid
was created by the
consulting company
Millward Brown in the
mid-1990s to illustrate the
five key stages of building
customer loyalty. Revenues
increase as customers move
from an awareness of the product
to complete commitment.

relaxing leather sofas, comfy chairs, and freely available newspapers. In the 1990s, the rise of the coffee bar on street corners became a social phenomenon that spread from North America to Asia, Europe, and beyond, because they met people's needs for a friendly gathering place.

Ethics and branding
Anita Roddick started the cosmetics store The Body Shop in the 1970s when her husband was traveling across the Americas, and she needed to support herself and her family while he was away. She had little business experience, but had a gut instinct that her products had to be different to sell. Mass production had brought choice to consumers, but interest in the sourcing of ingredients, how

products were made, and broader ethical issues was growing. Roddick sold natural products in refillable bottles, and aligned the brand with a number of causes. The Body Shop became globally successful because it was uniquely associated with social responsibility; respect for human rights, the environment, and animal protection;

and fair trade for suppliers. Despite the strength of branding, there has been a backlash against the dominance of some brands. Naomi Klein's 1999 book *No Logo* sparked the no-brand movement, which highlights globalization and the exploitation of workers in less-developed countries who make branded goods, such as sneakers.

Japanese retailer Muji has consistently followed a no-brand strategy. At the heart of its ethos is *kanketsu* ("simplicity"). Product packaging is plain and the company spends little on marketing of advertising, relying on word of mouth. Ironically, this has served to differentiate the company and its products, creating a loyal following.

Today, technology is changing the way that consumers perceive brands. Social media and the Internet encourage consumers to share feedback and interact. Big global brands, such as Apple, can influence consumer behavior and have the potential to change society. But organizations also recognize that consumers have greater choice than ever before, and are focused on creating brands that can engage with them on a personal level. ∎

The Starbucks brand is instantly recognizable. In the 1990s Starbucks marketed itself as a relaxing spot between work and home, as well as a place to drink fresh coffee.

THERE IS ONLY ONE BOSS: THE CUSTOMER

MAKE YOUR CUSTOMERS LOVE YOU

IN CONTEXT

FOCUS
Customer loyalty

KEY DATES
1891 Trading stamps are introduced in the US to encourage repeat shopping. Customers are rewarded with stamps that can be collected and redeemed for goods.

1962 Sam Walton opens Wal-Mart, with the slogan "Satisfaction Guaranteed."

1967 The first toll-free 1-800 customer service centers are launched in the US.

1981 American Airlines offers the industry's first frequent-flyer program to reward customer loyalty.

1996 With the growth of the Internet, live-chat and email customer support is introduced for online shoppers.

The idea that the customer determines how successful a business becomes has been accepted by numerous entrepreneurs and management experts since the late 19th century. Logically, if customers are happy with a product or service they will make repeat purchases and give recommendations to their friends and family. This helps the business to grow, and in effect pays the wages of employees.

Like any love affair, the intensity of a relationship between supplier and buyer is emotional as well as physical. The process involved in building passion and trust between the two parties

See also: Porter's generic strategies 178–83 ▪ Understanding the market 234–41 ▪ Focus on the future market 244–49 ▪ Promotions and incentives 271 ▪ Maximize customer benefits 288–89 ▪ Fulfilling demand 294–95

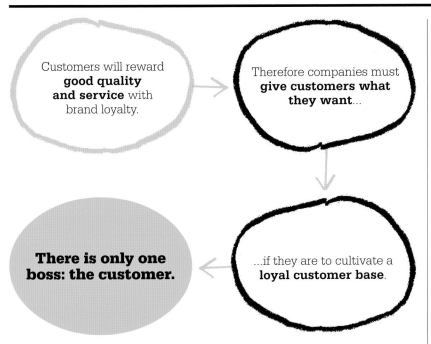

Customers will reward **good quality and service** with brand loyalty.

Therefore companies must **give customers what they want**...

There is only one boss: the customer.

...if they are to cultivate a **loyal customer base**.

Exceed your customers' expectations. If you do, they'll come back over and over.
Sam Walton

requires not just creativity on the part of the business to promote an emotional connection with the customer, but also practical know-how to ensure streamlined production and distribution systems. These practical aspects include such things as: order cycle time; availability of products; convenience of ordering; flexibility of delivery times; the look of the packaging and the ease of opening it; the simplicity of the returns process; and the accessibility of customer service personnel to deal with problems or questions.

Customer satisfaction
Historically, the process of wooing customers took place face-to-face on the store floor, and department stores led the way at the turn of the 19th century. Selfridges in London was designed from scratch to give shoppers, especially women, a rush

of excitement. The store not only offered desirable products to buy, but a complete experience that allowed customers to fantasize about a more luxurious lifestyle.

One of the most powerful emotional drivers in wooing a customer is money—the promise of getting more for less is hard for

most people to resist. Coca-Cola is credited with introducing the first such enticement in 1887, with a coupon for a free glass of cola.

In the case of Wal-Mart founder Sam Walton (1918–92), saving the customer money was at the core of his business plan and this strategy is credited with making him one of the most successful merchants of the late 20th century. "The idea was simple," he explained. "When customers thought of Wal-Mart, they should think of low prices and satisfaction guaranteed. They could be pretty sure they wouldn't find it cheaper anywhere else, and if they didn't like it, they could bring it back."

The importance of quality
The quality of the product or service being sold is another emotional force for customers. Unlike price, which must be consistently kept low for sustained customer commitment, quality »

Selfridges department store was a destination as well as a place to shop. It featured cafés and a roof garden, and Harry Selfridge exhibited items such as John Logie Baird's television in the store.

must be kept high for a long and happy marriage between producer and end user. The founder of Selfridges, Harry Gordon Selfridge, advised: "Remember always that the recollection of quality remains long after the price is forgotten. Then your business will prosper by a natural process."

In the early 1980s, industries first quantified the impact of product quality on profitability through studies such as PIMS (Profit Impact of Market Strategy). Before this time, "quality" was not usually a high priority for industry leaders, but as research continued to show the clear link to profitability, product quality became an essential factor in strategies for attracting and keeping customers.

Paying a premium

Even though a company may not have the biggest share of the market, it can still generate the biggest profit if its customers perceive the product quality to be so high that they are willing to pay more for it. In the smartphone market, for example, Apple's iPhone has a relatively small share but garners around 50 percent of the profit. Making a desirable product

and building an emotional experience around it can be enough to make customers love you—so much so that they are prepared to pre-order, wait, and line up. This is demonstrated most clearly in the fashion world, where customers willingly suffer the indignity of scrambling for limited-edition handbags or shoes, or—in the case of luxury brand Hermès—wait years for a bag. However, for most businesses this is the exception.

Customers expect providers of goods and services to do everything possible to win them over and keep them happy through

Customers are willing to line up for bargains, such is their loyalty to particular brands. In Italy, shoppers wait outside a Burberry store in Milan on the first day of the sale.

all the stages of the buying process. Although acquiring new customers is always an important part of marketing strategy, more income is usually generated by existing customers. These customers will continue to buy the same product or service, or may begin purchasing other products from the same provider. The business world has come to recognize that some customers are more profitable than others, and it pays to woo profit-inducing customers and entice them to spend more.

In online retail, repeat purchase can be encouraged by email campaigns tailored to the buying history of the customer. In the mail order or direct mail industry, mailings with special offers or cross-selling promotions for complementary products serve a similar function, while in a store the astute involvement of the sales staff can directly provide an emotional rationale for an additional sale, though they are also a cost to

The Likert scale, created by US psychologist Rensis Likert in the 1930s, is designed to measure attitudes. The five-point scale offers responses to a statement, and participants pick the response they most agree with. Considered a good way to get customer feedback, the scale has been criticized for giving skewed results due to its forced set of choices.

Strongly agree   Agree   Neither agree nor disagree   Disagree   Strongly disagree

the business. Making your customers love you therefore hinges on both the quality of the product or service and the benefits for the customer in remaining loyal to a particular brand or company, whether that's for convenience, a bargain, or a feel-good factor.

Cultivating loyalty

Pioneered by the airline industry with its frequent-flyer programs, the idea of loyalty programs is especially important to retailers. A successful loyalty program will not only offer customers a "money-back" type of incentive, but will also enable the business to gather data about customer preferences, spending habits, favored brands, and reaction to promotions. Retailers use this data to make decisions about what products to stock. Through its loyalty program, US department store Nordstrom records the size and color preferences of customers, as well as birthdays, anniversary dates, and other personal information. It offers "Fashion Rewards"—points earned for every dollar spent with its store card. When a customer has accumulated a certain number

The customer can fire you by simply deciding to do business elsewhere.
Michael Bergdahl
US director for people, Wal-Mart
(1954–)

of points, they receive "Nordstrom Notes," which can be redeemed against future purchases. Many other stores around the world run similar loyalty programs.

Online challenges

Retailers who exist online potentially have more to gain from loyal customers, but first they have to overcome the lack of an immediate emotional connection provided by the ambiance of a physical store.

For example, Zappos, the online shoe seller, uses its call center to forge relationships with customers and win their loyalty. For founder Tony Hsieh the call center is not a running cost, but an opportunity to market. Call center employees do not read from scripts—they seek to make an emotional connection with customers. Their reputation for going out of their way for customers is now enshrined as part of the brand. Simple tactics such as sending goods ahead of schedule, and a 365-day returns period, have helped to build a repeat purchase rate reported at about 75 percent.

CEO of Amazon Jeff Bezos paved the way for the development of customer satisfaction in the digital era. Bezos was able to overcome some of the potential stumbling blocks of Internet retailing, such as customers not being able to touch the products and having to wait for delivery, since its customer service includes next-day delivery and free returns. The company has consistently ranked at the top of the American Customer Satisfaction Index. As Bezos asserts, "If you make customers unhappy in the physical world, they might each tell six friends. If you make customers unhappy on the Internet, they can each tell 6,000." ∎

Customer loyalty and store cards encourage repeat purchase of products and also provide businesses with the opportunity to gather data about their customers' shopping habits.

Is the customer always right?

Department store owners Harry Gordon Selfridge (1857–1947), who founded Selfridges in London in 1909, and Marshall Field (1834–1906), who in 1865 started the store bearing his name in Chicago, are both credited with coining the phrase, "the customer is always right," which has come to mean that it is cheaper to retain a customer than find a new one. In an era of overblown product claims it was an approach designed to attract the burgeoning middle classes.

However, since the 1990s, marketers have adopted a more discriminating approach to customers in the belief that the customer is not always right.

Each customer can be measured by their individual return on investment (ROI) or lifetime value, allowing customer-service efforts to focus on the more profitable patrons. Using ROI, some businesses differentiate between customers who are always right and those who are not worth listening to.

WHITEWASHING, BUT WITH A GREEN BRUSH
GREENWASH

IN CONTEXT

FOCUS
Business ethics

KEY DATES
1985 Scientists announce that they have discovered a hole in the ozone layer.

1986 First use of the term "greenwash" in an essay by US environmental activist Jay Westerveld.

1990 By the 20th annniversary of Earth Day, a quarter of all new household products coming on to the US market are advertised as "recyclable," "biodegradable," "ozone friendly," or "compostable."

1992 The Federal Trade Commission, in association with the US Environmental Protection Agency, publishes "Guidelines for Environmental Marketing Claims."

1999 The word "greenwash" enters the *Oxford English Dictionary*.

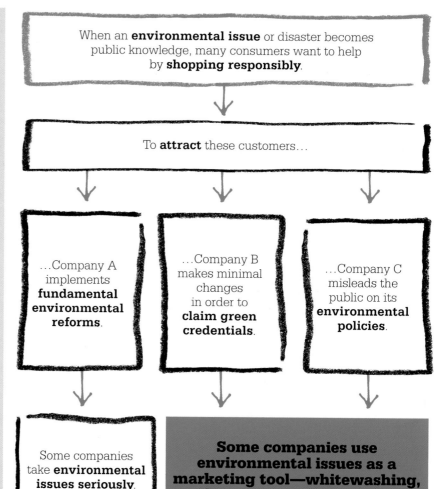

When an **environmental issue** or disaster becomes public knowledge, many consumers want to help by **shopping responsibly**.

To **attract** these customers…

…Company A implements **fundamental environmental reforms**.

…Company B makes minimal changes in order to **claim green credentials**.

…Company C misleads the public on its **environmental policies**.

Some companies take **environmental issues seriously**.

Some companies use environmental issues as a marketing tool—whitewashing, but with a green brush.

See also: Crisis management 188–89 ▪ Avoiding complacency 194–201 ▪ Morality in business 222 ▪
Creating an ethical culture 224–27 ▪ The appeal of ethics 270

The notion of "greenwashing" emerged during the rise of the environmental movement in the 1990s, and it refers to the perceived practice by corporate and government sectors of adopting an environmentally friendly veneer. In the same way that public-interest issues are described as "whitewashed" when they gloss over difficult aspects or cover them up, so "greenwashing" is defined as putting a surface gleam over environmental topics to detract from any serious discussion or definitive action.

Environmental activist and New Yorker Jay Westerveld was the first to use the word in print, in a 1986 essay about the practice of hotels asking guests to avoid using too many towels, in order to reduce laundering and help the environment. Westerveld interpreted this as a ploy to save money rather than the planet.

Growing movement

Until the 1980s, business managers mostly treated environmental issues as potential obstacles to be circumvented or public relations problems to be solved. However, in 1985, news of the hole in the ozone layer led to a successful consumer boycott of aerosols propelled by chlorofluerocarbons (CFCs), which were considered one of the main threats to the ozone layer. As the ground swell of consumer support for the environmental movement grew, marketers saw an advantage in aligning their products and corporate identity with green issues.

The marketing world first seemed to embrace the concept of safeguarding the environment after the release of the Brundtland Report in 1987 (see box). The 1990s were forecast as heralding a green revolution, and businesses rushed to associate themselves with environmentally friendly products and processes.

Green companies

Businesses such as The Body Shop and Volvo had already adopted green strategies as early as the 1970s, and because the media were looking for stories with an environmental angle, these companies frequently appeared in the press. Their publicity made the adoption of green policies and products even more alluring.

At the same time, there was growing evidence that consumers did not believe everything they read or saw and had developed a general scepticism about the business world's green intentions. However, the corporate world still saw a commercial advantage in being green, and marketers began to adopt strategies to try to connect with eco-aware consumers.

Greenwashing has appeared in surprising places. The nuclear industry has tried to dispel its reputation for being dangerous by presenting nuclear power as a remedy for global warming. Arms manufacturer BAe announced in 2006 that it was making "lead-free bullets." Marketers need to remember that the public is generally able to distinguish between policies and practices that are genuinely eco-friendly, and those that are simply greenwashing. ▪

Shades of green

In the years after the release of the 1987 United Nations Brundtland Report calling for protection of the environment, the volume of green advertising and campaigns increased dramatically. Between 1989 and 1990, green product launches in the US doubled. They continued to expand through the early 1990s, buoyed by market research showing that consumers were interested in environmentally responsible products.

By the mid-1990s, however, several key studies revealed that there was an inconsistency between consumer intent and consumer action when it came to paying higher prices for green products. There were also worries over the negative effect that green strategies might have on the attitudes of shareholders.

These factors may have led to a form of greenwashing where organizations make genuine but minor changes to products or processes to present a green face, but do not let environmental issues dent the bottom line.

The incidence of … greenwash—outright, purposeful untruths … is probably not that high. But there's an awful lot … that gets close.
Andrew Winston
US environmental strategist

PEOPLE WANT COMPANIES TO BELIEVE IN SOMETHING BEYOND MAXIMIZING PROFITS
THE APPEAL OF ETHICS

IN CONTEXT

FOCUS
Business ethics

KEY DATES
1867 Karl Marx claims that capitalism was built on the exploitation of labor.

1962 US president John F. Kennedy outlines the Consumer Bill of Rights: the right to safety, the right to be informed, the right to choose, and the right to be heard. This is extended and adopted by the United Nations in 1985.

1988 The Fairtrade Foundation is launched.

2008 A study in the journal *Psychological Science* claims that humans are neurally programmed to prefer fair treatment.

2012 The London Olympic Games restricts its food retailers to using only Fairtrade brands of tea, coffee, sugar, wine, chocolate, and bananas.

The appeal of ethics is based on a basic human preference for a fair deal. Business ethics—the moral principles and rules of trade—has been an area of study since the early 1900s. Early attention focused on workers' rights and conditions, and whether they were paid a "fair wage." In the 1960s, consumers also demanded rights too, and they wanted to know more about a company's reputation and approach.

However, it was not until the 1980s that ethics began to be reflected in the market, with the

Mayan coffee sold under the Fairtrade label provides consumers with a guarantee that coffee farmers have been fairly paid for their product.

founding of the Fairtrade Foundation. This introduced a labeling system for products that had been produced and traded without exploitation. It gave consumers the ability to choose products on ethical grounds when making a purchase.

From the 1990s, as corporations pursued globalization strategies and increasingly outsourced production to low-wage economies, consumers became more aware of the issues involved, and the implications of their buying choices.

Unilever publicized its ethical goals in its 2010 "Sustainable Living Plan," which promised it would halve its environmental footprint and source all of its raw products sustainably by 2020. Others have since followed suit. Although consumers know that some companies may fail to make good on these kinds of promises, they often choose to believe them, because, as Facebook founder Mark Zuckerberg observed, "people want to use services from companies that believe in something beyond simply maximizing profits." ∎

See also: Play by the rules 120–23 ▪ Morality in business 222 ▪ Creating an ethical culture 224–27 ▪ Understanding the market 234–41 ▪ Greenwash 268–69

EVERYBODY LIKES SOMETHING EXTRA FOR NOTHING
PROMOTIONS AND INCENTIVES

Marketers often use the offer of a free gift, prize, discount, or bonus to sway customers into buying merchandise. This strategy is known as "incentive marketing" or "sales promotion." It is commonly used to launch a new product, regenerate interest when sales growth is flat, or to help build the company's reputation or brand.

US industrialist William Wrigley was a pioneer of incentives aimed at encouraging purchases. In 1892 he started marketing his chewing gum offering gifts, or "premiums," to successfully woo customers away from the established brands. It was a tactic he returned to often to stimulate sales growth.

Push and pull
In modern marketing terminology, Wrigley used "pull" incentives: gifts or price reductions that stimulate consumer demand, so that retailers are forced to stock more of the product. Marketers can also use "push" incentives: these are compensations targeted toward the retailer or wholesaler, so that they will, in turn, direct consumer attention toward certain products.

Both push and pull incentives can cause a short-term lift in sales, but over time their impact wears off; promotion fatigue sets in, or the incentives become too expensive. The success of a promotion is measured by looking at return on investment (ROI). When this begins to fall, or the company's reputation suffers from a surfeit of promotions, the strategy is no longer working. ∎

One thing I've learned is that you can't push technology. It has to be pulled.
Bill Ford
US industrialist (1957–)

See also: Understanding the market 234–41 ▪ Creating a brand 258–63 ▪ Generating buzz 274–75 ▪ Marketing mix 280–83

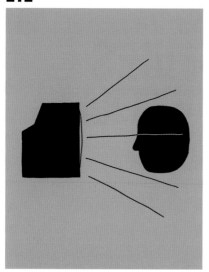

IN GOOD TIMES PEOPLE WANT TO ADVERTISE; IN BAD TIMES THEY HAVE TO

WHY ADVERTISE?

IN CONTEXT

FOCUS
Advertising

KEY DATES
1729 Benjamin Franklin, scientist and Founding Father of the United States, advertises his company's inventions in the *Pennsylvania Gazette*.

1840 The world's first advertising agency is founded in Philadelphia, PA.

1939 Coca-Cola uses Santa Claus in its ad campaign, helping to create the rotund figure so well known today.

1955 The iconic Marlboro Man ad is launched and is hugely successful, despite research that links lung cancer to smoking.

1994 HotWired becomes the first website to sell banner ads; a year later the first server able to track and manage ads is released.

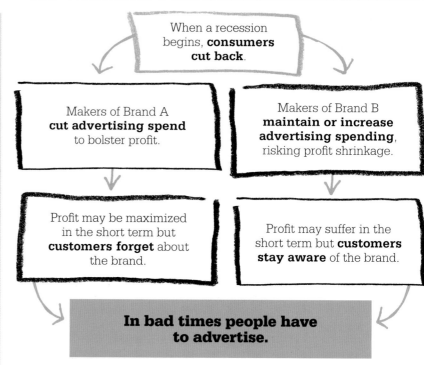

When a recession begins, **consumers cut back**.

Makers of Brand A **cut advertising spend** to bolster profit.

Makers of Brand B **maintain or increase advertising spending**, risking profit shrinkage.

Profit may be maximized in the short term but **customers forget** about the brand.

Profit may suffer in the short term but **customers stay aware** of the brand.

In bad times people have to advertise.

In the corporate landscape advertising is sometimes seen as a waste of money, and expenditure on it is often the first part of the budget to be cut back during a recession. The point that advertising executive Bruce Barton (1886–1967) was making with his much-quoted statement "In good times people want to advertise; in bad times they have to" is that advertising should be employed as part of an ongoing effort to build relationships with existing and prospective customers.

Barton, who was responsible for some of the key American advertising campaigns of the 1920s

Have a break – have a Kit Kat

Kit Kat advertisements in the UK like this one from the 1960s have used the slogan "Have a break—have a Kit Kat" for almost 60 years. The phrase is now synonymous with the brand.

Barratt, his son-in-law, was more of a risk taker. He understood the importance of staying in the public arena and of constantly evaluating changing tastes in the market.

An outstanding example of image building through long-term advertising is Nestlé's Kit Kat. Most people in the countries where this slogan was used will probably be able to finish the product's tagline, "Have a break—have a Kit Kat." One reason the slogan is so well known in the UK is that it has been in use since 1957, forming an important part of the brand's advertising and marketing ever since.

Staying power

It could be argued that the company that stops advertising risks disappearing from the public consciousness, perhaps even more so today when most people are

> Early to bed, early to rise. Work like hell and advertise.
> **Ted Turner**
> US media mogul (1938–)

bombarded with information and images on a daily basis. Research into viewer reactions to television commercials has shown that even when consumers have been overloaded with information, and are ostensibly uninterested in, or immune to, advertising messages, they are still likely to register positive feelings toward advertisements that reinforce previous brand preferences. This would seem to support Barton's view that effective advertising requires an enduring commitment. ▪

through the 1940s, believed that cutting advertising spend was foolhardy. Instead he pointed out the advantages of a continual presence in the market through constant advertising. To survive commercial ups and downs, a business needs to maintain a constant presence in the mind of the consumer.

Barton believed that it is a false economy to advertise only when the market is booming and the company has the budget for it, and then to cut back when profit margins are reduced. If a company withdraws from advertising, the consumer may forget about them, making it a tough job to win them back later when the economy is buoyant again.

Building a brand

Barton was not the first to prize the value of advertising in developing an indelible image for a company or product. Thomas Barratt (1841–1914), sometimes dubbed the "father of modern advertising," created a number of campaigns for the UK soap maker Pears in the late 19th century. These advertisements helped make the brand synonymous with soap. While owner Francis Pears was extremely wary about spending money on advertising,

Edward Bernays

Remembered as a pioneer of public relations, Edward Bernays (1891–1995) was able to link special events, press releases, and the influence of third parties to promote his client's products.

A nephew of Sigmund Freud, Edward Bernays was fascinated by psychology, often employing psychoanalysts to provide evidence for his campaigns.

He famously conducted a successful campaign for the American Tobacco Company in the 1920s, which radically

altered opinion, lifting the taboo on women smoking in public.

Bernays loved competitions and to promote soap for Procter & Gamble he created a soap-sculpting contest for children.

He set up surveys, gathered expert opinions, and arranged business luncheons to change public opinion. Other clients included car manufacturer General Motors and Philco, an early pioneer of television.

Bernays also sought to raise the profile of public relations and establish it as a serious profession in its own right.

MAKE YOUR THINKING AS FUNNY AS POSSIBLE
GENERATING BUZZ

IN CONTEXT

FOCUS
Word-of-mouth marketing

KEY DATES
Early 1970s US psychologist George Silverman pioneers the study of WOMM. He noted the persuasive power of peers within research groups testing new pharmaceutical products.

1976 UK biologist Richard Dawkins articulates how trends spread through a natural process of imitation.

1997 The spread of the webmail service Hotmail becomes one of the first examples of online viral marketing.

2012 Beverage manufacturer Red Bull sponsors Felix Baumgartner to make the highest-ever skydiving jump, which attracts 8 million views of the live feed on YouTube—a social-media record.

Word-of-mouth marketing is the most effective.

Using online communities and social media, marketers can **generate buzz** for their product.

The best ideas "catch on" and **spread quickly**.

Although the catchphrase is contemporary, the idea of "generating buzz" is a long-standing concept in sales. In a sophisticated market populated by savvy consumers who no longer trust most of the messages presented by advertisers, word-of-mouth marketing, or WOMM, has become a vital tool for anyone in business. The strategy is to use the consumer's own voice—the words of the ordinary person—to do the selling, rather than the voice of the big brand or the omnipotent mass communicator.

Back in 1973, Madison Avenue advertising legend David Ogilvy recognized that ad campaign jingles, catchphrases, and fashions could "catch on" and become part of social culture. "Nobody knows how to do it on purpose," he believed, though he was certain that word-of-mouth marketing was valuable, calling it "manna from heaven." He also knew the power of a good laugh. "The best ideas come as jokes," he mused. "Make your thinking as funny as possible."

Spreading the message
In the 21st century, WOMM strategies are predominantly used online via social media. Modern marketers are able to purposefully spark word-of-mouth campaigns within online communities, but they also understand the impact of Ogilvy's advice about using humorous, quirky, and offbeat ideas to get a reaction. Today, people still share their firsthand experiences with friends, but they also share

See also: Understanding the market 234–41 ▪ Creating a brand 258–63 ▪ Why advertise? 272–73 ▪ Benchmarking 330–31

From a single user sharing images or opinions with friends, and those friends passing the data to their friends, with modern technology ideas can spread rapidly and ultimately reach millions of users.

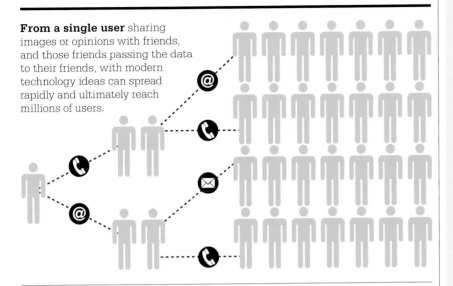

Memes and imitation

In 1976 evolutionary biologist Richard Dawkins put forward the theory that, just as genes are responsible for replicating physical characteristics, cultural information such as ideas, behavior, or style, can also be transferred from person to person. Dawkins referred to this cultural data as "memes." These memes, like genes, can spread, mutate, or die out in society. As Dawkins describes it, "Just as genes propagate themselves in the gene pool by leaping from body to body via sperm or eggs, so memes propagate themselves in the meme pool by leaping from brain to brain via a process which, in the broad sense, can be called imitation."

Marketers have applied the theory to online behavior. An Internet meme can be a photo, image, video, website, word, or symbol, which originates from a single user or group of users and builds momentum when it is imitated by other Internet users. By piggybacking on existing memes, brands can gain massive exposure for relatively little cost.

pictures and videos online, so information is easily spread. Tactics to manipulate this trend include guerrilla marketing, which uses low-cost unconventional methods with a surprise element to provoke comment, and viral marketing, which typically employs social media to spread a brand-sponsored video, or encourages influential bloggers and others to recommend products.

In *The Tipping Point* (2000), British social commentator Malcolm Gladwell outlines the power of social epidemics and how the smallest impetus can trigger a mass phenomenon. According to Gladwell, the title of his book refers to a "magic moment when an idea, trend, or social behavior crosses a threshold, tips, and spreads like wildfire." This describes modern "word-of-mouth" marketing, though it originates in broader ideas about how ideas replicate in human culture. As Gladwell explains, "ideas and products ... messages and behaviors spread just like viruses do."

Kick-starting the process

Marketers can mimic this process by encouraging customers or influential members of online communities to kick-start the imitation process and become "brand champions," sometimes by offering incentives in return for reviews and recommendations. Industries in which trends are paramount for success are at the forefront of WOMM online. Fashion e-tailer ASOS utilizes Twitter and Facebook to propagate customer recommendations and provide entertainment. In its 2011 "Urban Tour" campaign, ASOS marketers created videos showcasing the world's best street dancers and in-line skaters. The videos enabled click-through shopping and were platform-neutral to ease their spread on social-media channels.

Sneaker brand Nike has been at the forefront of the trend, producing videos with enough "wow" factor to send them viral. The two-minute "Touch of Gold" video (2008) featured soccer player Ronaldinho showing off his skills wearing Nike cleats. ▪

Today, the potential to persuade is in the hands of millions...
B. J. Fogg
US behavioral scientist

E-COMMERCE IS BECOMING MOBILE COMMERCE

M-COMMERCE

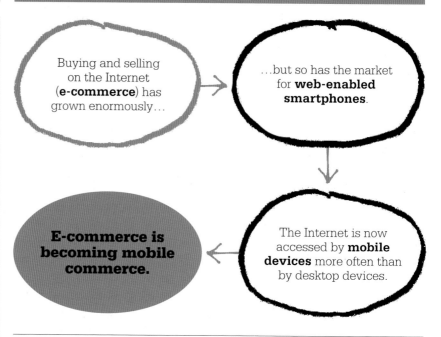

Buying and selling on the Internet (**e-commerce**) has grown enormously…

…but so has the market for **web-enabled smartphones**.

The Internet is now accessed by **mobile devices** more often than by desktop devices.

E-commerce is becoming mobile commerce.

The term e-commerce (electronic commerce) refers to all buying and selling done on the Internet. M-commerce (mobile commerce) specifically involves transactions that are made through a mobile telecommunications network. These transactions can range from the small, such as making an eBay purchase, to the potentially huge, such as trading stocks and shares.

M-commerce works in a similar way to e-commerce, with websites and apps adapted or originated for mobile and handheld devices. It can also include direct carrier billing, when purchases can be added to a cell-phone bill. Another function is tap-to-pay, where a customer makes payments using a mobile device that has been installed with credit card information via a program such as Google Wallet.

See also: Reinventing and adapting 52–57 ▪ Understanding the market 234–41 ▪ Lean production 290–93 ▪ Applying and testing ideas 310–11 ▪ The right technology 314–15

"
Consumers no longer go shopping, they always *are* shopping.
Chuck Martin
US CEO of Mobile Future Institute

The customer holds the device against a paypoint enabled with a technology called near field communication (NFC); this establishes a radio connection between the two devices to complete a transaction.

Growth of m-commerce

The value of online sales made on mobile devices is predicted to grow exponentially. North American research specialist Forrester forecasts US m-commerce sales to show compound annual growth of 48 percent in the five years from 2012 to 2017, with the value of m-commerce over the same period increasing by 250 percent on smartphones and more than 425 percent on tablets.

In the UK, which leads Europe in the growth of m-commerce, Barclays PLC expects m-commerce to grow by 55 percent over the same five-year period, while traditional online sales will grow by only 8 percent and in-store sales by 1.6 percent.

Emerging markets

The sudden and explosive growth of m-commerce can be attributed to several factors. Consumer adoption of smartphones and tablets is increasing; more and more people access the Internet with mobile devices rather than with desktop computers; and customers have become more used to shopping on the move, enjoying the convenience and immediacy it provides. People are also placing more trust in the service.

Given that the biggest increase in smartphone sales has been in emerging markets such as China, India, and Africa, it is not surprising that these regions are considered growth hubs for m-commerce. In China, expanding ranks of middle-class youths are fueling a rapid expansion of mobile transactions, while in Africa, e-commerce has been virtually bypassed in favor of m-commerce. In some African countries, in the absence of a conventional banking infrastructure, cell phones have created an informal banking system.

In 2007, the leading mobile network provider in Kenya, Safaricom, set up a mobile banking service called M-Pesa. Money loaded onto the phone can be used to make purchases or transfer funds. Currently, M-Pesa operates in Kenya, Tanzania, Afghanistan, South Africa, and India, with plans by Safaricom stakeholder Vodafone to roll out the service internationally. As this example indicates, the long-term implication of m-commerce could be a global cashless society. ▪

Mobile banking

The banking sector has helped to power m-commerce from the start, when Merita Bank of Finland launched the first cell-phone-based banking service using SMS in 1997. Since then, the key challenges for developers have been security (providing a safe environment for transactions); technology (developing cross-platform banking apps that will work on any cell phone); and innovation (finding new and improved ways to link digital banking with retail suppliers and provide a personalized service for consumers).

La Caixa bank in Spain has introduced contactless ATMs, allowing customers to withdraw cash with a tap of their cell phone. They can also buy tickets to events, select seats, and show a QR code to access venues. In Australia, Commonwealth Bank customers can make tap-and-go payments at retailers. Mobile banking is evolving so users can make payments irrespective of which bank they use or which retailers they go to.

Using M-Pesa, the cell-phone money-transfer service, is common in Kenya. Funds are transferred by SMS into an electronic wallet on the phone to be used at stores and agents nationwide.

TRYING TO PREDICT THE FUTURE IS LIKE DRIVING WITH NO LIGHTS LOOKING OUT OF THE BACK WINDOW
FORECASTING

IN CONTEXT

FOCUS
Forecasting

KEY DATES
1939 A quantitative method of forecasting is developed, using past sales correlation.

1959 Project RAND, a think tank assembled by the US Air Force, creates the Delphi technique for forecasting using expert opinions.

1970 British mathematicians George Box and Gwilym Jenkins develop a sophisticated model for picking out trends from historical data.

1980s Computerized forecasting models appear, such as INFOREM and E3.

2003 Sunil Chopra and Peter Meindel at Northwestern University, IL, emphasize the link between accurate forecasting and supply-chain management.

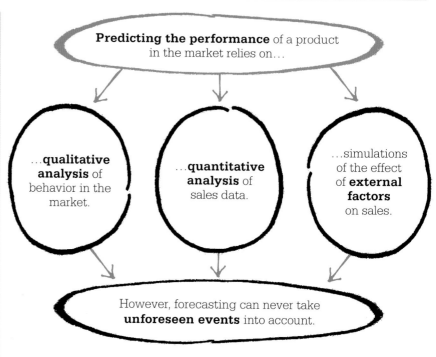

Predicting the performance of a product in the market relies on…

…**qualitative analysis** of behavior in the market.

…**quantitative analysis** of sales data.

…simulations of the effect of **external factors** on sales.

However, forecasting can never take **unforeseen events** into account.

F orecasting sales is one of a marketer's most important roles. Other management departments in a company will make critical decisions that affect the entire organization, based on the information that the marketer provides about the anticipated performance of a company's products in the marketplace.

Marketers first suggested the idea of using economic models to forecast regional sales in the 1930s, and from the 1950s onward the idea of quantitative and qualitative approaches emerged. Qualitative forecasting relies on the expertise of managerial staff and their acquired knowledge about market reactions. Quantitative forecasting

See also: Crisis management 188–89 ▪ Balancing long- versus short-termism 190–91 ▪ Contingency planning 210 ▪ The marketing model 232–33 ▪ Lean production 290–93 ▪ Time-based management 326–27

uses numerical data such as sales patterns. Also in this category are equations that make assumptions about future sales by drawing on a company's historical data, and market research that indicates the number of potential customers for a particular product or service. In addition, marketers look at external factors beyond the company's control, such as the state of the economy, and make simulations of how quantitative forecasts would be affected by external factors.

Unforeseen circumstances

Even the most carefully planned forecast can be thrown out by unforeseen events. In the travel industry, for example, it is difficult to predict performance because factors such as weather and world events have a significant impact on customer choices.

The effect of world events can be seen in the sale of luxury watches to China. From 2009 to 2011, high-end watchmakers in Europe enjoyed growing sales in China, but from late 2012 a dramatic decline

> The only thing we know about the future is that it will be different.
> **Peter Drucker**

began—as much as 24 percent in a single quarter. This was partly due to a slowdown in China's economic growth, which exporters might have been able to take into account; but what could not have been expected was a high-profile incident in the Communist Party's crackdown on corruption. A party official in Shanxi province was fired after images of him wearing various luxury watches were found on the Internet; one timepiece was worth more than $32,000. The story made front-page news across China in

September 2012. Luxury watches became publicly associated with corruption, and demand slumped.

Is forecasting worthwhile?

Management consultant Peter Drucker was scornful of forecasting. "We must start out with the premise that forecasting is … not worthwhile beyond the shortest of periods," he wrote in *Management: Tasks, Responsibilities, Practices* (1973). He had reason to be wary, having declared in a 1929 economic journal that stock prices were bound to keep rising, just a few weeks before the Wall Street Crash. International auditing company KPMG maintains that most companies produce unrealistic forecasts that can be off by up to 13 percent on average.

According to KPMG, better data management, scenario planning, and forecasts that are continually updated rather than made long-term can increase accuracy. Despite the difficulty of accurate forecasting, it remains the primary means by which marketers drive the business decisions of a company. ▪

Shares on the stock market are affected by many factors, including some that are difficult to predict—such as world events, severe weather, and global economic forecasts.

Accurate forecasting

Producing an accurate forecast depends on the company's required lead time—the time from order placement to customer delivery. The longer the lead time, the greater the error in forecasting figures. One theory holds that if lead times are reduced by 50 percent, forecasting errors will also be reduced by 50 percent.

Since the 1990s management theorists, including Dr. Edmund Prater at the University of Texas, have advocated that forecasting accuracy can be optimized by creating a demand-driven supply chain, which uses information and technology to shrink lag times between supply decisions and actual demand. Thus the need for forecasting is reduced when business activities become more demand driven. For example, when Wal-Mart asked stores to place orders every two weeks rather than monthly, inventories reduced because accurate forecasting increased in line with the shorter time frame.

PRODUCT PLACE PRICE PROMOTION
MARKETING MIX

IN CONTEXT

FOCUS
Marketing strategy

KEY DATES
1910 Professor Ralph Butler introduces the term "marketing" in the title of his university course.

1920s Marketing becomes further established as a recognized field of study.

1948 James Culliton identifies the idea of the marketer as a "mixer of ingredients."

1953 Neil Borden coins the phrase "marketing mix."

1960 E. J. McCarthy sets out the Four Ps as the ingredients of the marketing mix.

1990 Robert Lauterborn advocates the Four Cs in place of the Four Ps.

2013 Philip Kotler keeps the Four Ps alive, adding a fifth P—Purpose.

The marketing mix concept is a theoretical framework designed to help businesses plan, and put into practice, effective strategies for launching and selling their products and services. The crystallization of goals helps define a clear role for the marketer, separating the marketing function from other activities within a company.

Businesses need to consider a number of factors when bringing a product or service to the market. They must make decisions about aspects of the product (such as its type), its place of distribution, price, and promotion. These factors are the "ingredients" that together make up the "marketing mix" and

See also: The marketing model 232–33 ▪ Product portfolio 250–51 ▪ Promotions and incentives 271 ▪ Fulfilling demand 294–95 ▪ Quality sells 318–23

When an organization decides to **launch a new or updated product,** marketers must figure out the **selling strategy**.

They must also consider the **external market forces** that affect the marketing mix.

They must carefully calculate the **proportions of the elements** (such as product, place, price, promotion) in the **marketing mix**.

The marketer must **weigh the forces** and **juggle the elements** within the constraints of the **resources available**.

each can be adjusted by the marketer to influence the reaction of the consumer to the product or service being sold. The marketer must also take into account external market forces, such as customer behavior or competition, which will have an impact on the marketing mix.

Building the mix

Harvard Business School professor Neil Borden first coined the term "marketing mix" in 1950, using it in 1953 in his presidential address to the American Marketing Association. Borden credited fellow professor James Culliton as being the first to introduce the idea of the marketer as a "mixer of ingredients" in 1948. Inspired by Culliton's ideas, Borden began using the term to describe what Culliton's "mixer of ingredients" should design.

In an article in 1964 titled "The Concept of the Marketing Mix," Borden advised that when marketing managers build a marketing program, they should

make two lists: the first one itemizes the important elements or "ingredients" that make up marketing programs; the second outlines the external forces that may have a bearing on the first list.

The first list includes ingredients deemed essential if the company is to win sales—product planning, pricing, branding, distribution, promotion, and so on. The second list includes market forces, such

The marketing manager, as head chef, must creatively marshal all his marketing activities to advance the short and long term interests of his firm.
Neil Borden

as the behavior of consumers, retailers, competitors, government policy, and other external factors.

In Borden's model, the marketing manager should weigh the effect of external forces, then juggle the marketing elements from the first list to achieve the best possible program to fit the resources of the company. Borden advocated that to really get a grasp of all the marketing considerations, the manager should draw up a chart showing the elements of the marketing mix.

Both Culliton and Borden inspired further development of the concept within the academic community. In 1960, a marketing professor at Michigan State University, Edmund Jerome McCarthy, set out what would become the definitive word on the marketing mix. He condensed the mix ingredients into an easily remembered mnemonic, the Four Ps: Product, Place, Price, Promotion. In his classic text, *Basic Marketing* (1960), McCarthy elaborates on »

The Four Ps, key ingredients of the marketing mix, need to be in careful balance with each other and the mix as a whole. Alternative "ingredients" have been proposed as necessary components of the marketing mix, but the core Four Ps have endured.

PRODUCT
Evaluate customer needs; establish where and how the product will be used; decide on branding and packaging, and how the product will differ from others in the market.

PLACE
Decide how the product will reach the market; the channels of distribution; methods of storage; handling and transportation; and how to emulate or differentiate from the competition.

THE MARKETING MIX

PRICE
Set the price point based on market norms; perceived value by the customer and how sensitive they are to price; and competitors.

PROMOTION
Look at when and where to reach the target market; the optimum medium (television, radio, or press); and evaluate the techniques of competitors.

the nature of the Four Ps. "Product" refers to developing the right product or service for the target market, whether it is a laundry detergent, an accountancy service, or a political party's policy, and also includes branding, packaging, warranties, and anything else related to the product offering. "Place" refers to how the product will get to the target market, so it is available when and where it is needed—in other words, the channel of distribution and the logistics of transportation, storage, and handling. "Promotion" is communication about the product with the target market and others in the distribution chain—public relations, advertising, sales promotions, and so on. "Price" includes price-setting based on competition within the market, the cost of the entire marketing mix, and what price level the customer will accept. If price is rejected then the marketer's efforts are wasted.

An enduring formula
From the 1960s, the Four Ps became the undisputed means by which marketers made their strategic decisions. The approach has become an institution, mentioned in almost every marketing textbook, and still dominates management thinking.

Other additions or alternative mixes have been proposed, though none has yet replaced McCarthy's original premise.

In the 1990s, for example, advertising professor at the University of North Carolina, Robert Lauterborn, argued that the Four Ps articulated the seller's view rather than the buyer's view, and was therefore outdated in the customer-centered marketing of the late 20th century. He reimagined the Four Ps as the Four Cs: Customer solution, Convenience, Communication, and Customer cost.

Professors Jagdish Seth and Rajendra Sisodia then posited the Four As: Acceptability, Affordability, Availability, and Awareness. By 2005, academics Chekitan Dev and Don Schultz claimed that the Four Ps were no longer relevant; that consumer decisions were motivated by emotion and a desire for value, rather than for a specific product to fill a need or a particular price point. Other commentators have also pushed for a framework more applicable to e-commerce. On the other hand, Carolyn Siegel, author of *Internet Marketing*, states: "Although many attempts have been made to replace or expand the

Marketing mix is the pack of four sets of variables, namely product, price, promotion, and place variables.
E. J. McCarthy

> Marketing mix represents the setting of the company's marketing decision variables at a particular point of time.
> **Philip Kotler**

Ps, they've endured as an effective method for organizing the major tactical tools marketers can deploy in a competitive marketplace."

The four Ps in practice
In an industry such as fashion, which by its nature needs to be forward thinking and to embrace e-commerce and m-commerce, the Four Ps are still in evidence. To cater for the immediacy demanded by fashion-conscious customers, UK street-wear fashion brand Bench has focused on "Place"—in this instance the speed at which the product can reach retail outlets. Rather than relying on the usual trade-show route and showroom invitations, Bench uses a more direct approach. Sales people take samples to retailers, and send orders directly to headquarters while still with the retailer. An automated system then generates purchase orders to the manufacturing site within hours. From the customer's point of view (both individual consumers and retail outlets), styles arrive quickly, keeping the brand fresh. For the

Fashion store Zara concentrates its marketing mix on "Place." It is able to deliver new designs to its store floors in just under two weeks.

company it means greater efficiency, more accurate revenue forecasting, and a greatly reduced risk of being overstocked at the end of the season.

The marketing mix of fashion chain Zara embodies the Four Ps. Because of an emphasis on "Place" (distribution), new products are delivered twice a week, and there are only 10–15 days from the sketching of a new design to the item's arrival on the store floor. Such a streamlined approach to "Place" means that "Product" reflects immediate trends; "Promotion" happens on the instant channel of the Internet; and "Price" is kept low due to the emphasis on "Place."

Marketing guru Philip Kotler has acknowledged alternatives to the Four Ps, but maintains that they still make a useful framework. More recently, in 2013, he suggested a fifth P—Purpose. This is not only the purpose of a business to make money, but also a higher purpose of being a good corporate citizen. This fifth element is a concept embraced by Zara, a company that has kept 50 percent of manufacturing in Spain rather than subcontracting it to Asia. Not only can the business react more quickly to changing fashions, it can also be applauded for keeping employment local. ∎

Marketing pioneers

Neil Borden recognized the importance of creating a marketing methodology— a set of stated intentions for marketers to follow. When he put forward his marketing mix concept in 1953, he drew on theories developed by earlier marketing thinkers.

Ralph Butler, professor at the University of Wisconsin, pioneered the use of the term "marketing" by developing a course on selling called "marketing methods" in 1910. A few years later in 1915, H. W. Shaw wrote *Some Problems in Marketing Distribution*, in which he identified the tasks of production and distribution.

Paul Cherington and Paul Ivey, among others in the 1920s, further consolidated marketing as a field of scholarly pursuit, laying the groundwork for marketing as a college course in its own right. In the 1920s and 1930s, Paul Dulaney Converse described key elements of the marketing mix—distribution, pricing, and advertising—and emphasized the need to coordinate marketing activities.

DELIVER THE GOO

PRODUCTION AND POSTPRODUCTION

ING
DS

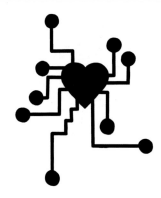

Market globalization and fast-paced technological change have raised customer expectations, and companies can succeed or fail depending on their ability to deliver the right goods at the right price, at the right time, via the right distribution channels.

If getting it wrong can be costly, getting it right takes time. It means constantly evaluating every part of the production process to see where it can be made more efficient without a perceived drop in quality or sales. Henry Ford was the first industrialist to recognize the value of offering customers "more for less," and made it his business to make improvements to his cars every year, while simultaneously dropping their price. Today, many use a "low cost, good quality" strategy to attract customers, especially during times of recession.

Low-cost efficiency
One of the most effective ways of lowering costs while maintaining value is to reduce waste. Known as "lean production," it entails identifying and cutting waste across the process, from production to delivery. Lean production developed from the ideas of Joseph Juran, a management consultant

who developed innovative ways of improving quality and efficiency at the same time. In the 1950s, the Union of Japanese Scientists and Engineers invited him to lecture to hundreds of top-level executives, who quickly put his ideas to practical use. Toyota was among the many businesses who implemented his methods. The company's approach ultimately grew into the "just-in-time" production system that is widely used today.

Stock control plays a large part in the "just-in-time" system, and is vital to a balanced cash flow. Too much stock in the warehouse represents money that is doing

Manufacturing is more than just putting parts together. It's coming up with ideas, testing principles and perfecting the engineering, as well as final assembly.
James Dyson
UK inventor (1947–)

nothing; if there is not enough stock to meet demand, customers may search out alternative suppliers.

Cost reduction is the holy grail of production managers, and one way to achieve this is to simplify production methods. This involves removing unnecessary and costly steps, or innovating so that stages become faster or less wasteful. Entrepreneur Michael Dell saved time and money by cutting out the retailer and letting customers design their own computers; these were produced to order ("just in time") and sold directly to the end user.

Creativity and innovation
Innovation can come from any part of the business. The Japanese idea of kaizen—meaning continuous improvement—is an ancient philosophy, but it was first used in an industrial setting by Toyota in the 1950s. Founder Elji Toyoda expected all employees—from the factory floor to senior executives— to constantly come up with ideas for improving products or production.

This idea took hold around the world. Companies recognized value in setting up teams to increase creativity. However, large companies often limit innovation—or at least the testing of its validity—to an R&D (research and development)

department. They can focus on the changing needs of markets and respond appropriately, making sure they benefit from the premium price of innovative products, and build a brand loyalty.

More recently, companies have also begun to value the creativity of their customers. Using an approach known as "open innovation," new ideas are welcomed from all sources, and customer feedback is valued in the product-development process. The opportunity for customers to post product ratings and reviews online allows ready access to customer feedback. Some even use online crowdsourcing to refine the design of products.

The rise of "big data"
Computer systems can collect and yield vast amounts of accurate data, which can translate into valuable information about employees, production lines, and markets.

Data collected about customers is often referred to simply as "big data." Customer buying preferences and habits can now be tracked with incredible accuracy—from their movements around a website, to where and how they like to buy products and services, both online and in stores. This gives an accurate picture of their overall market, while also targeting individual customers, offering them products in tune with their preferences.

The cost of quality
Companies aim to satisfy customers to get repeat business and good "word-of-mouth," which can hugely boost sales. Those that operate in the fast-moving-consumer-goods (FMCG) market, selling such things as chocolate, beer, and cereals, rely on quality for creating customer loyalty. In the service industries, following this "added-value" approach can be problematic. If competing companies raise the quality of their product or service to a level that would be unprofitable to match, this would signal the need for new strategic thinking.

However, high-quality goods can last for a long time without needing replacement, and this was a problem addressed by industrial designer Brooke Stevens. He suggested that companies could increase sales by creating in consumers the "desire to own something a little better, a little sooner than necessary." This seems especially true today, when new models of products such as smartphones are produced regularly—well before their predecessors are defunct.

For a smooth, fast route to a high-quality product, companies need to make best use of time and resources. This has led to the development of a way of working known as "time-based management," which involves utilizing time in the same way as raw materials. It is often used with critical-path analysis, which identifies all the stages of a project and puts them into a logical order, saving companies time and money.

Finally, businesses can improve processes and sales by observing the best practice of competitors in their field, using a process known as benchmarking, which takes the "best from the best" so companies can deliver the best products in the best way to satisfy customers. ∎

Improvement usually means doing something that we have never done before.
Shigeo Shingo
Japanese industrial engineer
(1909–90)

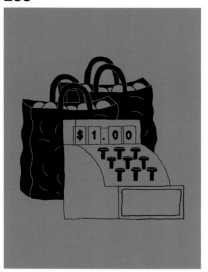

SEE HOW MUCH, NOT HOW LITTLE, YOU CAN GIVE FOR A DOLLAR
MAXIMIZE CUSTOMER BENEFITS

IN CONTEXT

FOCUS
Raising quality

KEY DATES
1850 Consumer choice theory is developed by UK economist William Jevons—according to this theory buyers seek out products that offer the best value for money.

1915 US businessman Vincent Astor establishes the first supermarket, in Manhattan, NY.

1971 Businessman Rollin King and lawyer Herb Kelleher set up Southwest, the world's first low-cost airline, in Texas.

1995 The Liberal government in Canada, under the leadership of Jean Chrétien, manages to cut public spending by nearly 10 percent in their attempt to provide taxpayers with more for less.

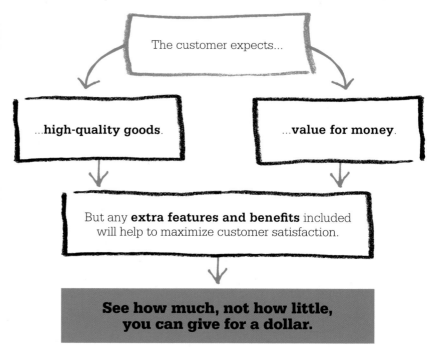

The customer expects...

...**high-quality goods**.

...**value for money**.

But any **extra features and benefits** included will help to maximize customer satisfaction.

See how much, not how little, you can give for a dollar.

Henry Ford spotted a gap in the market for a mass-produced car that ordinary Americans could afford. The Model T Ford was launched in 1908 and was still selling well nearly 20 years later. During this period, Ford regularly improved the car. For example, the first version of the Model T required the driver to crank the engine by hand to start it, but later models had an electric starter. Ford did not opt to make customers pay more for this better product. In fact, he did the opposite. The price of a Model T Ford fell every year from 1909 until 1916. Ford saw the importance of offering more for less. When cost-savings were made on the production line, they were

See also: Your workers are your customers 132–37 ▪ Porter's generic strategies 178–83 ▪ Lean production 290–93 ▪ Applying and testing ideas 310–11

immediately passed on to his customers by way of lower prices, which helped to boost sales.

Successful companies are able to attract customers by supplying high-quality goods and services at prices the buyer is willing to pay. Companies such as Dollar Tree in the US or Poundland in the UK base their business model on offering their customers as much as possible for $1 or £1—for example, in June 2013 Poundland launched the world's cheapest bra, which retailed at £1. Offering more for less can be an effective business strategy, provided that the price covers costs. Low prices that offer excellent value for money attract customers away from rivals.

More for less

Budget supermarket chains, such as Lidl and Aldi in Europe, have used this strategy to great effect. These businesses have been able to grow their market share at the expense of larger supermarket chains. Since the financial crisis,

Lidl's supermarkets are basic, with a limited range of products, some of which are displayed on warehouse pallets. However, the products themselves can be of a high quality.

I don't understand why anyone would hold something up and proudly say, 'I paid more for this than I needed to.'
Paul Foley
Managing director Aldi UK (1958–)

inflation has regularly outstripped pay raises, and households have responded by seeking out retailers that offer them more for less.

The secret to Lidl and Aldi's success is not solely due to their low prices. They also offer high-quality products. For example, in 2012, Lidl launched its own designer aftershave called G.Bellini X-Bolt for $6.35 (£3.99). In blind tests the fragrance beat famous brand names, such as Dior Homme, D&G The One, and Hugo Boss Bottled, which cost up to ten times more.

The stores focus on offering good value stock rather than an attractive shopping experience. They offer products on pallets direct from the warehouse, and do not spend time or money displaying their goods attractively. They also do not stock popular brands that shoppers will find elsewhere; most stock comes from less well-known suppliers that the stores can obtain at competitive prices.

The challenge for entrepreneurs is to offer outstanding value for money, while also keeping costs low enough to trade profitably. ▪

Hyundai

The car manufacturer Hyundai is the fourth-largest in the world and the third-largest *chaebol* (conglomerate) in South Korea. Its success is a direct result of its policy of offering customers a good deal at a competitive price.

One way Hyundai has grown its market share is by offering the longest warranties in the auto industry. Long warranties are an obvious selling point, because if a new car breaks down during the warranty period the buyer can return it to the manufacturer, who will repair it free of charge. Hyundai's warranties guarantee the engine for ten years, cover the bodywork for seven years, and offer free roadside assistance in the event of a breakdown for five years. Despite these long warranties, Hyundai still charges relatively low prices for its vehicles.

Hyundai cars are also well equipped. Features such as Bluetooth connectivity, heated side-view mirrors, air conditioning, and LED running lights are all standard. Hyundai competes by offering its customers as much as possible for the price charged.

COSTS DO NOT EXIST TO BE CALCULATED. COSTS EXIST TO BE REDUCED

LEAN PRODUCTION

IN CONTEXT

FOCUS
Waste reduction

KEY DATES
1908 The Model T Ford automobile is mass produced on an assembly line by the Ford Motor Company in Detroit, MI.

1950 W. Edwards Deming trains engineers and managers (including Akio Morita, the co-founder of Sony) in process and quality control in Japan.

1961 Robots are first used on an assembly line at a General Motors plant in Ewing Township, NJ.

2006 US management consultants McKinsey & Company publish an influential report urging governments to apply lean production techniques to the delivery of public services so taxpayers get more for less.

I n business, ideas for new products and production techniques tend to emerge during times of crisis when the old products and methods have become unprofitable. This is the case with "lean production," a method of planning for demand by reducing waste, developed in Japan by the Toyota Motor Corporation in the 1950s. At that time, Toyota was a relatively inefficient producer of cars. Like many other Japanese companies, Toyota was struggling to overcome the shortages created by an economy that had been devastated by war. Looking for ideas, Toyota sent a young engineer, Eiji Toyoda, to the US to

See also: Reinventing and adapting 52–57 ▪ The value of teams 70–71 ▪ Creativity and invention 72–73 ▪ Leading the market 166–69 ▪ Maximize customer benefits 288–89 ▪ Simplify processes 296–99 ▪ Time-based management 326–27

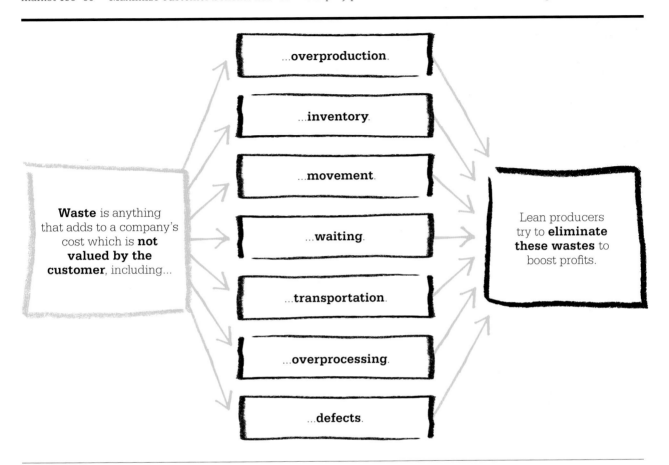

Waste is anything that adds to a company's cost which is **not valued by the customer**, including...

...**overproduction**.

...**inventory**.

...**movement**.

...**waiting**.

...**transportation**.

...**overprocessing**.

...**defects**.

Lean producers try to **eliminate these wastes** to boost profits.

visit Ford's Rouge plant in Detroit, MI. Toyoda spent three months studying the mass-production technique pioneered by Ford at the Rouge. On his return, Eiji reported that he was impressed by the scale of production that Ford achieved— the Rouge was so big that it required its own railroad, hospital, and several fire stations. However, he also believed that the factory was riddled with *muda*—the Japanese term for wasted effort, materials, and time. Toyoda and his colleagues set about developing a new production system that sought to replicate the output and economies of scale achieved by Ford, but in a less wasteful manner.

Seven types of waste
Shigeo Shingo, a Japanese industrial engineer who worked with Toyota in the 1970s, identified seven types of waste, or *muda*.

The first type is overproduction. Traditional manufacturers have a tendency to mass produce in advance of sales. These companies try to forecast what they think demand will be for their product, then they make the goods that they expect to sell. The main problem with this system of manufacturing, however, is that it relies on accurate forecasting of demand. If the forecast does not accurately match demand, the company could be left with mountains of unsold stock.

The second example of *muda* is inventory waste. In addition to stockpiles of unsold finished goods, many mass producers keep stocks of raw materials and work-in-progress to reduce the risk of production being halted. Stocks of raw materials are held in case a supplier fails to make a delivery, or to protect against the possibility that some of the raw materials might be defective and unusable. Stocks of work-in-progress, or semi-completed products, are held just in case a machine on the production line breaks down. These can then be inserted into the process to ensure that production continues. However, holding stocks of raw »

Holding goods in stock is a cost for a company, since warehouse space and employees need to be paid for. In addition, cash tied up in stock could be in the bank instead, earning interest.

materials and work-in-progress is considered wasteful because of the associated space and staff costs.

The third type of *muda* that Shingo identified is movement. In some factories, workstations are badly designed, and employees spend time doing things that do not add value to the product, such as looking for tools, walking from one part of the factory to another, or bending to pick up parts. This type of waste increases cycle time—the time taken to produce a unit of output. Longer cycle times lead to lower productivity, which in turn drives up unit labor costs.

The fourth *muda* is time spent waiting. Delays may occur when machines on a production line are poorly coordinated, resulting in bottlenecks. Time might also be wasted resetting machinery to produce a different part.

The fifth *muda* is transportation. Time and money spent moving work-in-progress from one factory to another will drive up costs, and this is unlikely to add value to the product, so it is wasteful.

The sixth example of *muda* is overprocessing. Consumers will only pay for the product features that they value. Producing complex, overengineered products is wasteful because it creates additional costs without any extra revenue.

The final *muda* is the production of defective items. Substandard products signify waste of time and resources, and mean that further inspection processes are required and the products must be reworked.

In addition to the seven types of *muda*, Toyota identifies two other potential problems: *mura* and *muri*. *Mura* is uneven flow in a process, leading to unbalanced working practices. *Muri* is the overburdening of people or equipment.

Lean strategy

Using these insights, production engineer Taiichi Ohno developed the Toyota Production System (TPS). This lean production method counters waste in the production process by producing more using less. It enables a manufacturer to increase output without having to pay for extra labor, raw materials, or capital. Alternatively, a business can use lean production techniques to make a better-quality product that will sell for a higher price.

Muri, mura, and *muda* are three Japanese terms identified by the Toyota Production System as problems to avoid. *Muri* refers to the overburdening of individuals or teams, which is inefficient; *mura* means an unbalanced work flow, which can cause bottlenecks in supply; and *muda* are all the areas of waste in a system.

MURI
Overburdened

MURA
Unbalanced

MUDA
Waste

JUST-IN-TIME

A just-in-time supply system eliminates *muri, mura,* and *muda* from the production system, so that teams receive materials as they need them and waste is avoided.

Lean producers try to eliminate overproduction and waste stock by using the just-in-time (JIT) system, in which production only happens in response to a customer order. Companies that use just-in-time never produce output for stock, and if there are no orders from buyers, production stops. Thus, production is pulled through by the consumer, rather than being pushed through by the manufacturer. The same principle is extended to raw materials and bought-in components. Lean producers run with minimal buffer stocks, relying instead on daily, or even hourly, deliveries from suppliers. However, the absence of a stock of raw materials means that a faulty shipment of components could bring an entire factory to a halt. So to make just-in-time work, lean producers require reliable suppliers that produce zero defects.

Lead times

If products are to be made to order rather than supplied from stock, there is a risk that a long lead time (the time between an order being made and delivery to the consumer) could result in customer dissatisfaction and consequently falling sales. Therefore, to run lean

production effectively, companies need to shorten the cycle time taken to make their products. To accelerate the pace of production, managers will need to control the movement *muda*, the waiting *muda*, and the transportation *muda*. At its simplest, this could be achieved by redesigning workstations and production lines so that employees have all the tools and components to complete the task close at hand. Likewise, bottlenecks in production can be eliminated by deploying more machinery or more labor at the problem area.

Overprocessing

Lean producers tackle wasteful overprocessing, the sixth *muda*, by applying a process called value analysis at the product design stage. Companies using value analysis attempt to identify product features that create cost but have no value for the consumer. If these features can be removed to create a simpler, cheaper product, profit margins will rise. At the same time, revenues should not fall, because the features that have been removed were not valued in the first place.

It could be argued that the business model of a no-frills hotel, as seen in the Malaysian company

Workers on a production line will be much more efficient if all the components they need are within easy reach. Time spent searching for items increases the movement *muda*, which incurs a cost to the business.

Tune Hotels, is based on value analysis. For Tune Hotels, affordable rooms are its priority. To achieve this, services that push up the price of a room but are viewed as nonessential by customers, such as air-conditioning or toiletries, have become optional add-ons. The chain focuses solely on core qualitites such as cleanliness and safety, valued highly by the customer.

To eliminate the seventh *muda*, defective products, lean producers seek to create high-quality items. This requires managers to trust workers to spot any fall in quality. Employees have the authority to stop the production line in order to solve the problem, and production only restarts once the source of the problem has been found and fixed.

High product quality, achieved by lean production, leads to lower costs. By solving problems at their source, companies spend less time and money on reworking defective products to bring them up to the required standard. ∎

All we are doing is looking at the time line, from the moment the customer gives us an order to the point when we collect the cash.
Taiichi Ohno

Regardless of how much workers move, it does not mean work has been done. Working means that progress has been made.
Taiichi Ohno

IF THE PIE'S NOT BIG ENOUGH, MAKE A BIGGER PIE
FULFILLING DEMAND

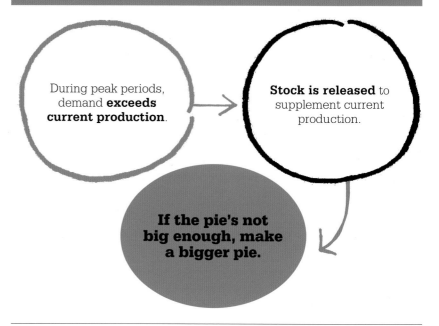

During peak periods, demand **exceeds current production**.

Stock is released to supplement current production.

If the pie's not big enough, make a bigger pie.

The success of a company can depend in large part on the effective management of its stock. Customer demand in most markets varies throughout the year. During busy periods, companies may not be able to produce enough to satisfy consumers. If companies fail to match supply to demand, potential buyers have to find alternative suppliers and sales will be lost. Additionally, once consumers have tried out the opposition, they may switch loyalty and never return. Sales may never regain previous levels, even after supply has been addressed, leading to lower profits.

Types of stock
Companies keep stock as an insurance policy—it enables them to deal with sudden surges in sales or a sudden drop in output. In addition to inventories of finished goods, manufacturers may hold stocks of raw materials, to create parts of the

See also: Luck (and how to get lucky) 42 ▪ How fast to grow 44–45 ▪ Avoiding complacency 194–201 ▪ Promotions and incentives 271 ▪ Why advertise? 272–73 ▪ Forecasting 278–79 ▪ Lean production 290–93 ▪ Simplify processes 296–99

final product or to replace defective materials. This strategy ensures that production can continue in the event of a delay from the supplier; companies are more likely to hold stocks of raw materials if their supplier is unreliable. They may also keep stocks of "work-in-progress," or semicompleted products. Work-in-progress stock can keep production flowing even if a machine on the assembly line breaks down.

Stock control

Good stock management balances meeting product demand with minimizing stock-holding costs. If a company runs out of stock, it may have to turn orders away, or deliver late and risk losing returning customers. In 1993 toy manufacturer Bandai was caught off guard by the popularity of its Power Rangers figures, and had to impose a "one figure per customer" rule in the UK until manufacturing could catch up with the huge demand.

On the other hand, if a company is overly cautious and holds too much stock, it incurs unnecessary

costs: warehouse space is expensive, and employees are needed to manage it. It can also lose value if it perishes or becomes technologically obsolete. There is also an opportunity cost associated with holding stock; the cash tied up in stock could be earning interest, or be invested elsewhere.

The goal is to hold just enough stock to meet demand, with minimum delay to the customer and at minimum cost to the company. A sophisticated computer program at McDonalds, called Manugistics, helps the chain forecast sales and ensure the correct quantity of stock is ordered for the week ahead.

Buffer stock

Most companies hold buffer stock—stock that exceeds the amount needed to meet current demand. It takes time to replenish stocks, so companies will reorder from suppliers well before their inventory falls below the buffer level. The longer the lead time—the time between placing an order and the goods arriving—the greater the

Because of our inventory management, Dell is able to offer some of the newest technologies at low prices while our competitors struggle to sell off older products.
Paul Bell
US former senior executive, Dell, Inc.

amount of buffer stock needed. If demand is stable and predictable, the need for large quantities of buffer stock is reduced.

Online companies may not need a storefront. However, unless their product can be digitally downloaded, many will still require a physical storage facility, with the same need to manage inventory and keep buffer stock. ▪

Surplus buses and other London and Olympic-themed models went unsold after optimistic oversupply caused a glut in retail outlets.

Hornby

To help recover the nearly $14 (£9) billion cost of staging the London 2012 Olympics, the UK sold rights to produce Olympics merchandise. Hornby paid for the right to produce official 2012 toys, including Corgi models of London taxis and buses, its model trains marked with the Olympics logo, and the Olympic mascots Wenlock and Mandeville.

Hornby produces most of its products in China and India to take advantage of low costs. However, outsourcing production has

lengthened its lead times: it takes six weeks to transport freight by sea from China to the UK. Hornby has to supply customers from stock, rather than current production, so sales of Olympic products had to be predicted well in advance.

Forecasts proved to be extremely optimistic. Hornby hoped to make a profit of $3.2 (£2) million from the Olympics. In the end, the contract cost it $2 (£1.3) million. To sell off stock, Hornby was forced to cut its prices by as much as 80 percent, ruining its profit margins.

ELIMINATE UNNECESSARY STEPS
SIMPLIFY PROCESSES

IN CONTEXT

FOCUS
Streamlining processes

KEY DATES
3rd century BCE The Romans mass-produce lamps. Instead of hand making them, they use two-part molds.

1760 The Industrial Revolution begins, moving from hand-production methods to specialized machines.

1730s US statesman Benjamin Franklin writes about waste reduction in industry in *Poor Richard's Almanack*.

1900s Ford revolutionizes car manufacturing with mass production and standardization.

2010 In *The Art of Invention*, US inventor Steven J. Paley states that it is easier to innovate by adding complexity, but the best results come from simplification.

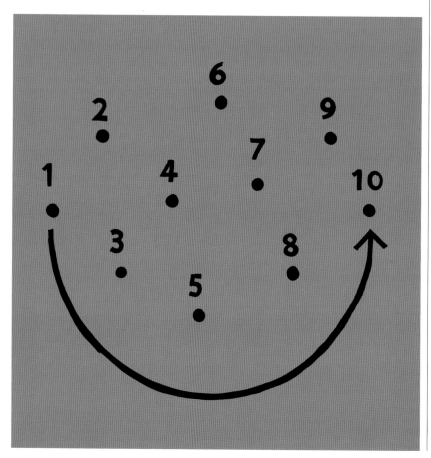

There are several ways that companies can improve their profits: they can increase their revenue, reduce their costs, or use a combination of both methods. If the cost of producing goods or services can be reduced, without negatively impacting revenue, total profits will rise. A good way to lower costs is to simplify the method of production by removing any expensive and nonessential steps that will not adversely affect the consumer's perception of the quality of the product. More straightforward— and therefore more cost-effective— production methods have been a goal for centuries. An early example

See also: Stand out in the market 28–29 ▪ Creativity and invention 72–73 ▪ Thinking outside the box 88–89 ▪ The learning organization 202–07 ▪ The value chain 216–217 ▪ Lean production 290–93 ▪ Kaizen 302–09

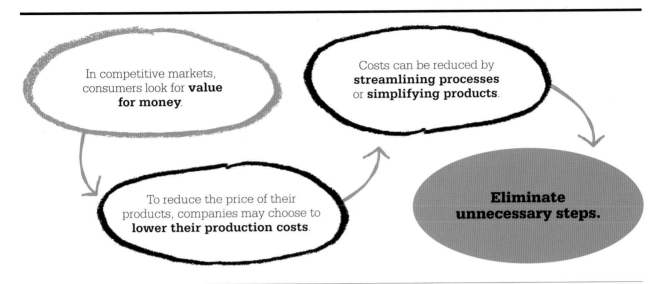

In competitive markets, consumers look for **value for money**.

Costs can be reduced by **streamlining processes** or **simplifying products**.

To reduce the price of their products, companies may choose to **lower their production costs**.

Eliminate unnecessary steps.

of a process that was successfully simplified is steel manufacturing. During the Industrial Revolution, huge quantities of steel were needed to build bridges, ships, and railroads. Steel was in short supply because it was expensive to produce. In Britain, steel had been made in high-temperature, coke-fired furnaces since the 1740s. Small quantities of iron were loaded into small clay crucibles (containers that withstood heat) and placed inside the furnace. After three hours, impurities were scraped from the crucibles, leaving the steel behind.

Simplifying the process
In the 1850s the production method was simplified by the British engineer Henry Bessemer. His so-called Bessemer process did not require crucibles. Instead, the impurities generated from heating

iron to create steel were removed from the metal by blowing air through the iron during the production process. Bessemer's simpler production method was more fuel efficient. As a result, the cost of making steel fell from as much as $97 (£60) per ton to $11 (£7) per ton.

In some cases, simplifying a process can mean using different materials. In 1946 in the US, James

Watson Hendry invented plastic-injection-molding technology, which was used to produce one-piece chairs and tables much more cheaply than wood.

Mass production
In the early 1900s, Henry Ford revolutionized manufacturing by standardizing the method used to make cars. Before Ford's »

Steelmaking was revolutionized by Henry Bessemer's new converter. It raised the temperature of the iron so that more impurities could be removed during the oxidation process.

assembly line, cars were made by teams of highly skilled craftsmen who produced custom-made cars using little more than hand tools. The components used by early manufacturers were usually nonstandardized. This meant that workers would spend time adjusting components so that they could be assembled. Ford removed this stage by designing the world's first standardized car. Mass production of the Model T, made from a standard set of components, began in 1910 in Highland Park, Michigan.

Ford's second great innovation was the conveyor belt. In the past, skilled workers had to move around the factory locating raw materials, components, and tools. In some factories workers were hired to push partially assembled cars from one workstation to another. Ford believed these were unnecessary steps that could easily be removed. People were taken out of the production process and were replaced by specialized machinery, including a conveyor belt that took the work to the worker. Each

Henry Ford made use of the conveyor belt on the assembly line at his factory producing the Model T. Workers specialized in one task with one set of tools, which lay within easy reach.

> Almost all quality improvement comes via simplification of design, manufacturing, layout, processes, and procedures.
> **Tom Peters**

employee was asked to perform a single task, using the same tool, over and over again. As a result, there was no time wasted searching for, picking up, and putting down an array of tools.

Finally, Ford removed variety from the production process. Each Model T produced was identical; Ford believed in simplicity of product, even down to the paint color, which speeded up production. Time spent resetting and cleaning machines between batches was avoided. A standard product made it possible to institute continuous-flow production, and the amount of time taken to produce a car dropped from over 12 hours to just over one and a half hours.Ford's decision to simplify production by removing skilled labor and time from the process enabled him to produce his cars at a lower cost, which he then used to reduce the price, and that created a mass market for the Model T.

Custom production
In more recent times, computer manufacturer Dell achieved stratospheric rates of growth in the 1990s by streamlining its supply chain. Michael Dell, the founder of the company, based his business

model on gaining a cost advantage over his rivals. He did this in two ways. First, Dell specialized in selling custom-made computers; customers could design their own machine, which Dell assembled in response to a specific customer's order. Dell held virtually zero stock and production was pulled through by the buyer. The main advantage of this just-in-time method was that Dell no longer had to pay the costs associated with storing stock. When a product was finished, it was sent straight to the customer.

Going direct to the buyer
Dell's second cost advantage was that, unlike other PC suppliers, it did not sell its products to specialized retailers; instead, it sold directly to the consumer via the Internet. This meant that the company no longer had to lose some of its profit margin to third parties. When Dell sold a computer for $400, it received $400. Eliminating retailers did not have an adverse effect on Dell's market share. In fact, the reverse was true. Most computer buyers preferred the flexibility of being able to build exactly the sort of computer that they wanted, and also appreciated the convenience of home delivery.

> Simple can be harder than complex: you have to work harder to get your thinking clean.
> **Steve Jobs**
> **US Co-founder of Apple (1955–2011)**

Dell's simplified business model delivered lower costs, enabling the company to gain market share by undercutting the prices charged by rival computer suppliers.

The success of Dell's model of selling directly to consumers was adopted by companies in other industries. In 1996, Amazon, now the world's biggest online store, began selling books online without the need—or costs—of running a bookstore.

However, since 2000 Dell has lost ground to a revitalized competition. Some companies copied Dell's idea to sell computers directly to customers, while others, such as Hewlett-Packard, were able to nullify Dell's price advantage by making their production process more efficient. The resurgence of Apple has also dented Dell's market share. Apple produces a range of products to suit different budgets, and also allows its customers to make some adjustments to the computer's specifications.

Simpler services

Companies that sell services also work to improve efficiency by trying to remove unnecessary steps from their production systems. Sometimes these changes are needed to ensure

Dell computers were not sold by computer retailers; instead they were available directly from the manufacturer. Dell took the bold step of cutting out retailers to undercut the competition.

a company's survival. For example, in the past, many independent food venues offered meals produced in a traditional, labor-intensive manner, cooked from scratch with fresh ingredients. Some business chains, looking to capitalize on the growing demand for low-cost food, adopted a simpler approach. They began to serve food that had been bought in a prepared state and simply heated in a microwave in response to a customer order. There was no need for trained cooks, and no time spent preparing fresh ingredients. Removing these steps cuts costs and enables the establishment to offer lower prices to consumers without losing profit margins.

However, innovations such as these can be cyclical. A rising market for freshly prepared food has led to new fast-food chains selling meals prepared on the premises. In the current climate, many companies are looking to cut costs by streamlining processes. But the businesses most likely to survive are those that can lower prices, but not quality, for the consumer. ■

Simplicity—the art of maximizing the amount of work not done—is essential.
**Principles behind
The Agile Manifesto (2001)**

Michael Dell

Born in 1965 in Houston, Texas, to an orthodontist father and a stockbroker mother, Michel Dell was a natural entrepreneur. He made his first $1,000 by dealing in stamps at 12-years-old, and sold newspaper subscriptions for the now-defunct *Houston Post*. Dell attended pre-medical college in Texas in 1983, but soon left to focus on his computer business, which he named PC's Limited. Dell opened his first international subsidiary in the UK two years later, and in 1988 changed the business's name to Dell Computer Corporation, making it a public company and raising $30 million. In 1992, Dell became the youngest-ever CEO of a *Fortune* 500 business at 27. By 2000, the company's direct-sales website (launched in 1996) was generating revenue of $18 million per day. Dell resigned as CEO in 2004 to focus on his charitable work, but returned in 2007, taking the business private in 2013.

Key works

1999 *Direct from Dell: Strategies That Revolutionized an Industry*

EVERY GAIN THROUGH THE ELIMINATION OF WASTE IS GOLD IN THE MINE
JURAN'S PRODUCTION IDEAL

IN CONTEXT

FOCUS
Waste reduction

KEY DATES

1969 The Spittelau incineration plant in Vienna opens to burn trash collected from the city. The award-winning design means that the energy created can be used to provide hot water to a local hospital.

1931 Walter Shewhart summarizes his work on process quality control at Western Electric in his book *Economic Control of Quality of Manufactured Product.*

1994 In *The Empty Raincoat,* Charles Handy predicts the rise of telecommuting, whereby employees work from home to reduce office space.

1999 Salesforce.com and Google develop cloud computing. This foregoes the need to run expensive servers on which to store their data.

Reducing waste increases efficiency by **improving the productivity** of capital and labor.

⬇

Efficiency gains created from cutting waste cause **average unit costs to fall**.

⬇

Lower unit costs can **help a company grow** because lower costs can be used to either:

⬇ ⬇

Fund **price cuts**, which will hopefully **boost sales**.

Or **improve profit margins**, which can be used to finance **new product development**.

⬇ ⬇

Every gain through the elimination of waste is gold in the mine.

In business, waste is anything that adds to a company's costs that does not create a higher output level, or lead to improved customer satisfaction. Any money generated from a reduction in waste can help a business grow by improving its competitiveness.

Joseph Juran (1904–2008) was born in Romania and moved to the US when he was a child. He became an expert in quality in business after working at Western Electric in the 1920s and being trained in statistical sampling and quality control. Juran identified waste as a factor that undermined profit. He urged businesses to constantly look out for opportunities to reduce waste. For Juran, the best way to do this was to improve product quality and the reliability of the production process.

Reducing waste

Waste in business ranges from investing in expensive machinery that does not meet the required output level because it breaks down regularly, to producing finished products that fail internal quality audits and are not good enough to be sold. If waste of this type can be reduced it should be possible to raise output without having to hire extra workers, spend more capital, or buy in additional raw materials and components.

According to Juran, lower costs can help a company grow in two ways. First, if average costs can be decreased, the business could choose to pass on the reduction by lowering prices to consumers. For example, if an initiative to reduce waste leads to a 10 percent fall in average costs, the management could opt to cut its retail prices by the same magnitude, and still earn the same profit margin. Cutting prices can help a business grow: undercutting the competition on price is likely to attract market share. Furthermore, even in markets where there is little competition, price cuts will make a product more affordable. The lower price will widen the brand's appeal, and potentially create growth by enlarging the target market.

Reinvesting profits

Reduced unit costs can help a company to enlarge its profit margins. If such savings are not passed on to the consumer, they could be used to increase the profit earned from the company's current sales volume. The additional profits made from reducing wastage could be reinvested into the business— the goal being to increase sales and to achieve growth. An efficient way to make use of the cash saved by reducing waste might be to fund a new advertising campaign.

Alternatively, companies might reinvest a significant proportion of their profits into scientific research and new product development. Theories about the life cycle of products, technological advances, and changing consumer tastes suggest that most products have finite selling lives in the market. If these investments pay off, the next generation of products will incorporate the latest must-have features and benefits that will appeal to consumers and translate into high sales. ▪

Paint robots at this Volkswagen factory help reduce employee costs, and can be programed to use the minimum amount of paint required.

Volkswagen

In 2012, Volkswagen announced its intention to become the world's most environmentally friendly car manufacturer by 2018. To achieve this goal, the German company set out to reduce waste during the production process.

When cars are produced, sheet steel is cut out to form parts of the chassis. If this process is not managed effectively, expensive steel can end up being wasted as off-cuts. The management at Volkswagen achieved a 15 percent reduction in the amount of steel used to produce each car by investing in new cutting machinery and by changing the dimensions of the steel sheets to reduce off-cut waste. In the paint shop, the amount of paint used to produce a vehicle was halved by installing state-of-the-art painting robots.

These savings meant that Volkswagen could reduce their prices. For example, the price of a Golf Cabriolet was reduced by approximately $10,600 in June 2013. Reductions like this contributed to a 6 percent rise in global sales by May 2013.

MACHINES, FACILITIES, AND PEOPLE SHOULD WORK TOGETHER TO ADD VALUE

KAIZEN

IN CONTEXT

FOCUS
Improving efficiency

KEY DATES

1882 Scottish shipbuilders William Denny and Brothers Ltd. becomes the first company to use a suggestion box to garner ideas from its work force.

1859 English naturalist Charles Darwin publishes *On the Origin of the Species*, and outlines his theory of evolution as a process of gradual changes.

1990 In "Re-engineering work: don't automate, obliterate" in the *Harvard Business Review*, MIT professor Michael Hammer argues that to stay ahead, companies need to periodically redesign production methods.

1997 Japanese founder of the Kaizen Institute, Masaaki Imai, writes *Gemba Kaizen*, stressing that kaizen works best when factory-floor workers provide ideas for ongoing improvement.

In Japan, *kaizen* is an ancient idea that has become part of the culture. In its everyday usage, the word means an enhancement or a change for the better. In a business context, kaizen is more of a philosophy; according to the kaizen way of thinking, companies should strive to increase efficiency through a process of continuous improvement.

The majority of kaizen advances are built around people and their ideas, rather than investment in new machinery. Employees use kaizen to produce hundreds of new ideas every year, aimed at improving the efficiency of the business. In isolation, each kaizen idea might only have a marginal effect on productivity and general efficiency, but together these changes add up, creating a critical competitive advantage. Ideas for continuous improvement should come from all quarters—from managers and employees alike.

The Toyota Way

Kaizen was first deployed on an industrial scale by car manufacturer Toyota in the 1950s, as part of the now famous Toyota Production

> Before you say you can't do something, try it.
> **Sakichi Toyoda**

System (TPS). This system was designed to reduce *muda*—the Japanese word for waste. One of the forms of *muda* identified by Toyota was wasted employee talent; Eiji Toyoda wanted more from his work force than just blind obedience and hard work. At Toyota employees were valued and trusted—so much so that the company expected their factory-floor workers to fix problems associated with quality, and come up with ideas to improve efficiency. According to the Kaizen Institute, founded by Masaaki Imai to implement the philosophy, the goal of any kaizen plan should be to

Toyota

The Toyota Motor Company (TMC) was established in 1937. It produced several models of sedan cars at its Honsha production plant following business precepts set down by founder Sakichi Toyoda, which included, "Always strive to build a homelike atmosphere at work that is warm and friendly."

Following World War II, the company faced a financial crisis and, for the first time in its history, had to layoff employees. In 1951, Toyota implemented a creative ideas suggestion system based on

the principles of kaizen. This, along with its principles of "customer first" and "quality first," helped the company thrive, and they began exporting their first cars to the US in 1957.

In 1962 management and unions signed a joint declaration stating that their relationship should be based on "mutual trust and respect."

By 1999 production in Japan had reached 100 million vehicles. Today the company continues to be guided by the twin pillars of continuous improvement and teamwork.

See also: Take the second step 43 ▪ Reinventing and adapting 52–57 ▪ Beware the yes-men 74–75 ▪ Make the most of your talent 86–87 ▪ Is money the motivator? 90–91 ▪ Lean production 290–93

persuade all workers that they have been hired for two jobs—doing their job, and then looking for ways to do it more efficiently.

Gemba is a Japanese word meaning "the real place," in a business context *gemba* refers to the place where value-added is created. Kaizen is founded on the conviction that the production-line worker is the *gemba* expert who knows where the problems are. Therefore, most of the ideas for kaizen change should come from the factory-floor workers, rather than from management. This is because difficulties and abnormalities can only be analyzed and fixed at the *gemba*, not from the desk. Kaizen philosophy recognizes that a company's greatest resource is its employees.

Quality circles

Kaizen is more likely to be effective if workers are asked to work as teams, rather than as isolated individuals. The process of coming up with good ideas and solutions is often the product of the synergy created by people that have different skill sets, qualifications, or ways of seeing the world. Working as a team on kaizen projects is known as being part of a "quality circle." The quality circle consists of a group of people who usually work together—for example, on the same part of an assembly line—as well as individuals from other parts of the business who can bring different perspectives. For example, an engineer could provide advice on technical matters, while sales-team members can give the group an insight into the customer's point of view.

In 1964, Toyota established quality circles at its factory in Toyota City, Japan. The quality

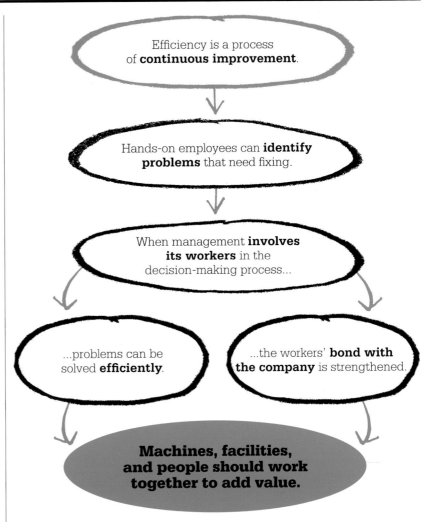

Efficiency is a process of **continuous improvement**.

Hands-on employees can **identify problems** that need fixing.

When management **involves its workers** in the decision-making process...

...problems can be solved **efficiently**.

...the workers' **bond with the company** is strengthened.

Machines, facilities, and people should work together to add value.

circles still meet regularly, at least once a week, to discuss any of the problems they have noticed on their section of the production line. Each morning employees are expected to attend an *asa-ichi* (morning) meeting with a positive attitude, before the regular working day begins. At this meeting they discuss quality problems and possible solutions to those problems. One of the main tools used by Toyota's quality circles to generate

kaizen ideas is the "fish-bone" diagram. This is a graphic device that uses the outline of a fish skeleton to plot all the various aspects of a problem and then explore a number of solutions. Quality circle members are asked to identify possible causes for the problem, and each suggestion is classified into one of six categories: Manpower, Methods, Machines, Materials, Measurement (inspection), and Mother Nature »

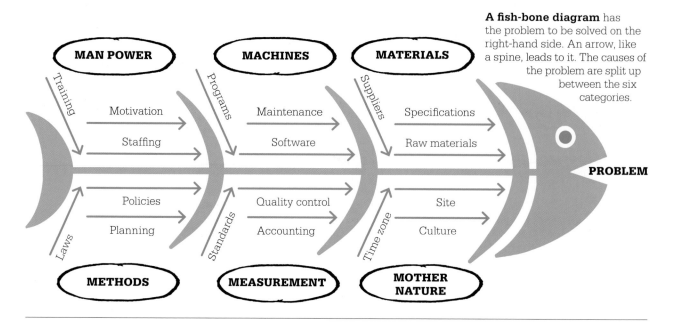

A fish-bone diagram has the problem to be solved on the right-hand side. An arrow, like a spine, leads to it. The causes of the problem are split up between the six categories.

(environmental factors). Solutions to each of the possible causes of the problem are evaluated by the circle using the "five Ws," which are the five questions: Why, When, Where, Who, and What.

Japanese companies do not tend to give cash bonuses to workers in return for their ideas. In order for kaizen to be truly effective, workers must feel a sense of pride and fulfillment when contributing their suggestions. New employees are told when they start working with the company that kaizen is an expectation: an everyday part of company life. In businesses that use kaizen successfully, employees' commitment to contributing ideas is usually secured via programs of job enrichment, which tend to produce high levels of employee motivation. According to motivational theorists such as Frederick Herzberg, workers enjoy problem solving, decision making, and the opportunity to advance and grow psychologically while at work. Therefore, it follows that workers should enjoy taking part

in kaizen improvements and, consequently, financial bonuses should not be necessary.

Empowerment
One way managers empower their workers is giving them the authority to make decisions that affect their working lives. Empowerment is more far-reaching than delegation, which merely involves giving permission for an employee to perform a specific task. An employee who is empowered has been given the freedom to decide what to do and how it should be done. Empowerment is essential to any kaizen program because it enables good ideas from the factory floor to be implemented immediately. Once the kaizen philosophy is in place, good ideas and their subsequent improvements should keep on flowing through—the number of ideas made every week increases because workers are able to observe the effects of their own solutions. To work effectively, kaizen requires a business culture where trust,

loyalty, and mutual respect exists between the management and the work force. This avoids a potential downside to the philosophy: the fact that in a market where sales are flat, employee ideas that lead to an increase in productivity could represent a threat to jobs. Workers are hardly likely to discuss labor-saving or cost-cutting measures if they are talking themselves out of a job. In many Japanese companies the kaizen culture used to incorporate a promise from the

A company will get nowhere if all the thinking is left to management.
Akio Morita
Japanese founder of Sony (1921–99)

> We will try to create the conditions where persons could come together in a spirit of teamwork, and exercise to their heart's desire their technological capacity.
> **Akio Morita**

management that workers would have a job for life with the company. Throughout the 1980s and 1990s this was the case at Sony. During economic downturns, when sales fall, most companies try to protect their profit margins by making layoffs that are designed to cut costs. Sony rejected this approach because it felt that laying off its own workers would break the bond of trust needed to make kaizen work. According to Sony's

co-founder, Akio Morita, "The most important mission for a Japanese manager is to develop a healthy relationship with his employees, to create a familylike feeling within the corporation, a feeling that employees and managers share the same fate." During the boom years Sony used the productivity increases made possible by kaizen to increase output, enabling the company to branch out into new markets.

Kaizen heads west

In the fall of 1984, following US concerns at the growing dominance of the Japanese car industry, the Massachusetts Institute of Technology (MIT) undertook a five-year, $5 million research program into the global car industry. The study produced a new way of looking at production, a new buzzword, and a best-selling book—*The Machine That Changed the World,* authored by James Womack, Dan Jones, and Dan Roos. The study confirmed the US car industry's worst fears; Japanese car producers led the way in terms of

> Excellent companies don't believe in excellence—only in constant improvement and constant change.
> **Tom Peters**
> **US management writer (1942–)**

minimizing the assembly hours per car, the amount of stock held, and the assembly defects per 100 cars. The book attributed Japanese success to a process called "lean production"—a vital component of which was kaizen.

Managers that had read *The Machine That Changed the World* tried to incorporate the kaizen way of thinking into their business model, and gradually the kaizen philosophy spread to North America and Europe. One of the early British adoptors was Rover. Under the guidance of Honda, who at the time held a 20 percent stake in Rover, the company introduced *gemba* walks at its Longbridge factory in 1991. Under Rover's *gemba* program, managers, supervisors, and assembly-line workers walked along the production line together, at least once a week, in order to look for inefficiencies, and to find solutions to the problems they had identified. *Gemba* walks were designed »

Discussing a problem with others is a more effective way to come up with solutions. Consulting people from other parts of the business brings different viewpoints and a wider range of options.

to remove the divide between managers and workers, the underlying philosophy being that managers, supervisors, and assembly-line workers should learn, discover, teach, grow, and make improvements together.

Kaizen in action

One of the first British companies to adopt quality circles was the pottery company, Wedgwood. From 1980 onward, 80 quality circles representing different parts of the business met for an hour a week. Each quality circle was empowered to identify its own problem, which it then spent up to six months solving. The solution devised by the circle was presented to the management and most were approved and then implemented. Employee motivation improved, which increased productivity. In addition, employee ideas reduced costs by cutting the amount of clay and paint wasted during the production process. According to Dick Fletcher, the man who led Wedgwood's quality circle program,

for every $1.60 (£1) the business spent on quality circles, Wedgwood's costs fell by $4.85 (£3).

Another business that has employed kaizen techniques to good effect is India-based Tata Steel. The company made improvements to the productivity of its gear-cutting machinery, which led to increased production.

The antithesis of kaizen

A very different approach from kaizen is Business Process Reengineering (BPR). This is based on infrequent—but very capital-heavy—investment programs that are designed to create a great leap forward in terms of productivity, reductions in unit costs, or improvements in product quality. Unlike kaizen, companies that use BPR do not endeavor to make regular small changes. Instead the goal is to radically rethink the whole production process every five years or so to make it more efficient. Typically, this is in response to a crisis. Once the company using BPR has caught up with its rivals,

Investment in robots in the workplace can be a large-scale, costly undertaking, which frequently results in job losses. This sort of BPR activity can alienate the work force.

a period of stability follows, until complacency sets in again, and the next crisis arrives, and prompts another round of BPR.

Rather than approaching employees for ideas that lead to improvements in efficiency, companies that use BPR only use ideas that originate from managers and highly qualified consultants. The work force is relatively passive: change is imposed from the top and often includes large-scale layoffs. This is because companies that use this approach often try to boost efficiency by investing in automated production systems that replace labor with capital. Those that favor kaizen argue that it is better to try to improve efficiency by making small but regular changes, rather than by instigating less frequent but more radical BPR changes. In competitive markets, companies that rely on BPR struggle to match the less dramatic but steadier growth achieved by kaizen. Companies using BPR can

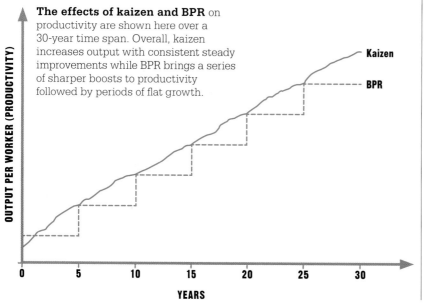

The effects of kaizen and BPR on productivity are shown here over a 30-year time span. Overall, kaizen increases output with consistent steady improvements while BPR brings a series of sharper boosts to productivity followed by periods of flat growth.

OUTPUT PER WORKER (PRODUCTIVITY)

Kaizen

BPR

0   5   10   15   20   25   30

YEARS

be slow to catch up because during the time it takes to develop, install, and test new systems, companies using kaizen have moved on, boosting productivity to an even higher level. This may be seen as analogous to the fable by Aesop in which the plodding tortoise trumps the sprinting—then delaying—hare. Increased productivity achieved by kaizen tends to be cheaper to obtain than productivity growth achieved by BPR. The source of kaizen improvement is people. Employee ideas are essentially free, unlike expensive new machinery for a new production system.

Is kaizen always effective?

However, in some companies kaizen does not work. Middle managers and supervisors who are inclined toward an autocratic leadership style typically resent kaizen: they enjoy making all the decisions and are sometimes resistant to change. Individuals with this mind-set will not want to delegate decision making to factory-floor workers. If their good ideas are constantly ignored by managers, employees will quickly become disillusioned and stop contributing. A company's industrial relations history can also affect the outcome of kaizen. In general, the chances of success with kaizen fall if there is a lack of trust between the management and the work force. Employees may see kaizen in a cynical way—feeling that the plan is just another management ruse to get more out of the work force without offering anything in return.

Kaizen is built on the premise that no production method is perfect; systems can always be improved through employee suggestions. But is this always true? Logically, businesses will try to use kaizen to fix key problems first. It could be argued that, over time, the benefits of kaizen are likely to fall steadily as any new problems that are tackled will be those previously considered less significant.

The rewards of risk

Technology and consumer tastes change. From time to time the old product, and with it the old methods of production, will need to be discarded in favor of something new and radical. Companies that favor kaizen may tend to eschew radical overhauls in favor of less dramatic change. The danger here is that they can end up being left behind by their bolder rivals. A good example of a company that suffered as a result of this approach is Nokia. For many years the Finnish cell-phone company enjoyed great success by sticking to its classic design of "Candybar" phones. However, in the meantime rival companies such as Samsung and Apple took greater risks, and as a result, out-innovated Nokia, taking away their market lead. ∎

Aesop's fable tells how the tortoise wins a race against the hare by slowly advancing to the finish while the hare sprints and then riskily naps. Kaizen can be viewed as the tortoise, making minor adjustments daily, while the hare can be viewed as BPR, making rapid, dramatic changes.

The tortoise demonstrates that **steady progress**, such as that achieved using **kaizen methods**, can be the better approach to winning the race.

The hare's overconfidence causes him to lose the race, much as the big, **bold changes wrought by BPR** can prove less effective in the long run.

LEARNING AND INNOVATION GO HAND IN HAND

APPLYING AND TESTING IDEAS

Scientific research leads to **technological breakthroughs**, which businesses use to...

...create new products.

...improve existing products.

...update processes.

To **innovate for the future**, companies must be **willing to learn** about new technologies and how they can be harnessed.

Learning and innovation go hand in hand.

Research and development (R&D) is any investigative and creative work intended to lead to new discoveries or to improvements in existing products or processes. Some companies, in areas such as computer software and pharmaceuticals, depend on scientific research to bring about technological breakthroughs and keep themselves on the cutting edge of their industry. Others apply R&D to improve existing products.

Filling a gap
In some cases, the direction of R&D is driven by market research findings that uncover a gap in the

See also: Gaining an edge 32–39 ▪ Kaizen 302–09 ▪ Quality sells 318–23 ▪ Planned obsolescence 324–25 ▪ Time-based management 326–27

market, as it did for the cereal manufacturer Kellogg's. Market research showed that there was a desire in the UK for a sweeter breakfast cereal made from nuts, which people perceived to be healthy. To meet this need, Kellogg's instructed its R&D department to design a new breakfast cereal; the result was Kellogg's Crunchy Nut, which has become the second most popular cereal in the UK.

There have been some cases in which market research pointed companies in the wrong direction. A prime example can be seen in the creation of Sony's Walkman. This portable audio cassette player was invented in 1978 by Nobutoshi Kihara, an audio engineer working for Sony. According to market research, the Soundabout (the name for the prototype Walkman) would never sell because focus groups declared that listening to music was a social rather than a solitary activity. However, Akio Morita, Sony's co-founder, told his R&D department to continue its

Innovate or die.
Damon Darlin
Business editor, *The New York Times*
(1956–)

work and ignore these findings. The Walkman went on to be one of Sony's most successful products.

More products, more often

Intense competition resulting from globalization, alongside rapid technological advances, has shortened the selling lives of many products. To stay in business in this tough trading environment, companies need to launch new products more regularly; those that are complacent and fail to innovate will be overtaken by their rivals.

It could be argued that managers who do not invest in R&D are setting up businesses to fail.

Companies such as BMW devote a sizable percentage of their turnover to R&D for motives that extend beyond self-preservation. Those that launch a new product first can charge premium prices and will benefit from monopoly profit until the competition arrives. In addition, consumers' brand loyalties are usually established early on. Companies that underinvest in R&D, fine to imitate rather than innovate, may have problems establishing a strong customer base.

There is more to effective R&D than spending money on technical breakthroughs. According to Akio Morita, converting these advances into products that provide value and benefits for consumers is more important than the breakthrough itself. Therefore, it makes sense for R&D to be done by a multi-disciplinary team that includes a representative from marketing, who understands the way the consumer's mind works. ▪

The global positioning system

Global positioning system (GPS) technology was developed by the US government during the 1960s and 1970s to enable the US Navy and Air Force to get an accurate geographical fix on submarines and aircraft.

In 1983, US President Reagan decided to give businesses access to GPS so that they could use it for commercial purposes. A number of companies saw the opportunities in this and began designing GPS satellite navigation systems for motorists.

GPS is an excellent example of a revolutionary, technology-driven innovation. However, in practice, most new product innovations are based on tweaking existing products to make them better. Companies such as TomTom, who make GPSs, use R&D to achieve evolutionary, rather than revolutionary, product development. The goal is to launch new products every year that are cheaper and better designed, and that have new updated features.

Satellites orbiting the Earth are able to provide data on time and location to a variety of GPS receivers based on or near the planet.

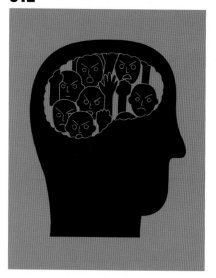

YOUR MOST UNHAPPY CUSTOMERS ARE YOUR GREATEST SOURCE OF LEARNING
FEEDBACK AND INNOVATION

IN CONTEXT

FOCUS
Open innovation

KEY DATES
1989 The Berlin Wall falls. Companies inside the former Iron Curtain must now respond to customer complaints.

2000 The travel website Trip Advisor, which enables users to rate hotels and restaurants, is founded by Stephen Kaufer.

2003 Organizational theorist Professor Henry Chesbrough publishes *Open Innovation: the new imperative for creating and profiting from technology,* which urges businesses to be open to learning from internal and external sources.

2009 US crowd-funding website Kickstarter is set up to encourage individual investment in small-scale business projects.

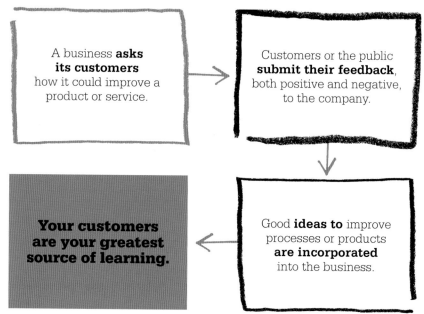

A business **asks its customers** how it could improve a product or service.

Customers or the public **submit their feedback**, both positive and negative, to the company.

Good **ideas to** improve processes or products **are incorporated** into the business.

Your customers are your greatest source of learning.

I n the past, companies required their own employees to design and develop new products. The knowledge was developed internally by the in-house research and development (R&D) department, and tended to be a closely guarded secret. This belief that a company should be in sole control of the creation of its intellectual property is known as closed innovation. In more recent times, a new approach has emerged. Open innovation is based on the idea that companies should be less private with their product-development programs, reflecting the view that its customers can make valuable contributions to the product-development process.

Internet feedback
The Internet has kick-started a sea change in how businesses get feedback from customers. Online

ratings and reviews allow companies to see what their customers like and dislike about a product.

In the IT industry, companies such as Apple and Microsoft use beta testing to enhance the quality of their new products. This process involves the software developer prereleasing copies of new software via the Internet. Members of the public who are interested in software and programing have the opportunity to road test the new product. They might point out bugs they encounter and offer possible solutions to the problems they have identified. The developer has the opportunity to improve the software before it is released, increasing the probability of the new product succeeding in the marketplace.

Crowdsourcing

The belief that companies can, and should, learn from their customers is growing. One example is the rise of crowdsourcing—a practice where companies get ideas, or even finance for a new product (crowd funding), from the public. There are different types of crowdsourcing. For example, some independent filmmakers finance their movies as crowdsourcing projects. Carmakers such as Citroën and Nissan have used crowdsourcing to enable car buyers to contribute ideas for the kind of product features that should be built into new vehicles. Citroën ran its crowdsourcing project via a Facebook app. Members of the general public were free to join the Facebook group—called C1 Connexion—and add their thoughts on six key aspects of the new car's design, including the number of doors, the color of the interior, and the equipment specification. Citroën kept its promise to build the car in line with the preferences expressed via the Connexion Facebook app.

There are several advantages to incorporating positive and negative feedback from members of the public and customers into the product-development process. The most obvious is that it is very cheap. In many cases companies do not pay for the ideas and opinions of crowdsourcers; interested volunteers

Ozzy Osbourne's official website hosted a poll for fans to vote for the next single from his 2007 album *Black Rain*. They were offered three tracks to choose from—the title song "Black Rain" won.

offer the information free of charge. If cash is offered in exchange for feedback, the amounts tend to be small. Those who use crowdsourcing as part of the product-development process also recognize that there will be experts outside the company who are not on the payroll, but who have valuable ideas and knowledge that should be harnessed. ▪

The more you engage with customers the clearer things become and the easier it is to determine what you should be doing.
John Russell
Harley Davidson president (1950–)

Wikipedia

The online encyclopedia, Wikipedia, was set up in 2001 by Larry Sanger and Jimmy Wales as a crowdsourcing project. Rather than hiring paid writers and editors, the founders of Wikipedia asked members of the public to create the product themselves by submitting their articles electronically.

By July 2013 Wikipedia comprised over 22 million articles, written in 285 languages by 77,000, largely anonymous and unpaid, authors.

Wikipedia is an open-source project, meaning that everyone with access to the Internet is able to write or make changes to it. Wikipedia does not charge its customers for using its product. Instead, the project is financed by donations from supporters. Many of these supporters argue that Wikipedia is superior to conventional encyclopedias because, unlike them, articles can be updated quickly and easily. Wikipedia has taken the concept of crowdsourcing to the limit—the entire product has been created by consumers.

TECHNOLOGY IS THE GREAT GROWLING ENGINE OF CHANGE
THE RIGHT TECHNOLOGY

IN CONTEXT

FOCUS
Managing change

KEY DATES
1822 English mathematician Charles Babbage designs "the difference engine"—the world's first mechanical, programmable, computer.

1951 The British food manufacturer J. Lyons & Co starts using LEO (Lyons Electronic Office), the first computer designed specifically for a business use—in this case, to track sales figures.

1981 US software company Microsoft develops the MS-DOS operating system.

1998 Banks and hedge funds in the US design computer programs to buy and sell shares, bonds derivatives, and other financial assets. This is the origin of high-frequency trading.

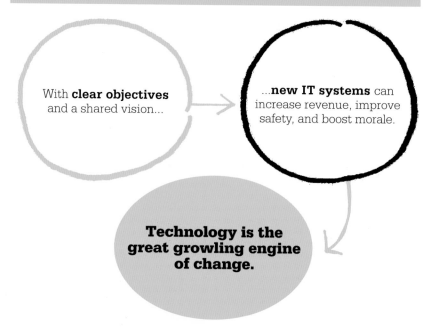

With **clear objectives** and a shared vision...

...**new IT systems** can increase revenue, improve safety, and boost morale.

Technology is the great growling engine of change.

No business today can survive without some form of computer system, but continual investment in new IT (information technology) can enhance a company in previously unimagined ways. IT can be used to boost productivity or increase reliability, or to decrease the risk of human error. Air India set out to improve efficiency in 2013 with a new computerized Crew Management System (CMS) that was designed to deploy pilots and cabin crew more effectively than a manual system. Under the previous system, some crew worked longer hours than others for the same salary, which created friction between crew members. CMS has enabled management to monitor crew deployment more closely. The hope is that by ensuring that staff are employed more equitably and

See also: Stand out in the market 28–31 ▪ Gaining an edge 32–39 ▪ The value chain 216–217 ▪ Forecasting 278–79 ▪
Kaizen 302–309 ▪ Feedback and innovation 312–13

> To err is human—and to blame it on a computer is even more so.
> **Robert Orben**
> **Comedy writer (1927–)**

eliminating favoritism, the airline will improve morale, which should have a positive effect on customer service, and eventually boost revenues. Air India also anticipates that CMS will enhance safety by improving the company's ability to meet strict international regulations relating to working hours.

However, not all new IT projects are successful. US investment bank JP Morgan lost $6 billion in 2012 because a new IT program, designed to help traders assess the risks of holding a range of financial derivatives, failed to work properly.

Managing change
So, how can big IT projects be best managed in order to achieve progress, rather than disaster? In 2005, research carried out by Lancaster University in the UK established that the chances of successfully implementing a new large-scale IT project increase

Police cars in many countries run Automatic Number Plate Recognition (ANPR) software. Suspicious vehicles are checked immediately and can be intercepted without delay.

when senior management is clear about what they hope to achieve from it. A clear set of objectives will help the IT designers to produce a system that effectively benefits the end user. Features that are not needed add to the cost of the project, and, in all probability, make the system less usable.

In Australia in 2005, a plan was introduced to improve productivity of traffic police by getting them to spend more time on the road, and less in the office. State governments equipped police cars with relatively inexpensive Automatic Number Plate Recognition (ANPR) cameras. Real-time information collected by police cars was fed, on the road, into the national database—CrimTrac. The system made policing more efficient because officers could use CrimTrac to identify, and pull over immediately, stolen cars or vehicles that had not been taxed or insured.

Factors for success
A new IT project also needs to be a shared vision. Customer-facing and factory-floor employees should

> As a rule, software systems do not work well until they have been used, and have failed repeatedly, in real applications.
> **David Parnas**
> **Canadian software engineer (1947–)**

know why the new IT system has been introduced, have a clear vision of the benefits of the system, and receive adequate training. In some organizations systems might fail because there is resistance to change—employees may fear losing expertise, or even their jobs. To overcome this, management needs to communicate openly and honestly about why the new IT system is needed. ■

WITHOUT "BIG DATA," YOU ARE BLIND AND DEAF AND IN THE MIDDLE OF A HIGHWAY
BENEFITTING FROM "BIG DATA"

IN CONTEXT

FOCUS
Analyzing data

KEY DATES
1995 US company Netscape Communications Corporation develops Internet cookies.

1997 NASA scientists Michael Cox and David Ellsworth devise the term "big data" to describe the challenge of processing and visualizing the vast amounts of information generated by supercomputers.

2000 Francis X. Diebold, an economist at the University of Pennsylvania, publishes his paper *Big data, dynamic factor models for macroeconomic measurement and forecasting.*

2012 Barack Obama's team uses "big data" to get him reelected to the White House.

2013 US whistle-blower Edward Snowden reveals that the National Security Agency was authorized to use "big data" to spy on US citizens.

A huge amount of **information** is gathered whenever **digital interactions** take place.

When this **"big data"** is organized and analyzed...

...it reveals the **viewing and shopping habits** of millions of people.

Without "big data," you are blind and deaf and in the middle of a highway.

Nowadays there is a huge amount of information that is routinely collected, stored, and analyzed by businesses and government. This "big data" includes sales data collected from credit or debit cards swiped at checkouts; web-browsing histories of actual and potential customers; information obtained from social media; and usage patterns collected from smartphones, digital video recorders, games consoles, and other personal devices that are connected to the Internet. Due to its size, "big data" can be expensive to store and organize on conventional databases.

Using "big data"
"Big data" can be used for market-research purposes to track and target consumers and identify profitable gaps in the market. One company that has made use of "big data" to increase revenue is Progressive Corp. The US insurance company has tried to increase its market share by offering lower car insurance premiums to drivers who install a device into the car's diagnostic port. The device measures how the car is driven—its speed, and the number of times the

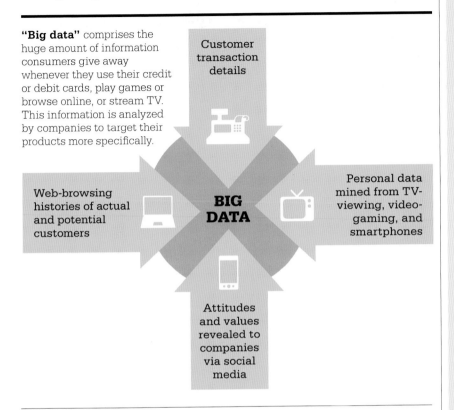

"Big data" comprises the huge amount of information consumers give away whenever they use their credit or debit cards, play games or browse online, or stream TV. This information is analyzed by companies to target their products more specifically.

Customer transaction details

Web-browsing histories of actual and potential customers

BIG DATA

Personal data mined from TV-viewing, video-gaming, and smartphones

Attitudes and values revealed to companies via social media

Internet cookies

Sales figures are an excellent example of "big data." US online retailer Amazon collects the browsing histories and purchasing data of its 152 million customers on a daily basis. Amazon uses "cookies," text files saved in a customer's browser, which help to track what kind of items each of its customers are interested in. This information is used to send recommendations that are likely to appeal to the customer, and so are likely to create additional sales for the company.

Cookies are used to create a unique ID that stores the customer's name, address, and credit-card number on the hard drive of their computer. When a customer returns to the website, the ID stored on the customer's computer is sent back to the business, which enables it to identify the customer and greet him or her by name. The ID also enables the online retailer to recall the customer's address and credit-card details quickly, speeding up the transaction and increasing customer satisfaction with the site.

---

car has braked suddenly or accelerated rapidly. The collected data is then sent, via a GPS signal, to the insurer for analysis. In theory, Progressive's use of "big data" will help them cherry-pick the most profitable customers in the market—those with safer driving habits, who pay their premiums but are unlikely to make expensive claims.

TiVo, a US company that makes digital video recorders, has used "big data" to create a new revenue stream. TiVo's boxes are connected to the Internet. This enables the business to collect huge volumes of data on TV-viewing habits at a relatively low cost. The data is subsequently sold by TiVo to advertisers. By correlating this data with sales figures collected from barcode readers at checkouts, retailers can assess the effectiveness of their TV advertising campaigns.

Product development

Netflix, the US media-streaming provider, has used "big data" to drive product development. In 2011, after evaluating the viewing habits of its 33 million subscribers, the company decided to remake a BBC series called *House of Cards*. Netflix knew from its "big data" that it would be wise to spend $100 million on a US version of the show because the original had been heavily downloaded. "Big data" was also used to make production decisions, including choosing director David Fincher. Fans of *House of Cards* also enjoyed watching Kevin Spacey movies, so he was cast in the lead role. ▪

It is a capital mistake to theorize before one has data.
Arthur Conan Doyle
UK author and physician (1859–1930)

PUT THE PRODUCT
INTO THE CUSTOMER'S HANDS
IT WILL SPEAK
FOR ITSELF
QUALITY SELLS

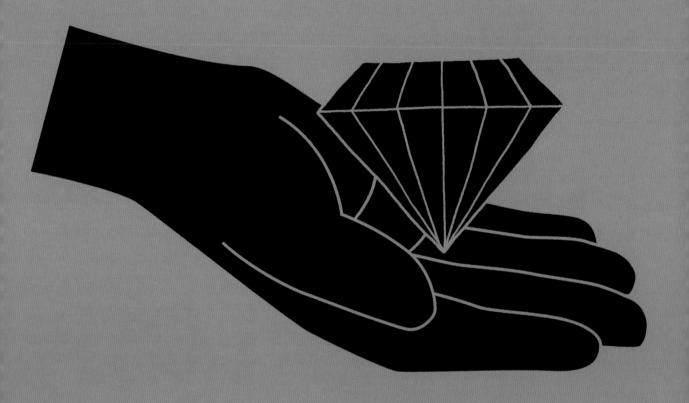

IN CONTEXT

FOCUS
Defining quality

KEY DATES
1924 German pen maker Montblanc launches its luxury *Meisterstück* ("masterpiece") fountain pen, which is still an icon of superior quality today.

1970 The Hamilton Watch Company develops the first digital watch. It succeeds despite its $2,100 price tag.

1985 Management guru Peter Drucker publishes *Innovation and Entrepreneurship,* which states that quality is the most important factor to affect sales. Drucker says that the consumer is the ultimate arbiter of a product's quality.

2005 Entrepreneur Richard Branson announces that he plans to offer the first trips into space. The price of $120,000 fails to deter rich and famous potential customers.

There is an adage that quality sells, and many companies believe that the best way to attract buyers is to produce a superior product. Businesses that put quality first believe that the other factors affecting demand, such as promotion, distribution, and the price, are much less important than the product itself.

At first this approach may seem irrational. In some markets, after all, low prices are critical. For example, Ryanair's competitive advantage over its rivals is based on its low-cost business model, which enables the airline to charge lower fares than its rivals. Yet some low-cost goods or services can represent a false economy for customers, especially if the goods are of poor quality, necessitating extra costs for the customer to repair or replace them.

Another possible way to boost revenue is to increase the volume of goods sold. Some companies attempt to achieve this goal by using advertising campaigns to steal market share from their rivals. However, the problem with trying to grow revenue through promotion is that it is usually expensive. In the UK, for example, in 2013 a 30-second television commercial cost up to $80,000 (£50,000).

Offering a quality product is an alternative to these low-cost or high-volume approaches. This strategy can achieve the same goal of boosting a company's revenues, improving customer retention by offering clients a product of a high standard that they will want to keep or to buy again and again.

What is quality?

To appreciate the role played by quality, it is first necessary to understand what is meant by this term. In a manufacturing context, quality is achieved when a company is able to supply reliable, durable goods that meet or surpass consumer expectations and are free of defects.

High-quality products inspire trust. Take, for example, high-quality car tires. They often have deeper treads than poor-quality tires, making cars that have them less likely to skid in emergencies or bad conditions. In this case the quality of a car tire could be the

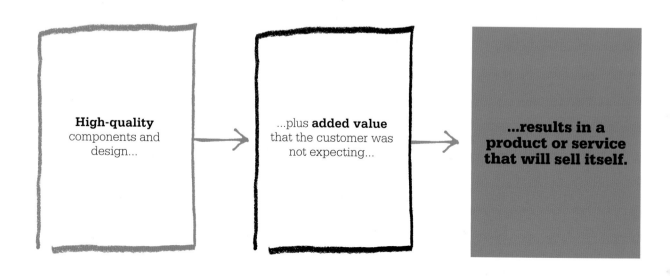

High-quality components and design... ...plus **added value** that the customer was not expecting... **...results in a product or service that will sell itself.**

See also: Finding a profitable niche 22–23 ▪ Gaining an edge 32–39 ▪ The weightless start-up 62–63 ▪ Leading the market 166–69 ▪ The marketing model 232–33 ▪ Creating a brand 258–63 ▪ Fulfilling demand 294–95

difference between life and death. Superior-quality tires, made from harder-wearing rubber compounds, also last longer than tires of lesser quality, which means that the driver will not have to face the cost and inconvenience of replacing them as frequently.

Great quality is not just about using the best components. Design is also crucial to achieving a superior-quality product, because design can offer the consumer new benefits for which they are willing to pay a price premium. In 2011 the Japanese tire manufacturer Bridgestone launched its new range of flat-run tires, based on an innovative design that enabled motorists to run a car with a flat tire for 50 miles (80 km) at a speed of 50 mph (80 kph). This feature enabled drivers to reach the closest garage to change a flat tire, rather than having to change it on the side of the road.

Businesses that have managed to incorporate differentiating features into their products can exploit the added value that these features provide by charging higher

Profit in business comes from repeat customers, customers …that bring friends with them.
W. Edwards Deming

prices. If in other aspects (such as function) the products are equal to their competitors, adding price premiums to products that are especially valued by consumers should lead to greater revenues and profits.

Quality wins out

Estée Lauder adopted the "quality sells" philosophy when she set up her cosmetics business in New York in 1946. When she was a child, her mother had lectured her relentlessly on how exposure to the

sun led to premature aging of the skin. The young Lauder took note and began making her own skin creams with her uncle, a chemist. Like many other successful entrepreneurs, Lauder genuinely believed that there was a need for her product, and in 1935 she began selling her first preparations: super-rich, all-purpose crème; crème pack; cleansing oil; and skin lotion.

In the beginning Estée Lauder did not use any advertising; she thought her products were so good they would sell themselves. She relied on her customers to promote the products. Customers would try her preparations, like them, and continue buying them. Furthermore, they would then recommend Estée Lauder's products to their friends. She gave this form of promotion a name: tell-a-woman marketing.

In more recent times, Samsung has also used the quality-led approach to great effect. The South Korean electronics manufacturer does not rely on glitzy advertising campaigns to create its competitive advantage. Instead, it appeals to a market segment who favors product quality over brand image.

In April 2013 the Samsung Galaxy 4 was launched. Very quickly it gained market share over the market leader—Apple's iPhone—because it was seen as a more technologically advanced product than Apple's latest model, the iPhone 5. The display offered around 100 more pixels per inch than the iPhone 5, and its built-in »

Customers who are loyal purchasers of a specific brand are valuable even if that product is a low-cost one. Quality is one feature that can inspire trust in and generate repeat business.

camera also surpassed the iPhone 5 in terms of functionality and pixels. In addition, according to research by the UK consumer magazine *Which?*, the Samsung processor was nearly twice as fast as that in the iPhone.

Samsung's prices were slightly lower than Apple's, but there were other producers of Android mobile phones that substantially undercut Samsung's prices without taking any of its market share. The key to Samsung's Galaxy 4 success was its superior quality.

Brand loyalty

Quality can be an important selling point even for low-cost products, since it helps build brand loyalty and thus ensures repeat customers. In markets for fast-moving consumer goods (FMCGs), manufacturers use superior product quality to preserve and extend their customer base. FMCGs are nondurable products, such as beer, toothpaste, chocolate,

and breakfast cereal, that are bought frequently by households and consumed immediately. Since FMCGs are purchased regularly throughout the year, the sales volumes achieved by a successful product can be immense.

A good example of an FMCG market is the one for toilet paper. According to research by US toilet paper manufacturer Charmin, 126 billion rolls of toilet paper are bought every year in the US. In a market this large, even a small share will translate into multimillion-dollar revenues. If consumers habitually purchase the same brand of a particular product over and over, rather than switching between rival brands, their brand loyalty will be invaluable.

High-quality brands are more likely to win brand loyalty than brands of an inferior quality. For example, households are more likely to buy Charmin toilet paper again

> Quality means fitness for use. Fitness is defined by the customer.
> **Joseph Juran**
> **US expert on quality management**
> **(1904–2008)**

and again if the product is softer and stronger than the brands sold by its rivals, generating higher volumes of sales and greater revenues. This means the business has increased its revenues without having to pay any of the marketing costs usually associated with acquiring customers.

Service and quality

Another indicator of good quality is providing a service in a manner that exceeds customer expectations. This might manifest as efficiency, or rapid response to customer concerns. The Zurich Insurance Group operates in over 170 countries and each month handles over 600,000 customer interactions via phone, mail, and the Internet. Its ambition is to be the best global insurer as measured by customers, employees, and shareholders, and it actively pursues quality assurance. Its iQuality program sets out how employees can pay more attention to customers, and find out more about their changing needs and expectations. It performs regular checks on the quality of employees' work and uses extensive market research to gain feedback on customer experience.

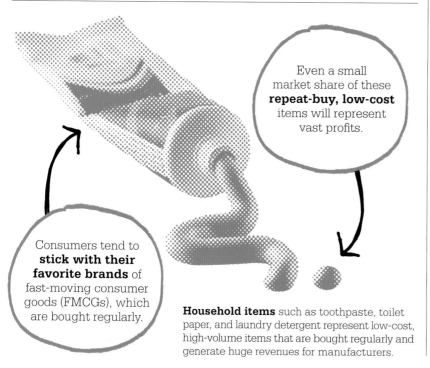

Even a small market share of these **repeat-buy, low-cost** items will represent vast profits.

Consumers tend to **stick with their favorite brands** of fast-moving consumer goods (FMCGs), which are bought regularly.

Household items such as toothpaste, toilet paper, and laundry detergent represent low-cost, high-volume items that are bought regularly and generate huge revenues for manufacturers.

Zurich also has protocols for reacting to unhappy customers; when several customers complained that payment was too slow when their policies matured, Zurich used the "five whys" to discover that the problem lay in a delay in sending out claim forms. The company put in an automatic system to send out the forms 10 days before policies matured, resulting in a 78 percent drop in complaints. Zurich has won many service awards, including two "Five-star Service Awards" based on 25,000 completed questionnaires.

Added value

Businesses can also create high-quality products by adding value. Value added is the difference between a product's price and the raw material cost of making the product. Companies can add value to their products with new features, innovative functions, or add-ons designed to benefit, and appeal to, actual and potential buyers.

In the hotel business, Ibis adds value by promising customers that their specially designed beds, mattresses, comforter, and pillows will give them a better night's sleep. The cost of these items is balanced against improvement in retention of customers, or by higher prices that create extra revenue.

Hotel guests are pleasantly surprised to discover luxury extras that they were not expecting. These could be complimentary services or products.

Other hotels have been even bolder in pursuing value added. In the premium segment of the market, hotels create additional value by redefining their core function. These hotels do not just sell a comfortable place to sleep; they sell an "experience," in which guests are offered a range of "delighters"— aspects of the hotel's service that delight the guest, but which are not usually expected. Examples include HD televisions; branded, high-end shower gel and shampoo; free champagne; and free slippers that guests can take home with them.

Adding value is a constant battle because a "delighter" can soon become an expectation. If a hotel fails to meet the constantly rising requirements of its guests, it will lose customers to its rivals. Successful hotels are constantly on the lookout for new "delighters" that will surprise their guests without becoming too expensive. Low-cost delighters are the ideal way to create value added, generate repeat purchases, and ultimately produce healthy profits. ■

Quality ... is not what the supplier puts in. It is what the customer gets out and is willing to pay for.
Peter Drucker
US management guru (1909–2005)

W. Edwards Deming

William Edwards Deming was born in 1900 in Sioux City, IA. He studied physics at the University of Wyoming before going on to receive a PhD from Yale. After leaving full-time education he worked for Bell Telephones, where he was part of a team working to improve quality control.

One of his key ideas was that the quality of bought-in raw materials and components matters more than their price because their quality will be a major factor in determining the quality of the finished product. Consequently, he argued, manufacturers should not choose their suppliers solely on the basis of the price charged. Ideally, companies should try to develop a long-running relationship with a single supplier, which is based on trust. This approach would be more likely to lead to better-quality materials.

In addition, Deming also believed that quality came from a production process that was stable and consistent.

Key works

1982 *Out of the Crisis*
1993 *The New Economics*

THE DESIRE TO OWN SOMETHING A LITTLE BETTER, A LITTLE SOONER THAN NECESSARY
PLANNED OBSOLESCENCE

IN CONTEXT

FOCUS
Maintaining sales

KEY DATES
1924–39 Lightbulb makers
Osram, Phillips, and General
Electric form a cartel, working
together to prevent any product
development that would
produce lightbulbs that could
burn for more than 1,000 hours.

1932 Bernard London writes
a leaflet titled *Ending the
Depression through Planned
Obsolescence*, urging the
UK government to pass laws
to limit the useful lives of
products to increase demand.

1959 Volkswagen uses the
tagline: "We do not believe in
planned obsolescence, we
don't change a car for the sake
of change," to criticize rival car
manufacturers who allegedly
did not build cars to last.

2013 Apple declares that the
original iPhone, launched in
2007, is now obsolete.

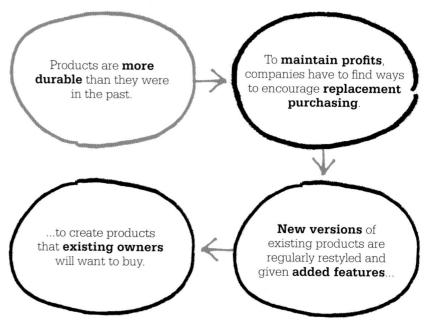

Products are **more durable** than they were in the past.

To **maintain profits**, companies have to find ways to encourage **replacement purchasing**.

New versions of existing products are regularly restyled and given **added features**...

...to create products that **existing owners** will want to buy.

Built to last may sound like an essential in any form of production, yet some manufacturers produce items that they know will become obsolete in just a few years. This policy ensures that customers continue to buy new goods. Products are replaced either because their components wear out or because they are surpassed by products with new features.

In the past, items such as lightbulbs or stockings were made to fail sooner rather than later. Nowadays, items such as printer ink cartridges, batteries, and components for appliances can be difficult or expensive to replace, making it tempting to buy a new version of the product instead. Many goods, such as pens or razors, have become disposable—cheap to make and easy to replace.

Updated styling

US industrial designer Brooke Stevens defined the term "planned obsolescence" as instilling in consumers "the desire to own something a little better, a little sooner than necessary." The strategy of planned obsolescence was originally developed by General Motors, who realized that advancing technology would adversely affect its future business. During the 1950s, it began updating the styling of radiator grills, taillights, and bodywork every few years to encourage drivers to replace their cars more often.

Over the last 30 years, as technology has advanced, cars have become even more durable and reliable. Today, new cars are built to last. With regular servicing the engine and transmission of a new car will still provide reliable service for over 250,000 miles (402,000 km). Typically, with average usage, this equates to an expected useful life of more than a decade. If drivers only replace their vehicle once every ten years, this would lead to low sales for car manufacturers.

To generate higher sales levels, many carmakers now set out to create planned obsolescence to

I believe in status symbols.
Brooks Stevens
US industrial designer (1911–95)

Obsolescence never meant the end of anything, it's just the beginning.
Marshall McLuhan
Canadian media theorist (1911–80)

speed up replacement purchase, by giving cars regular face-lifts. The redesigns are intended to encourage status-conscious motorists to ditch their still perfectly good vehicles for the latest body shape.

New features

Car manufacturers also employ various other tactics to persuade consumers to update their vehicles. New car models incorporate cutting-edge features such as touch-screen multimedia control systems for in-car entertainment, or additional safety systems, such as technology that warns about lane departure and potential collisions.

Phone manufacturers, such as Samsung and Apple, use planned obsolescence to increase revenue by persuading consumers to replace still-usable cell phones or tablets with something newer and better. In this highly competitive market, the rewards go to the company that creates planned obsolescence soonest, which gives them the fastest rates of replacement purchase. Samsung has used this strategy to great effect to boost profits. In July 2013 the

South Korean company posted record profits of $8.9 billion, up 47 percent from the year before. Over the same period, Apple's share of the smartphone market in Europe dropped from 30.5 to 25 percent. This was no doubt partially due to the popularity of Samsung's Galaxy S4, whose new features included the S-Translator, which enables the user to translate nine languages either from speech to text, or from text to speech.

Status anxiety

Soccer teams also take advantage of planned obsolescence. At the beginning of each season, most teams release at least two replica uniforms for fans to buy. The home and away shirts are restyled to be noticeably different from last year's uniform. This type of planned obsolescence is based on status anxiety. Many fans will choose to buy the new shirt to keep up with other fans, or to show loyalty to their team, even though the shirt that they bought a year ago may still look as good as new. ▪

Children in Zimbabwe wear soccer shirts donated by English soccer teams. Soccer fans in Europe will not buy last season's shirts because the styling is updated each season.

TIME IS MONEY
TIME-BASED MANAGEMENT

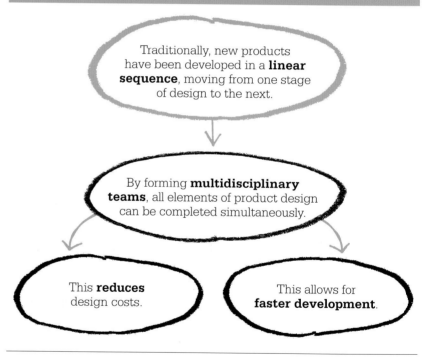

Traditionally, new products have been developed in a **linear sequence**, moving from one stage of design to the next.

By forming **multidisciplinary teams**, all elements of product design can be completed simultaneously.

This **reduces** design costs.

This allows for **faster development**.

Time has a monetary value. For example, if employees spend an afternoon in an unproductive meeting, their time costs the company money. There is also an "opportunity cost," since the meeting prevents them from doing other tasks that are potentially more productive. This is a typical concern of time-based management, which appraises the use of time in the same way that other models focus on raw materials and overheads. A time-based approach allows companies to manage labor effectively across the company, to gather true-cost data, and to cut costs by reducing the amount of time to develop and launch new products.

One way to reduce time costs on a project is to use a process called "simultaneous engineering." This

See also: Creativity and invention 72–73 ▪ Profit versus cash flow 152–53 ▪ Leading the market 166–69 ▪ The value chain 216–17 ▪ Lean production 290–93 ▪ Simplify processes 296–99 ▪ Critical path analysis 328–29

strategy involves working on all the design processes required to launch a new product at the same time, rather than in a linear sequence, and can reduce new product development time by months or even years.

Comparing approaches

Traditionally, companies have pushed new products through a linear sequence of development, where each department involved in the design works in isolation, completing their task before passing the product to the next department. In this way, the part-made product might move between design, engineering, and production departments.

However, this approach can lead to time-consuming mistakes. For example, when new cars are being designed, different departments might work on various parts in isolation and in a certain sequence. When the various subassemblies are finally put together at the prototype stage, the result is often unsatisfactory. And in order to correct one thing—such as a

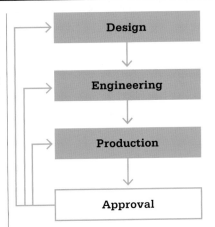

In a linear process of new product development, the evolving prototype or individual parts move separately, back and forth, between departments. This is time-consuming and costly.

In a simultaneous engineering approach, all departments are represented in one multidisciplinary team, working together to solve new problems, and saving time and money.

beautiful seat creating visibility problems once in position—parts may have to bounce back through several departments.

The alternative approach, chosen by time-based manufacturers, is to use a team of people from different departments, all working together on a new product from the

beginning. Project managers play a key role, since they must ensure that the multidisciplinary team members agree to the necessary design trade-offs at a very early stage in the development process. Design integrity is achieved the first time around without any reworking, slashing the amount of time taken to launch the new product.

Time-based management only works effectively in companies that employ flexible, multiskilled staff, who, in turn, respects each another's skills and value each other's input. A nonlinear process means that managers must be willing to work with a less rigid structure, and encourage a culture of trust.

This management approach forms the basis of many technology companies today, since it allows them to respond more quickly to changes in the market and customer needs, while providing employees with a more autonomous, creative, and productive work environment. ▪

Agile software development (ASD)

Within the software industry, changes in components and customer demands happen rapidly and repeatedly. This means that developers have had to find ever-faster and better ways of managing projects.

In 2001, a group of software developers met in Utah, to discuss how this might be done, and their conclusions form the basis of the agile software development approach. This recognizes the customer as the highest priority, and embraces

changing requirements (even at late stages of development) in order to give the customer the greatest competitive advantage. However, the founders note that this can only be achieved when "business people" take a flexible and trusting approach, hold daily face-to-face conversations with developers, and provide all the support they need. Coupled with regular reflection on team practice, these conditions will allow self-organizing teams to produce fast, brilliant designs.

A PROJECT WITHOUT A CRITICAL PATH IS LIKE A SHIP WITHOUT A RUDDER
CRITICAL PATH ANALYSIS

IN CONTEXT

FOCUS
Planning procedures

KEY DATES
1814 Napoleon's invasion of Russia fails because the Grande Armée is not equipped with the type of clothing needed to survive the winter.

1910 US mechanical engineer Henry Gantt invents the Gantt chart, which shows start and finish dates for all activities that need to be completed in order to finish a project.

1959 Morgan Walker and James Kelley publish their groundbreaking paper "Critical Path Planning and Scheduling."

1997 In his book *Golden Chain*, Israeli physicist Eliyahu Goldratt advises managers to plan for uncertainties by creating "resource buffers," which can be deployed to solve problems when they arise.

In a good strategy plan, **all the activities** that must be completed in order to finish a project **are identified**.

↓

These activities are ordered in a **logical sequence**.

↓

When possible, activities are planned to **run simultaneously** to save time.

↓

Critical activities that, if delayed, will stop the project from being completed on time **are highlighted**.

↓

A project without a critical path is like a ship without a rudder.

To minimize the amount of time needed to complete a complex project, managers frequently use a process known as critical path analysis (CPA). CPA was developed by mathematicians Morgan Walker and James Kelley, and was first used in 1957 by the chemical manufacturer, DuPont, to schedule a program of factory closures in the most cost-effective way. By following Walker's and

See also: Gaining an edge 32–39 ▪ The value chain 216–17 ▪ Lean production 290–93 ▪ Simplify processes 296–99 ▪ Time-based management 326–27

On this critical path network for a 20-day project, the nodes (circles) record finish times. The time the task should take is recorded at the top, while the time it must be completed by to keep the project on track is recorded at the bottom. Tasks B, D, and G form the critical path since they must be completed promptly; the other tasks all have more time than they need.

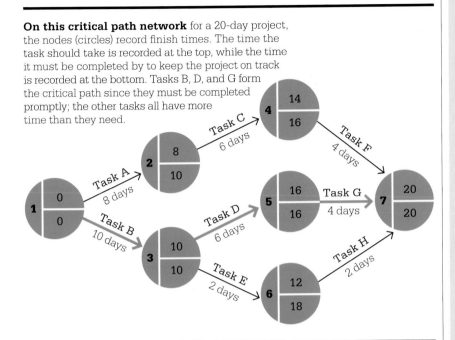

Kelley's advice, DuPont saved 25 percent in the shutdowns. In the early 1960s, NASA used critical path analysis to defeat Soviet Russia in the Space Race. Through careful project scheduling, NASA was able to advance its spacecraft and rocket-development programs.

Planning tool

CPA is a planning tool that plots a project's stages in a logical sequence, indicating which of the component activities need to be finished before others can start. It allows for activities to be scheduled simultaneously to save time. Activities that are critical to the project are identified—these are steps, which if delayed, will hold up the completion of the whole project.

Project managers illustrate this information visually, using a step-by-step network diagram. The most important part of the diagram is the critical path, which shows the activities where there is no float (spare) time. If a critical activity looks like it could be delayed, management will need to act, probably by employing extra people and machinery. These resources can be moved from noncritical activities that have float time.

Saving time and money

Manufacturers might use CPA to plan the launch of a new product. By identifying jobs that can be performed simultaneously, the manufacturer should be able to reduce the amount of time needed for development, allowing it to launch onto the market sooner. Completing projects earlier also reduces costs. For example, a company might use CPA to reduce the amount of money spent on hiring expensive machinery. By studying the network the manager can predict when to rent a piece of machinery and for how long. ▪

Sydney Opera House

One of the modern world's architectural wonders, the Sydney Opera House is a dramatic example of what can go wrong when projects are not properly planned and managed. When the world-famous performing arts center was opened in 1973, it was ten years late, and had cost 14 times more than its original budget.

In an attempt to open the building to the public as soon as possible, the government ordered building work to commence in 1959, before the Danish architect, Jørn Utzon, had finalized his drawings.

The decision to start construction work early led to a series of problems. For example, the podium columns that were initially used proved to be too weak to support the roof. As a result, time and money were wasted replacing these columns. Unfortunately for Utzon, it was initially his design that was unfairly blamed for the delays and cost overruns, rather than poor project management.

Architectural icon The Sydney Opera House is a feat of engineering and design, despite the difficulties encountered during its construction.

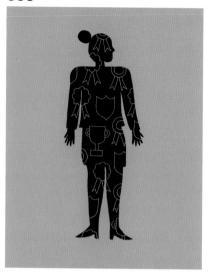

TAKING THE BEST FROM THE BEST
BENCHMARKING

IN CONTEXT

FOCUS
Competitive advantage

KEY DATES
240 BCE The Romans capture a Carthaginian ship during a storm. They build new boats based on this design and defeat the Carthaginians at the Battle of Aegus.

1819 Scottish industrialist James Finlayson sets up a textile factory in Tampere, Finland. His production methods are modeled on those used by Lancashire's world-class cotton mills.

1972 Ajax, the Dutch soccer team, wins the European Cup playing "total soccer," which allows outfield players to take any position on the field. Spanish team FC Barcelona subsequently adopts the same strategy and goes on to achieve great success.

To become an **industry leader**...

↓

...a company must identify its **most-successful competitor**...

↓

...and adopt the **best practices** of its rival.

↓

Take the best from the best.

If the performance of a company is adequate but unspectacular, it may seek to identify areas that would help it rise above the competition. The process of benchmarking allows a business to improve efficiency by comparing its performance against other organizations. The goal is to identify, and then learn from, best practice in the industry. Best practice might come, for example, from a competitor who achieves the lowest unit costs, the best customer satisfaction ratings, or the shortest lead times. The rival's approach is then carefully evaluated, including such factors as the equipment, training, and production methods used. Once understood, best practice can be adopted in the hope that it will raise the performance of the company to the level of the industry leader.

Cost effective

Some companies try to become more efficient via simple trial and error, but this can be slow and costly. One of the advantages of benchmarking is that it is a relatively cheap way to improve performance, because there is no need to replicate the expensive mistakes made by other

See also: Study the competition 24–27 ▪ Keep evolving business practice 48–51 ▪ Avoid groupthink 114 ▪ Ignoring the herd 146–49 ▪ Avoiding complacency 194–201 ▪ Simplify processes 296–99 ▪ Applying and testing ideas 310–11

businesses. Improvements can come quickly so that once the process of benchmarking has identified effective practices, these methods can be adopted. The changes should lift performance to the level achieved by the industry leader, so that any competitiveness gap is eliminated quickly. In the future, benchmarking can be repeated on a regular basis.

Benchmarking in practice

In the 1980s, the US photocopier manufacturer Xerox used benchmarking to restore its market share. For ten years, it had been losing customers to its Japanese rivals Canon and Ricoh. These companies had been gaining ground because they were able to undercut the prices charged by Xerox, without compromising on product quality. To identify what they were doing wrong, Xerox bought their rivals' products and took them apart. They discovered that Canon and Ricoh designed their machines so that they were made from a relatively small number of common components. Design

> Benchmarking provides an inventory of creative changes that other companies have enacted.
> **John Langley**
> **UK Barclays Bank executive**

simplicity enabled the competition to benefit from economies of scale; bulk-buying components reduced operating costs, making it possible for Canon and Ricoh to offer consumers lower prices. Xerox responded by simplifying its designs, so that the commonality of components across Xerox models rose from 20 to 70 percent.

Xerox's US management team also visited Japanese photocopier factories to learn more about their production methods. Upon their return, the team members adopted many of the production methods they had seen. Benchmarking also enabled Xerox to improve the reliability of its products. From 1981 to 1990, customer complaints fell by 60 percent. Over the same period Xerox's manufacturing costs fell by more than 50 percent, which enabled the company to match the prices charged by the Japanese, while maintaining its profit margins.

Raising standards

Governments have also used benchmarking to improve performance. For example, from 2000 to 2009, the Organization for Economic Cooperation and Development (OECD) surveyed education standards in 65 countries and identified that Finland achieved the highest rankings in reading, mathematics, and science. Teachers from around the world now visit Finland every year to learn more about the Finnish educational success. ▪

Ferrari's pit-stop crew has a clear chain of command, allowing them to refuel the car and change all four tires in less than seven seconds.

Benchmarking across industries

Some companies learn from another organization that operates in a completely different market. For example, in 2005, two doctors from London's Great Ormond Street children's hospital were struck by the efficiency of the Ferrari pit crew during a Formula 1 race.

Alan Goldman and Martin Elliot observed that only one person in the crew gave orders, avoiding time lost in discussion, and pit-stop routines were standardized. Crew members specialized in one task, which they practiced over and over, until it was perfect.

Goldman and Elliot changed working arrangements at Great Ormond Street by applying Ferrari best practice: clear job descriptions meant that each member of staff knew what their role was, and a leadership position was assigned for each shift. As a result, patient handover errors between the operating room and intensive care unit unit fell by 70 percent.

DIRECTO

RY

DIRECTORY

Business is all about succeeding, often against considerable odds, and to do so its practitioners have drawn on a range of insights from a number of related disciplines. It requires an understanding of people, numbers, and systems, so it is perhaps not surprising that a large proportion of its key thinkers come from the fields of psychology, mathematics, and engineering. Some of them have proved adept at turning theory into practice, building large businesses that continue to evolve and grow over the long term. The main part of this book has examined the work of some of those key thinkers in detail; here we look at others whose impact on the business environment is marked, from industrial designers and theorists to inspirational leaders and management gurus.

RICHARD BRANSON
1950–

Founder of the Virgin Group of businesses, Richard Branson was born in 1950 in Surrey, UK. In 1969 he started a mail-order record company called Virgin, which then expanded into retail stores. In 1972 he built a recording studio, and began his own record label. The Virgin brand expanded into diverse areas, and the Virgin Group today consists of more than 200 companies in more than 30 countries, including Virgin Atlantic airlines, Virgin Radio, and Virgin Galactic.
See also: Beating the odds at start-up 20–21 ▪ Creating a brand 260–65 ▪ Generating buzz 276–78

SUBIR CHOWDHURY
1967–

An expert on quality management, Subir Chowdhury was born in Chittagong, Bangladesh in 1967. He earned a degree in aeronautical engineering at the Indian Institute of Technology, Kharagpur, before studying industrial management at Central Michigan University, MI. His consulting work within diverse industries led him to develop the LEO (Listen, Enrich, Optimize) solution, popularized in his book, *The Ice Cream Maker*. This approach says that by making "quality" the responsibility of every employee, individual quality leads to process quality and organizational success.
See also: Quality sells 318–23

CLAYTON CHRISTENSEN
1952–

Clayton Christensen is considered one of the world's top management thinkers. Born in Utah in 1952, he worked as a missionary for the Church of Jesus Christ of Latter-day Saints in South Korea from 1971 to 1973. On his return to the US, he studied economics at Brigham Young University, Utah, and Oxford University, UK, before earning an MBA and doctorate at Harvard Business School. While working as a management consultant he helped found Innosight, a public policy think tank. Now a professor of business administration at Harvard Business School, Christensen has published widely; his first book, *The Innovator's Dilemma*, is an international best seller.
See also: Changing the game 92–99 ▪ Crisis management 188–89 ▪ Avoiding complacency 194–201

ROBERTO CIVITA
1936–2013

Brazilian media baron Roberto Civita was born in Milan, Italy, in 1936. His family moved to the US shortly after his birth, then to Brazil around 10 years later, where his father founded the Abril publishing company. Civita studied for several degrees at various US universities, in subjects as diverse as nuclear and particle physics, journalism, economics, and sociology. After stints working at *Time* and Abril, in 1968 he started *Veja*, Brazil's best-selling weekly magazine. His successful media and educational enterprises led *Forbes* magazine to estimate his net worth as $4.9 billion at his death in 2013.
See also: Rupert Murdoch 337

KATHLEEN EISENHARDT
1947–

Stanford University professor Kathleen Eisenhardt is a leading expert in strategy within high-velocity markets and industries, such as Silicon Valley. Originally trained in mechanical engineering (studying at Brown University, RI), Eisenhardt then earned an MSc in computer science and a PhD in business at Stanford. Her 1998 book *Competing on the Edge* (co-written with Shona Brown) is a classic text.
See also: Avoiding complacency 194–201 ▪ Coping with chaos 220–21

HENRI FAYOL
1841–1925

Born in Istanbul, Turkey, in 1841, Henri Fayol studied engineering at the Ecole des Mines de Saint Etienne in France before becoming a mining engineer. His innovative approach to technical problems and management led him to develop organizational theories that altered contemporary thinking. He was the first person to conceptualize the organization of an industrial company, and conducted groundbreaking work on operational excellence.
See also: Simplify processes 296–99 ▪ Critical path analysis 328–29

BILL GATES
1955–

William Henry Gates was born in Seattle, WA, in 1955. His father was a lawyer and his mother was active in the civic and corporate world. Gates began programming computers at 13 with his friend Paul Allen, with whom he later co-founded Microsoft. Gates studied law at Harvard University for two years before pulling out to set up Microsoft with Allen in 1975. As CEO, Gates built Microsoft into one of the world's largest companies. In 1994 he set up the William H. Gates charitable foundation, with an initial contribution of $28 billion.
See also: Leading the market 166–69 ▪ The right technology 314–15

PANKAJ GHEMAWAT
1959–

Born in Jodhpur, India, Pankaj Ghemawat lived in the US for 30 years before moving to Spain. He demonstrated academic excellence at any early age; he was accepted for a PhD at Harvard Business School at 19, finishing it in just three years. After working for a short time at consulting company McKinsey & Company, he returned to Harvard to become its youngest-ever professor. An expert on global strategy, he controversially questioned the idea of globalization, claiming that companies need to find a balance between "local" and "global."
See also: Understanding the market 234–41

SUMANTRA GHOSHAL
1948–2004

Organizational expert Sumantra Ghoshal was born in Kolkata, India. He studied physics at Delhi University and worked as a manager at Indian Oil before completing PhDs at MIT and Harvard Business School in the US. In 1994 he joined London Business School, where he became professor of strategic management. He wrote 12 books, two of which revolutionized corporate management: *Managing Across Borders* and *The Individualised Corporation*.
See also: Organizational Culture 104–09

GARY HAMEL
1954–

Strategist Gary Hamel got his PhD at the University of Michigan, MI, before joining the faculty of the London Business School in 1983. Ten years later he founded a consulting business in Silicon Valley, CA, to gain experience at the cutting edge of high-tech companies. Today he also works as a visiting professor at Harvard and Oxford universities. In 1995 he co-authored a best-selling book with C. K. Prahalad called *Competing for the Future*, which introduced the concepts of "core competence" to the business world.
See also: Protect the core business 170–71 ▪ C. K. Prahalad 338

JOHN H. JOHNSON
1918–2005

Media magnate John Harold Johnson was born in Arkansas City, AR. The grandson of slaves, he was unable to further his education because local high schools would not accept black students, but shone academically after his family moved to Chicago. After winning a scholarship to the University of Chicago, he became the editor of a corporate magazine. In 1942, using a loan secured against his mother's furniture, he began a black-oriented magazine that later became known as *Ebony*. In 1951 he started *Jet*

magazine, and by 1982 his holdings in book and magazine publishers, TV, radio, and cosmetic companies were large enough to make him the first African-American to appear on the *Forbes* 400 Rich List.
See also: Gaining an edge 32–39 ▪ Changing the game 92–99

JOSEPH JURAN
1904–2008

Born in Romania, Juran emigrated with his family to the US at eight years old. Academically brilliant, he skipped four grades at school, then completed a BSc in electrical engineering. By 1937 he was chief of Industrial Engineering at Western Electric but he was seconded to Washington, DC, to improve the efficiency of the lend-lease program (by which the US lent funds to the Allied Forces). He then returned to academia; in 1951 he published *The Quality Control Handbook*, which became a management classic.
See also: Lean production 294–95 ▪ Quality sells 318–23

INGVAR KAMPRAD
1926–

Swedish businessman Ingvar Kamprad is the founder of furniture retailer IKEA. Born in Pjätteryd, Småland, he started trading for fun as a boy, selling matches then stationery in his neighborhood. When he was 17, he was rewarded by his parents with money for good school grades, and the teenager used this to start his own business. Kamprad began by selling door-to-door, then started a mail-order service. In 1948 he began selling locally made furniture and the company expanded. Renowned for

products that are both stylish and inexpensive, IKEA has grown to encompass 284 stores in 26 countries by aiming to "allow people with limited means to furnish their houses like rich people."
See also: Changing the game 92–99 ▪ Anticipating demand 290–91

ROSABETH MOSS KANTER
1943–

Harvard professor of business studies Rosabeth Moss Kanter was born in Cleveland, OH. She studied sociology to PhD level before pursuing a career in business research. Kanter has taught at Harvard and Yale universities, and published many books on business management techniques, including *Men and Women of the Corporation*, which is regarded as a classic in critical management studies.
See also: Organizational culture 104–09 ▪ The value of diversity 115

PHILIP KOTLER
1931–

Generally regarded as the founder of modern marketing management, Kotler was born in Chicago in 1931. He earned his PhD in economics at MIT, and did postdoctoral work at Harvard University. Kotler was responsible for repositioning marketing within companies, moving it from a peripheral to a more central position. He also shifted emphasis away from price and toward meeting customer needs. Kotler is the author of more than 50 books, including the classic *Marketing Management* (1967).
See also: The marketing model 232–33 ▪ Understanding the market 234–41 ▪ Marketing mix 280–83

JOHN KOTTER
1947–

Harvard professor John Kotter is an expert on leadership and change. He initially trained in electrical engineering and computer science, but followed his first degree with a doctorate in business administration from Harvard Business School. Ranked number one "leadership guru" by *BusinessWeek* magazine in 2001, Kotter has written 17 books, including the best-selling *Leading Change* (1996).
See also: Leading well 68–69 ▪ Changing the game 92–99

ESTEE LAUDER
1908–2004

Estée Lauder was born to a family of Jewish immigrants in Queens, NY, in 1908. She was taught how to make beauty products by her uncle, a chemist. Beginning by selling her own products at local beauty salons, Lauder built a business that was valued at approximately $3.2 billion in 1995.
See also: Quality sells 318–23

KONOSUKE MATSUSHITA
1894–1989

The founder of Panasonic, Konosuke Matsushita was born in Wakayama, Japan. Following family financial misfortunes, Matsushita was sent to Osaka at nine to become an apprentice. In 1917, at 22, he set up his own business making electrical sockets, and in 1918 started a new company, which was later renamed "National" and then "Panasonic." His leadership style was extolled by

John Kotter in his book *Matsushita Leadership* (1997).
See also: John Kotter 336 ▪ Leading well 68–69

ELTON MAYO
1880–1949

Australian management guru and industrial psychologist Elton Mayo was born in Adelaide. At the city's university he studied medicine, philosophy, and psychology, and his research into the psychological causes of industrial unrest led to an invitation to join Harvard Business School, where he was part of the team that performed the celebrated Hawthorne experiments. These demonstrated that the perfomance of employees is influenced as much by their surroundings as by their skills.
See also: The value of teams 70–71 ▪ Is money the motivator? 90–91 ▪ Kaizen 302–09

ROSALIA MERA
1944–2013

Co-founder of Zara clothing retailer, Rosalía Mera was born in La Coruña, Spain, to a working-class family. She dropped out of school at 11 to work as a seamstress. At 13, she went to work in a clothing store where she met Amancio Ortega, who was to become her husband. Nine years after their marriage in 1966, they opened the first Zara store, selling inexpensive clothes based on couture designs. By 2013 there were 1,700 Zara stores around the world, and *Forbes* magazine named her "the wealthiest self-made woman on the planet."
See also: Gaining an edge 32–39 ▪ Reinventing and adapting 52–57

AKIO MORITA
1921–99

The founder of Sony was born in Kosugaya, Japan. He showed a love of mathematics from an early age, and studied physics at Osaka Imperial University. While in the navy in World War II, he met Masaru Ibuka, with whom he later set up the Tokyo Telecommunications Engineering Corporation. Renamed "Sony" in 1958, the company produced the first transistor TV and the game-changing Sony Walkman. Morita was an early champion of building an international business; It was the first Japanese company to build factories in the US and to have US members on the board.
See also: Gaining an edge 32–39 ▪ Keep evolving business practice 48–51 ▪ Changing the game 92–99

RUPERT MURDOCH
1931–

Media baron Keith Rupert Murdoch was born in Melbourne, Australia. He went to boarding school in Geelong, Australia, then traveled to Oxford, UK, to study economics. When his father died in 1952, Rupert was bequeathed a regional newspaper, *the Adelaide News*. Murdoch learned the trade through an apprenticeship at the *Daily Express* in London, then returned to Australia to take control of his paper. He drove circulation higher by delivering a more dramatic mix of crime and scandal; the increased revenues allowed him to begin buying more papers. Between 1968 and 2000 he created a global empire of mass media. Despite being involved in the newspaper "hacking scandal" of 2011–12, his business—News Corp—reported revenues of $34 billion in 2012.
See also: Stand out in the market 28–31 ▪ Roberto Civita 334

VINEET NAYAR
1962–

Indian businessman Vineet Nayar was born in Pantnagar, in the foothills of the Himalayas. He studied mechanical engineering, earned a MBA, then entered business. In 2007 he became CEO of HCL Technologies, where he practiced his controversial approach to management of "employees first," inverting the standard operational pyramid. Using this approach, detailed in a book of the same name, Nayar has transformed HCL into a $4.6-billion company with offices in 31 countries.
See also: Organizing teams and talent 80–85 ▪ Is money the motivator? 90–91

HENRI NESTLE
1814–90

Heinrich "Henri" Nestlé was born in Frankfurt-am-Main, Germany. He trained as a pharmacist, but in 1833 fled local riots to settle in Vevey, Switzerland. He continued to experiment, and in the mid-1860s began to produce a baby food that combined milk with wheat flour. The popularity of his "farine lactee" (the first formula for babies) allowed him to open sales offices and factories in the UK, France, Germany, and the US, while also acquiring local companies. Nestlé went on to invent the first form of milk chocolate and soluble coffee.
See also: Creativity and invention 72–73 ▪ Ignoring the herd 146–49

INDRA NOOYI
1955–

Indra Krishnamurthy Nooyi was born in Madras (now Chennai), India. After graduating with a masters in finance and marketing from the Indian Institute of Management, Nooyi completed a masters at Yale Management School, funded by working as a nighttime receptionist. She then spent six years as an international strategy consultant, before joining the telecommunications company Motorola as a director of strategy. In 1994 she became the chief strategy officer at PepsiCo, and was instrumental in positioning the company for growth in China, the Middle East, and India. She became the company's CEO in 2006, and chairperson in 2007.
See also: Balancing long- versus short-termism 190–91

TAIICHI OHNO
1912–90

Taiichi Ohno was a self-taught engineer whose insights and methods helped Toyota become one of the largest motor companies in the world. Born in Dalian, China, in 1912, Ohno started work at Toyota when he left school, and spent the rest of his working life there. He is best known for devising the "just-in-time" production system, where parts or products are not ordered until just before they are needed, rather than having large stock holdings on hand. He also advocated flexible manufacturing methods to allow tailoring for different international markets and to reduce waste. He is regarded as one of the production

geniuses of the 20th century.
See also: Anticipating demand 290–93 ▪ Lean production 294–95

PIERRE OMIDYAR
1967–

Founder of eBay Pierre Omidyar was born in Paris, France, to Iranian parents. He moved to the US with his family as a child, where he studied computer science at Tufts University. After graduating, he worked in software development for Apple before co-founding a company that developed business-to-business e-commerce software in 1991. Omidyar left to work for a mobile communication business in 1994, but continued to explore the possibilities of e-commerce for consumers in his spare time. In 1995 he launched Auction Web, which later became eBay. In 2012 it reported revenues of $22.6 billion.
See also: The weightless start-up 62–63 ▪ Changing the game 92–99

TOM PETERS
1942–

US management authority Tom Peters was born in Baltimore, MD. He studied civil engineering at Cornell University at a masters level, then earned an MBA and PhD in business at Stanford Business School. From 1966 to 1970 he served in Vietnam for the US Navy, then worked for the US government. From 1974–81 he was a consultant for McKinsey and Company, before leaving to work independently after the publication of his book *In Search of Excellence*, the business classic he wrote with Robert Waterman.
See also: Coping with chaos 220–21

C. K. PRAHALAD
1941–2010

Coimbatore Krishnarao Prahalad was born in Tamil Nadu, India. After completing a degree in physics at the University of Madras, Prahalad joined Union Carbide, and worked there for four years (he described this as a major "inflection point" in his life). He then studied for an MBA at the Indian Institute of Management followed by a PhD at Harvard Business School. En route to becoming a professor of business administration, he became renowned as a consultant, after his advice invigorated the failing Philips electronics business. He has published many best-selling books, including *Competing for the Future*, co-authored with Gary Hamel. He is considered one of the world's top management thinkers.
See also: Protect the core business 170–71 ▪ The learning organization 202–07 ▪ Gary Hamel 335

CARLOS SLIM HELU
1940–

Mexican business magnate Carlos Slim Helú was born in Mexico City. After studying civil engineering at the Universidad Nacional Autónoma, Mexico, he founded his own business, Inmobiliaria Carso, at 25. Through acquisition and shrewd management, he built on this to establish a large group of businesses—Grupo Carso—which included companies in the food, retail, construction, mining, and tobacco industries. International acquisitions and mergers followed, with partnerships with companies such as Microsoft, with whom Slim Helú joined forces in 2000 to launch

the Spanish portal, T1msn (now ProdigyMSN.com). In March 2013, *Forbes* magazine stated that Helú was the world's richest person, with a net worth of $73 billion.
See also: Effective leadership 78–79 ▪ Bill Gates 335

ALFRED SLOAN
1875–1966

Alfred Sloan was a groundbreaking industrialist who radically changed the ways that companies were organized in the early 20th century. He was born in New Haven, CT, and studied electrical engineering at MIT before joining a small company that manufactured ball bearings. By the age of 24 he was its president, and within another four years had led it from near-bankruptcy to an annual profit of $60 million. The company was bought by General Motors, which went on to make Sloan its president in 1923. He famously reorganized GM into separate, autonomous divisions, in a decentralizing process that was much copied. He was also the first to introduce a systematic approach to strategic planning. A renowned philanthropist, he died aged 90 of a heart attack.
See also: Simplify processes 296–99 ▪ Critical path analysis 328–29

BROOKS STEVENS
1911–95

Industrial designer Brooks Stevens was born in Milwaukee, WI. He had polio as a child, and occupied himself during long stays in bed by drawing. He later studied architecture at Cornell University, NY, before opening his own furnishings business. He said that

"planned obsolescence" was the mission of industrial design, and that design should make consumers want something "a litte newer, a little better, a little sooner than is necessary." Stevens was one of the most influential industrial designers of the 20th century.
See also: Planned obsolescence 324–25

ALVIN TOFFLER
1928–

American futurologist and writer Alvin Toffler was born in New York City, where he grew up and went to university. He and his wife, Heidi, embarked on many collaborative research projects, identifying current and future societal shifts. In Toffler's best-known book, *Future Shock* (1970), he envisaged a post-industrial future in which companies outsource labor, technology displaces the worker, and change takes place so fast that people cannot adapt fast enough to thrive.
See also: Reinventing and adapting 52–57 ▪ Focus on the future market 244–49 ▪ Forecasting 278–79

CHER WANG
1958–

Entrepreneurial thinker Cher Wang was born in Taiwan and sent to the US for school. She studied economics at University of California, Berkeley. After graduating, she worked for a computer company, where the heavy computer cases inspired her to wonder if computing could be made "smaller." In 1997 she co-founded technology company HTC based on this idea. By 2013 the company was making one in six of all smartphones used in the US.

An avid philanthropist, Wang is renowned for her remarkable insights into technology trends.
See also: Creativity and invention 72–73 ▪ The right technology 314–15

YANG YUANQING
1964–

Yang Yuanqing was born in Anhui province, China. While studying for a masters in computer science, he took a sales job at technology company Legend (now Lenovo). By 29 years old he headed up the company's personal computer business, and in 2009 he became CEO. Yang transformed the traditional company into a performance-oriented business with a diverse staff, supplier network, and customer base. In 2012 and 2013 he famously redistributed his bonus among the company's employees.
See also: Effective leadership 78–79 ▪ Changing the game 92–99

ZHANG XIN
1965–

Businesswoman Zhang Xin was raised in Hong Kong, and took on factory work as a teenager to save for an education in the UK. She received an MA from the University of Cambridge in 1992, then worked in investment banking. In 1995 she and her husband co-founded SOHO China, a property development company, offering prime properties to Beijing's new super-rich class. Success was not immediate, but SOHO China is now the country's largest and most profitable property company. In 2013 Zhang's net worth was $3.6 billion.
See also: Beating the odds at start-up 20–21

GLOSSARY

Acquisition The purchase of the whole or part of a business by another business.

Activity-based costing (ABC) A method of business accounting that analyzes overhead costs to determine which activities create which costs. This results in a more accurate analysis of costs than traditional **cost accounting**, which measures direct costs and then adds an estimate of **overheads**.

Asset Any economic resource that is owned by a company that can be used to generate value for the business.

Balance sheet A summary of a company's financial value, incorporating its **assets**, **liabilities**, and **equity** of the owners, which is usually published at the end of its financial year.

Bankruptcy A legal declaration that an individual or a company is insolvent, meaning that they cannot repay their debts.

Benchmarking A method of evaluating a company by comparing its perfomance and practices with those of the **market-leading** business or businesses.

Board In business, a term that refers to the board of directors of a company or organization. Board members are either elected or appointed to oversee the company's activities and performance.

Brand The perceived "identity" of a company or product that distinguishes it from the competition. This can include many things, from name, design, logo, and packaging to broader, external affiliations that may set it apart from its rivals (such as ethical trading standards and production initiatives).

BRIC economies An acronym for the four emerging economies of Brazil, Russia, India, and China. They are considered by some to pose a challenge to Western economic supremacy.

Budget A financial plan that lists all planned expenses and incomes of business unit, project, or venture.

Bull market A financial term describing a period in which **share** values increase, leading to optimism and economic growth.

Buy out Taking control of a company by purchasing a controlling interest of its **stock**.

Capital The money and physical **assets** (such as machinery and infrastructure) used by a company to produce an income.

Cartel A group of businesses that agrees to cooperate in such a way that the output of their goods or services is restricted, and prices are driven up.

Cash flow The incomings and outgoings of cash in a business, representing its operating activities.

CEO An acronym for Chief Executive Officer, the highest executive in a company. Appointed by and reporting to the **board**.

Closed innovation The idea, popular in the 20th century, that innovation in a company should take place strictly within its own walls, by its own employees, rather than drawing on knowledge, ideas, and expertise from outside.

Collusion An agreement between two or more companies not to compete, so that they can fix prices.

Commodity A term for any item, product, or service that can be freely bought, sold, and traded.

Comparative advantage The ability to produce goods or services at a lower opportunity cost than rivals.

Competitive advantage A strategy whereby companies position themselves ahead of competitors either by charging less or by **differentiating** their services or products from those of their rivals.

Conglomerate A **corporation** that is made up of two or more businesses that may operate across different fields and sectors.

Corporation An independent legal entity, owned by **shareholders**, that is authorized to conduct business. Corporations exist separately and apart from their employees and shareholders and have their own rights and **liabilities**: they can borrow money, own **assets**, and sue or be sued.

Cost accounting A method of business accounting that aims to determine costs by measuring direct costs and then adding an estimate of **overheads**.

Cost leadership A strategy whereby companies aim to offer the cheapest product(s) or service(s) in their industry or market and thereby gain a **competitive advantage** over their rivals.

Creative accounting Accounting practices that seek to portray a company's finances in either a positive or negative light through a range of accounting techniques. Although unconventional, and often used to depict artificial **profit** levels, such practices are generally legal.

Credit crunch A sudden reduction in the availability of credit in a banking system. A credit crunch often occurs after a period in which credit is widely available.

Crowdsourcing Tapping into collective online knowledge by inviting large numbers of people, via the Internet, to contribute ideas on different aspects of a business's operations. A related concept is "crowdfunding," which involves funding a project or venture by raising **capital** from individual investors via the Internet.

Default The failure to repay a loan under the terms agreed.

Deficit A financial situation in which a business's expenditure exceeds its **revenue**.

Demand The desire, willingness, and ability of consumers to purchase a product or service.

Differentiation A strategy whereby companies distinguish their products or services from the offerings of rival companies through cost, improved features, or marketing and promotion in order to achieve a **competitive advantage** in a crowded market sector.

Distribution The movement of goods and services from the producer or manufacturer through a distribution channel (such as a vendor or agent) to the end consumer, customer, or user.

Diversification A strategy to minimize **risk** and raise **revenue** by distributing expenditure across a number of different business units or products, and across a range of different **markets** and even geographical areas.

Dividend An annual payment made by a company to its **shareholders**, usually as a portion of its **profits**. Dividend payouts are made at the discretion of a company's directors.

Early adopter A business or a customer who uses a new product or new technology before others.

E-commerce Abbreviated from "electronic commerce," the buying and selling of products and services by businesses and consumers via the Internet and electronic systems.

Emotional intelligence (EQ) The ability to perceive, control, and evaluate emotions in oneself and in others. US psychologist Daniel Goleman noted that high EQ is common in business leaders and facilitates other leadership traits.

Emotional Selling Proposition (ESP) A **marketing** strategy that creates an emotional connection (such as pride, humor, or desire) between the customer and the **brand**, impelling them to purchase.

Entrepreneur A person who takes commercial **risk** in the hope of making a **profit**.

Equity In **investment**, the value of **shares** issued by a company; "equity" also denotes part or full ownership in a company. In accounting, the net worth of a company or individual, calculated by subtracting total **liabilities** from total **assets**.

First-mover advantage The benefits resulting from being the first business to enter a **market**.

Fixed cost A cost, such as rent or salaries, that does not change according to the number of goods or services produced.

Forecasting The use of past data to predict future trends and assess the likely **demand** for a business's goods and services.

Free market An economy in which decisions about production are made by private individuals and businesses on the basis of **supply** and **demand**, and in which prices are determined by the **market**.

Groupthink A quirk of group dynamics, in which individuals in a group place higher priority on achieving a consensus with one another than on effective and rational decision-making.

Hygiene factors A series of workplace factors identified by US psychologist Frederick Herzberg that, if poorly managed, contribute to job dissatisfaction. A separate set of factors—motivators—encourage job satisfaction.

Inflation The steady increase in the overall prices of goods and services in an economy.

Interest rate The amount of interest—the charge for borrowing a sum of money—paid annually by a borrower, measured as a percentage of the total amount borrowed.

Inventory Goods and materials that are held in **stock** in a warehouse or in any other similar premises. The term can also refer to the total value of a company's **assets**, including raw materials, and unfinished and finished products.

Investment In business terms, the activity of purchasing bonds or **shares** in a company. Can also refer to a company's expenditure on items intended to yield an increase in operational performance, such as new tools.

Kaizen The Japanese term for "good change," in business. It refers to continuous improvement to enhance productivity.

Leverage The extent to which people or companies fund their activities with borrowed money. When high leverage is widespread in the economy, the degree of debt can create a short-term boom; but this is often followed by a crash.

Leveraged buy-out (LBO) The acquisition of a business by a company or group of individuals using a large proportion of borrowed money.

Liability The financial obligations of a company to outsiders or claims against its **assets** by outsiders.

Liquidity The ease with which an **asset** can be bought or sold, without adversely affecting the asset's value. Cash is the most liquid asset, since its value remains constant.

Long tail A term coined by UK writer and entrepreneur Chris Anderson to describe how the overall sales of niche products at the thin "tail" of a demand curve may be greater than sales of the most popular products at the "head."

Market The consumers who buy a product or service. Also refers to any physical or virtual location where buyers and sellers trade goods, such as a store or a website.

Marketing Promoting the sale of products or services to consumers or other businesses. Effective marketing identifies, anticipates, and responds to customers' needs.

Market leader A product or company that has the largest **market share**.

Market share A business's percentage of sales in a specific industry or sector.

Merger The combining of two or more businesses to form a separate organization with a new identity. The goal of a merger is often to increase **shareholder** value beyond the sum of the two (or more) companies.

Micro loan A small loan made to entrepreneurs or small businesses.

Micropreneur An entrepreneur who starts and builds a small business of their own, often while on salaried employment.

M-commerce An abbreviation of "mobile commerce," the use of portable devices such as laptops and smartphones to conduct business transactions online.

Monopoly A **market** in which only one company is active. Monopoly companies generally have low product diversity, which they can sell at a high price due to lack of competition.

Niche market A small group of people with an interest in a product or service that is not addressed by mainstream providers.

Off-balance-sheet finance Accounting methods whereby some **liabilities** or **assets** are not recorded on a company's **balance sheet**.

Open innovation The idea that a business's talent base, and consequently its insight into new products and services, can be expanded by drawing on expertise from outside the company, often via social media and the Internet.

Operating margin A measure of profitability—the ratio of a company's operating **profit** to its **revenue**.

Outsourcing The contracting out of specific tasks or functions in a business to outside companies.

Overhead Any ongoing expense of a business, such as rent of premises; also known as "operating expense."

Positioning A **marketing** strategy that establishes a distinct position for a **brand** in the **market**.

Private equity A type of **investment** in which private **assets** or borrowed funds are used to finance private companies (those not listed on a public **stock** exchange).

Private limited company (Ltd) A company in which the **liability** of members is limited to the value of their **investment** in the company. The company's **shares** cannot be bought and sold by the public. Private limited company is a term used primarily in the UK. The closest US equivalent is limited liability company.

Product portfolio A strategy that involves assembling a diverse range of products or business units.

Profit The surplus of a company's **revenue** after all expenses, taxes, and operating costs have been met.

Publicly traded company In a publicly traded company the **liability** of members is limited to the value of their **investment** in the company. A publicly trated company's **shares** are traded on the **stock market** and can be bought and sold by the general public.

Recession The period of time in which the total output of an economic area decreases.

Reserves In business, **profits** retained by a company for future use and not distributed to **shareholders**.

Return on Equity (ROE) A measure of a company's financial performance, based on **profit** and the **equity** of **shareholders**.

Return on Investment (ROI) The ratio of money gained to the amount invested in the company.

Revenue Also known as sales and turnover, the income earned by a business over a period of time. The revenue earned depends on the price and number of items sold.

Risk In **investment** terms, risk is the uncertainty associated with an investment or **asset**. A high-risk investment, for example, may yield a high return; but if unsuccessful, it could cause the investor to lose everything. Operational risk is the risk of failure due to shortcomings in procedures, people, or systems.

Securities An umbrella term for a range of **investment** instruments that are traded on **stock markets**, such as bonds, options, and **shares**.

Shadow bank A nonbank financial institution—such as the treasury function of a business—that lends money to businesses. Shadow banks offer similar services as traditional banks, but are not subject to supervisory and regulatory burdens.

Share A unit of ownership in a company, signifying ownership of **stock**.

Shareholder An individual or organization that holds **shares** in a company. A shareholder is also known as a stockholder.

Speculating Making high-risk **investments** that could yield large returns, but bear a high **risk** of resulting in loss.

Start-up A business that has—or is being—launched from scratch.

Stock The **equity** stake of the **shareholders** in a business. The term also describes goods owned by a business that are held on its premises or in a warehouse, and are available for sale or **distribution**.

Stock market A place where bonds and **stocks** or **shares** in a company are bought and sold.

Supply The amount of a product or service that is available for consumers to buy.

Supply chain The people and processes involved in the production and **distribution** of goods or services.

Surplus An excess in **supply** over **demand**—when the production of goods, services, or resources exceeds their consumption.

Sustainability A strategy in which the business ensures that the resources it uses will be replaced, such as a paper manufacturer planting trees.

Synergy The supposed additional performance benefit that is achieved when two companies or units of a business are joined together.

Takeover The purchase of one business by another.

Treasury function Using a company's treasury (its financial operations department) to achieve the optimum balance between **liquidity** and income from the company's **cash flows**. Other activities can include **profit** generation, **risk** management, planning and operations, and **shareholder** relations.

Unique Selling Proposition (USP) A **marketing** strategy whereby companies distinguish their products from their rivals by offering customers something that their competitors do not or cannot offer.

Value chain The theory of US professor Michael Porter that the chain of a company's interrelated activities can be exploited to add value to its products or services. These activities relate to the flow of a product from production to purchase by the customer.

Venture capital Funds invested in a **start-up** at its earliest phase.

Viral marketing The launching of a product or service via the Internet or social media to attract rapid and widespread consumer interest.

Working capital The **capital** available for use in the day-to-day operations of a business, calculated as the difference between current **assets** and current **liabilities**.

INDEX

Numbers in **bold** refer
to main entries

D

E

N

O

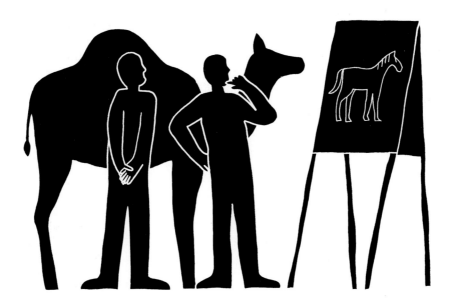

ACKNOWLEDGMENTS

Dorling Kindersley would like to thank Chris Westhorp for proofreading; Margaret McCormack for the index; Harish Aggarwal for jacket design; Alex Lloyd and Ankita Mukherjee for design assistance; and Alexandra Beeden, Henry Fry, and Miezan van Zyl for editorial assistance.

PICTURE CREDITS

The publisher would like to thank the following for their kind permission to reproduce their photographs:

(Key: a-above; b-below/bottom; c-center; f-far; l-left; r-right; t-top)

21 Getty Images: Bloomberg (bl). **27 Getty Images:** Al Bello (tl). **30 Getty Images:** Bloomberg (bl). **35 Alamy Images:** DPA Picture Alliance (tl). **36 Corbis:** Bettmann (tl). **38 Corbis:** Lucidio Studio Inc. (bl). **39 Corbis:** Karen Moskowitz (bl). **41 Alamy Images:** Everett Collection Historical (bl). **43 Alamy Images:** Ashway (br). **45 NASA:** JPL-Caltech (tr). **47 Getty Images:** MN Chan (bl). **50 Corbis:** Jenny Lewis (bl). **56 Alamy Images:** Eddie Linssen (bl). **57 Corbis:** Bettmann (tr). **Getty Images:** Chung Sung-Jun (bl). **61 Getty Images:** Charles Eshelman (tl). **63 Corbis:** Kimberly White (tl). **69 Getty Images:** WireImage (tr). **71 Corbis:** Ann Kaplan (bl). **Getty Images:** View Pictures / UIG (tr). **73 Getty Images:** Dave M. Benett (tr). **75 Corbis:** Bettmann (bl); Jade / Blend Images (tr). **79 Corbis:** Catherine Cabrol (bl). **85 Getty Images:** Paul Taylor (br). **87 Corbis:** James Brittain (tl). Warren Bennis (bl). **89 Getty Images:** Godong / UIG (tl). **94 Corbis:** Kim Kulish (bl). **95 Corbis:** David Cabrera / Arcaid (br). **97 Getty Images:** Bloomberg (b). **98 Getty Images:** Bloomberg (br). **101 Getty Images:** WireImage (tr). **102 Corbis:** Gonzalo Fuentes / Reuters (bl). **103 Corbis:** Porter Gifford (tr). **109 Getty Images:** Britt Erlanson (tl). **111 Getty Images:** Kris Connor (bl). **114 Corbis:** Arnd Wiegmann / Reuters (br). **121 Alamy Images:** Wavebreakmedia Ltd. PH07 (br). **123 Getty Images:** Bloomberg (tr). **125 Getty Images:** AFP (tl). **127 Corbis:** The Gallery Collection (tl). **129 Getty Images:** Bloomberg (tl). **131 Corbis:** Martin Harvey (tl). **134 Alamy Images:** Everett Collection Historical (tr). **135 Getty Images:** Yawar Nazir (bl). **137 Alamy Images:** Islandstock (tl). **141 Getty Images:** Bloomberg (tl). **142 Corbis:** Monty Rakusen / Cultura (tr). **144 Getty Images:** Giuseppe Cacace (tl). **145 Corbis:** Endiaferon / Demotix (bl). **Getty Images:** Bloomberg (tr). **149 Corbis:** Brooks Kraft (tr). **Getty Images:** Phil Boorman (bl). **151 Corbis:** Roderick Chen / First Light (tl). **153 Corbis:** John Eveson / Frank Lane Picture Library (br). **154 Getty Images:** James Nielsen (cr). **157 Corbis:** Alan Levenson (tr). **Getty Images:** Bloomberg (bl). **159 akg-images:** (bl). **165 Corbis:** (bl). **167 Corbis:** Frank Moore Studio (tr). **168 Corbis:** George Grantham Bain (tl). **169 Corbis:** Tony Savino (bl). **171 Alamy Images:** Lilyana Vynogradova (tr). **174 Corbis:** James Leynse (bl). **175 Alamy Images:** Allan Cash Picture Library (br). **176 Corbis:** Juice Images (tl). **181 David Tenser:** (br). **183 Alamy Images:** Allstar Picture Library (bl). **Getty Images:** AFP (tr). **184 Getty Images:** Cavan Images (cr). **187 Corbis:** Bettmann (tr). **189 Corbis:** Leif Skoogfors (tl). **191 Getty Images:** WireImage / R. Born (bl). **197 Alamy Images:** SiliconValleyStock (bl). **198 Corbis:** Ocean (br). **199 Corbis:** Bettmann (tl). **200 Courtesy of Victorinox, Switzerland:** (tl). **201 Alamy Images:** PhotoEdit (tc). **Corbis:** Brooks Kraft / Sygma (bl). **206 Alamy Images:** Brett Gardner (br). **207 TopFoto.co.uk:** (bl). **209 Getty Images:** Tim Klein (tl). **211 Getty Images:** AFP (br). **214 Corbis:** Imagerie / The Food Passionates (br). **215 Getty Images:** Allan Baxter (tl). **217 Fotolia:** Africa Studio (br). **219 Dreamstime.com:** Adistock (tl). **220 Getty Images:** Diana Kraleva (bc). **222 Getty Images:** Image Source / Dan Bannister (br). **226 Alamy Images:** Newscast (tr). **233 Getty Images:** wdstock / E+ (cra). **237 Corbis:** Steve Smith (bl). **238 Alamy Images:** Ashley Cooper (tl). **239 Rex Features:** Everett Collection (br). **241 Getty Images:** Justin Sullivan (br). **247 Corbis:** Timothy Fadek (bl). **249 Corbis:** C. Devan (bl). **Getty Images:** Duane Howell (tr). **253 Science Photo Library:** Hank Morgan (crb). **255 Alamy Images:** Interfoto (bl); The Natural History Museum (bc). **Getty Images:** Bloomberg (tr). **261 Getty Images:** AFP / EADS (tr). **262 Corbis:** Colin McPherson (bl). **263 Corbis:** Brendan McDermid / Reuters (br). **265 Rex Features:** Daily Mail (bc). **266 Getty Images:** Marco Secchi (tr). **267 Corbis:** Fotodesign Holzhauser (bl). **270 Alamy Images:** Guatebrian (cb). **273 The Advertising Archives:** (tl). **277 Alamy Images:** Benedicte Desrus (br). **279 Getty Images:** Junko Kimura / Bloomberg (bl). **283 Corbis:** James Leynse (br). **289 Alamy Images:** Marc MacDonald (bl). **Corbis:** Alexander Demianchuk / Reuters (tr). **292 Alamy Images:** Chris Pearsall (tl). **293 Getty Images:** Gerenme / E+ (tc). **297 Getty Images:** Science & Society Picture Library (br). **298 Corbis:** Bettmann (bl). **299 Getty Images:** George Frey / Bloomberg (tl); Andrew Harrer / Bloomberg (tr). **301 Alamy Images:** CoverSpot (bl). **304 Getty Images:** Kurita Kaku / Gamma-Rapho (bl). **307 123RF.com:** Hongqi Zhang (bl). **308 Getty Images:** Peter Macdiarmid (tr). **311 Alamy Images:** World History Archive / Image Asset Management Ltd. (bl). **313 Getty Images:** Jo Hale (tr). **315 Corbis:** George Steinmetz (br). **321 Getty Images:** Buena Vista Images / Stockbyte (bl). **322 Alamy Images:** Photosindia Batch11 / PhotosIndia.com LLC (cb). **323 Corbis:** Catherine Karnow (tr). **Dreamstime.com:** Weixin Shen (tl). **325 Getty Images:** Tom Shaw / Allsport (br). **329 Dreamstime.com:** Mishkacz (br). **331 Alamy Images:** DPA Picture Alliance Archive (bl).

All other images © Dorling Kindersley.

For more information see:
www.dkimages.com